Whatever Happened to Hollywood?

Jesse L. Lasky, Jr.

Funk & Wagnalls New York

First published in the United States, with additions, in 1975

Designed by Ingrid Beckman

Manufactured in the United States of America

Library of Congress Cataloging in Publication Data

Lasky, Jesse Lenard, 1910–
Whatever happened to Hollywood?

1. Lasky, Jesse Lenard, 1910– –Biography. 2. Hollywood, Calif.–Social life and customs.
I. Title.
PS3523.A735Z52 917.94'0924 74-16274
ISBN 0-308-10172-3

2 3 4 5 6 7 8 9 10

Also by Jesse L. Lasky, Jr.

NOVELS

Curtain of Life
No Angels in Heaven
Spindrift
Naked in a Cactus Garden

POETRY

Songs from the Heart of a Boy
Listening to Silence
Singing in Thunder

For Barbara
(alias Pat)
wife, collaborator, survival kit.
Through darkest Hollywood—to a new, old world.

The author wishes to thank
The De Mille Foundation
The British Film Institute
and
Jesse Lasky Productions, Ltd.
without whose support and assistance
this book would not have been made possible.

Ask yourself: "Had it been like this?"

Probably not. Not precisely. Memory is a poor camera. It filters the truth through layers of imaginings. We dare not measure recollections against fact.

The past is an abandoned stage. Its players are dead. All that we've kept of it are echoes and images. Some perhaps worth saving.

JESSE L. LASKY, JR.

Whatever Happened to Hollywood?

One

In the old silent movies the passage of time used to be indicated by a riffling of leaves on a calendar. This could take you backward or forward. Summer could plunge into instant autumn, or if you were meant to leap from time present to time future, a wind machine could blow a confetti of fake leaves off the branches of a prop tree. But to flash back into the past was even easier. It required only a *Dissolve To* wherever you wanted to be.

Dissolve To, then, a scene in medieval France. The year 1429, to be exact. We are in a long valley watching an earthshaking charge of armored knights. The dust is terrible. The thunder of hoofs roars nearer through whirling, powder-yellow clouds as they come on, riding stirrup to stirrup, wave upon wave, the long ranks representing the flower of French chivalry. Beneath bone-dry hills, clattering shields ricochet the sun's blaze from an assortment of mythological heraldry—griffins, unicorns, golden falcons crested above steel helmets. A forest of spears leafed with pennants descends. Harsh curses blast the water-blue dome of day. What could halt such a storm of magnificence? What force on earth could break this charge of panoplied power?

One word, called through a megaphone:

"Cut!"

Dust subsides on crested headgear. Chargers revert to sweating hacks. All eyes swivel to the wooden tower of scaffolding where the shirt-sleeved young man with pink bald pate stands in polished puttees and flared riding breeches, surveying the mounted lank-shanked cowboy-knights who are finding "extra work" far more profitable than cowpunching.

"Is there such a thing as an assistant director on this location?" The director general's voice is an angry bark through the megaphone.

"Yes, Mr. De Mille!" Three harassed individuals rush to the foot of the wooden platform. Cowboys in armor shift lazily in their unfamiliar chair-shaped medieval French saddles. Sweat scars dust-caked cheeks beneath vizored helmets. Their chain mail (woven string, painted silver) would be more comfortable in an arctic blast than in this sun-gorged valley of San Fernando.

Actors Wallace Reid and Hobart Bosworth trot their mounts over to get an earful of the rapid-fire corrections being given by the director to his assistants. Almost nothing had been right about that first charge!

"I want to get that shot again—from the beginning! If they can't sit horses better than that—get me someone who can! A schoolgirl with a spitball could unseat the whole army! And I don't want to see any more of those knights chewing gum!"

"Yes, Mr. De Mille . . ."

"And don't let me catch a glimpse of another wrist watch!"

"Yes, sir. That is, no, sir."

The assistants scurry away to relay instructions through the mounted ranks. Wranglers check tanned wrists above painted silver gauntlets and trot back up the field to their starting positions.

"Somebody get Joan of Arc over here!" barks the director. When he speaks, people jump and obey. A cameraman, cap worn backward so that he may peer more conveniently through his view finder, signals the adjustment of one of the great silver reflectors capturing the last strength of the waning sun.

A mustang bucks off a marshal of France to the delight of the cowpokes. A look from the director general and their rasping chortles subside.

The Maid of Orleans clanks over to the foot of the tower in her new suit of Hollywood mail, custom-built and authentically heavy. Real metal for the star. It is Geraldine Farrar, Metropolitan Opera diva, who had been lured to Hollywood's infant film industry two years earlier to star in the 1915 *Carmen.* She turns like a silver peacock for the director general's approval.

"How does it feel, Gerry?"

"A bit tight in the thigh, C. B." she complains.

He considers her critically from above. "Could you defeat the English army in it?" The question is dead serious.

"If I can mount my horse. But I'd hate to have to hit a high 'C.' "

"Of all the sins our films record, the human voice is not one of them." He finger-snaps a sweaty assistant to the foot of the tower. "I trust it won't require a kingdom to produce Miss Farrar's horse?" De Mille inquires, dangerously quiet.

"Right away, sir. And . . ." The assistant hesitates.

"And what . . . ?" Definite menace.

"The French army is ready when you are, sir."

"I've been ready since five o'clock this morning," growls the boss. He takes a step higher up the ladder, making a box with his hands to cut out the light, surveys the field. All wait. A few more minute corrections, then at last De Mille appears almost satisfied.

"All right, we'll try it again. Quiet, everyone!" Not that there was any sound recording to be quiet for, but the director would be shouting instructions during the filming.

"Positions, knights . . . !" Assistants dart among the formations for final instructions. Silence. The people who have come to watch this spectacular "location filming" stand up on the seats of giant touring cars that have brought them out.

There is a long moment—then the director's shout, "Camera . . . !"

Spurs drive into horseflesh. Again the ranks plunge forward in an unbreakable thundering charge. Some hundred yards in front of them a small boy has slipped away from the surveillance of parents and elders to salvage a gleaming object from the field, a wooden sword fallen among the horse turds and wounded wild flowers.

De Mille's gimlet glance spots him. "Hold the charge!" he roars.

A diminuendo of voices relays the order across the field. The knights rein in a few feet from the boy, who by this time is bolting for cover with his prize. The shot is ruined; some hundred feet of film up the spout.

"How the hell did that damned kid get out there?"

Nobody knows the immediate answer. The culprit has bounded away out of sight among the touring cars.

Kids have ever been fashioned to slide under circus tents, up trees, over fences, into holds of ships, anywhere they can get themselves into a bit of trouble. But this particular kid could, had he a modicum of wit, have spared his legs and the director's temper, for the enormous, dusty car top, folded back like an accordion, from which he peers out, belongs to his father, and De Mille's partner, Jesse L. Lasky.

Hollywood hadn't looked like the capital of anything when the Lasky Company arrived in 1913. Just an orange grove where they could rent a barn. Actually, my father and De Mille hadn't even come out together. My father had some reputation as a moderately successful producer of vaudeville shows on Broadway. He had started in show business with his first cornet lesson. Although never good enough to qualify for a position in Sousa's famous band, my father and his sister, Blanche, formed an act called "The Musical Laskys." Much later, he'd worked up to producing vaudeville acts.

As these acts grew more ambitious, my father began to search for talent further afield. He made trips to London to import music hall artists to America. One young acrobat eventually changed his name from Archie Leach to Cary Grant.

Around 1910, the year I made my first entrance, my father had bounded back from a Broadway failure called *The Folies-Bergère* with a big idea. He would produce an operetta based on the history of his home state. *California*—a musical pageant of Franciscan missions, Spanish dons, gold hunters, and railroad builders. To write it, he set out to hire the greatest New York playwright of the day.

William de Mille had prodigious Broadway hits to his credit. But William, the famous playwright's agent announced, was much too busy to write vaudeville acts. This theatrical agent—who happened to be William de Mille's mother—also happened to recall that the busy William had a younger brother, Cecil. If William was a success, Cecil was quite the opposite. Still struggling to gain his spurs on Broadway, but equally talented, insisted the agent-mother. Which was a way of saying that Cecil was almost a total disaster. A has-been actor, a would-be writer, a sometime assistant to theatrical manager David Belasco. Cecil was young, prematurely bald, currently unemployed, but dynamic. Motivated by her dual capacity, his agent-mother pleaded with my father to consider Cecil in place of the unavailable William.

My father wasn't very enthusiastic. The few brief meetings with Cecil had not resulted in mutual admiration. But agents can be persuasive, and one had to be nice to the mother of the important William. So Dad interviewed Cecil, and Cecil talked himself into a job.

Eventually, the two young men gave up trying to impress each other and began exciting each other's imaginations. They seethed with projects and dreams, mostly impractical, and one that De Mille brought along seemed the most impractical of all. There was a revolution going on in Mexico at that moment, and De Mille, who had begun to feel "stale" and restless, declared his intention of heading south of the border in quest of adventure that might stimulate new story material.

My father, a shade more conservative, perhaps because he was better established in show business at the time, was not anxious to part with a good friend and associate. He hastily proposed an alternative—which might supply equal excitement for a bit less personal risk. He suggested that they go into the movie business. Actually the suggestion had been coming to my father from a third young man, his dynamic brother-in-law, Sam Goldfish, a glove cutter and born salesman who worked in my mother's uncle's factory in Gloversville, New York.

The ironic part of it was that my father's sister, Blanche, had married Sam to get out of show business! She had become increasingly weary of the ups and downs, the heights and depths, the feasts and famines. She thought Sam would offer a stable businessman husband far removed from the hectic dream stuff of theater folk. She'd had her fill of "tours" and sleeper jumps and one-night stands in seedy hotels and tank towns, and sleazy managers miscounting the house and backstage dramas, and most of all the big, big ideas that never stopped being talked about at the dinner table. She could not have chosen a worse escape hatch in young Sam—who would later change his name to Goldwyn.

He had seen a two-reel "Western" movie, *Broncho Billy's Adventures.* That was in 1911, and two years later Sam hadn't stopped trying to push his vaudeville producer brother-in-law into taking the plunge in the newest show-business medium.

It can almost be said that the impetus that led to the birth of Hollywood was based on my father's wish to tempt his best friend away from the gunplay of a Mexican revolution.

That and the persistent Sam, who never would learn to take *no* for an answer.

It was the beginning of the end of Sam and Blanche's brief marriage—and the beginning of the adventure that would make a village in California show-business capital of the world! Still, as a beginning, it could scarcely have been more modest. The three young men, Lasky, Goldfish, and De Mille, formed a company capitalized at twenty thousand dollars from assorted brothers-in-law. Fifteen of this they promptly squandered on purchasing the screen rights to Edwin Milton Royle's play *The Squaw Man.*

Wisdom would seem to have dictated a trip across the Hudson River to Fort Lee, New Jersey, where most sensible one- and two-reel Westerns were then being ground out. But wisdom has never been the better part of showmanship or showmen. They decided on the radical idea of producing their first feature-length Western in the West. The authentic West! There cowboys and Indians could be hired—in costume—by a friendly wave of the hand. Cowboys and Indians who could ride and supply their own horses.

The novitiate film makers didn't originally plan on going all the way to the Pacific, however. There was plenty of authentic West much nearer. Places on the map with authentic names like Flagstaff, Arizona.

One likes to think of these starry-eyed young prophets envisioning a new world of fame and fortune in the potentials of the film business, but from their own verbal recollections this seems not to have been the case at all. They got excited—then cooled off.

Dad got cold feet. But Cecil had no reputation to protect. Again they ignited each other; or perhaps Dad's ever-abundant, if sometimes short-lived enthusiasm, resold Sam on his own idea.

The new company, the Jesse L. Lasky Feature Play Company, almost went under when they tried to cast a Broadway star in that first film project, *The Squaw Man.* Dustin Farnum, matinee idol of the day, positively refused to accept one fourth of the profits of the company in lieu of payment to star in the film. They had to raise another five thousand dollars. Brothers-in-law had to dig deeper. Eventually the money was raised and De Mille led the first film company west by train to Flagstaff, Arizona. Why Flagstaff? It sounded romantic. Since *The Squaw Man* involved cowboys and Indians, where better?

Where better? Anywhere! De Mille and his little film company arrived at Flagstaff to find themselves in the middle of a cattleman-sheepman war. Shooting a film was one thing. Being shot at by drunken wranglers was something else.

The first telegram back to a worried company president said: "Flagstaff no good for our purpose. Have proceeded to California. Want authority to rent barn in place called Hollywood for seventy-five dollars a month. Regards to Sam. Cecil."

Lasky was not happy. A native-born San Franciscan and the son of a native son from Sacramento, he had a natural suspicion of Southern California and especially Los Angeles. Besides, he didn't like the change of plan. If Cecil was off on a wild goose chase with the company's minute funds, perhaps he should not have been dissuaded from the Mexican Revolution?

The young vaudeville producer weighed this extravagance. He had tried to exert a practical guiding hand on the venture, but this young madman was drunk with power. Thank goodness he had at least taken the precaution to impose one restraint. Since De Mille had never actually directed anything before, Lasky had sent Oscar Apfel—an experienced director of one- and two-reelers—to oversee the production.

But "barns" . . . ? In unknown places . . . ! He bit hard on his cigar and telegraphed back: "Authorize you to rent barn but on month-to-month basis. Make *no* long-term commitments. Regards. Jesse."

On this economical note the most lavishly extravagant industry in history was launched in Hollywood. And with it: "The Jesse Lasky Feature Play Company." One barn. One truck. One camera.

From the beginning it was my father's credo that the "play was the thing." The play, not the player, the story, not the star. Perhaps it was unfortunate that this concept was later eroded by the "star system," but another showman, a pint-sized Hungarian-born Jewish boxer with flat ears and a talent for survival, had a stronger conviction.

Adolph Zukor's company, Famous Players, set out to sell the artist instead of the art, the diva instead of the drama. And because Famous Players had already starred such an immortal as Sarah Bernhardt, and also because little Adolph Zukor was ten years senior to the tall, blue-eyed, pince-nezed ex-vaudevillian, the marriage of the two companies in 1915 produced Famous Players-Lasky, with Zukor as president, Lasky as first vice president, in charge of production. Their company would for years hold an important place in the crazy world where I grew up, the place called Hollywood.

Two

Hollywood has variously been referred to as "a state of mind," "a dream factory," and "entertainment capital of the world." Perhaps it was something of all these and more; but to me it was, quite simply, a home town. I bicycled through its pepper-tree-lined streets, trapped rabbits and skunks in its then-wild hills, and resided somewhat impressively near the top of La Brea in a palatial old house with a billiards room and a projection room over the garage.

Hot, languid California summer, with skies breeding the drone of insects, and heat waves you could actually see. The dry eucalyptus clashed saberlike leaves. Sunflowers nodded enormously in the empty fields of weeds.

From 1914 into the 1920s, Hollywood grew from a handful of wooden bungalows in an orchard realm into a village where elaborate mansions reared themselves above streets of box-shaped stucco dwellings. Hilltops sported bogus Spanish haciendas where the stars, directors, and producers were grandly housed above the hovels of the technicians and extras who fed the growing factories. Although it was becoming self-conscious about its status as a glamour capital, it would long remain a small town where almost everyone knew almost everyone else, where gossip columnists weren't needed to spread the rumors and reveal sordid secrets of the hard-drinking, philandering cadre, whose overflamboyant appearances at public places made for unwelcome publicity. Entertaining in those days was mainly confined to the home. There was not yet an official censorship of the public product or of private lives.

In those early days, nightclubs were few; the Montmartre in Hollywood, the old Ship Café on one of the piers above the Pacific. In that nautical retreat Prohibition was flouted in hooch-filled teacups.

The "hard stuff" was delivered under the wharf by motorboats plied by rumrunners beyond the three-mile limit. And up the coast past Santa Monica, there was a village of castlelike sets from early costume films, Inceville. On a clear day, and they all were, you could see bevies of Mack Sennett bathing beauties being filmed in bonnets and bathing-costumed down to their stockinged knees. There was the Alexandria Hotel in downtown Los Angeles, where conservative Pasadenans might glimpse on a Saturday night outing such luminaries as Bert Lytell, Bryant Washburn, Florence Vidor, Wanda Hawley, or that promising newcomer Gloria Swanson.

But downtown Los Angeles was a considerable trip then. Stars preferred parties, like those given by Bess, my mother, and my father; dances for charity held on our tennis court, where new arrivals could be introduced to movieland elite. I'd be dragged away from my lead soldiers to meet dinner guests like slinky Alla Nazimova, well-padded Nita Naldi, or romantic Percy Marmont, British star of the first *Lord Jim.* The sophistication was wasted on me, but I did take a shine to Mary Pickford because she looked like a kid and had a pretty voice. Antonio Moreno and Doug Fairbanks, Sr., were personal heroes. But I never forgave Charlie Chaplin for failing to appear in baggy pants and mustache. William S. Hart taught me "quick draws" that he used in his cowboy films and inscribed a photo, "To little Jesse from his friend and partner, Bill Hart." I didn't flaunt it, because he'd said "little."

"Kid" McCoy, former middleweight boxing champion who sparred with Dad, was a true friend until the police carted him off one morning. After a particularly drunken party, he ran amuck, spraying bullets all over the street we lived on. He got ten years in the penitentiary for manslaughter, and Bess went up pretty high in my estimation because she made prison visits to him. He got out in half that time on good behavior. Shooting actors wasn't such a serious offense in those days. The "Kid" was rehabilitated as athletic director for the Ford Motor Company, and never took another drink in his life.

Hollywood crime would soon grow more convoluted, but life was still wonderfully simple and wonder-filled. When Dad's company hired its second carpenter everyone went down to the studio just to watch *two* men nailing up a backdrop. And probably because of the McCoy shooting, a second policeman was added to the one directing traffic at the intersection of Cahuengua and Hollywood boulevards.

What traffic? Dad often rode horseback from our house at 7209

Hillside Avenue down to his studio at Selma and Vine. One drugstore. One hotel—the Hollywood—and in World War I, one company of amateur infantry made up of studio employees, the Lasky Home Guard. My reward for good behavior was being allowed to don uniform and march with these undaunted warriors on Thursday night War Bond drives. We all had "war gardens," collected tinfoil for the Red Cross, and persecuted German spies—who could be instantly identified by their foreign accents. Our genial Swiss butler was an early victim of this witch hunt. At the instigation of our neighbors he was interrogated by the police. The experience drove him to drink and he became unemployable.

The presence of perpetual sunshine in cloud-free skies and the almost total absence of traffic were a great convenience for outdoor filming. Movie chases were everywhere. You could be crossing Hollywood Boulevard when careening carloads of Keystone Cops would tear down the street, banging blank cartridges and tossing out dummy victims. They would be followed by a camera car in which the cameraman, standing, would attempt to handgrind the action—not improved by jolting over badly tarred streets.

There were two private schools, from one of which I managed to get expelled. My punishment was enforced attendance at the other—to my embarrassment, called the Hollywood School for Girls. There were other unfortunate masculine students—Joel McCrea, Doug Fairbanks, Jr., Noah Beery, Jr., Bill Buckland—and we tried to avoid fraternizing with female schoolmates like Evelyn Flebbe (later Scott), daughter of one of Hollywood's first woman film writers, Beulah Marie Dix, and Margaret and Agnes De Mille, daughters of William, who had finally succumbed to the monetary temptation and rural charm of our town. There was Cecil's daughter, Cecilia, and my cousin Ruth, daughter of my former uncle, Sam Goldwyn, who had divorced Dad's sister, Blanche. All children of film pioneers. There were hardly any other kinds of people there.

My best friend, Bill Buckland, was son of the first film art director. Wilfred Buckland had developed techniques of stage lighting under the spectacular David Belasco. De Mille, who had also worked for the theatrical producer, persuaded Buckland to migrate west. Buckland was the man who originated interior lighting in the infant film industry. Until then, directors relied on natural sunshine controlled by metal-foil-covered reflectors and canvas sails, which were opened and closed to trap the angle of light. The innovation of arc lamps produced dramatic lighting and opened a new world for film makers.

I have seen Wilfred Buckland tie a couple of actors to the camera with ropes so that they could be kept in focus as they were drawn along by one of the first cameras to be placed on a "dolly," or platform on wheels. A man who had made suns rise and set on a theater stage was not likely to leave our early films to the whims of weather. Artificial lighting made it possible to tell day from night without the aid of the title "Came the dawn . . ."

Hollywood was growing up. And so were the children of the pioneers.

One day Dad came to me in the garage, where Bill Buckland and I were fashioning "coasters" to race precariously down the steep La Brea hill to Hollywood Boulevard.

"Jesse, I want you and Bill to start playing with the son of one of my best friends and neighbors."

"Do I have to?"

"Yes, you *do* have to! Douglas Fairbanks is a great friend of Wilfred's and mine. I have told him that you and Bill have invited Douglas Fairbanks, Jr., over to play with your gang."

I was shattered. "But Dad, he can't! Not tomorrow anyway—we've been working all summer building our coasters. He won't even have one, and we don't want anybody without a coaster to come to the race."

Dad considered the problem. He would pass it on to young Doug's father. Hopefully, we envisioned that this would kill the idea of having a stranger forced into our exclusive circle.

Next day, the big race. We assembled at the hilltop.

Fears of an invasion by Doug, Jr., were now far from our thoughts. Surely we reasoned, he couldn't have had time to build a roller-coaster overnight when it had taken us all summer!

Then our ears caught a suspicious sound. A small sputtering like a motorcycle, a chugging up the hill. We strained in horror to watch the approach of a coaster. But no ordinary affair like ours, stuck together from boards, sheet metal, and old wheels. This was a small automobile with its own gasoline engine, snorting up the steep incline under its own power. Behind the wheel, Doug, a scant year older than I, but by right of ownership of such a vehicle, far elevated in social status. It was the unlikely start of a beautiful friendship.

When Doug was about thirteen, Dad contracted him as a child star for Famous Players-Lasky. It was Doug's first job in films and it coincided with my first and only appearance as a thespian.

One day while walking my bike on lower La Brea I saw in the window of a junk shop a long flintlock pistol. Its upper jaw was missing, but there were definite traces of silver wire in the handle. The whole thing had an intriguingly early-eighteenth-century look. Caucasian, or Turkish? I inquired the price. Thirty dollars . . . ! A small fortune. How would a twelve-year-old kid get hold of thirty dollars, short of robbing my father?

Inspiration: In the early twenties when a film needed crowds, they simply nailed up a notice outside the studio and let the word get around. Anyone who wanted to work "extra" had only to appear and hope that one of the casting directors would designate him for employment.

I had heard that Douglas Fairbanks, Sr., was about to start shooting *The Thief of Baghdad.* I also knew that extras, or "atmosphere," as they were called, received five dollars a day for sitting about or filling a street scene. I had only to remain employed for six days, so I took myself down to the United Artists Studio on Santa Monica Boulevard. United Artists was owned by Fairbanks, Chaplin, Pickford, and Goldwyn (now parted from my father). These giants were seldom united and not always notably artistic, but their pictures were vastly successful. I joined the crowd of waiting would-be extras.

The thought of easy money for little effort attracted the dregs, whores, deviates, jailbirds, gamblers, petty thieves, fugitives, and those whose limited English denied them more exacting employment. All in all these "film extras" were a rag-tag, gypsy crew of easy-livers who drifted mindlessly from picture to picture. A grotesque face, a hump on the back, an authentic scar on the cheek, were the most desirable of qualifications. The stump of an arm or a leg, one eye, such blemishes were virtual insurance of employment. Hardly the environment for the scion of a Hollywood film tycoon. I knew instinctively that my father would not approve. My adventure had to be carried out with the greatest secrecy.

The assistant director's moving finger settled on me. The die, and I, were cast.

We dressed in huge tents, large enough to house small circuses, and soon enough they did. Dark body makeup was sponged over our nudity. Costumes and turbans and slippers with turned-up toes were passed among us. The whole thing was a marvelous adventure, if one could overlook and avoid the thievings, seductions, brawls, cheating at cards, etc. . . .

Two White Russian princes appointed themselves my guardians. Each informed me that the other was bogus and not to be trusted. I watched the seething skulduggery on all sides and avoided trouble. Nothing could be more fun than seeing sword swallowers and snake charmers practicing. A boy my own age tried to teach me to eat fire. It would, he assured me, enhance my future in the movie game. And then, on only the second day, I was singled out for a special chore.

A boy was needed to lead a camel. This propounded more problems than might meet the eye.

Our Baghdad set had highly polished floors and streets that glowed like obsidian. Between shots we all had to wear felt over-slippers so the shiny surfaces would not be marred, and I was warned, "If that camel pees or craps on the set, you're fired, kid."

The face of a camel offered few clues to the approach of its bodily functions. It became an obsession. I would watch him, then lead him off the set to be walked like a dog that couldn't be trusted. Then one day, the inevitable happened, right in the middle of a take. We were part of the background movement, me and my camel. In the foreground stood a long row of huge jars, the kind that wine or oil might be stored in. Doug Fairbanks had devised a brilliant "stunt." Pursued by the wicked caliph's guards, he was to make an escape by jumping from jar to jar. To pull off such a feat the inside bottom of each jar had been equipped with a spring platform that would turn Doug into a "Jack-in-the-box."

He rehearsed with his coterie of athletic henchmen, who always hung about in a muster of muscles. Eventually the difficult stunt was ready. Doug was a superb athlete and always did his own stunts.

At the cry of "Camera!" he hopped into the first jar and shot up and away, exactly managing the tricky leap that took him into the next jar. On and on he went, down the line, in and out of at least ten jars. The take was perfect. Except for one horrible mistake.

I had been so interested in watching Doug's fantastic feat that I didn't get the camel through the scene fast enough and he committed a spectacular indiscretion in full range of the camera.

"You!" screamed an assistant, bearing down on me. "What the hell do you think you're doing?"

"It wasn't me, sir!" I said. "It was the camel."

All attention turned to the camel-boy, including Doug's. A few bounds brought him over (Doug always seemed to move in bounds), and his dark eyes snapped and flashed surprise as he recognized me. He threw back his head and spilled laughter upward, much in the manner of the Robin Hood he had so recently performed. Well, if *his* son was playing the lead role in my father's film *Stephen Steps Out*—Jesse Lasky, Jr., deserved something better than nursemaid to a camel.

Photographers were summoned and stills made of us together. My career indeed seemed ready to soar. I might fill my wall with flintlock pistols!

Dad was not amused. He confronted me in golf plus-fours, his blue-gray eyes showing rare anger. In his hand was the Bulldog Edition of the Los Angeles *Examiner*—one of the local organs owned by his newspaper friend, William Randolph Hearst. The headlines read: "DOUGLAS FAIRBANKS JNR. WORKS FOR LASKY. LASKY JR. FOR FAIRBANKS."

He had, he assured me, through the offices of my Uncle Hector Turnbull, an executive at the studio, had the story squelched. It would go no further. Neither, it seemed, would my acting career. He had told Doug I would not be presenting myself for work on the following day, or any other.

In several weeks it would be time to return to school anyway, but not the school in Hollywood I had been attending. It seemed I was to be removed to a much safer distance from the film world. I would be sent to a preparatory school in New Jersey—Blair Academy, a boarding school far from the Hollywood fleshpots.

But when I opened my suitcase to begin packing for the dread banishment, inside it gleamed the flintlock pistol, its aged wood rubbed to a warm glow by my Uncle Hector. He started me off on a collecting binge from which I never quite recovered.

Hector Turnbull was a Scotsman who had married my father's sister, had been a newspaperman, a boxer, war hero, and finally a novelist and film executive. He was a square, tweedy man with a fantastic sense of humor, who in my young eyes was equally competent at giving Bobby Jones a good golf match, carving gargoyles from walnut, and satirizing the sting out of my not-always-perfect relationship with Dad. He also influenced me toward starting to write. In fact Heck could do just about anything except hold his liquor. Happily, his marriage to Blanche kept the drinking problem in hand.

It was a hard transition for me, leaving California for an eastern boarding school. I carried four talismans: the flintlock, a lariat from Dad (in case I managed to run away and join a rodeo), a Bible from Bess, and a photo of my pal, Doug Jr. I would see him again in the summers at the Santa Monica Beach Club. But his career was advancing with great speed. He seemed to grow up faster than the rest of us.

Bill Buckland and I enjoyed a longer childhood. I remember one early summer filled with lead soldiers, which, unlike those of other boys, marched, charged, and deployed on an actual model set of battlefields, ruined villages, and dark pine forests, from which our tiny hussars could surprise columns of infantry, all designed and built by Wilfred and set up on long trestle tables.

There was, however, a real enemy. My brother, Bill, aged three. He'd stagger in, a juggernaut in motion. One gesture could sweep away a village; another, wipe out a vast battlefield. And somehow he could not be barred from our sanctum, since we were never allowed to lock doors.

One day Bill Buckland and I decided to punish our nemesis. Pure violence had never been enough. This time, when he toddled toward our soldiers, we seized him by arms and legs and dragged him kicking and screaming to the window. Each holding an ankle, we dangled brother Bill above the rose garden two storeys below.

When we finally released the hysterical child, after many a threat to drop him head first, we felt secure that he would never again threaten our array of soldiers, and indeed for a while our wars were carried out in peace. And then one day the door to my playroom was kicked open and there stood brother Bill. But something was different, a mysterious evil expression as he moved toward us slowly, step by step. Had once not been enough? We'd shake him up and down out of every window in the room! But at that instant he whisked his hand out from under his jacket, clutching a huge, struggling snake.

In the rattlesnake-infested hills of California Bill Buckland and I had been taught terror of snakes as a practical precaution. Brother Bill had found our Achilles' heels. Waving his reptile like a saber as we sniveled and cowered, he knocked down three detachments of the Guard at Waterloo, doing a more thorough job then Wellington's infantry ever managed. My brother not only found a weapon, but a hobby of his own. From that time forward he was a collector of snakes with his own pits in our garden.

Of course his pets were always escaping, much to the chagrin of Bess and her guests. As he grew older he'd send to various parts of the world for specimens. Baby boas and myriad varieties of serpents, not all of them harmless, arrived by post in heavy packages. It was somewhat like receiving a terrorist letter-bomb today. We all tried to avoid opening anything.

In recent years, between assistant-director jobs, Bill earned a living training and supplying animals, birds, and reptiles for films and television.

Many a falcon that has ridden an actor's wrist was once a sky-riding eagle, captured and tamed by the boy who played with snakes.

Three

MY FATHER'S HOBBY WAS amateur exploration. This might seem a bit unusual for a film mogul, a breed universally known to devote its spare time to gambling and philandering. Not that this benign, dignified, quiet-voiced gentleman who presided so enthusiastically at our family occasions like Christmas, Thanksgiving, and birthday dinners was above the more addictive pursuits of happiness. Indeed, close scrutiny might have recorded that even as he spoke movingly of the virtues of love, honor, family feeling, and sense of occasion, he was stealing glances at his watch or sneaking to the telephone for a "quick business call" to some young lady. I learned eventually that Bess knew and tolerated his peccadillos and only on one occasion came near being pressed into that then-still-disgraceful practice, divorce. Bess had been reared in the un-lib idea that a man can do no wrong providing he never allows his wife and family to discover it. The Victorian sin still prevalent in America's early twenties was being found out. But aside from a nefarious indulgence of overblown romanticism, his wholesome, if not always harmless, pleasure was arranging outdoor adventures up mountains and down unknown rivers.

Dad fancied himself as an intrepid explorer, and, happily, had the wealth to indulge his whim. He would search the map of America for some wild mountain range or little-known wilderness, then plan his expedition like an invasion. He regarded these trips as a challenge, and his daredevilish appetite for risky thrills led him through any number of foolhardy exploits. He was lowered on lassos by cowboys to become the only man ever to have managed a descent down the arch of the towering Rainbow Natural Bridge in Utah. He completed three expeditions down the Colorado River, in the days when it was still an uncharted wilderness. He landed among hostile natives, reported to be cannibals, on the island of Tiburón off the coast of Mexico, and got his Bell and Howell smashed with a rock. We barely got out of that one alive. Yes, I was with him on most of those hare-brained adventures, and not by choice. The trips were becoming too dangerous to be considered fun. Dangerous, and uncomfortable. Dad was probably the first man ever to have led an expedition down the Rio de las Balsas in Lower Mexico—to the sea. For such hazardous river explorations he had "rapid-water boats" especially built and carried by trucks hundreds of miles. Canoes were mule-humped to lakes high in the Sierras that might never before have heard the echo of a human voice. My participation taught me a healthy respect for danger and a sensible appreciation of comfort. Twice I helped to pull Dad out of whirlpools after his canoe had spilled over trying to run impassable rapids alone. Alone, because nobody with a grain of caution cared to share such follies. But I had to. Once I nearly drowned with him when we attempted to swim across a stretch of the Colorado River which proved much wider than it appeared.

What drove a millionaire film tycoon who adored good food, wine, women, and pleasure to lay his life constantly on the line? Why should he or anyone spend huge sums of money to put themselves into situations that most people would sensibly do anything to avoid? Did we *have* to spend several weeks every year in the sheer discomfort of being eaten alive nightly by mosquitoes, reeking of insect repellant, scratching and learning at times to loathe each other because we were locked into a wilderness together? Did we have to spend hours wet to the skin, being knocked about in boats, sleeping on the hard ground? Was this necessary to him?

Perhaps this man, who spent his life fabricating thrills and adventures for the masses imprisoned in humdrum pursuits, needed something beyond the sheer reward of wealth itself. It was difficult to reconcile the daredevil of the Rio de las Balsas, the Colorado, Tiburón Island, with the suave, cool, mild-mannered executive on the other end of a cigar, but in many ways the adventurer was the more real figure.

Occasionally, before the expeditions grew as hazardous as they eventually became, he would include my mother. Bess's taste for adventure hardly ran toward crumbling mountain trails, smoky campfires, and savage armies of night-biting mosquitoes. But I remember one occasion when she was forced to accompany him with me. Her vote was required on a considerable investment. He was contemplating purchasing a large yacht. The fact that he was an imperfect sailor was not allowed to come into the question. It was known that Admiral Nelson had been seasick most of his time at sea, and even Columbus was reported to be more under the weather than over it during his later voyages! To convince Bess of the joys of life on the ocean wave, he borrowed a yacht and crew from Frank Garbet—a well-heeled film fancier and financier—and set out on a stormy run to Santa Cruz Island. It lay among the Channel Islands just in sight of Santa Barbara on the mainland. In 1924 Santa Cruz was considered to be a fairly rugged bit of terra firma populated mainly by wild boar and goats, and very occasionally used by motion picture companies on location, though most preferred a more convenient and civilized island—Wrigley's (chewing gum) Santa Catalina.

Never underrating the dramatic possibilities of running into dangers, until he ran into them, my father invited a favorite companion-in-adventure, "Kid" McCoy, the famous prizefighter. A useful man to have along, should the yacht be boarded by rumrunners, or even rival movie executives. But aside from a brush with *mal-de-mer*, the crossing to the island proved disappointingly unadventurous. Once on the beach, Bess was left to paint a few watercolors, and Dad, armed with a .30-30 lever-action Winchester; McCoy, armed with fists and hunting knife; and I, armed with a .22 revolver, set off into the hills.

My father's hunting exploits were generally pretty unsuccessful, but today a wild boar obliged by actually charging him. Three shots levered off with more than usual accuracy saved McCoy from a bout of knife against tusk. The boar was borne to Bess in triumph. She was setting up a cook fire in front of a lean-to that had in 1919 been part of a location set for *Male And Female*, the movie based on Sir James Barrie's play *The Admirable Crichton*. McCoy cut off a haunch of wild pig to be barbecued and Bess's enthusiasm for the adventure began to flag. But she put a brave face on it and went back to her painting while the hunters prepared the feast. I assisted at cleaning and quartering—a task sloppily managed with hunting knives and hammers.

As the meat roasted over a driftwood fire, a lovely sailing schooner hove into view. A half-hour later its anchor splashed a jet of blue-green water in the cove and a dinghy was rowed to the beach. Its skipper-owner would at that time have been recognized almost anywhere.

"It's Hamlet!" Bess cried excitedly. She had recently seen the most famous profile in America playing the tragic Dane. John Barrymore, immaculate in yachting cap, blue blazer, and white ducks, came up toward us; with him was an exquisitely sad-eyed young lady, Dolores Costello. The blonde American actress was the daughter of famous actor Maurice Costello. She was also John Barrymore's wife and costar.

"Be nice to Barrymore," Dad warned Bess. "I'm trying to get him to do *Lord Jim* for us!"

Effusive greetings were exchanged. All Hollywood greetings are effusive—even between deadly enemies.

"You and Dolores must join us for dinner!" Dad urged, adding with transparent modesty, "We're dining on a succulent wild boar I killed myself."

"Irresistible, Jesse, if you provide a worthy mead to wash it down."

Toasts were exchanged in California Golden State champagne of pre-Prohibition vintage, and the great actor sat down at the camp table as the sun plunged dramatically into an appropriately purple sea.

"Chilled it in a sea cave while we were hunting, John," my father enthused.

"Perfection!" the flamboyant Prince of Players enthused back, guzzling his second glass.

My father produced another bottle.

"Ahhh . . . You've always been a great producer, Jess!"

"The proof of that would be to do a picture for us, John. You and Dolores." No opportunity was being missed.

"Why not?" The hungry romantic drove fork and knife into the flesh of the boar. The knife broke and the fork bent double.

"It'll be tender enough on the inside," Dad the optimist assured quickly.

McCoy nodded confidently. Bess and Dolores said nothing. No fork or knife ever reached the inside to discover how tender it might have been. That blackened leather hide would have broken an ax or the teeth of a shark. Disaster was in the air but my father wouldn't give up.

"It's worth the trouble," he insisted. "Nothing can beat wild boar for flavor."

"It certainly has a wonderful aroma," John Barrymore conceded, preparing to lunge again. His hunting knife snapped at the hilt.

"It's the one I gave you for Christmas," Dolores said sadly.

"I'll put on some hot dogs," Bess suggested. But nobody seemed too hungry by then. Dad produced three long cigars and Bess provided a seashell for ashes. Everyone agreed that the tough old tusker should perhaps have been hung, then prepared well in advance and marinated in some rare rum.

In the night curtain, star formations blazed close to Santa Cruz. One star did not. John Barrymore turned down the lead in Famous Players-Lasky's *Lord Jim*—to do the film *The Sea Beast.* Percy Marmont was cast as Lord Jim instead. In fact, Barrymore never accepted any part in one of my father's pictures.

The boar's head was mounted and hung in our billiard room. Nothing more was said about buying a yacht. At least not until some seven years later.

One night Dad told the family he was going to screen for us "the greatest Western ever made," in our private projection room in the La Brea house. Hardly a modest description, since Dad himself had made the film. He was uncommonly proud of *The Covered Wagon.* Infallibly, the guardians of capital in the New York office had opposed making the film. Who but a madman, they said, would pour $782,000 into a "Western"? They were convinced that the public was perfectly satisfied with the usual low-budget "cowboy and Indian" offerings. Who needed an expensive Western? And yet Lasky had already spent a substantial sum purchasing the film rights to Emerson Hough's novel.

The film had taken months to make. Lois Wilson, J. Warren Kerrigan, Ernest Torrence, Tully Marshall, and Alan Hale, among the company of actors who crossed the plains, suffered scarcely less real harpships than the actual pioneers had done in their covered wagons. My father's attraction to Westerns was genetic. His grandfather had come west in 1848 in a wagon train that landed him in California. My ancestor was distinguished by being one of the few Forty-Niners who failed to find gold. But the spirit of the Old West ran high in the Laskys. I grew up hearing my grandmother's stories of stagecoach journeys up and down the State of California. She had, she insisted, been attractive and innocent-looking, and travelers had borrowed the use of her skirt to hide their valuables when passing through areas preyed upon by Evans and Sontag, the well-known bandits.

So it must be confessed that the audience who had gathered to see the first showing of *The Covered Wagon*—my mother, my father's mother, myself, my father, and Jimmy Cruze, the director who had been given the job because he was supposed to have Indian blood—

were nothing if not prejudiced. Cruze, tanned by the suns of Utah where the film had been made, sat wearing a huge cap that flopped over his enormous face. From the studio had come the film's editor, or "cutter" as they were then called. She was a young, dark, extremely serious woman in tweeds and flat golf shoes, named Dorothy Arzner. She had already made a good start by editing Valentino's *Blood and Sand*. She looked almost grim as onto the screen flickered Dad's silent Western.

When the last shot faded out we were weeping and cheering. My pioneer Jewish grandma, Sarah, started dancing around the tiled floor singing, "Oh, Susannah! Don't you cry for me. I'm goin' to Californee with a banjo on my knee . . . !"

The film had cost $782,000. A record for a Western. It was to become one of the largest moneymakers in silent-film history. Everyone connected with it shared in its fame, including Dorothy Arzner, who eventually became Hollywood's only woman director of the thirties. And when describing it to Adolph Zukor, who alone had supported Dad in getting reluctant eastern approval of the initial budget, Dad coined a new word. *The Covered Wagon* was the first "epic." A word never out of use since. It heralded a new style: war epics, gangster epics, sea epics, historical epics, biblical epics, and even cartoon epics.

But that night we were seeing history. Not merely the history that expanded a nation westward, but the moment when the giant industry could flex its muscles, spend more and more money on its films—and apparently do no wrong; *The Covered Wagon* sent all the studios on a rampage of "big" Westerns. And still the hardheaded businessmen in the East didn't get the message. As always they were resistant to anything new, anything untried.

Dad decided to explore fresher fields. He had not far to look. Someone had given him a copy of a novel about war in the clouds, called *Wings*. Nobody had as yet invaded the skies for filming. This novel offered a new concept. Man, the individual warrior, master of his own fate, fighting lonely sky duels above the vast, struggling mass-misery of trench warfare; helmeted, leather-clad knights of the sky, in goggles and scarves, perhaps trailing a lady's silk stocking wrapped about a throat.

"You can't send those boys up in those crates!" protested the squadron's youthful second-in-command, but of course someone did, and the "boys" who survived were a new kind of hero for the mass media. Hard-drinking, hard-loving young men, with insatiable appetites for dabauchery between bouts with the Von Richthofen Circus. John Monk Saunders set to work adapting his own novel for the screen.

The director was a particularly fortunate choice. Bill Wellman had himself been a combat pilot in the Lafayette Escadrille in World War I. He exuded the perfectly authentic qualities of toughness and courage.

But Dad was needing another sort of courage. New York was opposing the budget of *Wings;* in fact they were downright refusing to invest in this lunacy.

Millions sunk into a film about airplanes? Moving specks in the sky? The public couldn't be expected to show interest in something they could hardly see. How could they tell the good guys from the bad guys? Insert close-ups of the markings on the wings? Goggles made all the pilots look alike—Hun, Yank, or Limey. How could you root for men you couldn't recognize? Worse, Lasky wanted to get sound effects into the silent film. Sound effects . . . ! Hadn't many exhibitors protested that sound in films would keep the audience awake? People, they said, went to movies to rest, relax, and yes—in many cases get some sleep!

And the cast, Clara Bow and Richard Arlen—stars whose reputations were solid should not be risked in anything as revolutionary and unpredictable as an entire film about flying. It was all very well to use a newcomer fresh out of Paramount's talent school, like Buddy Rogers. To reassure them, Wellman and the screenwriter embellished the ground sequences. But this, too, increased costs. It would be necessary to borrow an army. At least a full division or so.

The American army happened to be available, since there weren't any wars going on. Government permission was arranged, along with the use of Kelly Field in San Antonio, Texas. This film was becoming too big for Hollywood! Some sensible New York executive decided that Lasky was becoming too big for his desk. Just let *Wings* fail, he confided to the head of Exhibition. But Dad had the backing of Adolph Zukor and Sir William Wiseman, English member of the board of directors.

The "shooting" had gone well, until they approached the battle sequence, "the St. Mihiel Drive." The final push that would win the celluloid war and provide the spectacle that meant solid BO (in this case—Box Office). My father decided it should be the greatest battle ever filmed (which would be outdoing history somewhat). Aside from the Infantry Division, Washington was providing tanks, artillery, engineers, and technical advisers. Famous Players-Lasky built an entire "ruined" French village on the plains of Texas. Since the action of the scene was to destroy the village, it could only be filmed once. And time was of the essence. It would be necessary to complete the Texas shooting within two days.

Everything was prepared. Explosions were set into position. At the pressing of a button vast sections of forest or village were to be blown sky-high. These areas were carefully marked. Assistant directors uniformed as doughboys, French *poilus*, British Tommies, and Huns would shepherd the troop movements to avoid accidents in the movie war. No less than ten cameras were hidden in ruined buildings, shell craters, trenches, half-destroyed tanks. Since they were to have only one go at it, all camera angles—close, medium, and master shots—would be photographed simultaneously.

The mayor of San Antonio had declared a holiday. The whole town had been humming for weeks with the advent of "them movie folk" trying to catch a fleeting glimpse of the "It" girl or of dashing Dick Arlen. Wellman had arranged for a vast grandstand to be built to accommodate almost the entire town. Seats were at a premium to witness the first French battle to take place in Texas. There hadn't been anything like it since the Alamo.

From the top of a hundred-foot tower set on a rise of ground, Wellman and Dad watched the preparations that would send a few hundred thousand dollars up in smoke. Wellman had arranged a "commence action" signal to his scattered hidden cameras and costumed assistant directors. In those days before "walkie-talkies" three waves of a white flag from the top of the tower could be seen clearly by those who mattered.

The weather was perfect, as it is on most days in San Antonio. Long awaited "photogenic" clouds decorated a sky soon to be filled with the screaming passage of shells and strafing, zooming planes. From their crow's nest, Dad and Wellman looked down upon the vistas of the French village and the zigzag of trenches where troops were poised to "go over the top." The planes were warming up to take off in waves from a nearby airport upon the relayed signal.

Texans swarmed into the grandstand. A flashy roadster whipped up to it and stopped. Out stepped an attractive young girl who happened to be, although nobody was immediately aware of it, the daughter of the mayor. She quickly identified herself and was offered a place of honor at the front of the grandstand. Seated there already were other young ladies whom she knew. Debs, before whom she wished to cut a rather special figure. Anyone could watch from the grandstand, she decided as her eyes swept up to the top of the wooden parallel where that privileged handful of film makers stood. That would be the place to watch from—if one happened to be the daughter of the mayor! She turned away from the grandstand, heading for the long ladder, where a harassed public relations man barred her way.

She made her point, quite firmly and clearly; she would not be swayed or argued out of it. She would inform her father, whose cooperation had made all this possible, if she were not allowed to see, and be seen, from the top of the tower! The PRO turned his back to seek higher authority. She seized her chance and scrambled up the ladder, climbing higher and higher to find a place at the railing. The film-men were too busy to notice her. The very fact that she *was* there seemed to prove that she should be!

Wellman peered over the scene, while he engaged in some further adjustments and corrections. The young mayor's daughter was becoming just a bit bored. Here she was, in the high place of privilege, and everyone was much too busy to pay her any attention. Worse, none of her friends had even noticed her. Something would have to be done about this! She shouted down, tried to catch *anyone's* attention. No luck. Finally she drew the white scarf from her neck and waved it . . . three times . . . in great sweeping gestures toward one special girl friend. The girl waved back, and she waved again.

Hell broke loose! The stupendous battle scene inexorably erupted into action. Tanks ground forward, artillery fired, explosions were ignited. Troops surged in waves over the top. The battle filled every corner of the Texas plain. The French village was blown to rubble, while the planes surged above into the sky. Individual dogfights began, none of which would be heard on the silent screen. Or seen either. Not a single camera recorded the scene, because the cameras had not yet been loaded.

It is known that the film *Wings*, which was extremely successful, did not, however, finally contain the colossal battle scenes that one might have expected in an epic of such scope. Some critics noted it with wonder, but only two men knew why.

In the final analysis everyone was happy. Even New York, who shared the profit and the glory. All of Hollywood was quick to share the idea. At RKO, Howard Hughes set out to make *Hell's Angels*. In it he "discovered" a beautiful blonde extra girl who had changed her name to Jean Harlow.

Nor had *Wings* been without its own "discovery." As the picture was unfolded over and over again around the country and around the world, people were moved and affected by a single incident. It was a scene in which the regular Dawn Patrol took off into the sky. The story made it evident that many of these lads who flew their fragile planes against Von Richthofen's Aces would not survive. Cast as an American aviator was a lank, towering beanpole of a cowboy. This striking young man had one poignant moment as he left to join the Dawn Patrol. Bill Wellman suggested he should pause at the door, give a sloppy farewell salute to the other members of his squadron. The cowboy-extra did this in a casual, graceful manner, tipping two fingers off his forehead in a uniquely, deeply personal way. The audience was aware this good-bye would be his last. He would never see his mates again. They were aware that this was a man going to his death—with a gesture fatalistic and charming. It was no more than one flash in a film. But it was not forgotten. The fan letters poured in. Who was he? What was his name?

Even hard-bitten exhibitors were writing in to the sales department about the lanky unknown who in less than two minutes of screen time had given *Wings* one of its most memorable moments.

Ben Schulberg, new head of the West Coast studio, asked the casting director—who asked his assistant—who asked the assistant director—who asked the director, Bill Wellman.

"Hell, if you don't know, I don't!"

The tough film director had been presented with a new sports roadster as a bonus for bringing in the difficult movie to box-office triumph. He couldn't care less about a nameless cowboy extra at that moment. Yet curiously enough, the Montana-bred cowboy was neither nameless nor merely an extra. Like so many others, he had simply got lost in the small world of Hollywood. Lost, after having played roles in several important films. This tall, bashful drifter from the open spaces (whom my father would later claim as his personal discovery) had traded in his saddle to try his luck as a cartoonist, then moved from drawing board into the seamy world of "two reelers." He played fairly important parts in *The Winning of Barbara Worth*, in *It*—Clara Bow's sex-epic, in *Children of Divorce*, and *Arizona Bound*. Then nothing. It could happen that way. A few rungs up the ladder, then a few months out of the industry's eye, and you might as well never have existed! No explanation. No logic. In filmland one good thing didn't always lead to another. But in those films, Gary Cooper had developed a direct, unactorish style that communicated a basic honesty. The strong, silent type. Few words—and important reaction close-ups.

Gary Cooper had been out of a job long enough to accept the smallest bit part in *Wings*. The impact he made brought him a five year contract with Famous Players-Lasky. When I asked Gary about it on the set of one of the two films I later wrote for him, he didn't remember the gesture at all.

Wings was the last of the silent spectaculars and the first movie to win an Academy Award. It advanced every one of its stars—including one who had begun as a messenger boy at the Marathon Street Studio. One day while motorcycling from lab to studio with a can of film under his arm, the messenger had a bad fall and broke a leg. The head of the legal department brought it up at the weekly production conference.

"You realize the kid could sue the studio for a million bucks?"

Schulberg, the studio manager, showed appropriate concern. The huge cigar hoisted itself to a worry-angle in the pink face framed by silver-white hair. "How much could he collect?"

"Depends on his lawyer, B. P. If some ambulance chaser hears the word "movie," he'll take us to the bank for our shirts!"

"So what do we do?"

"Offer a payoff. Now."

"Wait a minute . . ." B. P. Schulberg's gray eyes caught fire with an idea. "Why not offer him a part? Anything. In one of our pictures. He wouldn't sue his sponsors if he gets the whiff of a career in acting."

"But B. P., can he act?"

"If it saves us a few hundred thousand, he can act."

It is probable Richard Arlen wouldn't have sued anyway. In his parts, and in his life, Arlen was always the perfect gentleman. By such a lucky break as a leg that messenger boy got his foot in the door to stardom. What the studio was unaware of was that Dick had taken the messenger job to try to break into pictures!

Four

Before leaving for Europe our chauffeur, Pierce, told my father that our huge California-based Fiat, with its Bosch magneto, gold-plated fixtures, and rosewood dashboard, was showing its age. Not that we were down to our last automobile. A Locomobile and a Rolls-Royce town car were garaged in New York. The Rolls-Royce roadster, maroon with rumble seat, crouched in the California garage beside Dad's Packard Special. That gray, cigar-shaped racing car had been designed by Dad's racing pal, Ralph De Palma. Still, Pierce suggested, if Dad could find a replacement for the Fiat while in London it would be "only a good economical step."

So, in the cause of pure economy, my father, wearing striped trousers, pearl gray spats, leaning on a blonde malacca walking stick with initialed gold head, entered the London showroom of Rolls-Royce. The salesman pointed out a variety of cars but my father's eye was captured by a veritable house on wheels called the Prince of Wales Model. The only other like it, assured the salesman, had been built for the heir to the throne. The one gleaming in royal blue splendor before him was ordered by a maharajah who had been mildly incapacitated in a tiger-hunting accident and did not live to take delivery. An opportunity for an excellent buy. It would make a nice surprise for Bess, who was amusing herself antique-furniture-hunting with British playwright Eddie Knobloch; she was furnishing the Fifth Avenue apartment with Queen Anne, William and Mary, and early Georgian. Delighted, the vice president of Famous Players-Lasky signed the order form and hastened off to lunch with his friend and theatrical associate, producer Gilbert Miller.

In that first half of the 1920s Dad's company was churning out some seventy films each year. Not all good, but almost none financial failures. He had even decided to buy into or build a British film studio where "quota" pictures could be produced, the British government having wisely decreed that a proportion of the films released in England must be British-made, although this failed to prevent American companies from siphoning off their profits. (Though most of these were inexpensively made, they proved an ideal showcase for British actors, actresses, directors, and writers, many of whom later swelled the ranks of the huge foreign colony in Hollywood.)

Success was bringing impressive changes to the Lasky lifestyle. The California boy who had once supported himself by shooting ptarmigan to sell to the gold hunters in the Alaska gold rush was wallowing in celluloid gold. Dad now occasionally traveled by private railroad car attended by an impressive retinue of assistants, secretaries, an athletic trainer, and a private golf pro whose best efforts still failed to bring his erratic golf game under ninety. A sinister Prussian physiotherapist was having more success keeping Dad slim. Von Heim looked like a fugitive from a horror movie, and administered rubdowns with the sadistic enthusiasm of a professional torturer. To these he added sweat boxes and pummelings of raw salt which were supposed to stimulate virility. "Von is my hair shirt," Dad would affirm when the employment of this human Frankenstein came into question.

On the basis that women could never keep secrets, Dad's new production assistant, young Walter Wanger, persuaded him to replace his personal secretary with a male amanuensis named Randolph Rogers. He was called Randy, and the appellation was not inappropriate. Randy was a joyous dog forever in heat. The mere approach of a young woman ignited him like Guy Fawkes night. His eyes became wicked pinpoints of suggestion. It would be fair to say that this guardian of the outer office, with its eternal display of leg-crossing soubrettes, hardly enjoyed a tranquil moment. He was endlessly efficient, hopelessly lecherous, and totally charming. Mustache ends twisted to needle points, he was immensely proud of being a direct descendant of Cotton Mather, the witch-burning judge of Old Salem who used local ladies as tinder in the chill autumn of 1692. Randy remained with my father to the end, and when the lean years came, he worked on for nothing, sitting in the empty office—his loyalty had become Hollywood legend.

But the twenties were the prosperous days and they brought a change of address. From the rambling, creaky old mansion on La Brea to Dad's personal Versailles on the Pacific. An ocean-front house that would be gradually enlarged into a palace built on sand. And what sand! It could have been gold dust for what ninety feet cost him, but they were strategically located between the mansions of Louis B. Mayer and Sam and Frances Goldwyn (Sam was now a top producer at United Artists).

Other neighbors were Norma Shearer and Irving Thalberg, a fragile genius who had to have special air piped into his beach house. There were Doug Fairbanks, Sr., and his Mary Pickford—alternating their huge beach house with their town palace of Pickfair, high above Beverly Hills. There was Billie Burke, widow of Florenz Ziegfeld. She had been on the stage since childhood and in films since 1916. Her peformances of elegantly addled ladies hardly portrayed the real-life professional who had never in her life been late on a set or forgotten a line. There were Mildred and Harold Lloyd. The great American comedian had also entered films in 1916 and by the twenties was one of the richest stars in Hollywood. And one of the few who would die one of the richest. He never divorced the leading lady he had married, and like Doug and Mary, kept a palazzo on a high hill in Beverly Hills. He also kept a pack of dogs that were the terror of the beach colony.

Yes, colony. Where everyone knew everyone, entertained each other, and watched each other get richer and richer. But the largest house of all was the super-palace of William Randolph Hearst, the newspaper czar, who could buy and sell studios as a hobby. And did. I considered it a great thrill to be invited to swim in his Olympic-sized pool of *heated* salt water. His beach house was so enormous that tourists took it for a hotel and constantly stopped to apply for rooms. It was guarded by a small army of watchmen and it housed the incomparable Marion Davies. My friend Dorothy Parker once stopped before the Davies dressing-room at Metro, which resembled a small cathedral and had a statue of the Virgin placed above the huge entrance. The sight prompted Dorothy to pen these lines:

> Upon my honor, I saw a Madonna,
> sitting alone in a niche.
> Above the door
> of the glamorous whore
> of a prominent son of a bitch.

It is not reported that the newspaper giant, who was said to be quite capable of starting wars to feed his headlines, was deeply concerned.

I met Hearst with my father in his private car on the Santa Fe train rattling west from Chicago in 1926. The awesome octopus of the press fixed me with a penetrating glance above his glass of milk.

"What do you plan to do with your life, boy?"

"Jess wants to be a writer, W. R." This suggestion came from my father, who had always wanted to be a writer himself when he was not wanting to be a concert cornetist, a racing driver, or an explorer.

Hearst drew a pyramid and indicated the point: "If you write for the classes, you'll live in the masses." His pencil lowered to the broad base of the pyramid: "but if you write for the masses"—pencil moved up to the peak—"you'll live in the classes."

I never forgot the advice, and apparently never followed it.

Our Santa Monica beach house, 609 Ocean Front, was a two-storey hacienda surrounding a garden with a fountain. It originally had twelve guest suites, which should have been sufficient even for the opulent hospitality of those times, but my father enlarged it still further. We became a kind of hotel for the famous, excluding actual royalty, most of whom got the royal treatment at Pickfair, the Fairbanks place in Beverly Hills.

I can remember no time when we were not inundated with house guests. Among the string of novelists who, lured by the promise of profits and the prophets of promise, followed the film sales of their works and summered with us were Fanny Hurst and Louis Bromfield. G. B. Stern arrived from London bringing a gift of her newly published novel, *The Matriarch*. She had a fringe of gray hair, had hobnobbed with Rebecca West and Virginia Woolf, and had a walking stick which she assured me had once borne the weight of Lord Byron. She brought a breath of Bloomsbury to our beach and had wild arguments in our swimming pool with Joe Hergesheimer, the Pennsylvania novelist. He had migrated to Havana, then followed the sale of one of his books to California, which he insisted he hated but refused to leave. His ugliness—Dad described him as one tooth and a pencil—was offset by the magnificent good looks of the Homer of the jazz age, F. Scott Fitzgerald, who wore out his welcome at the beach house not because of his alcoholism but by too frequently beating Dad at golf.

Unfortunately the Hollywood environment was destructive to novelists. High earnings lulled them into complacence. Some unreality in the atmosphere, a lack of definition of seasons, too much sunshine, too few strong winds to blow alive the sense of frailty of man, the isolation and insulation drugged the senses and numbed the hard edge of purpose. Perhaps the hacks survived best, for Hollywood was their Kingdom of Heaven.

Like prospectors combing the Badlands for gold, the movie makers searched out the raw materials that could be fashioned into stars. A "find" was anybody who had the mysterious basic ingredient that could be trained, groomed, and developed into a film personality. Success in the search called for a shrewd instinct and pure luck. The searchers hardly knew what they were looking for until they found it. It. The him—or her—whom the public would take to their hearts and pay out hard money to see. Showmanship was never a science in which rules were followed and results guaranteed. Of thousands of attractive people, what combination of physical assets held the spark of stardom? Fortunes were invested in building "good bets" that never paid off. Anna Sten, Lillian Harvey, John Loder—all promising enough, but finally they missed the target and never became truly "big."

In silent days acting had never been all that important. Directors could wring emotional performances out of wooden Indians. If well lighted, and well cast physically, a dolt could rise to histrionic heights. Von Stroheim was known to lurk behind actresses, twisting their arms to get them to show the proper agony required in a close-up. "Takes" were short, and performances, unlike those on the stage, did not have to be sustained.

What the movie makers sought was some unidentifiable appeal to the senses, dream creatures who could communicate with the hearts of the lonely and the minds of the feeble. It is surprising how frequently really big drawing cards turned up in the deck. Once discovered, the factory took over. Time, money, know-how were invested in turning human creatures into national idols. They were groomed, styled, and guided. Many became glamorous robots. Many were destroyed in the process. A few died at the top.

When I was a kid my father came home one night raving about a tango-dancing gaucho he had seen in *The Four Horsemen of the Apocalypse*. Rex Ingram, who had directed the film, was an old family friend. Bess had helped the young Irishman when he first came to town, a shattered ex-aviator out of World War I. Rex had little to say for, or against, the Italian who had danced the memorable tango in his picture. In fact, he seemed reluctant to discuss him. Since *Four Horsemen* had been made for the shrewd Dick Rowland, head of Metro, it was a dead certainty that the young tango dancer had been locked into a long-term contract. Rex was of course delighted that my father liked the picture.

"Liked it! After *Birth of a Nation,* I consider it the most thrilling film I've ever seen!"

Then, one evening not too long after, Dad came home looking like he'd swallowed a cageful of canaries. His enthusiasm, generally uncontrolled, had never been greater. But his stories always had to start from the beginning—which meant food forgotten, and finally indigestion when he remembered some evening engagement, bolted his dinner, and ran.

"When I got to my office at the studio this morning a young man was waiting to see me." By the air of mystery and significance we could have guessed it to be the Prince of Wales.

"His name was Rudolph Valentino."

We looked ignorant.

"Rudolph Valentino! Who danced the tango in *Four Horsemen!* For goodness' sake, don't you remember him?"

Bess remembered him very well, but couldn't see why his waiting in the office should have been all that important.

"Because I just signed him up for life!"

"For life" usually meant five years—with options.

"Metro had him in their pocket and neglected to sign him. So Valentino just stopped by our studio looking for a job. We can make him the biggest star we've ever had!"

All stars were the biggest, in my father's expectations. Until they were proven less. But this time he certainly wasn't wrong. Because Roland of Metro had been too busy negotiating the sale of the company to the mighty Marcus Loew, or maybe because there had been rumors that Rex Ingram had found the young Italian "difficult" on the set, they had passed up Rudy. To find a "find" who had already been found was unthinkable. A carelessness impossible in the agent-dominated industry of later days.

Valentino's first film at the Lasky studio made history. *The Sheik* in 1921 even changed the hair style of most young American males. Young men swaggered about, even we younger ones, hair glued to our scalps with axle grease. Someone even made a quick fortune by inventing a hair strap that insured no possible ripple in our slick flat-tops. We were called "Vaselinos." Had flares sewn into our trousers for the bell-bottom gaucho effect. Practiced tango-dips with invisible partners in our arms.

We slithered about, crooning "I'm the Sheik of Araby . . . ," adding after each couplet the daringly witty "without pants on." Girls were called Shebas and dreamed of being abducted away to the desert by Rudy. White slavers could have done a roaring trade to Araby that year.

Blood and Sand, filmed in 1922 from the Vicente Blasco-Ibañez bullfighting saga, carried the Valentino craze to greater heights. The Italian had become a national fetish. And an increasing problem on the set. Ego-inflation was a disease few successful Hollywoodites could avoid.

When Rudy's first marriage fell apart, he wed Winifred Hudnut, stepdaughter of the famous cosmetic manufacturer. This flashy young lady was also an exotic designer in fashions and advertising under the professional name Natasha Rambova. Their union made Valentino slightly less accessible than the Pope. He placed all his affairs in his wife's hands, and even heads of the studio had to arrange to be received by appointment—made through her weeks in advance. Directors and producers could barely see their star!

"She won't even let me near him!" my father complained. "Vice president in charge of production, and I have to beg for an interview!"

"Why put up with it?" Grandma Sarah wondered.

"Because Valentino is the biggest thing at the box office since Wallace Reid. But now Rambova even insists on selecting his next picture. And she couldn't have made a worse choice. Valentino became what he is playing earthy tigers. Physical lovers smelling of the bull ring. And desert chieftains dragging women to his tent."

"That ain't bad," sighed Grandma.

"And now she wants him to play a mincing dandy in a powdered wig in the worst story Booth Tarkington ever wrote. *Monsieur Beaucaire*."

"So what are you going to do, Jesse?" said Grandma, always down to brass tacks.

"Nobody ever sets out to make a failure, Mother. We'll do the best we can."

The best was none too good. Valentino suffered a drop in popularity as Beaucaire, in 1924. The flimsy vehicle was more successful when Bob Hope selected it years later as a natural for unintentional comedy. Of course Rambova and Valentino blamed the studio for its lukewarm reception. The great lover sulked off screen without making another picture for two years. Eventually, he was persuaded to make films for another company. But for the moment the glow was off the worm, the bloom off the peach, the twinkle dulled on the star.

Only in *Son of the Sheik* did he regain some of his original popularity. This renaissance was interrupted by death. Of peritonitis, at the age of thirty-one. His funeral caused public riots, and launched legends of veiled ladies in black, appearing annually at his grave. His house, The Falcon's Nest, became a Mecca for female romantics. His memory lingered on. And on.

Such devotion prompted a search for a replacement. Every studio looked for a Latin lover whose bedroom glance could bring swoons and swell box-office receipts. Ramon Novarro came close to filling the pedestal. So did Gilbert Roland (whose name was fabricated as a combination of the popular Jack Gilbert and Ruth Roland). His studio threatened to take back its name and send him back to being Louis Alanso when Gilbert Roland asked for a raise.

But my father's problem of finding a Latin lover for his company had still not been solved. One evening in the mid-twenties, he, Bess, and I were dining at the Ambassador Hotel's Cocoanut Grove. My own craze for tangoing gauchos and galloping sheiks had somewhat abated by then. Most of my friends had hung up their headbands, turned in their jars of hair grease, and were considering crew cuts.

We were watching a dance contest of amateurs weaving in and out of the fake cocoanut palms of the fabulous grove. Bess became captivated by one of the tango dancers who bore a reasonable resemblance to the dead Latin lover. He wore the number 19 on his back, and glided to victory, insured by an ovation of applause. My father sent the head waiter to summon him over.

I always found such show-business tactics as offering screen tests to strangers unbearably embarrassing.

"How would you like to be a moving picture star, young man?" However sincerely meant, it seemed like hitting somebody in the face with pie in the sky.

On this occasion the proposal sounded even worse. "How would you like to become the next Valentino?"

The amateur tango dancer looked as though he'd been hit by a falling castanet.

"I'm Jesse Lasky," Dad assured him to show the offer was authentic. "What's your name?"

"Jack Krantz, sir."

"We'll change that, for a start! Something appropriately Latin."

"But I'm Austrian, Mr. Lasky. At least my family was."

"From tonight on, you're a Latin." My father's eyes flicked to the band he was just removing from his cigar. He offered one to the tango dancer. "A Ricardo?"

The young man accepted. The name and the cigar.

"Now for a last name. Spanish, maybe. A conquistador. Something romantic, easy to pronounce, and faintly familiar . . ."

Everyone at the table got into the guessing game. Balboa? Coronado? Magellan? All tried and discarded. Pizarro was a near miss.

"What about Cortez?" Bess suggested.

"Ricardo Cortez, you will be at the studio tomorrow at ten. We'll draw up a five-year contract!" My father must have had some faint misgivings because he hadn't said "a contract for life."

Cortez became a popular star of the twenties and thirties. But he never became another Valentino. The Sheik had ridden into his last sunset with the flower of womanhood dangling from his white-robed arms.

Cortez lasted much longer—because after he got older he made a successful shift from acting to directing.

Some Hollywood careers didn't find such happy endings.

An example of the corrosive effect of sudden success was our perennial house guest John Monk Saunders, who had written *Wings*. Johnny was probably the handsomest man who ever lived and he wasn't even an actor. He had been a Rhodes scholar, held an Oxford Blue for swimming and boxing, and had been an American Olympic swimmer. He married Fay Wray and their romance almost broke Bess's heart. She regarded him as her own special admirer. But he was a one-hit author, and his repeated efforts at screenwriting were becoming less successful.

One night while I was home from boarding school, Dad threw a huge party at the beach house: two orchestras, one playing only rhumbas; people dancing on specially built platforms above the sand, a fake moon wired above the festive scene because the real moon wasn't large enough that night. Life was more formal on the beach then, stiff white dress shirts, dinner jackets, spangled evening dresses. Those who had fabulous gems wore them so that those who hadn't would know they had.

The word had been whispered about that John Monk Saunders' latest film was a disaster. Overhearing the talk, the ex-Olympic swimmer challenged his detractors, whom he insisted could neither write nor swim, to three lengths across the pool in full evening regalia, with one length's start for anyone who needed it. Quite a few men accepted. Someone popped a champagne cork as a starter and off they plunged, patent leather shoes, boiled shirts, and all.

Johnny won this particular battle, but lost the Hollywood war. Like many others, he began to search for his luck in the bottom of a bottle. He died mysteriously in Florida in 1940, some said by suicide.

Happily, Bess had other admirers, like violinist Jascha Heifetz and Boris Lovet-Lorski, the Russian sculptor, who did busts of every member of the family except me, as a kind of singing for his supper in marble. But as house guests they were only two of a multitude, since everywhere my father went he would invite almost everyone to the beach house, and they all always turned up. In Nice one winter the film director Rex Ingram introduced Dad to Édouard Corniglion-Molinier, president of the French company London Films. Corniglion had us to lunch in Nice, and we had him to a summer in Santa Monica.

Dad, who was hopeless at names, was always sending me up the back stairs to Bess to be reminded to whom he was talking. But Bess was no better. I once heard her introduce Rouben Mamoulian, the director whom my father had just hired from the Theatre Guild, as Ernst Lubitsch—to Lubitsch!

The trouble was that just when you'd memorized one name another would arrive. Eddie Goulding, the English writer-director, came for a weekend and stayed for a month. George Gershwin came by for a drink and fell in love with Bess's concert grand. When she forgot his name she'd introduce him as Mr. Steinway. Erich Maria Remarque made our beach house his western front. Antonio Moreno, the aging Spanish lover of the silent screen, was one of Bess's special favorites—she said he was the only man who could still appear handsome smoking a cigar.

Sometimes we had house guests we didn't even know were there. I recall Dad seeing the French director Jean de Limur having breakfast on a tray facing the unfurling green combers of the Pacific. "Jean! Back again!" Dad exclaimed "But J. L.," Jean replied, "I never left. Where else can I be served an English bloater by a beautiful Swedish maid while watching Doug Fairbanks walk into the ocean on his hands?"

A rarefied atmosphere for a schoolboy home from the hardships of a New Jersey boarding school. I used to watch the procession of breakfast trays going to the various suites in the morning and wonder who would be joining Dad by the pool. Olympic-size, it was located on the sand, where on stormy days the disrespectful Pacific would hurl great waves at the sea wall. A strange sensation to be floating tranquilly in the gentle blue water and hear waves pounding against the side of the pool. Like being in the mythical eye of the hurricane.

And since nothing could be grown on the sand, truckloads of earth were brought into the patio. Bess had developed a special communion with flowers. She was accused of talking to them. "Naturally," she replied. "Why shouldn't I? I raised them."

"But do they ever answer?"

"Naturally, I'm their mother." End of conversation. She would sit in her garden painting in an old but glamorous straw hat, generally keeping her distance from the "show people," preferring her circle of sculptors, poets, and writers. One day one of Dad's guests who had somehow missed being introduced to her found her painting. "Are you hired to paint these pictures of the Lasky house?" he asked.

She thought about that for a minute and then nodded.

"How much does Lasky pay you?"

"A few million dollars," she smiled.

Droppers-in for a weekend or a week often included Maurice Chevalier and his chic French wife, Yvonne. His friendship with the Laskys started one night at the Casino de Paris in the springtime of '29.

Bess and Dad had fallen in love with Paris. In fact, they felt as though they'd discovered it. Most Americans treated Paris as a rather personal discovery in the twenties. The Laskys were entertained by stage producer Gilbert Miller, who kept a flat there and introduced them to the famous, among them authors André Maurois and Alfred Savoir. Bess added to her wardrobe, paints, and paintings, and discovered a star for my father's galaxy, the flamboyant singer with the straw hat, contagious grin, and personality transcending all languages. But France had already found him.

"Go back and sign up that singer, Jesse!"

"But Bess, suppose he doesn't even speak English?"

"He doesn't need to."

"Tell that to our New York executives!"

"When did they ever stop you if you were sure of something?"

"It's *you* who's sure!" But he became surer as the singer went on. It might have been the champagne, it might have been the atmosphere of a city that started getting into the blood when the boat train approached the station, it might even have been the need to reingratiate himself with Bess after some daring private peccadillo. They ended up in Maurice Chevalier's dressing room.

"How would you like to go to Hollywood and star in a picture?"

The smile flashed back in all the dressing room mirrors. "Would I meet Doog and Mary?" Yes, he spoke English—with an enchanting accent.

"It's a promise. Your first night in Hollywood." They shook hands on it. "I'll have a contract ready to sign tomorrow, at the Paramount Theatre Building."

Next day brought qualms in the sobering Paramount offices with Al Kaufman, the shrewd young dynamo of the Zukor clan. Kaufman had bulging eyes—and a sour look that became downright cynical at mention of Chevalier.

"You don't want to sign him, J. L.?"

"What's wrong with Chevalier?"

"He's been around Paris too long. Every producer in the business has seen him and turned thumbs down. Thalberg and Louis B. caught his act last month. Wouldn't touch him with a foot-long cigar."

"They could be wrong," Dad said, confidence waning.

"Don't bet on it, J. L. Americans won't understand that accent. It's thicker than Gruyère. Better reconsider."

Dad did. After all, Bess had never been noted for show-biz judgment. Even Dad's mother had warned him about getting too artistic. There had been the disaster of the Folies-Bergère when he'd lost his shirt.

Al Kaufman bounced up. "You want me to call off the appointment?"

"No, just the lawyer." It flashed into my father's mind how he had once turned down another prospect—on everyone else's judgment: a song-plugging piano player named Irving Berlin. "I hope you're right, Al. I'll see Chevalier and tell him the deal's off myself."

My father had the reputation of being able to fire people so graciously that they had been known to thank him for it.

The French secretary with her brightest smile announced the arrival of the Parisian singer. "I hope you can persuade him to make a picture for you, Monsieur Lasky," she bubbled.

Maurice stepped in, hand outstretched beneath the fatal smile. "My valise is packed, and also my wife!"

"Maurice, I'm going to have to postpone your trip to Hollywood . . ."

"No Doog and Mary?"

That smile. If every executive in the Industry was against Chevalier—than every executive could be wrong!

"Only for two weeks. I want to get to New York first. Prepare a proper reception for our new international star." Then he sent for the contract lawyer.

The news was cabled to New York. New York cabled back: URGE CANCEL CHEVALIER DEAL STOP PUBLIC WILL NOT REPEAT WILL NOT ACCEPT ACCENTS STOP EVEN RUTH CHATTERTON TOO ENGLISH FOR AMERICA STOP FRENCH ACCENT TEN TIMES WORSE STOP.

Dad decided that it was too late to stop. Girded for battle, he and Bess boarded the boat train for Cherbourg. Chevalier appeared at the carriage window grinning above a bouquet of roses tied with a tricolor ribbon. French fans engulfed him as the train pulled out.

"Aren't you glad you listened to me for once, Jesse?"

"I'll let you know when we get to New York." He was seeing visions of the New York hierarchy—Zukor, Wobber, and Kent. Men with faces carved of stone, cool, practical, eternally disapproving. They represented moderation, conservatism. They, the watchdogs against dangerous expenditure.

But even their misgivings fell away at Chevalier's reception banquet. Without rehearsal or advance warning, Chevalier, who had stepped off the ship only that morning, sang several impromptu songs at my father's request. By the third, he had the crowd in his pocket. The day seemed won.

Then came news from the story department of the West Coast studio. The screenplay for Chevalier's first film had run into writing problems. It would be at least another six weeks before it could be ready. With Maurice's salary of $1,500 a week, starting from the time he set foot in New York, faces lengthened again at the Paramount Building. The French star would cost the company thousands before he could even begin to study his first American script!

A troubled moment for the production head. Then his secretary announced Mr. Florenz Ziegfeld on the phone.

"How are you, Jesse?"

"Fine, Flo." Never let worry show through the optimistic facade.

"I heard your French performer at the banquet. He's sensational!"

"Thanks, Flo."

"So this morning an idea came to me while I was shaving. I asked myself, Would Jesse consider loaning me Chevalier for *The Midnight Frolic* I'm producing on the New Amsterdam Roof?"

The question called for a careful pause. No show of too-quick acceptance. "You asking me to postpone the start of his first picture, Flo?"

"I'll only need him for six weeks. It would be a great favor, Jesse."

"I don't know . . ."

"All right, Jesse, how much is it going to cost me?"

Quick calculations—six weeks at $1,500 per week: $9,000. Would Ziegfeld go that high? Play it safe. "What would he be worth to you, Flo?"

"Five thousand a week. Say, $30,000?"

"Flo, as a special favor to you—I'll postpone the picture! We won't argue about money."

"I'll never forget this, Jesse."

And never again did my father have to pay for front-row seats at the Follies. The studio made the loan-out and a profit on their new star before a camera turned.

Innocents of Paris in 1929 proved a great springboard for Chevalier. In it, he sang "Louise," composed for the picture by Leo Robin and Richard Whiting, father of Margaret. After that came a parade of musicals directed by Rouben Mamoulian and Ernst Lubitsch. He was often teamed with a discovery from a Shubert musical, Jeanette MacDonald.

But some of the best entertainment the public never saw. Ordinary Sunday nights at the beach house. They generally included some fifty guests. Joan Crawford, Doug Fairbanks, Sr. and Jr., Mary Pickford, Marion Davies, William Randolph Hearst, Billie Burke, Jascha and Florence Heifetz, Charlie Chaplin, Pola Negri, Joe von Sternberg, to name-drop a few. Impromptu entertainments were organized. One night somebody brought the entire Albertina Rasch Ballet to dance in the moonlight.

As applause melted away from the poolside patio, it was announced that still another great ballet company had arrived—with no regard for expense. The Ballet Russe de Santa Monica! A group of hairy-legged males had donned tutus and launched into a spontaneous burlesque that included Eddie Cantor, Harpo Marx, Doug Jr., Phillips Holmes, Carrol Case, Randy Rogers, and me.

In her book *Candle in the Sun*, Bess tells of stealing away at dawn to enjoy a cold turkey bone in her antique maple four-poster. Elsie Janis, Eddie Cantor, Kay Francis, and Jeanette MacDonald saw in the dawn around the bed—singing as the sun blazed through the delicate lace curtains. Chevalier raised his champagne glass and toasted Bess as his "Columbus."

In the waning twenties, life seemed to avoid endings. To parties. To pleasures. To the hope that each film would be bigger, better than the last. As everyone knew, the motto of the company was, "If it's a Paramount picture it's the best show in town!" With the money pouring in, the motto could not have been entirely wrong!

Launching a foreign star into our community generally required an artillery barrage of press and a healthy sprinkling of scandal and rumors. First the community had to be impressed, later the whole country, finally the world. Festivities often started in outlying Pasadena, where super-celebs like the glorious Swanson and her new husband, the marquis de la Falaise, would descend from the Santa Fe train onto a red carpet that stretched through the station to the cavalcade of limousines between ranks of cheering, flower-tossing fans, some of them not paid for by the studio.

Such producer-pandering to the stellar image impressed the public no less than it did the stars themselves. "Going Hollywood" meant incurring that peculiar swelling of the cranium causing the victim to see the world as not only his oyster but also his mirror. Movie Queens buzzed circles above the drones. Talented, and even untalented, importations reached our shores with more fanfare than world leaders.

In 1922, Pola Negri's arrival could hardly have been topped by the Second Coming. Having been mobbed, by careful prearrangement, at the dock, she was driven down Fifth Avenue to the old St. Regis Hotel behind a police escort of screaming sirens, totally paralyzing the traffic. Pola, born in Poland, made a star in Germany, and having acquired honorary membership in several Indian tribes en route, was somewhat disappointed with Hollywood itself. Despite having received the by now traditional red-carpet reception at Pasadena, she described it as a "sleepy small town of squat, undistinguished buildings." But if Pola Negri had felt let down by her first sight of our town, she soon made it her springboard to world fame.

Dad had always been lucky with his "discoveries." It was an irony that he made one of his greatest finds sight unseen. In 1929 one of his directors, Josef von Sternberg, had taken leave of the studio to make an Emil Jannings film for UFA in Berlin. Von Sternberg belonged to the "imagist school," which made highly effective use of symbols. He drenched his characters in atmosphere, creating a thick veil of illusion through which he built, with exaggerated tonality, grotesque visions. He created mood effects by shooting through gauze and fishnets and all his dusks were smoky. His very unsubtlety was an artistic weapon and his films were admired for their stylistic power. *Underworld, The Last Command, Dragnet, Docks of New York*, each in its turn had advanced the art of the cinema.

Joe was a short, somewhat hunched figure, opinionated, pompous, seemingly unhumorous, introverted, and vain. Like Erich von Stroheim, Joseph von Sternberg was a highly individualistic artist in film making. Having worked up from a "cutter," he was less extravagant, more practical, with a shrewder sense of public appeal. Joe established his reputation with *Salvation Hunters* in 1925, followed by *Underworld*—the first real gangster movie—and then *The Last Command* with Emil Jannings. Each was something of a masterpiece.

He had nothing of Von Stroheim's militaristic bearing, but he did affect an extremely impressive form of self-portraiture, as I was to discover.

One summer holiday from college, I got a job working as assistant to the censorship editor of Paramount. Geoffrey Sherlock, who later became guardian of Industry morals, sent me around to the producers and directors to point out possible pitfalls. Cutting offensive material after a film was made could damage the flow of the story.

Von Sternberg, normally a family friend, became understandably hostile at the sight of one whose mission was to bowdlerize his work. I was as welcome as a process server.

I found the moody genius posing like an eighteenth-century Bourbon monarch, simultaneously having his portrait painted, his head sculpted, and his every word recorded by a young woman journalist assigned to prepare an article entitled "The Director's Day." A still-photographer hovered on the periphery of his aggrandizing court, snapping "unposed" poses.

"Mr. Von Sternberg, there are three lines in your script that will bring censorship objections in Ohio," I began, not too happily.

He weighed this information like a threat to the imperial throne while shutters clicked, brushes slashed, and clay was slapped on clay.

"Tell the Ohio board of censors that I will not approve the script until they reject every word!"

I believe his movie survived Ohio, Pennsylvania, and the New England states unscathed. But Joe was a genius, even though he acted like one. Whether or not he had chosen his aristocratic nomenclature to replace plain "Joe Stern" from Brooklyn (as detractors suggested), he advanced the magic of storytelling on the screen. Perhaps he will be even better remembered for discovering and creating one of the all-time-great lady stars.

It happened like this.

My father received a letter from him raving about the young actress he was using in the Jannings film, being produced by UFA in Berlin. Dad took it seriously enough to ask Sidney Kent, East Coast VP in charge of sales, who was making a trip to Europe, to have a look at Von Sternberg's find. The cable came back: "She's sensational. Sign her up!" Dad did, without even having seen a still photograph of Marlene Dietrich. A fair demonstration of what he then referred to as "the Lasky luck." It was great while it lasted.

Of course a smashing party had to be given at the beach house to welcome his new star. She arrived complete, with, so rumor had it, lover and husband. All our ocean-front neighbors and illustrious film celebrities contrived to be there. The uninvited somehow invited themselves. The publicized triumvirate were fashionably late, as everyone expected them to be, and when they finally appeared nobody was disappointed.

Earthy, lusty, yet mysteriously sophisticated, the lady swaggered into the crowded room flanked by the two disparate males, bringing a breath of continental bistros, exotic places. She had a certain sloe-eyed magnetism that years and time would never dim. From head to toe she was a star, loaded with that particular magic that stars exude, and when all eyes had filled themselves with her presence the speculations began.

Was one of these two men her lover, one her husband? If so, which was which? The golden-blonde, blue-eyed young Teutonic athlete who might have stepped out of a Wagnerian opera, brimming with virility and bronzed from some Alpine ski slope, was her husband, Rudolph Sieber. The caved-in, disheveled, unkempt, gnomelike Von Sternberg was her admirer and discoverer. A Hollywood cliché was shattered.

In those days things were meant to be as they appeared. Our villains wore black, our heroes patted dogs and children. Audiences expected to know where they were from the moment the hero or villain walked on the screen. Subtleties and gray tones were not yet a part of our film making. We were still the myth makers who believed that all endings were happy, deserts were always just, virtue always rewarded, evil punished, and good triumphant.

Marlene was, of course, an instant success. To mystery she added a special warmth in which the exotic and erotic were tremendously alive. In her first American film, *Morocco*, she dressed in a man's dinner jacket and kissed a pretty girl on the lips, one of the first suggestions of lesbianism that was permitted to reach the screen. And

Boston Conservatory music student elopes to Atlantic City with vaudeville producer—the author's mother (Bess) and father, 1909. *(Author's collection)*

One of the first Hollywood locations—the authentic ranch house used in *Rose of the Rancho* (1914). *(Author's collection)*

The Squaw Man (1913, producer Jesse L. Lasky, director Cecil B. De Mille) was Hollywood's first major feature film. In this moment of violence Winifred Kingston protects Baby DeRue from assault by Dustin Farnum, while white-hatted Art Accord looks vehemently on. *(De Mille Foundation)*

Probably the first picture of the three original partners of The Jesse L. Lasky Feature Play Company in 1913. From right: Jesse L. Lasky, Cecil B. De Mille, Samuel Goldwyn. *(British Film Institute)*

Indians who took part in the Jesse L. Lasky production of *The Covered Wagon*, some of whom claimed to be survivors of Custer's massacre. From left: Sid Grauman; Lasky holding an Indian boy; James Cruze, the director; and Tim McCoy, who acted as interpreter and technical adviser. *(Jesse Lasky Productions, Ltd.)*

Film folk in a mood appropriate to the carefree days of Hollywood's youth. Among them are Jesse, Sr. (seated, right), Bess (seated, left), Douglas Fairbanks, Sr. (kneeling, right), and a very junior Jesse, Jr. *(Author's collection)*

The merger with Adolph Zukor's Famous Players Company brought a new respectability to the pioneers—the president (right) and first vice-president began to dress the part . . . *(British Film Institute)*

. . . It also brought a new prosperity. In 1916 Jesse L. Lasky bet Mack Sennett $5,000 he could drive his Stutz Bearcat across the continent in three weeks; he won the bet, but he wrecked the car. *(Author's collection)*

Later one of De Mille's senior scriptwriters, Jeanie MacPherson started out as a silent actress–seen here with Theodore Roberts in *The Girl of the Golden West* (1914, scenario and direction by Cecil B. De Mille). *(De Mille Foundation)*

Jeanie MacPherson with De Mille (right) and flying instructor, circa 1920. De Mille had taken up flying in 1916, and become so keen on it that he bought a plane—and an airfield. *(De Mille Foundation)*

Lois Wilson and J. Warren Kerrigan as they crossed the prairie to fame in the pioneering great western *The Covered Wagon*—a Lasky production directed by James Cruze. *(Author's collection)*

Another contribution to the war effort was the Lasky Home Guard—with Bill Buckland, left of the bandleader, and Jesse, Jr., to the right. *(Author's collection)*

the famous thighs covered in smartly tailored trousers started a fashion revolution from which there has been no looking back.

Some years later Dore Schary, one bright young executive, decided that actresses should no longer be glamour queens, but were to become the "girl next door." As a serious writer he put realism ahead of showmanship, and the trend he set was unfortunate for the old Hollywood. When the public was allowed to peer behind the magician's cape, it lost faith in the magic.

But there had been plenty of magic in the twenties, for those who still believed in it. One morning over a tray of kidneys and scrambled eggs, Doug Fairbanks was telling us about his plans to sail a schooner on a cruise to the South Seas with a camera crew. The expedition in search of pearls and adventure was not without solid commercial consideration, since every move Doug would make, from chinning himself on the bowsprit down to his most casual handstand on the binnacle, would be filmed. The magnificent physique was still intact, though he had begun to look just a bit puffy. Doug had been telling Dad about it when he unexpectedly swiveled around to me. His voice had a high-pitched rasp of excitement. The face that always appeared tanned, almost black, produced a white gleam of teeth in an irresistible grin.

"What about young Jess coming with me to the South Seas?"

"He's got to get back to school," my father said sternly. As on several other occasions, I could have murdered him.

"We'll be off in a couple of weeks. Have him back almost as soon as school starts." Doug turned his sharp eyes on me. "What do you say, young Jess?"

"Yes!" I exploded.

"I guess we could consider it," Dad conceded. I took that to mean he would let me go. After all, I'd been on some pretty harrowing trips with him.

For days my mind buzzed with outriggers, shark fishing, diving for pearls, coral pools. A few days later, in a fever of excitement, I phoned Doug to ask what special equipment I might need to spear fish. He was not available. Dad broke the news. Doug had sailed. Yesterday. Hadn't I read it in the papers? Naturally he hadn't meant to forget his promise, but perhaps he'd decided that with school starting soon the expedition might take too long. Perhaps he had even tried to phone me.

At that moment I should have learned a lesson about putting trust in the words of actors. The most charming breed in the world, perhaps the most well meaning, and frequently the least reliable.

Five

Two fertile minds were brunching with us at the ocean-front swimming pool: Eddie Goulding, the English director and master spellbinder at storytelling, and Joe Hergesheimer, the novelist, back again from Havana for another bout of California living. Dad, generally overwhelmingly effervescent, was quiet and gnawed by worry. He needed a story for one of his stars, Nancy Carroll—and he needed it by yesterday. So far the efforts of the studios both east and west had failed to produce any suitable material. Never one to miss picking the nearest available brain, he turned his attentions to Joe, whose face was lifted in ecstatic sun worship.

"Joe, I'm in trouble. Eddie here is going to direct the new Nancy Carroll film. Only we have nothing for him to direct."

Eddie nodded agreement as he stuffed his mouth with California cracked crab. Eyes still closed, Joe gnawed his pencil with his single tooth.

"Don't look at me, Jesse, I'm on holiday. In fact I'm searching for an idea for my next book. The publisher's already advanced me money on the title and I'd hate to give it back, since I've already spent it."

"What's it called?" Eddied asked with a spark of interest.

"*The Spanish Shawl*," said Joe, doodling on the L.A. *Times*.

The great British director fixed Dad with a cryptic eye. "You've asked everybody for an idea but me, J. L."

Dad turned on him. "You mean you have an idea and you've been holding out on me?"

"It's just come to me this minute," Goulding smiled, eyes drifting toward the blue-green expanse of Pacific past our pool and fixing on a form in the sky. "A seagull," he murmured. "One seagull!"

With that he began to weave a tapestry of words, a story pouring from him like spirit speech through a psychic medium. It was as though he didn't participate at all. He painted visions of scenes in a disconnected tone poem of highly dramatic effects. He engulfed us in mood: the rain on a dark street, patterns of lamplight in a deserted alley, the movement of night people among whom his heroine drifted like a displaced moonbeam, wonderfully detached, while the story grew around her—lurid and mysterious.

"I'll play Carroll with one breast hanging out," he proclaimed. "Finally at the end I will show her in an empty window looking from her own empty life into the emptiness of the city where there will be nothing left for her. And then, when you feel only emptiness, nothingness . . . one cello note?" He took in the rapt attention of his audience. "And now you are back in the street and it's day and bright. And this figure is coming forward. Moving! Moving out of the crowd. You recognize him and you can't believe it and it's unbearably wonderful! Magnificent! Right! True! Real! Because it's there." And so he talked on, casting his spell of words, binding us with the magic of his delivery.

A long silence, then Dad spoke. "I'll give you twenty-five thousand dollars for that story, Eddie!"

"I accept," Goulding replied.

"Go and put it on paper. I'll have the contract drawn up." My father rose to phone the legal department and get the agreement into the pipeline. Hergesheimer bit his pencil with his solo tusk because he hadn't thought of it.

There was only one trouble: Eddie could never put it on paper. Not that story—he'd forgotten it as soon as he told it. And we who had listened to his imagery, we who had been engulfed and enthralled, couldn't remember it either! Nobody could remember anything except odd phrases, occasional words. But what had it all added up to? The wonderful effect that it had upon us was the magic of Eddie Goulding himself, a magic which he could not solidify and put into form.

The money was never paid, the story never written. Ultimately a story was found, and Eddie directed Nancy Carroll's next picture, which succeeded anyway. Most films did in those days. Hollywood seemed to be using up material like ammunition on a battlefield.

Reading departments combed every magazine, covered every novel, viewed every play for suitable subjects. There was a long way to go, however. Television, the great devourer, wasn't even a gleam in the camera's eye. Huge stables of writers were recruited by every studio, assigned to come up with usable ideas and create original stories, although originality was never the most sought-after quality, and most pictures were copies of the most recent successful picture.

Now and again playwrights from Hungary or novelists from England would turn out some "ideal movie property" and be contracted and imported with the adulation paid a new star. Such a writer was Elinor Glyn, who had written a sensationally risqué novel called *Three Weeks.* When another film company beat my father to the screen rights, he concocted a title, *The Great Moment*, and persuaded Madame Glyn to come to America and create a slinky story for Gloria Swanson to fit that title. It would have been difficult for her to write a story that didn't! Disembarking from the *Mauretania* in New York, Glyn insisted on walking with Dad from the press reception to her hotel. Flaming red hair, green eyes, powder-white face, dripping with leopard skins, she looked more like one of her own heroines than an authoress as they made their way through the Fifth Avenue traffic. That was only the beginning.

Arriving in Hollywood in 1921, she held up the start of the movie of her script by exercising her contractual prerogative to have final approval in the selection of the leading man. Apparently none of those offered by Sam Wood, the director, had that mysterious quality she called "it." Only Rudolph Valentino himself qualified as the Glyn standard of male sex appeal. But since he wasn't available for this film, Dad pulled an actor named Milton Sills off another film. Glyn had met Sills at a party and assured my father that he had "it." She also met Valentino and lavished her sexual savoir-faire upon him, and even taught him a then-sensational bit of screen business—to press a kiss into the palm of a lady's hand!

But when it came to the big love scene in *The Great Moment*, which she had designed to take place on a leopard-skin rug, no written description in the script could do it justice. The scenario included the following instruction to the director, Wood. "Rather than describe this scene, Madame Glyn will personally enact it on the set."

No doubt she didn't underplay it—or any moment in her own life. When she couldn't prevail upon my father to remove Gloria Swanson as the leading lady she attempted to remold the already famous star into the sort of heroine she felt her script required. She tutored Gloria in her choice of clothes, movement, accent (although the film was silent), and even selection of reading material.

Inevitably, Charlie Chaplin met Madame Glyn at a Hollywood party.

"You don't look as funny as I'd expected," the green-eyed authoress breathed patronizingly.

"Neither do you," Charlie replied.

Glyn returned to England to become involved in a well-publicized White Russian espionage caper behind the Red curtain.

Film star Gloria Swanson, meanwhile, rose from success to success. When her contract with Famous Players-Lasky came up for renewal she was offered one million dollars a year, plus half the profits of any film she appeared in. It was the fattest offer ever made to any screen star—but it was not enough. Gloria's mind was set on forming her own company. Dad held an all-night conference with New York on the long-distance telephone. One may imagine some lonely Navajo herdsman drifting after his scrawny sheep or cattle while the wires above him crackled with the pros and cons of paying a lady more money to drape herself across a leopard skin than his whole nation had ever dreamed of earning. The final conclusion was that the star had become too big for the company. They would have to let Gloria go her own way.

Those troubled executives in the twenties foresaw that if they met such a price they would be starting a trend that could destroy their very industry. They would be fertilizing a golden egg to kill their goose. Later film executives were more shortsighted. They met stars' demands, thereby beginning a process which ultimately priced Hollywood out of existence. Worse was to come. There would be a day when the player would dictate the play in the game.

Gloria Swanson was probably the first of the screen stars to set up her own company. In this, she had the help of a young Bostonian who had for a brief time been one of Dad's production assistants. Joe Kennedy had a personal admiration for Gloria Swanson and gambled his own money in her company. Mistakenly convinced that the public would prefer her as a down-to-earth gal instead of a glamour goddess, Gloria selected as her first film for her new company *Queen Kelly of the USA*. The film was a disaster and never released. It was one of Joseph Kennedy's few financial misjudgments.

Gloria survived, too, becoming one of Hollywood's all-time greats. She shares with Marlene a certain ageless beauty. Perhaps, when one considers other really great stars like Greta Garbo and Ingrid Bergman, this agelessness may be seen as a common denominator. Or perhaps not so common.

Stars' names have never totally insured a film's success, but without them the risk of failure is considerably increased. Sometimes a producer regards the subject as the star (a best-selling novel, or a famous historical character). Carl Foreman recently cast the comparatively unknown Simon Ward as young Winston Churchill. It didn't always work that well, as when Darryl Zanuck cast Alexander Knox as Wilson, in 1944. Neither subject nor actor proved sufficiently enticing to the public.

Toward the end of the silent era, in 1927, my father hit upon "the greatest of all subjects for a moving picture," *The Rough Riders*, a story of Theodore Roosevelt. Every film project he instigated was always the "greatest"—until it was made. Roosevelt, man and president, had always held special personal appeal for my father. As a young vaudevillian, he once played before his idol in a theater in Washington D.C. On that occasion he was so nervous that when he did a "quick change" into Rough Riders' uniform and rushed back onstage, raised cornet to lips to sound a bugle call, he found his hands empty! He had left his cornet backstage.

Now he wanted to bring his hero to the screen complete with buck-toothed grin beneath down-curved mustaches and beribboned pince-nez: a face that had almost become interchangeable with the American Eagle. The "man's man," who spoke softly while carrying the big stick and mouthing "Bully! . . ." The statesman whose great white fleet flaunted the flag around the world in the best of times. The times when my father's cornet blasts had marched troops off to the Spanish-American War through the streets of his beloved hometown, San Francisco.

This biographical film would concentrate on one small but typical adventure of the Roosevelt saga. Upon the outbreak of war with Spain, Teddy, then assistant secretary of the navy, resigned to form and command a colorful regiment of wild and wooly warriors. His experiences with them in Texas and Cuba ideally typified the fiery personality of the future president. From the start, the problem was, Who among the Hollywood stars to cast?

Victor Fleming, vigorous "action" director, would guide the production. It would be filmed on the actual spot in Texas where Teddy had assembled his band of cowpunchers and hunters. Actors would be coached by some of the original members of the First U.S. Volunteer Cavalry, as the Rough Riders were officially known. Hermann Hagedorn, the Roosevelt historian, was hired as author and technical consultant. A half-million-dollar budget was approved (which, though generous in those days, would finally exceed more than twice that amount). And still the major problem remained unsolved. Who would play the part?

Fleming chewed his pipe in the office of the production VP. Between them rose a mound of stills, like discards in some giant's card game.

"We thought it was going to be easy, J. L. But we're no nearer finding a star than ever and we are a hell of a lot nearer start of production!"

"I've a crazy idea, Vic. Almost ashamed to try it on you."

"As long as you don't say, 'Let's use a complete unknown.' "

My father froze. "Well, I *was* thinking along those lines. I mean, an actual double. Spitting image, instead of an actor."

Vic scowled through orbiting smoke rings.

"Most of our stars never saw a stage—or a camera, until they got their break," my father reassured the director and himself. "They were football players, beach bums, photogenic nobodies, who learned to act by acting."

"You mean, I've got to teach him, too?"

"Remember, it's an action picture, Vic. And he doesn't have to talk."

Fleming recognized the euphoric process of self-salesmanship. Besides, he became intrigued by the possibility of getting a great natural performance, untainted by overacting.

"Okay, J. L. I'm willing. But where do we start the search?"

"I'll send the word to every Paramount exchange in the country. They can hold contests. Advertise in the papers. We'll pick our winner from the best photograph. Just think of the publicity value!"

In no time, photos of Teddy Roosevelts were pouring in from every corner of America. One was outstanding. From mustache to toothy grin he *was* Roosevelt. The contract was signed, and he left his small town somewhere in middle America and took the Santa Fe to Los Angeles. When he walked into the office, director and producer decided they had found their Rough Riding colonel.

But Frank Hopper shook hands rather too limply. He seemed noticeably withdrawn, insecure. They reminded themselves that being no actor, it might take him time to get acclimated.

Then, on the eve of production, Fleming made a troubled appearance in my father's office.

"It won't work," he confided. He didn't have to say what. "It's hopeless, J. L. He looks right, photographs perfectly in the tests, but he just hasn't got the rocks. He's everything T. R. wasn't! Shy, timid, afraid to face even the studio messenger boy! He's got to be thundering, bombastic, even if it is silent! Fearless! I tell you, we're in trouble."

"You're telling me! Hopper's contracted and publicized. We can't fire him now. Anyway, there wouldn't be time to replace him. New York would call off the production."

"But the man can't even look you in the eye! He's too frightened to ask his way to the bathroom. If he leads the Rough Riders up San Juan Hill, Cuba will return to Spain! Can't you pay him off, postpone the starting date, find the right man, or cancel the picture?"

"You've never had to deal with stockholders, have you, Vic?" Dad moaned.

At that moment the door was opened by a slender, graying man of distinguished bearing: Will Hays, former postmaster general in President Harding's cabinet, now embarking in the $100,000-a-year post of custodian of motion picture industry morals (to improve the national image after a few too many scandals had begun to hurt business).

"Can I come in, Jesse?"

"Glad to see you, General. We have a large problem."

Hays listened, a spark showing through squinting eyes. He looked like Uncle Sam, minus the beard. When the dilemma had been aired, he spoke.

"This may be out of the far end of the diamond, Jess, but there's a simple fundamental that might apply. So basic people forget it. A man reacts the way the world treats him. Other people are his mirror, he becomes what he sees in the way they look at him. Try it on him. Get Hopper in here, now! Instead of letting him see how worried you are, introduce him to me with the greatest respect. I'll act as though I'm meeting Roosevelt himself."

My father looked at Fleming.

"Try it, J. L. What have we got to lose?"

Dad reached for the key on his dictaphone. "Get Mr. Hopper over here, Randy. Right away."

When Hopper arrived, Hays proved at once he knew how to play the required scene. He had learned how with real presidents in his Washington days. When the would-be Roosevelt came cowering into the office, eyes darting nervously around, my father began with near reverence, "General, I have the honor of presenting Theodore Roosevelt."

"Proud to make your acquaintance, sir." Hays responded with a formal bow. "May I say, sir, the resemblance is perfect? But more than merely physical. I can see you have the same fearless nature, the same character and patriotism. You are the kind of man who would meet the challenge of war with the words 'Let us pay with our bodies for our souls' desire.' " Then he turned to my father. "Mr. Lasky, as former postmaster general of the United States, I count this as a proud moment, and I thank you for the honor of meeting this man."

Astonished at first, the new treatment hit Hopper like a bolt from the blue. Red, white, and blue. As he left the office and everyone rose, it could be noted that his posture had undergone a subtle change. His head was more erect, his step had acquired the slightest suggestion of a strut.

Orders were relayed throughout every department of the studio: The movie Roosevelt was to be treated precisely as though he were the real T. R. As told in my father's biography, by Don Weldon, *I Blow My Own Horn*, this was one of the rare occasions where grips, juicers, cameramen, assistant directors—everyone, in fact, but the star—was performing to the hilt.

Unfortunately, the worm turned too far. Under this ego-massage, the simple, smalltown storekeeper became almost unmanageable. The man was submerged by the megalomaniac monster demanding total attention, obsequious respect, demanding that every scene should receive his signature of approval before he would film it. Since he wasn't an actor, he couldn't take off his role, like a costume, at the end of the day.

His performance served the picture well enough, but as might be expected, it didn't lead to other parts. There just were no further calls for Teddy Roosevelt. Eventually, he drifted home to wife and family. Somewhere in a little village, where the dust of Main Street is occasionally stirred by a gust of prairie wind, a lonely man continued to strut and preen, to the amusement of his neighbors.

"Just ol' Frank Hopper lettin' off steam. Never been quite right in the head since he come back from livin' with them moom pitcher folk."

New faces. New stories. New directors. The creative raw material of the burgeoning industry. Famous Players-Lasky had two film factories now. Aside from the Hollywood Studio on Marathon Street, an East Coast studio had been opened in Astoria, Long Island. Astoria came under the direct studio management of sophisticated, Dartmouth-polished Walter Wanger, and operated in rivalry with the Hollywood plant under shrewd Ben Schulberg. My father presided over these warring factions as vice president in charge of all production. It was up to him to make the decision as to which studio would get which star and which story. The healthy competition advanced the fortunes of the parent company and kept Dad hopping to and from Europe in search of new talent.

And what talent! I was a bit too young to fully appreciate the famous visitors to our London hotel suites. One day, while my father was lunching at the Garrick Club with Sir Gerald du Maurier, Bess and I returned to the hotel to be confronted by two rather formidable pipe-smoking authors, waiting to see him. The great scribes rose, bowed to Bess like a vaudeville turn, and smilingly announced, "We're H. G. Wells and Arnold Bennett. Now, Mrs. Lasky, you must guess which is which."

Bess guessed wrong.

Her judgment of furniture, however, was becoming more accurate, but I couldn't understand why she wished to pack our New York apartment with more and more shipments of spindly chairs and chests of drawers that popped marquetry flowers in the steam heat of New York like a boxer spitting out teeth. Dad agreed, but he wasn't home enough to complain too bitterly.

Bess had become far too elegant for Grandpa, too. Her aging Russian-born father would always enter by the servant's entrance, much to her annoyance, and sip tea in the kitchen with the butler. He felt more at home there than among the, what he called, "bric-a-break." We were all rude invaders at Bess's personal court of musicians and poets, who drank pink champagne at her feet and complained about the vulgarity of the film business that made it all possible.

It was on one of these summer visits to Europe that I was afflicted with a mysterious paralysis. I couldn't walk for months. With little else to do, I took up writing verse. This in itself might not have proved too fatal except that one poem about Thomas Edison was actually published by the *New York Herald Tribune*. They even paid for it. Ten dollars. As a result I broke out in such a sweat of verse that even the publication of a thin volume by Boni and Liveright could not stem the flow. That Christmas holiday I stalked the New York apartment with a Byronic look and resisted falling in love. Easy, since despite being the son of a film tycoon I didn't know many girls.

Then my father involved himself in making the film *Peter Pan*. For some reason they had decided to shoot it in the Astoria studio. A more serious consideration was, Should they make it at all? Although the story was already a classic in England, Americans weren't familiar with it. Distributors were immediately uneasy about the title. Sir James Barrie, however, would not consider changing it, not even for Jesse Lasky. Distributors asked themselves, What would audiences in the sticks think of it? This assumption of rural naiveté frequently stunted the mental growth of film production. Happily, on this occasion, Barrie won.

But there was another difficult problem. Casting the lead. *Peter Pan* required a waiflike creature of gossamer fantasy and a kind of neuter charm. For the first time casting directors were shouting, "Find me a girl without sex appeal!" Herbert Brenon, the British director set to guide the film, had been testing every flat-chested, wide-eyed actress he could locate. Talent scouts cased drama schools and drugstores looking for elfin creatures.

Then someone found the perfect unknown, Mary Brian. There was only one thing wrong with the choice: Someone else at the studio had seen and tested another young unknown, Betty Bronson. Dad found himself juggling with an embarrassment of riches. The problem was resolved by giving Betty Bronson the part of Peter and Mary Brian that of Wendy.

The night Dad brought home Betty Bronson's photograph to show us, it was love at first sight for me! Second sight brought even deeper love, when I met her in Dad's office. Somehow I got up the courage to ask her for a date. She could hardly refuse, with Dad looming over us.

Dating in the twenties was a formal affair. I sent Betty a corsage of gardenias accompanied by a carefully worded card in iambic pentameter, collected her in our Locomobile, driven by Pierce. I wore my first tuxedo. This ritual was further complicated by the fact that America was still in the desert of Prohibition. I felt that a young man, if he were to be designated a man at all, would be expected to carry a hip flask. Although I didn't yet drink, I armed myself with one of Dad's flasks well filled with his best bootleg whisky.

Then the thought occurred, Suppose Dad saw the bulge in my pocket and stopped me at the door? I returned to his room and armed myself with a second of his flasks. He had a drawer full of them received as Christmas or birthday gifts. The chances of his missing one, or even two, were slight.

Of course the expected happened. As I was slipping out the front door in my racoon-skin coat and derby, I ran smack into Dad. Cool blue eyes penetrated my not-so-innocent grin.

"Jess," he said in his most stentorian tone, "you're going out with a very fine young lady and probably an important future Lasky star. I would be sorry to think that you might under any circumstances violate the laws of our country and carry a flask."

That he might violate these same laws did not at that instant occur to either of us. Perhaps that wasn't altogether pertinent. In any event his intuition was working at full throttle. He held out his hand. "If you have a flask, I would like to have it."

I presented him with one, and honor was satisfied. He patted my shoulder and I headed out the door. When I produced the second flask in front of Betty Bronson she was completely shocked. The future star was in fact an uncomplicated eighteen-year-old who thought she had fallen into the hands of a degenerate sixteen-year-old roué. I would have been delighted to have fulfilled the part to perfection, but I never got the chance. I couldn't get her to taste the stuff, and when I downed several swigs to prove how depraved I was, I became ill and had to send her home in a taxi. End of an affair. I was left with only my memories and an autographed photo.

But the event was not entirely untainted by commercial considerations. When I returned to boarding school, I had with me a suitcase full of her photographs purloined from the publicity department. These were dutifully inscribed to my various roommates. I had learned to forge my beloved's signature to perfection. Very shortly there was no one in the school who had not offered fifty cents to a dollar to get a signed photograph of the beautiful young star of *Peter Pan.*

The next summer Bess, sensing a dangerous trend in my character, decided I would be safer spending the holiday under my father's restraining eye. She insisted that since he was to tour the European film exchanges I must accompany him to start learning the business. I was delighted to learn that Randy Rogers would also be going, for my father's flamboyant secretary was the best of traveling companions, particularly when Dad wasn't around to cramp his style.

The shoe seemed to be rather on the other foot this time, however, for Dad suddenly decreed that Randy and I must travel one country behind him. It would be too boring, he explained, for a teen-ager to be stuck with all the business meetings and official banquets he'd be expected to attend. Randy was to guide me through the various film exchanges, where we could view the latest foreign product. This is how it was supposed to work: Dad went from Paris to Prague. We remained in Paris until he was ready to leave Prague, whereupon we went to Prague and he, to Vienna. We left Czechoslovakia as he was ready to leave Austria. The system worked perfectly from his standpoint. It gave him the freedom he required on his tireless searches for talent.

Randy, ever the soul of discretion, fabricated excellent excuses for how little time Dad would have with me. How much more fun I'd have on my own, without the parental eagle eye on my activities. We were scheduled to rendezvous in Berlin, at journey's end, and travel home together.

But the film exchange man who had booked hotel reservations and rail tickets made one mistake. Randy and I arrived at the old Donaplota Hotel in Budapest to find that Dad was still "in residence." Out for the evening, of course, but there, nevertheless. I was delighted, could scarcely wait to surprise him with my presence.

Randy seemed less enthusiastic, wrote my father a note, left it in his box and hustled me off to dinner and a movie, Hungarian in both cases. The movie turned out to be goulash and the dinner was strictly from Bela Lugosi. We returned to the hotel to find that Dad hadn't.

Randy and I shared a suite which overlooked a main street. I was awakened in the early hours by indigestion and gypsy music, the latter drifting up from the street. Dawn was rising over the Danube when I peered out the window. A dawn singing with czardas music growing louder and nearer by the note. Out of that hazy, golden Magyar morning materialized a curious parade. Four open black carriages crowded with musicians in bright red, yellow, and green costumes; a full orchestra dominated by violins and accordions, playing the sensuous, sighing music of the Magyars. Marching in front of the carriages was a motley procession. Arm in arm with gentlemen in rumpled dinner jackets came beautiful young actresses and gypsy singers in spangled gowns, drinking champagne from silver goblets as they danced down the street. Leading them all, an armful of talent on each side, was my father.

Awakened, too, Randy came into the room behind me. "Come away from the window, Jesse. He might see you!" Randy warned quietly. "I don't think he'd appreciate knowing that you know."

Randy managed to retrieve his message before my father saw it. He further arranged that the hotel would not mention our presence when my father checked out in the morning. Which would be about an hour later. Whatever Dad was getting out of his tour of the European exchanges, it wouldn't be much sleep.

Years later he confessed to me that the president of the company,

Adolph Zukor, had arrived at my father's suite that morning just as he was undressing for bed. Like a scene from one of his own comedies, Dad promptly pretended to be dressing for the day. The puritanical Mr. Zukor took note of his vice president's energetic devotion to the company's affairs. He liked to see an executive rise early.

Adolph Zukor, mini-mogul (as Norman Zierold, cinema historian, styled him), had migrated to New York from his native Hungary in 1888. His was the classic odyssey of the emigrant boy of fifteen with forty dollars sewed into his vest and a vision of opportunity in his brain. His eyes were doubtless fixed on Lady Liberty in New York Harbor, and having passed through the great faucet of Ellis Island he was soon studying English in night school. The American dream that would become the great cliché—but no less true for the contempt bred by later familiarity.

Young Zukor progressed from fur to films, a world then confined to exhibition in penny arcades. A little man of large ambition and impeccable morals, he became both father-figure to my father and respected president of America's foremost film company. He built a huge house in New City, New York, with a private eighteen-hole golf course. Weekends in the East, we used to house-party there, embarking on the Zukor yacht from a New York dock and cruising up the Hudson. His son, Eugene, captained the fine craft. Since guests were always handed out yachting caps upon boarding, we must have appeared a fair shipload of captains. One might consider this as a possible origin of the old Jewish mother's question to her companion: "But to a captain is he a captain?"

Having been transported by limousine to the Zukor estate, we would follow our small host, gray, soft-spoken, incredibly dignified, around his private golf course, in pursuit of the one achievement that eternally eluded him. He could never manage to break ninety! Frustrating also to the staff of private golf pros he employed for that single purpose.

My father treated him with a mixture of formality and reverence. When Dad was at the East Coast office, they would lunch together every day: first at Delmonico's, in later times at Sherry's, still later at the Astor, then the Ritz, following the change in fashionable goldfish bowls. They exchanged cigars and ideas and plotted the destiny of Famous Players-Lasky.

At one of these lunches, Dad was given an ultimatum of shattering consequence. "Mr. Lasky"—the partners over all the years never addressed each other but in the most formal terms—"Mary Pickford repeated to me this morning a conversation between you and Sam Goldfish."

The tone told trouble was coming. Pickford was Zukor's great star. Loyalty to him had compelled her to report a conversation she overheard.

Goldfish to my father: "Jesse, don't let Zukor butt into production! Our Feature Play Company always made better pictures than Famous Players ever did. Keep Zukor out of California, and you and I will make all production decisions!"

An unpolitic suggestion from a brother-in-law partner. It could have been ignored and forgotten, had it not been relayed to Zukor, but now the fat was in the fire.

"Mr. Zukor, I won't deny what was said, but Sam was excited. Sometimes he says things he doesn't mean. Anyway, I didn't take it as a proposal of Company policy—and neither should you."

Zukor was slow to anger and slower to forget. He reached to the breast pocket from which his cigar would have customarily protruded. He must indeed have been deeply disturbed this morning, for the pocket of the dark blue suit was empty. Dad supplied one from his. Zukor gravely accepted the flame.

"Mr. Lasky, I'm sorry to say what I'm going to say. Famous Players-Lasky is not large enough to hold Goldfish and myself."

"Mr. Zukor, I wouldn't be in moving pictures if it weren't for Sam."

"This I understand. But you will have to choose between Goldfish and me! Since you brought him into the Company, you must ask him to leave. Or I leave. I will be waiting in my house in New City in the country for your decision."

My father called it the hardest decision he ever had to make. Fire his sister's husband, who had nagged him into the business—or wreck the new amalgamation? Sam's plans had helped form the Company. Sam's salesmanship had saved the Company when more capital had been needed to finish the first feature film. Was the Company outgrowing its founders? My father thought of the vast web of stockholders, whose confidence in Zukor's leadership was the financial insurance of the future. Had Sam been other than he was, compromise might have been possible. But the hard-selling ex-glover could not play second fiddle to any man. It made him difficult to live with, yet his qualities of leadership and courage would make him difficult to live without.

When the decision was finally taken, they tried to soften the blow by buying Sam out for $900,000. It enabled Goldfish and Edgar Selwyn to form Goldwyn Pictures. Sam changed his name and eventually merged with Louis B. Mayer's Metro Pictures. But as always, he couldn't function happily in partnership. He left his name on Metro Goldwyn Mayer—and moved again.

This time, at United Artists, he became one of the all-time-great creative producers. His closest associate in the new amalgam was none other than the little girl star who had carried the tale of Goldfish's insult to Adolph Zukor. Mary Pickford!

Six

SOMEONE ONCE SAID that to be in the film business all you needed was fifty dollars, a broad, and a camera. This might almost be true today, when the vast industrial complexes have fallen to dust and history, and energetic young film-school graduates can grind away on any street corner and hope to win a festival award. Once a film is made, however, it still has to be distributed and exhibited in cinema houses. The dreamers and showmen conceived and gave birth, but the hard-headed businessmen had to make baby pay.

Until 1915 Famous Players-Lasky had distributed in the United States through the "States Rights" men—so called because they negotiated for the rights to sell films state by state. But in that year these independent distributors banded together to form Paramount Pictures. It was one of the first organized attempts to distribute films nationally.

Paramount. The name had been chosen by W. W. Hodkinson, the San Francisco exhibitor who formed the States Rights men into a distributing company. He had seen it on an apartment house. My father never cared for the name; to him it would have more appropriately suited a brand of cheese, or possibly woolen mittens. He and Zukor liked the terms of the new distributing company even less. Thirty-five thousand dollars in advance paid on each FP-L film against 65 percent of the gross.

With production costs rising, FP-L would find it almost impossible to finance themselves from such paltry advances. The contract of one star alone, Mary Pickford, called for ten thousand dollars a week, which with bonuses came to almost seven hundred thousand dollars a year! The production men began to realize that if they didn't rid themselves of the greedy distributors, they would be out of business. But how?

Zukor had the answer. Absorb them. The situation called for a discreet takeover that would make Paramount Pictures into a docile, obedient subsidiary. So in 1915 Adolph Zukor quietly began to buy up Paramount shares until FP-L had acquired a controlling interest in the stock, and Paramount Pictures became FP-L's subsidiary distributing company.

Certainly the power of the Lasky name and position seemed stable enough in the dawn of 1929, a year that could scarcely have started more promisingly. Like Zukor, my father had invested heavily in his company's stock. He had only to open the financial pages of the morning paper to watch himself grow richer. In 1927 *Variety* had estimated his fortune at twenty million dollars, the eighth largest in show business—doubtless an exaggeration, but what was a few million one way or another?

An inventory of assets at the beginning of 1929 suggested at least a comfortable future. He acquired a canyon in the Malibu Hills behind Malibu Beach Colony, where he planned to build a rambling hacienda in the old California Spanish style, with a private pier on the Pacific. He talked about palominos with silver-mounted black saddles and bridles that would carry the family down Lasky Canyon to the pier; about boarding the yacht, well stocked with rum drinks and dashing companions, and sailing to the beach house in Santa Monica. He would discuss such plans with his great pal the actor Leo Carrillo, who, as an authentic descendant of Spanish caballeros, could be expected to savor this dreamed-of life style. It was a season for dreams, with every penny tucked into the huge block of film company stock, half a dozen great office buildings in New York, and the market booming, ever upward. The great American depression was still to come, and the shock waves of the Eastern earthquake took a bit longer to roll West.

Even before it struck, many tycoons were aware of the troubles in their paradise. The sun shone on the high-salaried artists afloat in pools of affluence, but serious film makers could hardly have felt satisfaction with the order of things.

In my father's studio, the loss of Swanson for a paltry million now seemed a mistake. Stars like Gloria were worth any price. Others of whom much had been expected had turned out to be disappointments. Swanson's famous rival, Pola Negri, hailed as the most exciting actress of Europe, was giving stereotype performances in films that looked as though they were turned out by stamping machines. Perhaps it was the fault of bad scripts or misguided publicity—in any case, exhibitors were demanding that Negri's name be removed from the advertisements of her pictures! An investment in talent wasted, and the movie queen returned to Europe to recapture her artistic integrity.

Was it inevitable that studios would become factories of mediocrity, turning even important authors into overpaid hash-slingers? Men like Carl Van Vechten, Joseph Hergesheimer, Michael Arlen, paying Hollywood back with their worst work—then a bitter novel, and away to rediscover themselves. Was it the fault of a system, an environment in which power became too absolute? The rewards of favor too high? Why did so many of the best-laid plans of film men become mousetraps for thoughtless multitudes? Were the movies fated to become—in the apocryphal words of Sam Goldwyn—"positively mediocre"? My father was gnawed by a sense of the failure of his product, even when most financially rewarding. The search for another Garbo had been as unsuccessful as the search for a second Valentino. Perhaps that was the essence of Hollywood's failures: the attempts to remake the images in imitation of each other.

These were problems of which I was blissfully unaware on the beaches of Santa Monica's summers. I was too shy and always too easily enamored of the parading females whose beauty-masks were styled in exact imitation of the reigning favorite stars of the moment. Wherever you looked, a spurious Garbo, a Clara Bow, a Carole Lombard. The authentic Alice White, flapper cutie, left her bathing-suited imprint in the sands of time and mind as she winked at me, saucer-eyed, from an embrace with Jimmy Hall, her current leading man-lover. Would I always be too young for everyone? It seemed a strong possibility.

Evenings, we tried to drown youth in devilish debauchery that always had disappointingly harmless endings. Songs howled above ukuleles around beach fires where marshmallows were toasted to dripping molten gold. Sea roar in ears, we necked in rumble seats and attempted seductions that always failed. Callow, spoiled, confused adolescent years—but the events that would shake and tumble us into reality were approaching. Before they reached us, another kind of earthshaking experience visited our beach.

Some executive—I think it was Winnie Sheehan (newly arrived in California)—had procured an unexpurgated print of *Ecstasy* from Europe. The screening of it was heavily attended in our private solarium theater. At about the point where the heavenly Hedy turned her bare back to the camera and trotted off toward the lake, the house rocked. Yes, actually! Not just the potted banana trees and nude Hedy jumping around the silver screen, but walls, tiled floors, the whole house shuddered with spasms. We crowded under door frames while the sand heaved and rolled beneath the foundations.

"The Palisades will fall on us!" somebody screamed.

It seemed likely. There was nothing to hold those sheer cliffs of sandstone. You could see the log fences at the crest waving and undulating above us like matchsticks.

Then the first shock waves subsided. However menacing they loomed above, the Palisades had not slipped down to bury our colony. I think it was Janet Gaynor who spoke first. "I thought for a moment we'd got caught in one of Mr. De Mille's pictures!"

Some wild-eyed people ran by trailing rumors: Santa Barbara and Long Beach had been practically demolished. The rumors later proved true.

Jascha Heifetz cast his eyes sadly back to the theater. "Jesse, do you think we could continue running *Ecstasy?* If these are the last days of Santa Monica, I can't think of a better way to finish."

Everyone poured back to continue the picture. The shock waves returned at intervals, but the seductive lure of Hedy Lamarr, the beautiful unknown nude, proved more riveting than even a California earthquake.

The damaged beach area was soon repaired, but another kind of quake was coming. After it, no one would ever again be the same.

When the calamitous tide of Depression ultimately reached Hollywood, it resulted in more than the loss of fortunes. It brought a revolution of power—as if the music had stopped in a game of musical executive chairs. All were uprooted, most unseated, many destroyed. FP-L did not at first appear to be seriously affected. Even the stockmarket crash did not instantly break the public's moviegoing habit. There were still substantial takings at the box office. But the Company had an Achilles' heel, or rather an Achilles' necklace: those chains of glittering film palaces stretching from coast to coast, even throughout Canada. Although FP-L now had control of the distributor, Paramount, its exhibiting subsidiary, Publix, controlled these cinema houses under its ambitious executive, Sam Katz. Publix had bought heavily into many giant circuits, making the purchases partly with cash and partly with stock, redeemable upon demand at a fixed price. To the mighty parent company responsible for these purchases, it must have seemed like healthy expansion, ensuring even larger empires in which to exhibit its ever-growing programs of movies. After the crash the stock plunged far below the "fixed" price, but the Company was nevertheless obliged to redeem its pledge at full value, draining capital while stocks continued to fall. Inevitably, the Depression hit box-office receipts. The blood of the company was being drained and no more plasma was being pumped in.

In the tense uncertainty of the times, feuds grew between the subsidiaries as each one passed the blame down the line. Desperate to reestablish some sense of unity by reminding the distribution and exhibition departments that they still belonged to the same company, my father first suggested changing the corporate name to Paramount Famous Lasky. When this didn't do the trick, he proposed dropping his own name completely and calling the company Paramount Publix. It seems an unbearably childish way of trying to patch the deep wounds of an industrial organization with a bandage of pride, but it almost worked. Peace was briefly restored. The two worst contenders, Sidney Kent and Sam Katz, became equal vice presidents. But the company was short of money, and Katz set about to supply it, to the detriment of his rival.

While these protagonists were grappling in their power match, my father was having personal troubles. He'd bought over a million and a half dollars of company stock on margin, and now was forced to sell it for thirty-seven thousand dollars. Next went his towers of empty offices, untenanted glass window-eyes looking out on the dark days of New York at other windows through which other millionaires were plummeting like sparrows in a blizzard. Beach house and other properties secured a personal loan from Harry Warner of a quarter of a million. All of it went in efforts to save the stock. And the stock went too.

Bad got worse. Katz's powerful new Chicago financiers, elected to the board of directors, backed the Publix vice president against Sidney Kent, my father's strongest friend, who resigned, advising Lasky to do the same. It was not advice that he, as the Company's founder, was prepared to follow. He would stay and fight.

The new regime showed disconcerting concern for his personal problems, his bankruptcy, his health. It advised him to have a rest, a change, stay away from the Hollywood studio. In fact, it insisted on that. The handwriting was on the wall. Darkness moved on the face of Paramount, bringing treason in high places.

To help him shoulder the increasing load of production problems amid personal and corporate disasters, my father had taken on a new personal assistant, Manny Cohen. This young man had been an executive at Universal News Reel, where his record in documentaries was impressive. He plunged with zest into the facts and figures and confidential files, freeing my father to cope with major issues. A veritable glutton for detail, he converted himself into an inhuman dynamo, functioning day and night. He seemed, indeed, almost psychopathically anxious to die for the boss. Every day he spent more time in my father's office, familiarizing himself with the studio operations. His admiration for Lasky seemed unbounded as day by day he took a firmer hold of the routine of production.

It was not then surprising, when the meeting of the new board of directors was called to appraise the current crisis, that this young man should have been asked by my father to help him answer questions. From eighty dollars a share the stock had now fallen to a few pennies. Every film that had failed to bring in spectacular profits at the box office now appeared to have been poorly selected. It wasn't the fault of distributors or exhibitors, it wasn't the crash that was to blame, the board of directors decided, so it must be the production department's extravagance, bad judgment and miscalculation. It was guilty of not guessing what the public wanted (a feat toward which no showman would have dared aspire). The scapegoat had been found.

Hiller Innes, one of my father's most loyal assistants, walked out of that closed meeting with waxen pallor. Later he told Andrew Stone, the producer-director, what had transpired. In the rush of charges and countercharges, accusations and innuendoes, East against West, the vice president in charge of production was driven to the wall. One man could have helped him refute irresponsible charges hurled at him by the Publix men: his new assistant, who had made himself privy to the private files. But he allowed the attack to grow without one word of defense; then he joined it. Finally he led it.

When the votes were counted, Dad found himself sacked by his own company. His assistant was appointed to replace him as head of production. Zukor, too, was removed from high office and exiled to a humble company outpost in South America. But like many another former leader he would live to return from that exile.

With what may loosely be referred to as the tactics of Hollywood jungle warfare, the career of this new head of Paramount is interesting to follow. Not content with assassinating one by one the old giants who had headed the company—even those who had supported him against my father—he began to practice a diabolical brand of skulduggery. As the contracts of great stars like Gary Cooper, Mae

West, Bing Crosby (who were now Paramount's real assets) came up for renewal, the new production boss renewed them—but with himself. He negotiated private, personal contracts under which the services of the stars would be owed to himself rather than to the company of which he had become vice president. He carried out this maneuver with the greatest possible secrecy, but silence has never been a virtue in Hollywood. Actors and agents can never keep their mouths shut and the trade papers raised gossip to a fine art. Whispers reached the ears of the East Coast board of directors. They were stunned. Why would a top executive gut his own company, unless he thought the ship was sinking and he would escape on the only lifeboat—crowded with stars?

No Little Red Riding Hoods to be bamboozled meekly by a shrewd wolf, they kept their discovery more secret even than he kept his manipulations. Not a voice was raised against him. No word of criticism escaped the boardroom. On the contrary, a testimonial dinner was organized in Cohen's honor at the Ambassador Hotel in Los Angeles. Everyone of prominence in Hollywood attended. Speeches were made praising his unstinting service, his sage new leadership, his selfless dedication to saving Paramount from the storms of Depression and mismanagement.

All night he bathed in praise.

Next day he climbed aboard the Santa Fe Chief to attend a similar function in New York. He never made it. Halfway across the continent he was cut down by a telegram brought to his drawing-room on the train, informing him that he was fired.

Since he held the personal contracts of many top stars, the board of directors offered him an independent production deal, but they retained final approval of any project he might launch. That approval, readily given in minor matters, was however, withheld at key moments, sabotaging his projects and building for him an image of incompetence. Eventually his contract stars wearied of his production problems and rejoined the parent company, and he rejoined the temporarily unemployed. But like many people in Hollywood who have made a reputation, even a bad one, he was not long inactive. He found another backer and set up as an independent.

What a homecoming it was for me, from my university in France! My preparations for life had fitted me to order dinner in several languages, drive cars too fast, play polo and tennis, and open champagne bottles. I returned to the beach house to watch our fleet of Rolls-Royces being driven out of the cavernous garage by our creditors.

The great palace, now empty of servants, gaped around us like the belly of Jonah's whale. We had not yet been chucked out ourselves, but even that was imminent.

In this tragic atmosphere my father came home to Hollywood, bankrupt, jobless, and bereft of the sister who had since vaudeville days been the mainstay of his strength and his most valued adviser in show business. For Blanche had died three weeks before. Only a week prior to that sad event, Hector Turnbull had managed to goad the new head of Paramount into settling his contract for a considerable amount of hard cash. With this, he and Blanche planned to fulfill their dream of retiring to Pennsylvania on the old farm he had rebuilt with his own hands. He would go back to his first love of writing novels, and the terrible tensions of Hollywood politics could be forgotten. But when Blanche contracted pneumonia and died suddenly at the Ambassador Hotel, Hector took to the bottle. It was an act like ritual hari-kari—a deliberate, steady, self-destructive course, from which no one could dissuade him. I was alone in California, too young to cope with the iron determination of the uncle I loved more than anyone. I stayed with him, but I couldn't stop the drinking, or the mindless, uncaring gambling away of his settlement money from Paramount.

One night at a Sunset Strip gaming house I watched him lose twenty thousand dollars in cash. Next morning I went to the owner, a notorious racketeer, and offered him a deal.

"Look, my uncle just lost his wife. He's trying to drink himself to death and I can't stop him. He's also throwing away all the money he has across your tables because he doesn't care. He doesn't want to win, he wants to destroy himself."

The gangster shrugged, chewed his cigar. "What do you want me to do, kid?"

"Couldn't we set a limit? Let him lose, say, a thousand dollars a night. He'll play till he passes out, he'll lose it all, but in the morning you could give it back to me, less the thousand. Then I could slip it back to him, and there'll be something left when he pulls out of this."

He pushed the cigar hard into the ashtray. "Okay, kid, you got a deal . . . but don't put any of the change in your own pocket, huh?"

And so each night we'd go to the gambling joint and he'd throw away his money until he'd drunk himself unconscious. Then I'd take him home in a taxi and the following morning I'd return to the casino, find the boss, and give him my accounting. He never argued with my figures and always paid promptly. My uncle began to think he had a bottomless pocket, but it hardly mattered to him. The system worked for a while, but in the end Hector was too bent on self-destruction. Finally he eluded everyone I had tried to enlist to protect him. They picked him out of the gutter in downtown Los Angeles, his pockets full of cash. He had not been able to throw it away fast enough.

Bess's first words to me as I set down my valises were, "Watch Dad, Jess. I'm so worried about him. Oh, he hides his depression very well. You wouldn't think to look at him that anything was wrong. But I know him. Why, he even stays home nights now! I've offered to sell everything that I have, my jewelry and furniture, but the prices one gets for such things today! Really, Jess, you wouldn't believe it. My string of pearls, the second most perfect after Mrs. Ford's. My emerald ring, the largest in the country—why, they offer you nothing for these things now. Anyway, I can only say to you we must wait and see what's going to happen. Nobody seems to know. Yes, they'll take the house. We don't know exactly when, but it will happen soon. Anyway, watch him. Just keep your eyes on him!"

I did, but not closely enough. One bleak morning, Bess's voice roused me from studying the "help wanted" column. I was not equipped to put an airplane engine together blindfolded, which seemed to be the only available opening.

"Jesse, Jesse, he's gone! He's out there, he's swimming in the ocean. He's beyond the waves!"

Dad had suddenly plunged into the surf and was swimming with strong steady strokes in the direction of Japan. I came rushing down the stairs, kicking off my shoes, jumped into the Pacific and swam desperately to reach him before he could get beyond the limits of his endurance. In a way I knew it was the kind of death he would choose. Clean, lonely, empty, and considerate. To vanish in his beloved ocean without having caused anyone trouble, pain, or mess. I swam harder. The memory of another such swim with him across what had looked to be a narrow width of Colorado River during one of our annual expeditions came back to me. We had both almost drowned then. Better luck for the devil today, no doubt. Hard strokes finally brought me up to him, or perhaps he had slowed and was treading water. One imagined an almost bottomless depth of ocean below us. The shoreline was distant enough to make return a serious worry. He looked around at me with a vague, distracted stare. "What are you doing out here, Jesse?"

"Well, I thought I'd swim out and join you."

"Join me?" he said. His whole manner was detached, as if he were thinking about something far away. Here we were, treading water together a long way from shore. There were no words to voice the fear that I felt. We were breathless in the cold deep green-blue water, highlighted around us with blotches of foam. And then suddenly he smiled.

"Oh!" he said. "I see! You're dressed, aren't you? Well . . . ! So you thought I was going to . . ." he broke off, laughing above the sound of the surf behind us.

"Well, I thought you might be just a little far out of your depth, Dad! A little far out for a dip, aren't you?"

His eyes swiveled back to shore, as though distance was something he had quite overlooked.

"I didn't realize I swam so far! You see, I have the greatest idea for a new picture. I want to make a picture about a romance in a zoo. Remember Budapest, when we were there? Well, actually *we* weren't there together because you arrived after me, didn't you? Yes, anyway it was an idea for a story somebody gave me on that trip . . . *Zoo in Budapest!*" he said, treading water. "I optioned it. A great romance . . . A strange kind of boy. A young boy who was, kind of . . . like one of the animals himself. Closer to the animals than to people. And the girl, an orphan. Oh, it could be wonderful! I even like the title, what do you think of it? *Zoo in Budapest?* Well? What do you think Jess? What do you think?" A wave broke over our heads.

"I think, we'd better start swimming for shore."

As we swam slowly back toward the Santa Monica beach, he inclined his head to me. "You know something Jesse? You worry too much. You're worse than your mother." My father regarded all fears, concerns, and alarms as a kind of maternal inheritance. He may have been right.

By the time we reached the shore he'd reached a decision. He still had friends. He would set up his own production unit and start all over again!

With the family in chaos, the country in the doldrums, I thought hard on Thomas Wolfe's advice, "You Can't Go Home Again." It was time for me to move out of the nest.

London and Paris, Princeton and Dijon, New York and Madrid, Morocco and Mexico. Names that lay behind like stepping stones that had brought me to the cheerless present in depression-bound Hollywood. I had once vaguely thought of joining the diplomatic corps. I had learned a few languages inadequately, indulged in superficial travel, drifted from school to school in America and Europe. I had imagined myself outposting the American "Empire" in some Kiplingesque kraal in a not too uncivilized corner of the globe, resisting the seductions of exotic lady spies while softly humming "My Country 'Tis of Thee" to the tune of "God Save the Queen." I had indulged in the experience of actually working, when during a vacation from college Dad got me an assignment as an apprentice "title writer." It was to the great Herman Mankiewicz, older brother of the later famous director, Joe. Herman needed me like a kangaroo needs a pogo stick, but it was a case of nepotism in full cry. I supplied such sterling lines as: "On the far-flung borders of Russia a demoralized army struggled to hold back the German storm, while another storm took form behind it. Red Revolution!" Herman had not passed that one. The summer convinced me not only that Herman needed no assistance but that I had no real calling for film-title writing.

Experts like Mankiewicz and George Marion, Jr., were paid great sums for their creative know-how. Titles could make up for the shortcomings of the films themselves. If the film didn't work as a tragedy, it could be turned into a comedy merely by inserting carefully chosen captions. But sound was on the way in. The title writer would soon be as obsolete as the armorer or the carriage maker . . .

. . . as the barn where *The Squaw Man* had been produced, which stood only a short distance from the corner of Hollywood and Vine, where I now stood, waiting for fate to tap me on the elbow. I could recall that on the streetcars of the Pacific Electric Line (whose network later established the boundaries of Greater Los Angeles) there was a sign prohibiting the shooting of rabbits from the rear platform. But that had been long ago, when our village still slept in hot, clean air scented faintly by orange blossoms like an expectant bride soon to become pregnant with the future. Here, on a famous corner that was also part of my personal history, I was back home—and broke.

I'd just come from the jewelers, where I'd sold some of my father's keepsakes which he would have been too embarrassed to dispose of himself; Dunhill lighters, cigarette cases with diamond monograms, platinum watches. Inscriptions that read: "To my esteemed boss, Rudolph Valentino." "To the man who set my feet on the road to success, Buddy Rogers." "To a great gentleman from a grateful one, Walter Wanger." Expressions in keeping with the flamboyant times. Baubles sold now for the weight of their gold, not their sentiments. A drop in the ocean of the family debt, and now all these stopgap geegaws were gone.

Only my empty, travel-worn pigskin valise attested to the plush days of high living in far places. Proudly it still bore the stickers of the great continental hotels. The Adlon, Berlin; The Donaplota, Budapest; The Ritz, London; The Georges Cinq, Paris; The Negulesco, Nice; hotels in Vienna, Madrid, Marrakesh, Prague, and New York. There were ship's tags, too, from the *Isle de France*, the *Paris*, the *Olympic*, the *Majestic*, floating hostelries of elegance where privilege had been carefully defined by classes: first, second, and third. It had not seemed unnatural then for a descendant of steerage immigrants to sit at the captain's table. Money was a great equalizer in the twenties. But if there had been a nouveau riche, there was now a nouveau poor. We sons of privilege who had ordered our shirts from Sulka's, our suits from Leslie and Roberts, who had paraded through our boarding schools dressed by Brooks Brothers, DePinna, and Finchley, sported derbies and chesterfields to tea dances at the Biltmore and monstrous raccoon-skinned coats to football games, our hip pockets weighted with flasks of hammered silver, who had danced at the debutante parties, scarcely knowing the names of our hosts but invited because we went to the right (or nearly right) schools, who had necked with the daughters of the Blue Book and groped chorus girls from the Vanities and Ziegfeld Follies in rumble seats, we—the gentlemen boozehounds tempered by the hangovers of Prohibition hooch after vomiting under the moonlight from throat and pen, we who had been flung ingloriously from the speakeasies of Manhattan when our money ran out on weekends—we had now become obsolete before ever having been useful. We drifted in a Depression-bound world as extinct as Mesozoic reptiles lost in an age of ice.

Standing on that corner, I looked forward to nothing, backward to all. At which moment the expected tap of fate, right on cue, reached my elbow.

Fate, in this case, wore loose, worn-out clothing, had a breathless voice and the face of a fragile gargoyle. Hair sparse as mountain grass, live blue eyes, hands that darted in birdlike gestures and a smile warming the whole, wildly enthusiastic thin face. He looked as though he might not have long to live.

"Pardon me, but have you actually been to all those places?" he inquired.

"All what places?"

"Those hotels in foreign countries. The ones on your suitcase."

I glanced down at the tags. "Yes." I wondered why he, or anyone, would have bothered to notice this evidence of wanderings about the "upper world" of the late twenties.

"Have you got any job at the moment?"

Of course I hadn't. Neither job nor place to live. Neither prospect nor purpose, nor plan. He seemed delighted.

"Then you might consider a proposition I've got for you?"

I considered the ragbag with the snapping blue eyes. I waited.

"You see," he said, breathing heavily between every word. "My wife and I own some apartments on Vista Street. Vista Street . . . you know where Vista Street is? Well, it doesn't matter. Some are empty at the moment. I mean, you could live in one of them and we'd give you meals, free, too . . . if you worked out for me. I mean . . . if we got on and everything."

I contemplated the strange expression, the birdlike gestures, completely mystified as to what sort of work he had in mind which could involve my past travels. He looked harmless enough, however, for me to accompany him home.

The explanation came in his pleasant, tile-floored gray-beamed, spurious Spanish Colonial apartment. Jack Preston was a writer. But not *just* a writer: an incurable, compulsive, fanatical fiction machine who was producing a series of novels for the old Macauley Company.

"Potboilers, I suppose you'd call them. Five hundred dollars advance per book against royalties," he told me. "Of course they generally don't sell that much, but they're good yarns. The kind of stories people can read and forget their troubles."

"Sounds great," I said. Anything would have.

"They get published and that's the best you can say for them. Used to paper my walls with the rejection slips, but writing is the thing I've always wanted to do. Don't know why. I say to my wife, Vi, I say, a man might make a lot more doing something else. I once did."

Jack had been born and raised in western Canada, migrated down to the American Middle West as a newspaperman, then drifted to Los Angeles, the great mousetrap for dreamers, madmen, prophets, and fools. That was all he had seen of the world—and it offered nothing of the world about which Jack wanted to write. The star he set his course by was more Michael Arlen than Sinclair Lewis. His brain seethed with White Russian princes, wild American debutantes, glamorous lady spies, profligate polo players who breakfasted on champagne and chorus girls, commissionaires dripping with braid who "deus ex machinaed" at luxury hotels, whisky-soaked correspondents who wrote poetry on the zinc bars of Montparnasse bistros, bullfighters with hips like ballet dancers, and ballerinas whose carriages were drawn by adoring students rather than horses. There were war correspondents and randy English noble ladies, beachcombers and sinuous South Sea sirens in slinky sarongs. The whole phony circus of twenties pulp fiction pulsed in Jack's dreams.

Jack was prepared to overlook the fact that I had never rubbed torsos with pearl divers in the South Seas—one couldn't have everything—and so I became the "ghost" of a writer.

For uninterrupted privacy, Jack had set up his office in the rusting chassis of an ancient automobile, which was parked amid nettles and sunflowers on tireless rims in the vacant lot behind his apartment house. Here we toiled from dawn to dusk over a pair of antique Underwoods mounted on two-by-four boards straddled across glassless window frames. A bare light bulb dangled from a diaper pin attached to the tattered cloth ceiling, its cord snaking back to his kitchen. An atlas, a dictionary, and a Roget's *Thesaurus* completed the furnishing of our immobile office. With Jack's energy and my know-where, books fairly flew from our keys. Imaginations seethed, backs ached, and with each new effort my contribution was permitted to grow. We became a full-fledged collaboration and it would have been unthinkable to Jack not to offer credit where credit was becoming due. I was soon turning out entire books under my own name and ghosting books for other nonliterary authors. The phantom could afford to go to the opera! The books were terrible, but there was a new breath of hope in the air, a stirring of tubers after long winter.

Seven

THEN ONE DAY the Depression had run its miserable course. Its end had come gradually, like a seasonal change, but if one had to tie it to some great moment, it would have been the inauguration of Franklin Delano Roosevelt. When he told us we had nothing to fear but fear itself, we swallowed the platitude and felt better. He came to appear remarkably fallible after we had been led into still waters. But in the early moments of the subsiding storm, most Americans thanked God for Franklin D.

The sun was shining again in California. The banks had reopened. Hollywood, perhaps by the very nature of its geography, most lightly jolted of all American villages by the Depression, was flexing its bank accounts, planning larger extravaganzas than ever, and plunging back into the business of making the public forget the recent turbulence that had briefly shaken the all-American dream.

Dad's old friendship with Sidney Kent bore ripe fruit. Kent had become president of Fox Films and he arranged an independent producer's berth for Dad, who immediately set about producing *Zoo in Budapest* with Gene Raymond and Loretta Young.

On the strength of my published pulp I wangled a lowly job in the reading department of Fox's Western Avenue Studio, that unfashionable factory where the B pictures were ground out. Western Avenue was the eastern perimeter of Hollywood where it melted into Los Angeles. Its very location was an embarrassment to anyone trying to look like a big frog in the Hollywood pond. Fading stars were sent to this foreign legion outpost when they began to lose box-office appeal and no longer commanded top salaries. Here John Gilbert, Garbo's once-great screen lover, struggled to switch his career from acting to directing. His high-pitched voice had brought giggles instead of sighs. The advent of sound had ruined many, but no one more completely than Gilbert.

I joined the reading department feeling like a remittance man who had been shipped away to prove his mettle or go under. The studio was presided over by an efficient ogre named Sol Wurtzel. It was said around the town that when you joined the Western Avenue lot, you had gone from "bad to Wurtzel." Nepotism flourished here, too. There were some half dozen other Wurtzels nurtured on the payroll, ranging from children to Sol's grandfather. This old man's main occupation was picking up fallen nails carelessly dropped by studio carpenters on the sound stages or the walks between. The economics of this task may seem difficult to comprehend in a world of such extravagance, but nails could be used again, and besides, they punctured tires.

Grandpa, a mellow sage who had outlived any real usefulness, went about his task quite happily, warmed by the knowledge that his job was secure. Or almost. The old gentleman had one unfortunate idiosyncrasy. He was kinky about pinching young ladies on the bottom. Since his vocation kept him in a low-bent position, his targets were always at eye level. Aware of his aberration, the dancers and extra girls took a perverse delight in exposing him to temptation. Perhaps they felt that Grandpa was always there in a pinch. Eventually the word reached Sol who maintained a puritanical regime. He warned his grandfather "one more and you're out!"

Bravely the old man fought temptation, until one day a pair of blondes went hip-swinging by in red satin shorts. They paused near the old man to exchange a cigarette and a wink, teetering on stiletto heels. Visions of sugar plums danced through his venerable head—and he lost it.

That afternoon Sol had him on the carpet. It must have been a poignant scene, the didactic dictator dismissing the profligate patriarch. The old man had finally touched bottom.

Nobody could turn out B films so cheaply, so quickly, so efficiently as Sol Wurtzel. His studio was the ideal training ground for anyone with a spark of production talent. Unfortunately, at twenty-one, I had none.

Wurtzel was an impressively large-framed man with a rough manner and an almost perpetual grimace which the uninitiated might take for a smile. Such an error would be to one's sorrow, for he was an authentically tough character. All the same, he was singularly fair and even honorable, compared to many of the film monsters of his day, when survival often depended upon ruthlessness.

He had come west with the great Winnie Sheehan, once the secretary to New York's police commissioner. Sheehan was rumored to have taken the rap for a murder. True or false, he had been rescued by William Fox from a police department bribery scandal and worked his way up to a salary of $130,000 a year, a stately home in Beverly Hills, a stable of rare Lippizaner horses, and marriage to the opera diva Maria Jeritza. When Sheehan took over as head of Fox film production he made Sol king of the B's.

To a parvenu in the practical world of film production, my boss was terrifying and my job in the reading department the true bottom of the totem pole. My desk was the rubbish bin. I covered pulp magazines, unproduced plays, unreadable books, and original film scripts submitted by unknowns. Any submission that might vaguely be considered of importance was given to a more senior reader, which was practically anyone. I hacked out synopses and opinions which almost nobody bothered to read. It seemed I had fallen into a backwash of stagnant security, a limbo from which one might neither rise nor fall except by some miracle.

In the early thirties, the town of Agua Caliente was the principal watering place south of the Mexican border, developed with capital from that powerful movie brotherhood the Schencks, and Jack Dempsey. As if Hollywood needed one, Agua Caliente was an oasis of sin.

We already had a fair reputation for lurid happenings. Wallace Reid, an early star of FP-L and an American image of wholesomeness, had died of a drug overdose. The jovial Fatty Arbuckle (also one of Lasky's valued stars) reportedly crushed a call-girl to death beneath his huge bulk during a private party after the screening of his latest family comedy, in San Francisco. Next came the unsolved murder of William Desmond Taylor, the gentlemanly British director. Taylor, considered a model of decorum and propriety, was used by my father as window-dressing whenever he wanted to show off Hollywood's refinement. And yet an hour after leaving a conference with Dad, that distinguished gentleman was found murdered. The failure of the police to solve the case gave the newspapers an opportunity to cast suspicions on almost everyone. The most likely suspect, his valet-chauffeur, vanished, never to be found.

Yet another unsolved crime rocked Hollywood, this one with implications so sinister that for years it was mentioned only in guarded whispers. The roughly assembled fragments of jigsaw gossip revealed that an important film maker named Thomas Ince was shot to death on William Randolph Hearst's yacht. It was rumored, without confirmation, that the bullet had been aimed at Charlie Chaplin in a fit of jealousy over Marion Davies. Some even whispered that it was because Louella Parsons had witnessed the shooting that she secured herself a lifetime job as Gossip Queen on the Hearst chain of newspapers. "Hollywood, Follywood," the poets said.

But when things actually became too quiet in the old town, Agua Caliente offered horse racing, a superb golf course, a flashy casino. It also offered whores, pimps, con-men and the fleshpots of neighboring Tijuana. In Caliente the lush bungalows were temples of discretion for the indiscreet.

I was a little surprised when my father asked me to spend a weekend there with him, but maybe he guessed I needed a break from the Wurtzel regime.

We were shown into a sumptuous suite, all pink adobe, stucco, and wild, flower colors—like moving into a fresco by Diego Rivera. In double time we were out on the first tee, Dad moving at his usual frantic pace. His drive this morning was a hard three hundred yards down the fairway. He set off after his ball at a dead run, only to be brought to an aggravating halt by a twosome dubbing slowly along in front of us. Far too slowly for Dad. Impatiently, he signaled for permission to go through and hurried forward at furious stride, caddies panting behind. As we came up we saw a handsome, gray-haired, olive-complexioned man and a breathtaking platinum blonde, whom my father greeted enthusiastically. It was Jean Harlow. She introduced her stepfather, Signor Bello, but we weren't looking at the dapper Italian. She filled the eye and imagination with the impact of her looks and personality. I never saw a star with more personal magnetism. Many had it on screen, brought to life by the camera, like fireflies ignited to view by darkness. They needed the attentions of makeup people, wardrobe, and finally a director to supply the spark that came through the camera's eye. Not so Jean Harlow. Her stardom was of the immediate moment of her presence, of stunning good looks, of unbounded vitality that needed no grafted additions or embellishment. She caught and held anyone who happened to be near by an intoxicating attraction, a fascination quite unforgettable. It was in voice, eye, and a knowing way of smiling that implied the utmost concept of excitement possible between man and woman. Individual magic that worked all the time, on and off the screen.

Bello suggested that instead of "going through" we should join them and play the remaining holes together. My normally erratic golf settled into a golden groove. Hooks, slices vanished; drives rocketed straight down the fairway. Everything was working. I felt inspired. I was!

That evening I was wedged into the tuxedoed throng of suntanned males crowding the crap table where Jean was throwing dice as though she'd invented them. Wearing a spectacular white satin gown cut to the navel, she sprawled the dice for twenty-four passes in a row across the green baize. Who was looking at the dice? I was betting with her, on her, beside her. Silver-dollar stacks sprouted ceilingward. My profits were becoming considerable and I wasn't even trying.

Finally Jean surrendered the dice and flashed me a glance of unexpected warmth. "Basta!" she sighed.

"You roll great dice," I blurted. Not very scintillating dialogue.

"You play good golf," she smiled.

I helped her collect a leaning tower of silver Liberty-heads that weighed down her beaded handbag.

"Perhaps we could have a game when we get back to town?" she suggested, favoring me with so devastating a glance that I thought she might be looking at someone else.

"Dice?" I inquired.

"Golf," she smiled. "That is, if you don't mind playing with an old lady." I think she must have been about twenty-three at the time.

All I could do was stammer something to the effect that I'd love to play with her. I was too inexperienced to give it a double meaning. She suggested we meet the following Saturday at the Riviera Country Club in Los Angeles.

"At two o'clock," she said as she was swept away by half the men in the room. Bello followed, bearing her white fox fur like a consolation prize.

The glamorous star was near the peak of her fame. Her career had been briefly clouded by the tragic death of her second husband, Paul Bern, found on Labor Day, 1932, naked before his bathroom mirror with a bullet in his brain. His mysterious suicide note to Harlow had not satisfied the L.A. police. Only the desperate efforts of L. B. Mayer and his great publicity chief prevented her being indicted on a murder charge. But no one who knew her really doubted her innocence. When told of her brilliant producer husband's death, Jean, who was spending that evening at her mother's, tried to throw herself from a balcony. But the meaning of that suicide note was never explained by Jean, which left an open field for salacious conjecture by journalists, gossips, and biographers.

Her attraction was so great that it was supposed that Bern, a highly sensitive, moody person, had found himself physically inadequate to satisfy the earthy siren.

Very possible. But when I met her, the shadow of tragedy had begun to fade. She had made *Red Dust* with Gable, close friend and rumored sometimes lover; she was scheduled to appear next in *Bombshell* and reach an even higher summit of popularity. Ahead lay a third marriage to Harold Rossen, the great cameraman, which would end unsuccessfully, and the famous romance with Bill Powell.

Of all this I was scarcely aware when at the age of twenty-two I was dated in Agua Caliente to play a round with Jean Harlow at the Riviera Country Club in Santa Monica.

However, once back in town at my ignominious desk, sober consideration prevailed. Of course Harlow wouldn't remember a casual date, carelessly made in the heat of a weekend of fun and fancy. Even I couldn't believe that the most important star in Hollywood would date a nonentity, the lowest reader in the least of filmland's studios. So ludicrous was the idea that when Saturday came I made up my mind that there was no point in turning up at the Riviera. Imagine walking up to the Caddy House and asking if Jean Harlow was looking for me!

Well, she certainly wouldn't show up, and I didn't intend to slouch around the club with egg on my face. So I decided to catch up on the extra reading at the sweatshop. Two readers were home sick and I'd inherited their stacks. I sat there in the midst of my customary mental paralysis when the phone on my desk jangled. I answered it.

A low feminine voice said, "Not very nice of you to stand up an old lady!"

"Is it . . . Jean?" I stammered. "No, you can't be!"

"What, furious? Well, I should be. It isn't exactly polite."

I couldn't believe it even then. Still, I hadn't told anyone, so who could be pulling my leg? "Jean? Is it really Jean Harlow?"

"Uh huh," she allowed flatly. "Start explaining."

"My God!" was all I could produce.

"What a memory . . . !"

"I didn't dream that you'd really . . ."

"Really what?" she asked.

"That you'd actually . . ."

"Actually what?"

"Be there. At the club . . . I mean, for golf!"

"I see. Well, you're not forgiven." But her tone suggested that I might be. I ran out of the office and beat every red light from Western Avenue to the sea.

I don't know what I expected from our liaison. At twenty-two life had provided me with no frame of reference by which I could fathom such a femme fatale. Still, if any moment in time deserved to be frozen in memory, why not that afternoon in Brentwood Hills, striding with Jean Harlow after golf balls at the dawn of a fantasy experience—one that I was too immature to savor or deserve?

One meeting led to another, and, never asking why, I accepted the joyous miracle and made myself available whenever she rang. Rarely did *I* have the courage to phone *her*.

For weeks we went everywhere together, dined in the flashy restaurants on the Sunset Strip, slummed ostentatiously in Venice Amusement Park or on the Santa Monica Pier. Jean enjoyed the sensations she created everywhere, the riots of demonstrative fans. No Garbo, hiding her light from the world, when local police had to extract us from the too-physical adulation of autograph hunters, she was unruffled and vastly entertained. Fun was to her the unexpected, the unplanned, the unconventional.

In the rush of these moments, all thrill and buoyancy, we never discovered each other at all. For the moment her attitude was "to enjoy." And I? I dared to hold her hand and kiss her hello and goodbye. I didn't conceive of venturing further. Perhaps that was my attraction. Everything about me seemed to amuse her. Even my third-hand wreck of a car. One evening at the Trocadero the doorman opened the door for her and the handle came off in his clutching white cotton glove.

I found myself spending fewer and fewer hours reading down the stacks at the studio, until one day a growl from Sol Wurtzel burst the dream.

"Junior . . . !" Sol sounded angry. He always did. This time he was!

"Where have you been keeping yourself? You don't work no more nights?"

"Sir?" I tried not to look him in the eye.

"You look asleep. You don't go to bed any more neither, huh? Jesus Christ, I seen mummies in the prop department looked better than you! Are you still on my payroll?"

"Oh, yes, sir!" I assured him.

"With your eyes closed? Your father's a great producer even when he's not employed. You got a chance here to learn something about this business and what do you do?"

"Nothing, sir."

"You're goddamn right you don't do nothing! Half the time you ain't even at your desk! This job you could learn something from. But you got less ambition than anyone I ever knew!"

I was sorry—appropriately appreciative of the opportunity he'd given me. I assured him I wanted to learn the film business. My mouth was full of humble pie, my mind full of Jean.

"So tonight," he roared, "I got to select stock film. You want to learn something? You be there! Projection room number one at eight o'clock. With me!"

Finality, total. He was gone before I could word an excuse, had I dared, which I didn't. So I never told him that I had a date, or with whom. Instead, I phoned Jean, bleating apologies and explaining that I certainly would lose my job if I didn't appear tonight for the screening with Sol.

She took it more calmly than I expected. In fact she had a suggestion; she would come to the studio. Oh, not to the projection room, of course. She'd wait in my office. Since she had the script for her new film, it would afford her a quiet hour or two to study. When the screening was over we could go out for a late dinner and maybe drop in some fun place after.

It worried me just a little bringing Jean to my shabby reader's attic as we mounted the stairs in the silent studio. For reasons of economy, no doubt, the lift was out of operation at night. We entered the cluttered office where the old typewriters slept under worn oilskin covers. Through the window I pointed out the building where I'd be screening. She would be able to see me come out, could perhaps come down to meet me. I left her ensconced with script, cigarettes, her feet on my desk, and went down across the quadrangle to join Sol in the main projection room.

His mood was less than jubilant. He'd had fifty thousand dollars cut from the budget of his current film by Winnie Sheehan and was ready to eat nails. I was the nearest available whipping boy; he used my ignorance of the mysteries of selecting stock film as an excuse to work off his rage.

"Junior, I don't know what you got on your mind but it ain't film. Stop looking at that door like you had some place better to go! If we don't find what we want we're gonna be here all night."

All night! I had sick visions of returning to my office to find a bowlful of angrily crushed cigarette stubs and no Jean. With the aid of the film editor, we were selecting footage from old films: mob and crowd scenes which were intended to match up with close-ups of the actors in Sol's new film. It was an old trick, still useful in the low-budget field, which spared the producer the need to film scenes requiring large numbers of extras. But there were always complications when matching close-ups with stock and finding existing stock to fit the script's requirements. Lighting and costume also had to be taken into account. What use I was to Sol that night is dubious, but when he noticed me sneak a nervous glance at my watch he ordered another five reels. It was hours before we emerged into the darkness of the quadrangle.

An empty studio at night can be the most deserted place on earth. Sol's eyes swept across the dark windows of the three-storey executive building, searching for a light some profligate employee might have left burning. Unbelievably, he found it. A lighted window on the third floor. He stared incredulously. Could someone have missed the constant reminders on the bulletin boards?

"Who left that on?"

"The light?" I asked uneasily.

"The light, of course the light! Junior, make a note. I want the name of whose office it is and I want it on my desk at nine o'clock tomorrow morning."

"You can have the name now, sir. I turned it on before I went into the projection room."

"You . . . ?" he glared.

"You see, sir, I have a date. A lady is waiting for me up there. I didn't think you'd mind if I let her read in the office while we were . . ."

The lips twisted into the proverbial grimace, for somehow he found this wildly entertaining.

"Junior's got a dame, huh? My book reader's got some cheap dame," he rasped. "You getting it tonight, huh, Junior? Saturday night he gets laid?" The heavy humor echoed loudly through the night across the quadrangle. Jean must have heard, because suddenly my office light went out. Moments later she emerged from the building some fifty feet away and walked toward us. It was a walk that the world had not ignored. A way of carrying the head, a poetry of seductive motion.

Sol looked. Then he gawked. "Junior . . . ! She looks like, like Jean Har . . . But she can't be!"

"Yes, sir."

"Don't give me crap!" he exclaimed. His feelings were quite logical. In his studio, the factory of B pictures, the idea that the Queen of MGM could be waiting for a twenty-two-year-old reader . . . ! But she was now too close for doubt.

"May I introduce Miss Harlow, Mr. Wurtzel?" I must admit to a certain note of triumph.

Wurtzel stared, mumbled, stared some more. Then he told her how glad he was to meet her and why hadn't Junior, the schmuck, brought her to the projection room? She was deliciously gracious. She wouldn't have dreamed of interrupting our work and so forth and so forth. Eventually Jean and I made our apologies and took off to enjoy what was left of the evening.

Next morning a message was waiting on my desk and my phone was ringing and both said that Mr. Wurtzel wished to see me at once. "At once" presumably meant, at once! Bob Yost, head of the reading department, favored me with solicitous interest. Now what trouble? Trouble was easy enough to come by in that studio.

The seriousness of the occasion was emphasized by the fact that I was ushered into the sanctum without a moment's wait. I resigned myself to dismissal for Heaven knew which breach of the plentiful regulations. Sol glared through glasses, and this time to my surprise I felt almost sure that the grimace was in fact a true smile.

"Junior, all night I've been thinking. How would you like to be my personal assistant?"

How would I like sainthood? "Your assistant, sir?" I could not fathom such glory.

"Sure. Certainly. Why not? You'll have a private office next to mine. Already I gave orders one should be vacated for you. Also you got to have your own secretary. And your name on the intercom here." He stabbed a finger at the box through which his orders were customarily barked to department heads. "I want you to get"—he sought for and found *le mot juste*—"involved!"

"In what, sir?"

"In everything! Preparation. Budgets. Schedules. Scripts. Art direction. Sets. Rushes. Editing. Music. With me you will be in on all decisions, and particularly"—the special meaning-filled grin—"in casting."

"Casting, sir?"

"Sure, why not? You might get ideas for some stars we could maybe borrow or something. Who knows?"

Clarity came with a flash. Who indeed could know? In quick

mirage I saw myself casually suggesting to Jean over a taco in Alvera Street, "I said to Wurtzel the other day that you might do a guest appearance in his new film."

"Of course, Jesse, anything to be near you," she would reply, flashing me an engulfing smile. The intoxication of power swept reason aside.

Sol was still talking. "Lastly, Junior—what about a raise in salary?"

"If you really feel—I should have one, sir."

"Oh, you should! You will! You have!" He cleared his throat. "What do I pay you now?"

"Twenty-five dollars a week, sir."

"From now on you get two-fifty."

My mind boggled. "Two hundred and fifty . . . dollars?"

"For a start—and one more thing before I forget. Winnie Sheehan wants you to come to his party tonight. Bring anyone you like. A girl friend, maybe."

"Like Jean Harlow?" I suggested.

"Why not? She's a nice girl."

Sheehan, in charge of all production at Fox! Wurtzel's big boss. The tough, power-oriented Irishman responsible for many extremely successful and artistic films, although his critics liked to suggest that his greatest contribution to the studio was its superb police force, drilled like grenadiers and inclined to overreact to such crises as parking violations. An invitation from him was like a royal command. Would Jean accept? Happily, she did.

Our entrance into Sheehan's party caused no slight stir. People who had never known of my existence suddenly became old friends. It was "Jess, old fellow" from virtual strangers. There seemed no altitude to which my current stock might not rise, like the champagne bubbling over the rim of Sheehan's solid gold goblets. Even my father, who had recently signed a four-picture deal with Sheehan, regarded me with new respect.

Would I, he suggested, bring Miss Harlow to dinner at the house? It was not difficult to read his mind. What a star for his next picture, if she could be borrowed from Metro.

Aside from the sheer joy of being with her, Jean was catapulting me into a new dimension of space—importance. Imagination readily envisioned a kind of young Thalberg-cum-Walter Wanger, rocketing to the top rung of the ladder.

Suddenly my opinion was sought by Sol on almost everything. And because he would ask for it, his underling producers began soliciting my support for their particular projects. "Say, Jess, could you give this script a quick read before S.W. sees it? You know, so if he asks you, you could say a good word." In the next few weeks everyone seemed to require consultation and advice. My phone hummed. My secretary fought off appointments. Agents besieged me with actresses, writers, scripts, new songs. The world had become a very friendly oyster.

Then one day the oyster turned sour.

It started the evening we dropped into one of the Beverly Hills bistros for a dance. That dance was my downfall—in more ways than one.

The night before, Jean had happened to express a fondness for tall, dark, athletic men. Well, I couldn't compete with her friend, Gable, but I was dark and devoted to athletics. I was also five feet six in my highest heels, and you couldn't wear cowboy boots out on a date. Not in those days. Then I got an idea. Newspapers, bunched up and stuffed into my shoes, could add another vital two inches! (Those were the days before Adler Elevators lifted the spirits of small men.)

Jean gave no sign of noticing my enhanced stature when I kissed her hello at the great white hilltop house. She did say, "You look marvelous, darling. You're going up in the world."

"You did notice!" I said, taken aback.

"What?" she asked.

"With Sol, I mean," I put in quickly. "Ever since that night at Fox Western, you've been my rabbit's foot."

"You got a raise!"

My mind flew to the overstuffed shoes upon which I was teetering, but happily it was not them to which she referred. I nodded.

"And he looks like he's ready to reach for his checkbook every time I step in the office."

"I'd like to be in your shoes."

"Oh, no you wouldn't! I mean, helping run that place is not like being an MGM star."

Her perfume was so strong it made me reel—which was precarious in my lofty position. She was wearing one of her Adrian-designed white dresses, which set off the silver-platinum hair.

"You never looked more beautiful," I told her. She took the compliment in stride.

"We'll have fun. I want to have a lot of fun tonight."

It seemed a dead certainty. We started with drinks strong as her perfume on her balcony. The darkening evening made Hollywood that jeweled carpet the bad novelists always described it as. A sparkling stillness, as though the Milky Way had been upended and lay at our feet.

At the nightclub, all went perfectly through charred steaks and Waldorf salad, until the orchestra lunged into a tango. "Like to tango, Jean?"

It was the only dance I ever considered myself to have mastered, having been carefully indoctrinated by Arthur Murray himself in the days when he still personally polished each pupil.

"I like everything," she replied, as we walked out to the floor. "Every dance. Every drink. Every role. Well, almost. I could have lived without pies in the face in those Sennett movies. Did you learn your tango in the Argentine, Jess? Traveling with your father?"

"No, I did most of my tango dancing in Paris. And Spain. Traveling alone." I was doing my best to project the image of the international "homme fatal."

The music oozed from accordions, she curved into my arms. I started a sinuous glide—and fell flat on my face. The overstuffed shoes had come off at first slither. I rose, diminished by a mere three inches, but it could have been three miles for the unintentional entertainment I had provided everyone in the place. You were always part of attention's center with Jean. She had disentangled, and avoided dropping with me. Now she was laughing, it seemed from the navel!

"You need a saddle horn on those shoes, Jess! Or buy a pair that's been broken!"

What was broken was my heart and confidence. Not that she was being mean. As anyone who ever worked with her knows, she had no meanness in her.

The shoes minus stuffing had me down to earth by the time I drove her home. She was complaining of a slight headache, and we'd done our share of drinking to deserve it.

"I am now about to read the corniest line in movie history," she threatened. "Come up with me while I change into something comfortable."

I did. And she started to. That bedroom . . . soft shades of ivory, rugs matching walls. Someone had unkindly called it "the platinum house that hair built." Probably someone who had never been inside. The bed was a French import, antique, and canopied. Fit for a king—or a king's lady. Huge. A white bear rug beside it. Also huge. Pink dressing table holding a fair arsenal of perfumes. She picked one up and sprayed it all over me.

"Like my perfume straight and my liquor strong." A line she had used in some interview or other.

The wardrobe held a collection of shoes. She had a love for beautiful shoes and the means to buy all she wanted. There were white fox furs, silver fox coats, minks. She stepped into the dressing room, leaving the door open. In the mirrors, white flesh, sheer silk, flashing. I waited.

"Somebody's got loose with a hammer in my head. Think I should lie down. Why don't you relax. Stay awhile."

But instead I hurried out of the room—to return in a moment. "Got something for you," I called through the door.

"Nearly ready." She came out of the dressing room in a fantastic peach-colored negligee.

I handed her two aspirin and a glass of water. The glass was pink and silver.

"How old are you, Jesse?"

"Twenty-two."

She climbed into the vast bed. On the floor sprawled pages of the script for her next picture, *Bombshell.*

"When I was sixteen I was married," she said. "My first husband couldn't stand me wanting to work in pictures. I guess he was jealous of them. Why are all men jealous?"

"Lack of confidence, maybe. Like being—too tall or—my father always called me Shortie."

"I wouldn't have noticed," she said kindly.

I noticed the aspirin were still on the bedside table. "How's your head? Would you like me to read you to sleep?"

She looked at me a long moment. "If there's one thing I can't stand, it's reading in bed. Be a good boy and go home."

The moment had passed when I might have been any other kind of boy.

Next day I phoned Jean at her studio dressing-room to check on the time for our usual evening date. The colored maid who'd been with her for years said she couldn't speak to me. Another phone call brought the same answer. And another and another. "Couldn't" had obviously become "wouldn't." By the tenth phone call I knew it was over; Jean Harlow wouldn't be seeing me again.

The word traveled quickly, sped by Louella Parsons, whispered at the Mocambo, the Troc, and other currently fashionable nighteries. It was exchanged on sets where cast and technicians waited interminably between shots. The awful truth filtered back to me. Jean had mended her rift with William Powell. Only a temporary rupture, the columnists agreed. No one would remember that for a brief moment in her life Miss Harlow had amused herself with an altar boy in the temple of her fame.

I thought again about her earlier marriage to the brilliant young producer Paul Bern, right hand to Irving Thalberg. I recalled my own embraces with the sex queen, which I had been too naive, too inexperienced to consummate. Perhaps what she had needed at that moment in time was a playmate, not a bedfellow.

But more than Jean had ended for me. Only hours after my abortive phone calls, Wurtzel got word on the grapevine that we were no longer "an item." A note was placed on my desk reducing me from Sol's executive assistant back to the reading department, and with it, my salary reverted to twenty-five dollars a week. Again Bob Yost was snarling at me with no more respect than if I had never emerged from behind my stacks of unread stories, books, and pulp magazines. Sol seemed to have forgotten I existed.

I never saw Jean again. A few years later, returning from Europe on a French freighter, I was briefly disgorged into the banana heat of some South American port with an hour ashore to browse over souvenirs. A newspaper headline exercised my feeble Spanish. It proclaimed the death of a great star of the "Peliculas" at twenty-six. The generally accepted cause of Jean's death was from a uremic infection brought on by the powerful hair bleach she used. Norman Zierold, Boswell of *The Hollywood Tycoons*, blamed her mother, who, a Christian Scientist, had failed to summon medical aid until too late. At that moment in South America, the cause seemed hardly important—only the fact that she who had been so gorgeously alive was gone.

Her memory began to sprout legends. One may be worth repeating because it could have been true. Lady Margot Asquith, wife of the prime minister and a leading London hostess, was famous both for the celebrities and near-celebrities who were included in her invitations and for her quotable quips. Once she gave a luncheon party for my father. Arriving tardily as was his habit, he was promptly introduced: "Ladies and gentlemen, the late Jesse Lasky!"

When Jean Harlow met her, Jean is said to have said, "Ah, Margo*t*"–accenting the *t*–"I've certainly looked forward to meeting you."

Whereupon Lady Asquith replied, "Thank you, my dear, but the *t* is silent, as in Harlow."

But I have kindlier memories of the Lady who made me king for a day.

Eight

Our town was correctly noted for sudden rises and falls. In the upper echelons they called it "being as good as your last picture." But a studio reader had no "last picture," good or bad. He chewed the cud of mental monotony. And when submissions of story material were slack one rested eyes and bottom, or tried a hand at some writing of one's own. As an alternative to watching the flies scale the summit of the water cooler, I decided to peck out a play.

Everyone had heard how Noël Coward could dash off a London stage success in the course of a weekend, but those who lack the Master's talent should avoid such time-schedules. The first quick draft of *Private Beach* came out suffering from anemia of plot and character, but a writer friend, Gladys Unger, helped me build it into a submittable dramatic stage piece. The play was set in the "notorious" playground of Malibu, where the film colonists escaped from themselves to each other. I used a theatrical device in which the characters would make their entrances down the aisles in bathing costume, dripping from having been hosed down outside the theater, as though emerging from the surf. Amazingly, a local management offered to produce it.

The director selected a bombastic extrovert to play the central character, a Hollywood producer. My antihero, it must be confesed, too closely resembled my current puissant, galvanic boss, Sol Wurtzel. In fact, he was dead on. I could only hope S.W. would not hear about the production.

But the play was being produced in a Beverly Hills theater not far from his lair. Still, I consoled myself, even if it did come to his attention, surely he wouldn't trouble to attend. The scribblings of so humble a member of his organization would not merit two hours of his valuable time. But as rehearsals moved toward opening night and publicity filtered into the local papers, sure enough, some misguided friend brought it to Wurtzel's attention.

"Junior . . . ," he hissed as I tried to slither from view across the quadrangle one day, "somebody told me you wrote a play."

"Er, no, sir, not really. That is, I . . . I merely helped. A c-c-c-co . . . collaboration, you see. Anyway, it's no good. No good at all!"

"Of that you ain't the best judge!" His grimace had never been less deceptive. The subject definitely had to be changed.

"You know, sir, I read a very interesting book yesterday that would make a wonderful Western. It's about two midgets who escape from a circus and become gunfighters."

Wurtzel was not to be that easily sidetracked. "Do I get tickets to the opening night or don't I?" he queried.

"Well, sir, I really wouldn't dream of wasting your time and . . ."

He cut me off. "Or do I have to buy them?"

"But it's so bad, you see, sir, Mr. Wurtzel. You wouldn't believe how bad this play is . . ." I insisted.

"So what's the title of this bad play?" he asked.

"*Private Beach*," came my weak reply.

"Military stuff, huh? Sounds interesting. Leave two tickets for opening night with my secretary." And he was off, striding across the quadrangle.

I considered hari-kari, or resigning before I was annihilated. Still, there was a grain of hope left. Having made his point about the tickets, Sol would surely have something more important to do on the night. An out-of-town preview, or an important poker game at Hillcrest Country Club, or a sudden ulcer attack. But none of these salvations took place.

Opening night arrived and Sol was definitely planning to come. A tactical rethink was imperative. I slipped backstage to the dressing room of the overexuberant actor who was to play the Wurtzel character. A half-empty bottle of bourbon reared itself above overflowing ashtrays. His red face glared through a square of light in the dressing-table mirror. Lips pinched as he applied too much makeup. No subtlety or understatement obscured any facet of this thespian's art.

"Would you mind," I began, "just for tonight of course, *under*-playing it?"

The tomato-boozy face swiveled a glare. "What was that?"

"Er, just this one night . . ." The plea was accompanied by a limp smile.

His face contorted into strawberry rage. "Listen, no kid playwright is going to squeeze my balls, opening night!"

"That was not my precise intention," I began. "It's only that he's . . . that is . . ."

"Say, do you know how many audiences I've faced?" The question hardly seemed pertinent. "More than you've had pimples on your ass!" he informed me. "Now get the hell out of my dressing room!"

The situation was beyond human intervention. Nothing for it but to slink into the darkest corner at the back of the house and pray for a friendly catastrophe.

The house lights had just lowered when Sol arrived, looking like the offspring of Goliath and Queen Kong. From the beginning the play went raucously too well; laughs in right and wrong places rocked the house. A noisy time was had by all, especially the cast, the heavy-handed performances becoming even more violent with every mirthful burst. At last, the final curtain and applause, lustily led by members of my family. But where was Wurtzel? Not in his seat! Had he slipped out then? During one of the gauche sallies of that half-crocked ham stalking the stage had Sol stomped out, cigar brandishing like a saber? Would he at this very moment be telephoning his lawyer?

My mind provided a harrowing pattern of dialogue. "I want that kid in jail, Sam! Behind bars!" for of course his lawyer would be named Sam. Wasn't every good theatrical lawyer? Maybe he could even get my father fired as well!

A hand fell on my shoulder. Bone and muscle weighted with unquestionable authority. "Junior!" he snarled.

I spun around into the full broadside of the famed grimace. Teeth flashing like cannon from gunports. "Sir . . . ?"

"You think I don't know who that was? That producer in your play?"

"But it wasn't anyone," I insisted. "Not anyone real. Only a figment of my imagination. A composite character drawn from—oh, someone in a book, or somewhere . . ."

"Don't give me that. I know who that gonif was! Knew the minute he stepped on the stage. Knew the first word out of his mouth! You think I'm stupid?"

"Oh, no sir, but—whooooo?"

"Sam Goldwyn!"

Sol was still chuckling when he crushed my hand over the contract that brought my first sale of an original story to films. The picture was produced (after considerable alteration) as a musical, starring Alice Faye.

The film script, written by somebody else, was titled *Music Is Magic*. As I recall, there wasn't even a beach scene in it. I further recall that it was one of Sol's few financial failures. Still, in honesty I suspect the film was an improvement on the original play. It should have taught Sol to let sleeping readers lie. It didn't.

The Bible tells us that King Saul, when he was sorely troubled, caused the boy David to soothe him by singing to His Majesty with a harp. Sol Wurtzel, King of the Fox Hollywood studio, one day again decided to make me his David. I was chosen to read his film scripts—aloud. My only previous thespian experience, as a camel boy in *The Thief of Baghdad*, hardly qualified me to bring dramatic rendition to, "Meanwhile, back at the ranch . . ." but either for reasons of tired eyes or on a whim, Sol once again reached out for his reader, and I found myself in the exalted inner office.

The embarrassing aspect of this task was that too frequently Sol would have these readings performed in the presence of the screenwriters, who sat glowering at my interpretations of their deathless dialogue.

One day I was in Sol's office reading a Western, mercifully uninhibited by the presence of the writer. The speeches were traditionally terse, sparse as prairie grass.

"Sheriff: Plannin' on makin' a long stay in this town, stranger?

"Cal: Haven't rightly decided, Sheriff."

I read on, quite enjoying it. "Sheriff pauses. One finger hooked in his gunbelt inches slightly toward the Frontier Model Colt, swinging butt forward on his thigh. Sheriff: 'I wouldn't be too all-fired sure that decision is going to be up to you, Cal Slocum, alias John Blackstone!' Two hands flicked to their hips . . ."

"Junior!" Sol's voice cut in. I stopped, feeling shot down in full flight.

"Sir?"

"What's happening to my goddamn door?" I followed his frozen glance. The door of Sol's office, which was under no circumstance permitted to be unbarred without previous announcement and the permission of his secretary, was very slowly and silently inching open. There was something inexplicably sinister in the movement. To mind flashed a quick compilation of Sol's potential enemies. If one had done in his secretary, it would not be inconceivable that . . .

The door stopped about a quarter of the way open. We sat transfixed. The head of a corpse was suddenly thrust through the opening! It was totally bald, blue-white, the face wedged downward to the floor. One could see only the ghastly head—scarred and hideous.

"Junior—see what *that* is!" Sol whispered.

Quaking with fear I arose and forced my numbed legs to bring me over to the door where the thing was wedged. I was not sure at all what to do, but made myself take hold of it, turning it so one might see the face. Then I yelled, as its teeth sank into my hand! The corpse had bit me!

I jumped backward as though struck by a rattlesnake. Sol watched, eyes glazed.

Then the head I had been holding slowly swiveled around and lifted into recognition.

It was Harpo Marx.

A good friend of Sol's—he was playing one of his practical jokes. He had stopped by the makeup department on the way over and had his head "done-up." Of course everyone had a good laugh. Except me.

That joke perfectly typified the antics of Hollywood in those halcyon days when every court had its jester.

Perhaps the greatest of all practical jokers was Sid Grauman, the showman who built and operated three of the most formidable "Movie Palaces" in Hollywood. It's not surprising that a man with the sort of imagination that could perpetuate Rin Tin Tin's pawmark in the cement forecourt of Grauman's Chinese Theatre, close by the impression of Jean Harlow's shapely foot, would go to the most elaborate lengths to play a trick on a friend.

One afternoon he phoned my father in the greatest urgency to ask a favor. It seemed that a body of important exhibitors had convened on Hollywood and Grauman was hosting them at his Million Dollar Theatre in downtown Los Angeles. Knowing Dad's reputation for being eager and ready to speak extemporaneously at the drop of an introduction, he begged Dad to address the convention on the current state of the industry. Dad readily agreed.

Arriving at the backstage entrance, my father, late as usual, was bustled by Grauman to the footlit stage. Grauman had scarcely time to give him more than a few quick words of introduction before Dad stepped out, squinting across the haze of footlights at the sober-suited audience. They were wonderfully still and attentive. He launched into a few warming jokes, and was a bit annoyed not to get his usual laughs. Well, if they wanted a serious lecture they would get it. For the next hour he pounded them with facts and figures. Hard facts! Put the blame for bad business where it belonged—on sales and distribution! He was candid about the problems of production and urged a closer alliance between the creative and marketing bodies of the Industry. He held them quite spellbound. They scarcely seemed to move. Not even a cough interrupted their rapt attention. Dad finished on a splendid note of optimism and awaited their applause.

Silence! Could he have so spellbound them that their hands were paralyzed? Only the Gettysburg Address had been *that* successful! He turned to where Sid waited in the wings. Grauman urged him to return to the stage for a question period. But there were no questions.

When the house lights were raised, Dad's audience was revealed as a houseful of wax dummies.

Sid was also the butt of a few jokes, albeit somewhat feeble ones. Rudolph Valentino had a go at him at the opening of one of his films at the Grauman's Egyptian Theatre. When introduced, the Sheik came on stage wearing pajamas. He apologized that he had overslept, then stripped the pajamas off—to reveal to the shocked audience the white tie and tails he wore underneath. The Impresario was not vastly amused. Besides, Grauman was occupied with one of his own superjokes.

A craze for Egyptian archaeology, fashions, and architecture had swept our town since the discovery of King Tut's tomb. Sid Grauman employed a young Afro-American, bound and bandaged him to resemble an ancient mummy, then secreted him in a mummy case which was to be opened "for the first time" on stage for an invited audience.

It all started wonderfully well. Sid assured the audience that he had spared no expense in bringing the rare object from the tomb where it had been unearthed—directly to the stage of Grauman's Egyptian Theatre. Tonight the newly found mummy, perhaps a royal Nile king, would be revealed after his sleep of ages!

The attendants carefully opened box within box. The idea was that when the final mummy case was opened the mummy would suddenly leap out and shriek at the audience, whereupon the audience might be expected to shriek back. It didn't quite happen that way. When they reached the final mummy case there was a dramatic pause. It was here that the hired mummy was supposed to do his shocking "Jack-out-of-the-box" act, but when the lid was pried open the mummy was stiff as mummies generally are.

Sid Grauman shouted for a doctor in the house. The audience at first thought *that* was funny, but eventually one was brought up and the man revived. The air vents in the case had been insufficient and the man had become temporarily asphyxiated while waiting to be released from his "sleep of centuries."

But the great showman's sense of humor seemed to have survived even that bad joke. During the Depression days, when he was invited to a gloomy gathering of industry heads, his arrival provided the only laugh of the evening. He came by hearse and was delivered to the conference room in an open coffin.

Some practical jokes were not without an element of serious danger, like the one played on Ernst Lubitsch, the great director who for a time was head of Paramount production. Lubitsch was famous for having made a series of movies unequaled for high comedy with a Continental flair.

He was known to be excitable, highly creative, fearless, dynamic, and extravagant. But the lively, uninhibited, bouncy little German had one secret terror. He would never travel by airplane. He had what was in those days a quite sensible fear of flying. Normally such a necessity could easily be avoided, but when he became head of Paramount production, time became of the essence. Want to or not, the moment arrived when Lubitsch was forced to make his first flight.

The occasion was a "sneak" preview of an important new motion picture, a first, out-of-town screening before an unsuspecting audience, who are invited to criticize the picture. Unfavorable comments are then weighed against praises as a guide to further editing and finishing. Generally speaking, the more important the film, the further away it is "sneaked." Then, as now, no film maker wanted to face the tough Hollywood reviewers and Industry opinion until ready.

In this case, the film was extremely important. One of the new Mae West pictures. The studio decided to sneak it in San Francisco. And of course, Lubitsch, as production head, could not spare the time to go up by overnight train. A private plane was chartered by the studio to fly him and his staff.

The fear-filled day dawned. Lubitsch sank his teeth into a large cigar and committed himself to the air. He was just trying to master his fears when the plane ran into a spot of turbulence over Santa Barbara. Lubitsch clung to the arms of his chair for dear life.

And then the door of the pilot's cabin flew open and two pilots ran down the aisle. As they reached the emergency exit they opened the hatch and, turning to Lubitsch, shouted, "We don't know what you're going to do, but we're getting the hell out of here!"

Then they jumped. The horrified Lubitsch saw them parachuting toward the earth, bit clean through his cigar, had a minor heart attack, and passed out. The two "pilots" were of course stunt men whom some wag had secreted in the pilot's compartment. But the "joke" almost killed its victim.

Nine

VICE!

Personal or public—filmed, or hidden behind the closed doors of its mansions—had always been a constant threat to industrial Hollywood. The Arbuckle case and others had shown that overpublicized sin could be a serious business liability. It could bring box-office rebellion against a star's image. The film makers had to protect themselves against the well-aimed mud pies of professional gossip mongers, who throve on who-was-doing-what-to-you-knew-whomisms. Like opportunist birds picking through the castings of careless cattle, the columnists isolated tidbits of bawdy carnality and careless corruption.

It was never very difficult to find. The roaring twenties had ukuleled itself and its rolled-hosed flappers into memory's nostalgic museum. The vamps had come and gone, along with Elinor Glyn and the fifty thousand dollars she had pocketed for that two-letter-word film title. "It" had come to mean the indefinable allure that could turn strong men into slobbering slaves of desire. But the shrewd showmen knew precisely how far to go with the spectacular depravity of Rod La Rocque and Nita Naldi before drawing the line, or getting the line drawn for them by the censors. They had to in order to survive. They knew how to pack their films with generous doses of undisguised abandon and as much naked flesh as they could get away with. They got away with it and salvaged their public images with last-minute screen redemptions and punishments of sin. No barriers on showing man's bestial side, as long as you ultimately spanked his lapses of virtue. And so the promulgation of the essential myth of Hollywood: that evil always bore the seed of its own punishment, as did virtue that of its own final reward. The credo spawned the wonderfully permissive fairly tales and ensured the "happy ending." Its banner was "escape." Canned escapism from the sordid bumps and hard grinds of a world emerging from war and depression.

This was all very well, as long as the movie makers themselves didn't get caught kicking a sacred cow. They might portray dissoluteness, but the private lives of the stars had to be above serious reproach. Perhaps it was condoned for a screen vamp to enjoy the hint of off-screen intrigues, but stars who portrayed noble characters were expected to be dutiful family folk, devoted parents, patriotic citizens, and regular churchgoers.

Such considerations weighed heavily on the mind of Cecil B. De Mille even back in 1927 when he set out to produce his great religious epic *The King of Kings*. The selection of the actor to play the Messiah, in particular, was undertaken with appropriately publicized responsibility. Clearly he must be a person of spotless reputation to perform that most holy of roles.

After an infinity of screening and testing, the lot fell upon H. B. Warner. It was an ideal choice. Aside from physically resembling the generally accepted concept of the Savior, the distinguished British actor was a man noted for clean living and sobriety, his morals as pure as an angel's, his character and abilities flawless. And to ensure that no fallibility of the flesh would cast a shadow on the key performance, Warner, in what must have been the first use of the morality clause in a contract, was bound by a legal pledge that no breath of scandal should touch him during the making and exploitation of the sacred film. There were too many deeply religious people who were troubled by the fact that Christ should be portrayed in a movie at all, let alone that his portrayer should be subject to human frailty. The clause was in fact a bow to the ecclesiastics being lured aboard as technical advisers and guardians of doctrine, for official religious approval was essential at every stage of preparation and production.

Filming began with that perfect combination of showmanship and public religiosity that De Mille no doubt learned from his early training under the master of theatrical morality, David Belasco (the famous New York producer, known for bringing virtue's shining light to the stage, had even affected a reversed collar to enhance his clerical image).

A stream of press releases assured one and all against the possibility of any offensive treatment of the subject. In an effort to please all the people all the time, accredited representative authorities, Catholic,

Jesse, Jr., and his first movie idol, Antonio Moreno, taking time out from filming *The Spanish Dancer* (1923). *(Author's collection)*

The Exodus as filmed on the sands of Santa Cruz by Cecil B. De Mille in the silent version of *The Ten Commandments*. . . .

. . . and Rod La Rocque, in a bravura performance as the pharaoh, drives through the Pacific surf. *(De Mille Foundation)*

These costumes worn at an early Hollywood costume ball were from the Lasky film *Berkeley Square*. Jesse, Sr., and screenwriter Hope Loring, wife of Louis Lighton, scenarist of the trend-setting Clara Bow movie *It*, are the couple on the left. The courtier gazing so soulfully at Bess Lasky, wearing Heather Angel's costume, is actor Gene Raymond. *(Author's collection)*

Jesse L. Lasky with his children—Betty, Bill and Jesse, Jr.—on possibly the most expensive piece of beach on earth—Santa Monica in the 1920's. *(Author's collection)*

Publicity shots taken on the set were eternally pompous. Here, Lasky with visiting lion Admiral Richard E. Byrd, the polar explorer, and Will H. Hays, whose censorship of the film industry brought a touch of ice to Hollywood excesses *(Author's collection)*

Geraldine Farrar as *Joan the Woman* in 1917, stalwart on a field of dying cowboy extras who had been drafted into uniform for the duration. *(British Film Institute)*

Left, Betty Bronson, star of the silent *Peter Pan* and also of Jesse, Jr.'s teenage fantasies, both circa 1924. *(British Film Institute)* Right, in jazz-age uniform, her greatest fan. *(Author's collection)*

On the set of *The Great Moment*, producer Lasky with British novelist Elinor Glyn (she was famous for her leopard skins) and star Gloria Swanson. *(British Film Institute)*

Bess and Jesse Lasky at their fabulous house on La Brea Avenue around 1917. The swimming pool and tennis court were both among the first in Hollywood. *(Author's collection)*

Protestant, and Jewish, were present on the set during the filming of every scene. There would be no deviation from either authorized doctrine or good taste. The scenario, by Jeanie MacPherson, at that time De Mille's number-one writer, had, with a few minor changes, passed the scrutiny of the highest church authorities.

As the hour of production neared, the mood of the whole studio took on the sanctity of a cathedral. On that first day when H. B. Warner walked out on the set in flowing white robes, some of the onlookers and film makers actually fell to their knees, so perfectly did he look the part.

Several months into filming, De Mille was busy lining up a shot, giving his usual total attention to detail and background, when one of his assistant directors slipped to his side, ghost-pale. He whispered into the director's ear, "Boss, better come and have a look at your Christ."

The way he said it brooked no delay. With booted stride De Mille reached the star's private dressing room. He opened the door.

In the violet-filtered light of the specially installed stained-glass windows lay H. B. Warner, bare, beatific and splendidly besotted. And not alone. His body was entwined with the alabaster limbs of an equally naked girl extra, in what was unmistakably the aftermath of an epic production far removed from that which C. B. had planned. She turned her deliberately sober attention to the stunned director general with the smile of the serpent celebrating his successful take-over bid in Paradise.

De Mille, who told me the story himself many years later, was not reluctant to admit that few moments in his life had required a quicker need for decisive action.

Instantly reassuring himself that the incident was so far unknown to any but the participants, the assistant director, and himself, he quietly ordered the dressing room to be cordoned off and guarded by the most trustworthy of the studio's special police.

Assorted monsignors, ministers, and rabbis were swiftly shunted away to a far-off projection room, "to view important newly arrived film from the Holy Land," with which California locations would have to be matched.

Thus, when the director general confronted the enterprising young woman, it was alone in his office. The question was perfectly simple. How much? The alternatives had been instantly considered and as instantly dismissed. He was over the proverbial barrel, and he knew it. One word of this escapade would not only be the end of his film, it would rock and possibly destroy the entire film capital, whose already smirched image would bear no further tarnish at this time. In those pre-permissive days, every scandal was another knife-stab into an already perforated Caesar. De Mille also knew he would not dare to answer her demands with a legal charge of blackmail. No matter how compliant the public prosecutor might be, how could De Mille keep it out of the press?

Unless he wanted to consider having her abducted to Mexico, both of them knew there could be but one answer: Pay up and shut up! In this spirit the hard bargain was reached.

The young woman had the wisdom not to press her luck too far. She vanished from Hollywood, no doubt to become one of those early expatriates astounding some exotic corner of the earth with Yankee largesse.

H. B. Warner? A platoon of doctors soon had him dried to the sandals, and under De Mille's falcon eye he resumed a life-style more appropriate to the character he portrayed. The film was completed and is still considered a classic early treatment of the most revered of subjects.

A story more often told alleges that Sam Goldwyn was warned by one of his story editors that a certain hit play he wanted to film might not be suitable screen material since the leading female character was a lesbian.

"That's all right," my one-time uncle reportedly replied, "we can change her into an Italian."

Throwing stones at the glass houses of Hollywood was a national sport. But snipping our films to the varying requirements of different state censorship boards brought constant headaches. No two censors seemed to agree on exactly what would most corrupt an audience. The definition of vice varied not only from state to state but from country to country around the world. In Japan, a screen kiss was considered deeply offensive. In Ohio you couldn't show female undergarments fluttering on a clothesline. Nowhere at all could married couples be photographed sharing a double bed. Movie makers tried to tailor their cloth to suit almost everyone, and the results were sometimes pathetic.

While protecting the public reputations of their stars, the producers developed a growing reputation as hopelessly lecherous wolves themselves, forever ambushing the Goldilocks' who crowd into town in search of fame and fortune. No doubt the status did them too much credit; still, these men exercised an extraordinary kind of business power.

Consider the extent of the power of a mogul whose job it was to select perhaps one out of the hundreds of pretty, talented aspirants. Candidates were often ready and eager to trade their charms and offer their bodies in exchange for what they considered their "big chance." How many young hopefuls would not sleep with anyone who even pretended to have the power to grant them a screen test when the rewards of success in filmland were beyond all reason? There was less emphasis on training and dramatic experience then, and too many stories of discoveries made at soda fountains. Girls ran away from respectable homes to reach Hollywood, penniless and desperate to "make good," "make it big," "make it quick."

To protect some of these neophytes, my mother and several other well-intentioned matrons organized The Hollywood Studio Club, where "decent" girls could find inexpensive lodging and board if they obeyed the rules: not being out late in the evening, never entertaining men except in the Club lobby and then only during prescribed hours. No doubt my mother and the other good ladies were protecting the girls from their own producer-husbands. Many a star emerged from the cloistered sanctity of the Studio Club less scathed than might otherwise have been possible.

This ambivalent climate of sin and sanctity, public morality and private license, for whatever morally destructive effect it had on the tycoons themselves, was frequently disastrous to their progeny. It would appear that the sons and daughters of the old film makers had a higher proclivity to maladjustment than other offspring of success. My old friend, Carl Laemmle, Jr., son of Universal's founder, was forced by his pioneer father to head the entire studio when he was just twenty-one. What a birthday present! Warm, kind, desperately anxious, totally unequipped, he could not finally come to grips in that jungle of power-playing politicians and was forced out by his father to be replaced with his own brother-in-law, Stanley Bergerman. Carl became a prey to hypochondria and opportunists. The pimps and spongers clustered like locusts. They swarmed to his decaying estate like the rats in his cracking, unusable swimming pool. Gentle young Carl walked me across his weed-ruined tennis court talking about plans for independent productions that even he knew would never come to light. He was dying of disappointment—because he had failed the expectations of his father and been put on the dust heap before he was twenty-five. He never married although he had been deeply in love with an actress, for his father had disapproved.

There were others: unhappy homosexuals, targets of blackmail and thieving rogues, some hounded to suicide without even the protection of the law. Beating and robbing "queers" was almost regarded as a patriotic duty by the police in those days, and some of the most outwardly normal young men proved to be the most inwardly troubled.

One such person haunts the memory, not only because of the young man's pathetic problem but because his father was among the non-monsters of our old film world. He was decent, efficient, and honorable. His role in one of the great studios in the years during and after World War II did much to bring a final stability to the last golden age of Hollywood. This man shared nothing in common with the lecherous, power-drunk moguls of the Hollywood scene. He had even been happily married to the same woman all his life.

His son, an attractive young man, had come through college and war service with a superb record, the ideal candidate to be trained to fill his father's shoes at the head of the company. He was duly launched into one department after another, in order to learn the complex problems of production.

In accounting, he showed a quick grasp of the mathematics of budgeting and payroll maintenance. He was shifted to location, then set construction, film editing, and casting, and in each he progressed swiftly to a grasp of the problems indigenous to that department. He was completing his apprenticeship with distinction.

Then, one day, he was picked up by the police during lunch hour, seated in his superb sports car, exhibiting himself to a bevy of Hollywood High School girls of the average age of fourteen.

The incident was totally and successfully hushed up. Political pressure was brought to bear and the case was never entered in any official reports.

His father consulted psychiatrists and was given the most lucid possible diagnosis. Actually, there was nothing very rare about this case—the symptoms fitted the aberration almost too perfectly. The exhibitionist was young, and came from a family with puritanical and extremely proper attitudes toward sexual matters. Certainly he had been excessively prudish about his feelings.

The physicians picked their words carefully. It seemed, they further explained, that this young man's case could be said to prove the Solomonic truth that for all things there is a season. His exposures seemed to occur during the warmer months, since his offense was primarily an outdoor activity. Maybe he would grow out of it, they indicated hopefully. Most exhibitionists tended to be in their early twenties. In his case alcohol, although never in itself the cause, led to a slackening of moral restrictions. His psychiatrist urgently warned against drinking.

At first this expensive analysis seemed to be helping. If the analyst was not ready to pronounce the young man cured, he was nevertheless considered to be fit and ready to return to his studio activities. Then one day during lunch hour he vanished again.

The police answered a call to another local high school. Again high influence hushed it up. And then, several months later, another call. Gradually subterranean knowledge of his tragic condition was beginning to leak out. But such was the power of a Hollywood executive that there was no leak to the press. Family dignity was outwardly preserved.

The fact that the unhappy happenings generally took place during lunch hours seemed to incorporate two logical elements. It was during lunch hour that the young man might be tempted into several drinks at one of the convenient bistros across the street from the studio. And it was at lunch hour that the greatest number of little high school girls were likely to be parading themselves, as they shared sandwiches on the steps of their schools or campuses.

So "bottle guards" were provided to prevent liquid temptations. Since the young man himself was a perfectly willing teetotaler unless someone deliberately set out to ply him, they were generally successful. Until a certain end-of-film party.

For those readers unfamiliar with this institution, it was the custom for the producer, director, and stars to put up the money to supply booze and free eats to all members of the film company, particularly the hardworking "grips," electricians, prop men, makeup people, carpenters, and all the generally anonymous "crew" who handle the physical end of filming. These parties also provided a kind of "speakers' corner" where the lowest member of the crew could let off steam if he felt the need against the not always approachable upper-echelons, with verbal gloves off. Loaded with a well-earned snootful, some burly electrician who had spent his days high up on the catwalks could vocally let the boss have it right between the eyes. This alcoholic democracy was a healthy tradition, and if some high-salaried director or star was subjected to a modicum of abuse—or possibly an overabundance of affection—he or she bore it in good spirit, and may even have rehired the offender on the next picture.

But there was always the danger that the "big boss," no matter how congenial he might appear in absorbing the shoulder thumps and outspoken opinions of the lowly, could just happen to remember some too well aimed barb next day and forget to forgive.

The timing of departures from these studio bashes was a delicate calculation, as sooner or later the company milque-toast, who normally wouldn't have dared cross his wife on the choice of his necktie, would stumble up to John Wayne (or whoever happened to be around), fix him with a glittering, intemperate eye, and declare with unsubtle invitation, "You ain't all that tough, John!"

The Duke, or whoever, was expected to take such nimble repartee with genial good grace, though many of the old-time leading men were every bit as tough as they looked.

This particular end-of-production party was held on one of the studio's half-dismantled sets. Things got off to a roaring start: threats, broken glasses, huge displays of affection, shouted confidences, and the usual melting of barriers. The executive's son with the unmentionable penchant was present. So were his protective guardians. So was I. A small orchestra was playing. Everyone was guzzling the free drinks when someone slipped the young man a loaded orange juice. One, two, perhaps three. The bottle guards themselves had become careless, it seemed, because suddenly there was an outcry—the heir apparent had unzipped his trousers in front of the youngest female members of the cast.

Everyone tried to close in on him, but the great soundproof doors were open to the warm California night and he slipped out, running desperately through the dark jungle-maze of sound stages and standing sets. Every man sober enough to pursue formed into an instant posse. His father summoned available members of the studio police. The lad had to be caught before he broke loose in the surrounding city!

A ludicrous hide-and-seek ensued. We were running in all directions, bumping into each other, sprawling over the great python coils of lighting cables. A perfect comedy chase, except that the cause wasn't funny.

The studio police cornered him in the parking lot before he could reach his car. He was brought down with a football tackle and held firmly until his father reached the scene. And a pathetic scene it was.

The crown prince of this major company looking up at his father, who could only murmur, "Why, son? Why?"

Tears flowed down the young man's handsome face. "Dad, Dad . . . I was only"—he choked on a sob—"looking for some place to take a leak."

I don't know if he was ever finally cured. He is dead now, as is his father.

I have known the others: the drug victims, the perverts, the well-meaning, misdirected, badly aimed projectiles of their fathers' ruthless power drives. I've seen the neurotic wrecks, overdriven like engines unable to attain the high-speed ascendancies they thought their fathers demanded of them—because the fault was not always the father's, it was as often due to the son's inability to accept his own mediocrity.

There were always outstanding exceptions. Budd Schulberg, son of the mighty B. P., became one of America's first-rank novelists, drawing on the experience of his own growth through the dream factory to write *What Makes Sammy Run?* and the immortal *The Disenchanted*. Richard Zanuck was given the highest post at Twentieth Century-Fox by his father, Darryl, to become one of the best studio heads Twentieth ever had. The successful second-generation actors and actresses are too well known to bear discussion.

In other businesses nepotism has been an honored tradition. Sons followed in their father's footsteps because they made loyal assistants and trustworthy successors; because, expected to carry on the job, they had assimilated it by association. But nepotism in show business has too often meant the abuse of opportunity through the misuse of influence.

It is curious to recall how much influence and power came to be wielded by a few people who had nothing to do with actual film production.

Before television served up its generous helpings of hair-let-down celebrity interviews, stars could only be met off-screen in press columns, fan mags, and radio. Columnists provided the principle peepholes into private lives. And through those peepholes, came power. What power! Stars and executives cringed before public revelations by the gophers of gossip. They wooed the great rumor mongers with corruptive flattery and self-destructive cooperation. The Winchells, Parsons, Hoppers, and a host of lesser satellites with varying degrees of responsible reporting employed networks of informants that would do credit to the White House Plumbers. Most columnists affected a stewardship of public morality. Winchell, the flag-wrapped pundit of patriotism, persecuted Reds with the fervor of an inspired Inquisitor. For him, saving America from pinkos and perverts, protecting women and children from the turpitude of tawdry entertainers, became a highly lucrative calling.

As always, salvation had a salacious wrapping. Nothing was more provocative than the misdemeanors of the privileged. To see them spanked in print was both edifying and entertaining.

Perhaps the most successful of the Gossip Queens of the West—and the least principled—was Louella Parsons. Her blunt assaults on reputations terrified film folk, large and small. A few, like Ingrid Bergman, managed to rise phoenixlike from the destructive fires of her slander—which could be as tastelessly unintentionally funny as it was damning: "But tell me, Ingrid, what everyone wants to know, is *whatever* got *into* you?" This on radio, after the famous affair with Roberto Rossellini.

Her malapropisms were endless. Example: When Rita Johnson was accidentally hit by a hair dryer and knocked unconscious, Louella's reportage was also unconscious. "Poor Rita Johnson is still in a comma. . . ." But when Hollywood laughed it dared not laugh too loud. The stucco walls had ears.

Louella's husband was a studio doctor. "Docky," as he was unlovingly known, had his own brand of terror. Hundred proof! No quarter given or dared asked, when some ailing starlet laid her life in the hands of this film physician. Something like falling into the cavern of an intoxicated Mad Hatter of medicine. His wife's power assured him an uninhibited field of operation. Who would dare complain about his prescriptions when one destructive comment in Lolly's lively column could slow down a rise to stardom?

Docky even served the state boxing commission as consultant medic. Friday nights he would be in his glory at the Hollywood Legion Stadium, beloved by punch-drunk pugs, for he was unstintingly generous with a buck or a bottle.

So was Louella with her parties. She was the only person in Hollywood who could be sure of 100 percent attendance. An invitation was a command. Appearances were *de rigueur*. An absence was career suicide. She had her own shooting range for sitting ducks.

I once attended one of those request nights. Several of us stood at the front door ringing the bell. The butler, usually quick to respond, was obviously busy elsewhere. At last the door was opened by Louella herself. We were treated to the unedifying spectacle of Docky—stretched full length across the threshold. You had to step over him in order to enter or depart the house. Snores like roars—he was no doubt slumbering off a celebration that must have begun at breakfast.

Agnes Moorhead did a lively little hop-step over him. Joan Fontaine skirted him like a puddle of pythons. I watched, fascinated, as Louella gave the exquisite June Duprez a hand over him. June managed a tasteful smile as she high-stepped the obstacle in a Howard Greer gown, as though treading between eggs. A foot in the face would have spelled film finis.

Louella swept her husband's position with an untroubled glance and unhesitant explanation. "Poor Docky's had a beer!"

It was a more generous conclusion than many published in her column.

Ten

WHILE I WAS ON HOLIDAY in England a friend of my family, actor Cedric Hardwicke, got me an introduction to Gaumont British, one of the largest film companies of the day. They needed an American to write dialogue for the transatlantic characters in their films. In those years the languages were a bit further apart, more xenophobic, more insular. American was a foreign language to the English. Slang was neither comprehensible nor interchangeable. And I got the job.

London was the Athens of the thirties, of T. S. Eliot, Auden, Spender. Inspired by my surroundings, I had indulged myself to write an extremely limited edition of extremely experimental poetry, for which a friend had done original water-color illustrations. John Gabrial and I were two bachelors on the town, and what a town, and what a time! Dating ballet dancers, attending performances at Sadler's Wells where we roared and cheered like a football crowd at Frederick Ashton's or Robert Helpmann's latest choreographic achievement, going to after-theater suppers with dancers like Anton Dolin and Alicia Markova.

I had spent long weekends in the country, playing tennis, shooting pheasants that came rattling out of the wood before the sticks of the beaters like golden-feathered rockets. I had house-guested at castles with haunted rooms, like Narworth, and stayed at eighteenth-century country houses where gentlemen sipped port before joining the ladies. I enjoyed conversations with MPs and cabinet ministers. What a time to have been in England, present at the funeral of one king and the abdication of another. Heady stuff for a young scribe, this gentle glow of civilization at its peak. The final glow? Everything had begun to seem so *après moi le déluge*-ish, within the still-fixed orbit of a caste system where servants could yet take pride in their profession.

It was not easy to tear myself away when my contract finally ended. I lingered on like a melody. My work permit expired and still I remained, unable to give up the life I had fallen in love with. As usual I'd spent more money than I'd earned. In fact, I was broke when I mounted the gangplank of the glorious *Ile de France*. (Many years later my friend Andrew Stone purchased the *Ile* to sink her in a Japanese harbor for a spectacular sequence in *The Last Voyage*.) But on that voyage she was one of the greatest sparkling luxury palaces afloat.

I was standing at the railing at Cherbourg, where we had called before turning nose across the Atlantic toward New York, watching the passengers come aboard. Suddenly the longest car in the world, a silver-gray Mercedes Benz, slid up to the gangplank. From it descended a tall, handsome man, festooned with an Astrakhan collar, Homburg, and enormous dark glasses. If his purpose was anonymity he failed totally. He could hardly have created a more spectacular appearance if he'd worn a toga. I recognized him immediately as my dashing comrade of coaster days, Doug Fairbanks, Jr.

Dismounting with him from the block-long car was a goddess swathed in pale mink. She, too, wore dark glasses, and if he looked like Rupert of Hentzau, she looked like Catherine of Russia on an illicit rendezvous. It was Marlene Dietrich. The dramatic duo committed themselves to an earth-shaking farewell embrace, much to the delight of the assembled voyeur-voyagers. And then Doug unfurled himself up the gangplank to appear again at the first-class railing, where he blew Marlene a flamboyant last kiss. As he turned away from the rail, feeling, I suppose, secure in his incognito, I called up to him from my lowly perch on the second-class deck.

He stared down in amazement. "Good God, Jess! How did you ever recognize me?"

"It wasn't easy," I lied.

"What on earth are you doing down there, anyway?"

"Crossing home, Doug, same as you."

"Not in second class, old man?"

"Conserving the old pocket, old man," I apologized.

"Good God! Come on up at once. We'll have a drink."

Doug, of course, had the nearest thing to a Royal Suite. He welcomed me with booming hospitality and bucketed champagne, gloriously iced. I really couldn't be permitted to continue my crossing in some dreary cabin with a total stranger when, he insisted, he had more than enough space for both of us. This I could not deny.

Besides, he confided, the ship was overflowing with amusing people, titles fairly dripping from his lips: dukes, earls, counts, countesses, actresses, American blue-bloods. One might have thought I had boarded a floating weekend with the Aga Khan. It was to be the most exciting of all possible crossings, and I must share it with him! Captain's table, cocktail parties given and attended. Doug, ever the soul of generosity, was as good as his word, in fact better!

Our crossing must have set some kind of record for international snobbery. We entertained. Were entertained. And since Doug was brushing up his fencing for a film, and I had once captained the Hun School of Princeton's fencing team, we daily fought our way ostentatiously around the promenade deck. Our mornings were pure *Mark of Zorro;* our evenings, the last days of Versailles. We recovered with massages, sweat baths, workouts. We were at it from noon till dawn.

And as the *Ile* came tug-hooting into New York harbor past enigmatic Dame Liberty, I stood for one last poignant moment with Doug at the railing, deeply moved, my appreciation for his bounty overflowing.

"Doug," I said. "It's embarrassing, but I really must say something. I must say—how deeply I feel. No . . . really, I can't tell you what this crossing has meant to me at this time."

"Not another word about it, old man," he shrugged magnanimously.

"No, I do insist! I must say it. You, my old school friend—lifting me up from what might have been a really depressing crossing. Why, you gave me the best time, the best of friendship and fun, I could ever imagine!" I meant every word of it.

"Forget it, old lad. We will speak of it no more."

"I can't! I won't! In fact—I insist!" And now I was more than a bit carried away by intoxicating gratitude. "I certainly wish I could pay my own share," I said from the depths of my poverty.

"If you feel that way, old boy, of course I'll send you a bill for your half."

And he did.

I never told Doug I had to borrow the money to repay him. In those days everyone always still assumed the Laskys could afford anything.

There is always a temptation to sentimentalize the passing of old Hollywood, particularly if you happen to have seen one of those well-documented reports on television of the auctions of ancient "props." A paddle-wheel steamer that supported the pageantry of the great *Showboat;* the *Bounty*, where once Clark Gable led a mutiny against Charles Laughton. Judy Garland's red dancing slippers from *The Wizard of Oz*, rotting pyramids of old World War I fighting planes. The list is endless; the prices reached, incredible—the stuff of dreams, going, going, gone. The film capital hardly took a sentimental view of itself in 1937 when the production of movies had attained the status of a major American industry. It was right up there at the top with steel, oil, and automobiles.

Still, the town itself could be said to have retained what a hometown boy might consider its original charm. The spurious bungalows and apartments of its Egyptian period, dating from the Tutankhamen craze of the twenties, looked a bit shabbier. The great, bowler-shaped restaurants of the Brown Derby chain were still favored gathering places of the stars and tourists who wanted to get a glimpse or an autograph. There were only two Brown Derbys then, one on Wilshire Boulevard and the original on Vine Street. The old Hollywood Hotel was still a favorite residence for visiting actors. The original barn where Dad and De Mille had produced *Squaw Man* had not yet been moved to the main Paramount lot on Marathon Street to be maintained as a historical landmark. Beverly Hills was beginning to probe the watery blue sky with stone fingers of skyscrapers—limited to sixteen storeys because earthquakes were always expected. The fashionable and privileged were pushing ever westward—through Beverly Hills, Holmby Hills, Westwood, skirting the base of Bel Air—toward land developments to come, like Brentwood. You could, if you were susceptible to the smooth talk of the real estate salesmen camped under giant umbrellas, buy huge tracts of the huge San Fernando Valley for almost a song. The few who did have been singing ever since. One of my father's stars, Francis Lederer, bought miles of this "worthless" dry valley bottom. Years later, when his career declined, he found himself a real estate millionaire from having been a sucker at the right moment.

In 1937 the studios were churning out A's and B's to fill the popular double bills. People wanted their money's worth; but it was a safe bet that if you could see two for the price of one, one would hardly be worth seeing. In the Valhalla of the A's lived those pampered gods and goddesses, the stars, who were not expected to be brainy, politically conscious, or even very choosy about the roles the great studios assigned them. They were expected to accept that Papa knew best, Papa being Louis B. Mayer, Jack Warner, Harry Cohn, David Selznick, and Darryl Zanuck. The stars were handsomely rewarded for doing what they were told. So they occasionally did.

The image of the serious, probing Actors' Studio actor was not yet with us. The player did not ask for psychological meanings from his director. The influence of the Strasbergs in New York, of Stanislavsky and the great Russian analysts of the theater, had not yet permeated the public's darlings. If the winds of change were blowing, they hadn't quite made it over the range of dry mountains that rose behind Hollywood like a theatrical backdrop, seeming to isolate us from the outer world in the oversimplifications of our boy-meets-girlism. Cowboy actors still indulged in the unabashed showmanship of a pair of bristling Texas longhorns mounted on the hoods of their automobiles. Tom Mix had his white tuxedo cut with a "western flare." One stalwart had a silver-mounted saddle set in the back seat of his chauffeur-driven Dusenberg, to make him feel at "home on the range." Bill Hart had passed on the squint-eyed look above his pearl-handled six-shooters to Ken Maynard, Bill Boyd, Gene Autry, and a host of others who helped create the fantasy of an American cowboy-frontiersman that never existed.

The wonder is how slowly the impact of the brewing storms in the outer world reached Hollywood. But reach us they soon would. The Spanish civil war, Mussolini's invasion of Ethiopia, the stirrings of German-American Bunds inspired by the rise of National Socialism in the Fatherland, all were beginning to make some members of the film community conscious that there might be larger parts to play than mere participation in escapist fantasy. And as we became conscious we became vulnerable. Vulnerable to propaganda from right and left. The politically unsophisticated film folk of the thirties became ready-made victims for causes, good and bad. Our hearts and pockets would become increasingly available for bleeding. And as will be seen, all of the blood takers were not as altruistically polarized as one had wanted to believe.

To creative people, whose beginnings were generally humble, the sudden influx of wealth can bring a curious kind of guilt. Here, for writing, directing, performing, we were earning more money than some heads of government. Show folk always had been quick to dig into their pockets for a worthy charity, but in the thirties it was "causes" that caused us to whip out our checkbooks. The fight against fascism in Italy and Spain, economic injustices at home. Like all good Americans, we were opposed to all forms of human oppression and were ready and willing to sign petitions for or against almost anything. Against lynching (I don't recall anyone signing *for*), against oppressive uses of migratory cheap labor from Mexico. We were beginning to feel the need to grow up out of the profitable world of fairy tales and do something about something. The trouble was most of us weren't quite clear just what. One of Ring Lardner's sons joined the Abraham Lincoln Brigade and went off to get himself killed in Spain. Arthur Caesar, a top writer of the day, who had won a Congressional Medal of Honor for courage in World War I, flung himself through a plate glass window to attack single-handed an anti-Semitic meeting of the German-American Bund. The Los Angeles Police threw him in jail for disturbing the peace.

Of all creative film groups, perhaps the writers were most alert to the gathering storms. And our village had always lured writers, to try their hand at films for huge rewards or just to relax and enjoy the benefits of endless sunshine. Christopher Isherwood and Aldous Huxley were there. Liam O'Flaherty had joined John Ford to prepare the film version of *The Informer*. Thomas Mann and Stefan Zweig had come as political refugees from Europe. Dorothy Parker, married to writer Alan Campbell, dominated the politically conscious section of society; she was a founding member of the League for Democratic Action (which was later to be branded a Communist front in the McCarthy days). Thornton Wilder, the mighty Chicago novelist and playwright, was doing a film for Sam Goldwyn, who was prepared to buy the best at any price. Samuel Hoffenstein the poet, S. N. Behrman, Irvin Shrewsbury Cobb—the great humorist after whom The Brown Derby named one of its best salads—Ben Hecht, Will Rogers, Fitzgerald. If it was sometimes considered a creative graveyard, our "cemetery" found few who turned down its invitations. Inevitably, the growing intellectual weight of the community began to infiltrate the product itself.

An art form that had enjoyed little praise since *The Cabinet of Dr. Caligari*, the movies were feeling growing pains. Still, most showmen kept an unblinking eye on box-office receipts. Over and over the writer was reminded that the masses bought entertainment—not art. "If you have a message, send it by Western Union" overrode all objections. A curious marriage it was, the creative, liberal thinkers and the profit-oriented tycoons who held the reins of power. But the bankers and stockholders were content. They were getting one hell of a ride for their money!

That was the Hollywood I returned to from London in 1937. I needed a job and had decided to start looking at the top.

Eleven

GOD. THAT'S WHAT MANY WHO WORKED FOR HIM called him, the great man behind the huge cluttered desk. Everything you could imagine was on that desk: photos of presidents he had helped elect, gifts from grateful stars, tokens of esteem from oil tycoons whom he had financed, decorations from foreign governments, endless awards, plaques, and props from one or another of his movies. And when you saw him, bald and benign, you could believe the legends—and the jokes, like the one about the psychiatrist needed in heaven because "God thought he was Cecil B. De Mille."

And under that desk, a terrible weapon: a light which could be kicked on to blaze in the face of some nervous actress, putting her on the spot. But when you walked into that office your attention wasn't distracted by the vast array of objects, but was riveted upon the man himself. An enormously attractive person most of the time, he exuded charm enough to render humans of either sex defenseless, rather as certain insects stun their victims. We could all become his victims, I thought. His victims, his audience, and even, at times, his would-be assassins. I had heard how he could fall into explosive rages or equally make one feel that the simple achievement of a word combination to be spoken by an actor was equivalent to the conquest of Everest. And he was loyal to his staff. "Staff"—the word engulfed his employees like a monastic order, raising them above the tedium of long hours and frenzy for detail.

On this occasion I had crossed an ocean and a continent to ask him a question: Would he give me a job? He was beginning to prepare the script for the first version of *The Buccaneer*. De Mille fingered the thin volumes of thin verse I'd sent him from England. "Do you believe in God, Jesse?"

"Yes, sir. I think so."

"Think so? But you don't know?" There was a dangerous—yes, ominous—threat behind the question. A man might be burned at the stake for less than certainty.

"I believe in you, sir."

"Not a bad beginning," he allowed, thumbing one of my books. "You write fair poetry. I wonder if you could write drama. Could you?"

"I think so, sir." I had seen his film of *The Crusades*, starring Henry Wilcoxon and Loretta Young, at the Curzon Cinema in London and had decided I wanted to write for him when my assignment at Gaumont British had drawn to an end.

"Think, do you? You're not very sure of anything. The universe, or your place in it. Or who put you into it. Or why!"

I averted my head from the penetrating, hypnotic glance. "I guess not, sir."

"And have you brought me some samples of dialogue you *think* might fit into my next film?" He was a man who could swagger while seated behind a desk.

I pulled out some pages—a scene I had prepared based on the rough screenplay outline his office had sent me when I'd applied for the interview. They had suggested that I prepare improvements as a sample of my screenwriting abilities. He took it benevolently: Zeus accepting an offering. He scanned it, then read aloud slowly. Deliberately badly. If an actor had given such a reading De Mille would have thrown him out of the office. He was making my dialogue sound like drivel—which no doubt it was. His eyes flicked up and I saw the blue-white rage that would be there on so many occasions. One hand slipped into the desk drawer and came up holding a revolver. He offered it, butt forward.

"If you want to destroy me, Jesse," he hissed, "use this. It's quicker!"

He could afford such self-indulgence. At this time De Mille was at the top of his field as the master of spectacles. He was so rich and important it was rumored he had solid gold fixtures in his bathrooms. D. W. Griffith may have attracted more critical attention, but no man had produced as many financially successful and visually exciting extravaganzas as De Mille. Out of seventy-one films to date, I believe he only turned out one real financial loser, and it was one of his few attempts at doing a rather "intimate" study of people. A definite non-spectacle called *Four Frightened People.* De Mille always referred to himself as the fifth.

For his great films he had devised what proved to be an infallible formula. He packed the screen with impressive pageantry, supported by complex plots and subplots, and into each scene he measured out a careful soupçon of pure suspense. He drew his sense of scenic composition and balance from such carefully studied illustrators as the great Frenchmen Gustave Doré and Job. It did not concern him in the least that in the opinion of "serious" film makers his works were considered as artistically significant as Barnum and Bailey's Circus. He feared only one thing—that an audience might be bored. To insure against such a dreadful possibility he would over-pack his vistas, over-costume minor players, and give his actors so much "business" that the fascinated public hardly bothered to listen to the deathless dialogue. Long before I dreamed of becoming a De Mille writer I was a fan of his films. I found the splash and dash of his primary colors, the sense of heroic dimension, the uninhibited interpretation of history in the interest of drama and panorama, totally irresistible.

Dramatic license, an infinity of freedom to pack every foot of film with excitement! I knew that he and his writers pored through history and research to root out fascinating trifles that could be worked into a line of dialogue or an unusual prop. How, when soaked with research, they took to their typewriters, knowing they could do exactly as they pleased, as long as it pleased Mr. De Mille. A renowned professor once protested at one of his extravagant dramatic liberties in the first *Ten Commandments.* "Were you standing there beside Moses when it happened, my dear doctor?" De Mille inquired with devastating politeness.

I was not then aware that three top writers were already at work on *The Buccaneer:* Edwin Justus Mayer, the playwright; Harold Lamb, author and historian; and C. Gardner Sullivan—sometimes referred to by De Mille as "The Great Carpenter," not for any likeness to Jesus, but because he was noted for the difficult task of constructing and planning the series of "shots" which De Mille (unlike most directors) wanted laid out in advance to save time on the set.

Besides these veterans, Jeanie MacPherson had done the original adaptation of the book *Lafitte the Pirate* upon which the film was supposed to be based. Poor Jeanie had already begun to age out of favor; yet it was typical of De Mille loyalty to his friends and longtime workers that he did not cut them adrift after their best powers were beginning to wane. Besides, Jeanie had always been madly in love with him and had in the past held an important place in the court of women used and enjoyed by the great man. With such a formidable array of screenwriting talent, my chances of getting aboard what little work might be left were dubious in the extreme, but this I didn't know at the time.

The star was to be Fredric March, playing Jean Lafitte, the pirate leader. In the supporting cast was a superb player whom De Mille would use later many times, Akim Tamiroff—to appear as "Dominique You," the famous gunner of Napoleon who became Lafitte's chief lieutenant. The picture was set against the background of that senseless war between Britain and the United States which began in 1812. The story had an ideal De Mille–type theme. The pirate, released from prison by General Andrew Jackson, leads a collection of cutthroat scum in one day of glorious patriotism beneath a more-than-amply waved and bullet-perforated Stars and Stripes—at the battle of New Orleans. Whether or not the enlistment of the pirates turned the tide of battle and saved New Orleans and the United States from losing the war did not concern De Mille. Nor did the fact that the United States and Great Britain had already signed a mutually agreeable peace treaty, so that the battle of New Orleans had no historical pertinence, no matter how bravely fought. Such ironies were unimportant. What mattered was the fact that the adventure offered an ideal blend of legend, romance, undiluted swashbuckle with a smattering of history—pure spectacle, backgrounding strong personal drama.

Having declined the offer to shoot De Mille, I waited while he resumed looking at my pages. And then the pained expression was suddenly replaced by a flash of pleasure. He had found a combination of two words that changed my life.

In the story, a young girl has been forced to "walk the plank" clutching her small dog. His barks are heard by Tamiroff in the longboat. I suggested that Tamiroff should cup his hand to his ear, picking out the dog's voice above the sounds of wind and water, and shout to Lafitte, "You hear that, boss? A barking fish!" A more entertaining way of leading to her rescue, I thought, than merely having someone hear the girl's cries for help.

De Mille considered how Tamiroff would read the line with basso profundo Russian accent, and the director's entire attitude changed—even becoming just slightly apologetic; the De Mille of instant charm, vastly likeable.

"Barking fish," he said softly. "That's a De Mille line, Jesse. Not just words, but an original way of moving plot. I can use that! And I can use ideas like that."

Visions of sugar plums did a hectic gavotte through my brain. "You can, sir?"

"The line, yes." I waited, and hope held its breath. "The line, but not you, Jesse. Make too much trouble with my authors if I put you on this late in the script. I can't waste time with a lot of offended feelings right now."

Not then or ever, as I would learn. He arose, striding the office like a caged Zeus, burnished boots flashing leather lightning beneath the flare of his well-cut riding breeches.

These melodramatic trappings had become his trademark, smacking of the circus ringmaster, the cavalry leader, the man of action, ever trapped in the heat of epic events. This costume would become the cliché of the old-time film directors, but for De Mille it was both totally practical—since directors were always scrambling about over barriers, through dust, brush, or mud—and highly individual, making him instantly recognizable in the midst of a large and active set, crowded with extras, crew, animals, and onlookers.

From the belt of his riding breeches invariably hung a collection of leather-cased watches which told him what time it was anywhere in the world—a personal eccentricity, like the pocketful of "golden eagles" (obsolete twenty-dollar pieces), which he would jangle as a warning of shortening patience, not unlike the rattle of a poisonous snake. His shirt was open to a still-muscular throat, and his bald head did not diminish strong good looks in the Roman imperial style. He was physically fascinating to all, literally all, women. Actress, female writer, socialite seeking a contribution to charity, or the highly competent women on his staff—all found him quite irresistible if he bothered to turn on even a modicum of charm. All that charm vanished, however, when he fell into one of the sudden insane rages that could sweep him without warning.

As he considered what he would do about me, I tried to focus on the crowded walls of his office. They were "redressed" regularly before every production so that he could saturate his eyes with his current film. This afternoon they were hung with a huge storyboard with movable cards outlining every scene, various piratical props, superb water-color paintings of every character by Dan Grosbeck, pirate scenes from Howard Pyle's great illustrated book. Desks and table tops were equally a-clutter with model sets, pistols, cutlasses.

"Barking fish," he muttered. I was getting pretty sick of the phrase, since it hadn't been the key to a needed job anyway.

"No, I can't take you on this time. My authors have already sucked me dry of the last drop of blood in writing money. However . . ." The long dramatic pause and the hypnotic eyes. "I'll work in some of the suggestions you've made here. And I'll send you a gift. A token. And I'll make you a promise, Jesse . . ."

"You don't have to send me anything, sir . . ."

He ignored the interruption.

"The promise. Next picture I make, whatever it is, you can be in at the birth. It may be a year, or whatever, but when we've got *The Buccaneer* behind us—I'll send for you and give you a chance on the writing team."

"Thank you very much, sir."

"Maybe you won't!" There was a curiously ominous note in the words, as though I would be given an assignment more dangerous and fraught with perils than I might dream. Then the shadow was gone, and he smiled again.

"How is your father? We don't see much of each other . . ." The remark was not without calculated significance, for they were not at the moment on the great footing of friendship that once had been.

"He's fine, sir."

The intercom buzzed tentatively and he knocked open a key with a snarled, "Yes?"

"It's your Washington call, Mr. De Mille."

"Put him on." "Him," I realized, might quite possibly be the president of the United States. De Mille's support of Republican presidential candidates was highly solicited by the National Committee. He had himself turned down, after due consideration, the offer to run for governorship of our state as a Republican candidate. He had decided, "I can reach more people with my pictures than from any State House."

Unquestionably true.

Politically a shade to the right of Louis Quatorze, he had nevertheless graciously loaned an open touring car to that Democrat Franklin D. Roosevelt, since it happened to be the largest available touring car in Los Angeles. Never inhibited by friend or foe, he had presented that president with a silver fifty-cent piece of rare type "for your foreign policy, Mr. President," and then handed him a Buffalo nickel —"for your domestic policy."

Home that evening, I dared wonder, not if De Mille would call me in that dim future at the gestation of his next epic, but more immediately—what would be the gift of the Magi? In the De Mille tradition, an elephant load of gems seemed not an impossibility—or, and what would have been most welcome, a modest check, perhaps?

The doorbell's ring put an end to suspense. One of his chauffeurs delivered a case of superb champagne—Bollinger '28. It would go very nicely with the hamburger and chili we were living on at the moment.

Twelve

WITH A PROMISE instead of an assignment from De Mille, I headed for an agent friend who might help me find a writing job. In Hollywood somebody said you could be forgotten while you were out of the room going to the toilet. Out of sight, out of memory; as simple as that. So having been working in England without credits of great importance was a kind of death. It was easy to imagine the response the agent would get when he let it be known that I was back in town and "available."

"Great, but what's the guy done recently?"

"Well, before Jesse went away he was at Fox and . . ."

"Sure. Sure. But who've you got new? I gotta have a fresh approach on this one . . ."

Thus aware of the constant threat of oblivion, one had left town at one's own risk. The condition seemed to apply to almost all creative talent. You were always "as good as your last picture" and your last picture had better have been good! And recent. Writers, actors, directors, and even producers all knew the unwritten rule of the game.

Stay fresh! Like dairy produce. Be the answer to the cry for "a fresh face," "a fresh mind," "fresh ideas."

To supply this magic "freshness," talent scouts scoured the country for young hopefuls. They ransacked the little theaters, the drama schools, the beauty contests, the radio talent shows. Young writers were lured from New York publishers' lists, or from universities, or from the slick magazines, *Cosmopolitan*, *Saturday Evening Post*, and *Collier's*. Those days of mass film production burned up talent as television does in our own time.

But your fresh script of last year could go as stale as last week's cod. Credits that had been could make you a "has-been." There were, of course, those exceptional few who had risen to the giddy heights of permanent establishment. And for the true "greats" there was a kind of stratosphere where the laws of gravity no longer applied. A Gilbert, a Garbo, a Gable, a Garland . . . a Capra, a Borzage, a Ford. And even a few writers, the handful who could do what they pleased, when they pleased, and ask what they would—and get it!

It was the man in the middle who felt the most insecure. And with reason. We were the replaceables. One had to appraise one's altitude like a balloonist to be sure that high was high enough—that the welcome mat would be out and the fatted calf simmering on the front burner.

To make things worse, extravagance seemed to be congenital to the climate. Like orange juice. People who earned enormous salaries might suddenly find themselves between pictures—for years—yet everyone was susceptible to the American disease. Think big! Go for broke! Bet high and sleep in the cactus. No matter that in betting on yourself you were often buying ulcers on the installment plan. That didn't stop anyone. There was always the allure of that new car, new house, new swimming pool. Didn't everyone who wasn't a nobody have one? Hollywoodites rode to the guillotine in platinum tumbrels of status consciousness. Being a star meant dressing the part, driving the part, living the part, and for many, everything but acting the part. Economy, saving for the lean years, was practiced mostly by the never-would-be's, and the occasional Harold Lloyd.

And so yesterday's stars and directors and writers might often be seen stalking the sun-blistered pavements like zombies. Avoided, shunned, they learned that unemployment was a kind of leper's bell.

With all our lushness and opulence, we never ceased being a community of the walking dead.

"Waltz me around again, skullhead—around, around, around!"

It certainly made for a "buyer's market" for those seated firmly in the saddles of success. Casting couches and the waiting rooms of outer offices were never empty, unless the Gods went off to their golf clubs, bored by sheer satiety.

Actresses on the skids, embalmed in desperation, only fought for the chance to sleep their way up again. "Talent I can buy for a dime!" Writers and directors who hadn't quite made it, or who had been cut down in their prime by bad reviews or box-office failure, were too ready to whore their way back aboard by drowning their talents in movie garbage. Obsolescence, the great killer, spread like barnacles on a putrid hulk. Such conditions made "the trades" as important as papal bulls. The two daily film newspapers, *The Hollywood Reporter* and *Daily Variety*, told who was up, who was down. They were so powerful they could actually exert blackmail in the form of paid personal advertising. For a mere couple of hundred dollars you could buy the spectacle of your name in a quarter-page ad in the middle of a section devoted to the premiere of your latest film. Just in case someone might miss the fact that you'd been working. You knew damned well that the fast-talking young space vendor who popped into your office just before your picture got its first public showing had no influence whatever on the almighty reviewers. But a large segment of Hollywood folk paid for the blackmail ads and hoped for the best. It was like buying an expensive rabbit's foot. Everyone knew that the only people who worked were the ones who were working.

My problem at the moment was a bit different. I'd gone away too far and stayed away too long. I needed a writing assignment and fast. But I might as well have brought back bubonic plague. The handful of producers I'd worked for in the past suddenly became unreachable by telephone. Had I been more astute I could have plumbed the depths of my descent by the failure of headwaiters to remove the ever-present "reserved" sign from tables in prestige filmland restaurants when I entered. As it was, old acquaintances not only forgot, their shoelaces became suddenly untied at my approach. Nowhere as in our Hollywood was the smell of success as deeply sought by the lungs of the beholder.

I consoled myself that it would have been worse had I been an actor. At least writers weren't important enough to be considered "poison at the box office." Unless you were a Ben Hecht or a Dudley Nichols you just weren't considered at all.

My agent friend, a member of a then all-powerful agency (housed in a building in Beverly Hills that resembled the Virginia residence of George Washington), regarded me across a genuine antique American Colonial desk. Hooked rugs, shelves bursting with books by his successful authors, his desk groaning with manuscripts. It was a mark of his humanity that he even bothered to see me. But I had invoked the magic word "friendship," and somewhere beneath the panderer's sharkskin beat a compassionate heart. It was not perhaps the most desirable quality in an agent if he had to go out and do battle for you. His compassion might extend to the producer. Any agent who would represent me, I shouldn't want, I thought, watching Harry select a straight-grained gold-banded Barling from a triple-tier rackful of expensive pipes. He leaned back, resting Harris-tweeded shoulders against the superb stamped leather of his armchair, and contemplated me sadly.

"Beware of Jews wearing lifts," someone once paraphrased. But Rock didn't need lifts. He was a six-foot, Harvard-trained lawyer. His Hollywoodese, semi-Brooklyn, show-biz way of talking was pure affectation, so that his producer clients would never be made to feel inferior. He would, of course, one day be a producer himself, and then elegance and literacy could out.

Our dialogue went something like this:

"Jesus, baby, where you been? You were supposed to be gone one month. You should have come back instead of crapping around England."

"I told you on the phone, Rock. I did a couple of polish jobs. One for a new director, Alfred Hitchcock."

"Whoever heard of him?" snarled Rock.

"And I did some work on a script by R. C. Sheriff, who wrote *Journey's End*," I said, hoping to reestablish my prestige.

"Your journey should have ended sooner! You missed a couple of good scripts here that might have done you some good. Christ, I mean, you know how it is! Six months, was it? Seven? They forget, pally, they forget."

I knew. I was more than ready to concede that I hadn't done my career any good by staying abroad. I listened with the utmost respect; agents like Rock were desperately important. He closed his eyes, searching for my salvation.

"If you brought back any original screenplays we might do something," he tried hopefully.

I had not. I had been enjoying my travels too much to get down to hard work—except for the polish jobs. I admitted I had been a spoiled, lazy bastard.

"So don't ask for a f—ing miracle, pally. I can't sell what you haven't got. You said you saw De Mille last week. So wait. Meantime we'll keep our ears to the ground till something breaks."

"What will break will be me, Rock! The next De Mille picture could be a year off. Two. You know that. Even if he remembers to put me on."

He nodded. He knew.

"So in your situation it would be hard to insult you."

"What do you mean?"

"You want to work, and you're not feeling over-particular?"

"I've got to. I'm just married. And my wife likes Saks Fifth Avenue." In fact, I had recently married an American ballet dancer from Mexico City.

He finger-combed a profusion of lustrous black hair. "Could you come up with a story line for a Valley studio, like by tomorrow at three o'clock?"

"What kind?"

"Kind, schmind. The grapevine says they've got a commitment with a red-headed dame somebody's banging. They've also got a starting date and a script everybody hates. So if you had a really fresh idea—in solid step-outline—I could pick up that phone and say look, one of my boys has got a really fresh angle for a sexpot lead. A starring vehicle, see what I mean? You'd have yourself a job tomorrow."

I saw. And I poked in the cluttered writers' attic of my mind for something old, something new, something borrowed . . .

"Rock, I'm not saying it's impossible—but by three o'clock tomorrow . . . ? That's cutting it a little thin!"

His shrug was a threat of removal from the orbit of his interest. "You want the assignment? Or shall we forget it?"

"What makes it all that sure—you could sell me? I mean if I do come up with a story. They could hate it."

"They haven't got time to hate it. So go burn the midnight oil. I'll call up and make the appointment. Look, they're not expecting *Gone With the Wind*. Just a fresh angle on girl meets boy. Somebody lays somebody. They lose each other. They get together. You know. Just so it's fresh and you could script it really fast."

The mental attic had thus far produced only a title.

"I may have something. Do you think they'd go for a title like: *The Redhead?*"

"I love it. It's fresh!"

I didn't tell him that it was the singular of the title of one of my father's famous old vaudeville acts, produced about twenty-five years before.

"They'll go for it," he beamed; then his face was suddenly overcast—even ominous. "One thing I should maybe warn you."

"They pay in coconuts?"

He ignored the attempted humor, polishing the straight grain against the grease of his nose. "It's a B picture. B minus. They've already shot their wad paying for the script that they can't use."

"So there's nothing left to pay for the script they will use?"

"They've got about five hundred bucks left. For screenplay and story."

He did not miss the sag in my face.

"It's take-it-or-leave-it time, old chum. I already tried to get them up a couple of hundred higher. For one of my other boys they wanted. They wouldn't play."

I could understand why his "other boys" had passed up this challenging assignment. I could see also that Rock was losing interest. Hardly surprising. His fifty-dollar commission out of my five hundred wouldn't have paid for one of his straight-grain pipes.

"Okay," I sighed. "I'll do it."

He beamed. "You're being realistic, Jesso. So the money's *bubkas*. Look at it like this. You'll be doing them a favor. Next time we won't let 'em forget it. We hit 'em for the jackpot. True?"

That logic sold more talent down the river in Hollywood than coal to Newcastle! Because the next time, they'd say, "He worked for peanuts. Why should I pay him more?"

If there was a next time.

I looked around the lush office. Everywhere genuine antiques. Well, Rock was doing me a favor. Any other member of the agency wouldn't have given me the time of day. Rock was a friend.

"Too bad Lincoln freed the slaves. They could have had me for five strokes of the lash," I suggested, rising to go.

"Four, baby. Things aren't all that great right now for writers."

The phrase was familiar. So was the condition. Would there ever be a time when things were—that great? Always more scribes for sale than buyers. Yet, had we only known it, those days were heaven compared to what lay ahead.

At 3:45 next day I had the assignment. I would have had it by 3:10, but the producer kept me waiting in his outer office thirty-five minutes while he interviewed a potential starlet. When she came out I went in. Like an Alka Seltzer after a night out. I don't even know if he heard the story idea I presented. I read it from a carefully-constructed outline blending action, suspense, and what I hoped would be considered "freshness." At the price Rock had agreed to accept for my services, the story hardly mattered. There were few Hollywood writers who would have got out of bed for that price, and he knew it. Not anyone with established "credits."

With two hundred and fifty dollars in advance, I broke speed records turning out the script. I needed the other half. It wasn't good but it was fast. Again the wait in the outer office, while he auditioned a pretty unknown fresh off the train—who must have been just dying to break into Hollywood. When she finally left, I was ushered into the presence. He sagged behind his desk, drained, eyes wriggling like nervous worms.

"All night I been up reading your goddamn script," he bleated, stabbing my masterpiece with the wet end of a chewed cigar. "I got to tell you the truth. I do *not* like it all that much. So this morning I drove by the house of our vice president and left it for him to read. He just called me, and he ain't happy." Surreptitiously he rebuttoned his wide-open fly.

"He wants changes. We kicked it around and came up with something solid. Something you could fix in a couple of hours. New characters and a different setting. Make it Alaska. The Gold Rush, maybe. The dame deals faro or some crap like that. The hero's a young prospector—who's got a hard-on, see? The heavy's using her to cold-deck him—and the guy is out on his ass—with his last poke of dust in her stocking, you get the idea? Give the story some balls."

"It would take some considerable rewriting," I said.

"Read your contract. We got the right to ask for changes. If you don't make 'em—you can pee on my desk for the rest of your fee. There's plenty hungry writers who'll do it for less."

So I did it. It seemed the vice president was never satisfied with the setting or the characters—or even their names: I did one version with the Foreign Legion—a "tits and sand" saga, as they were called. Another set in a phony Baghdad, a far cry from my original version, which was a smalltown boy-and-girl story. Anyway, they finally seemed satisfied and paid me off. I found out later that all four scripts were actually produced as low-budget films. Four scripts for the price of one. Still, I was lucky. Other writers frequently never saw more than the down payment at the start of a job. Others never saw a dime.

Screenwriters, in those days the unsung drones, got less credit than they do now. The gray gnomes of the industry, somehow we usually managed to emerge, though indispensable, as pretty unimportant. For the most part the scriptwriter was and still is the most undercredited member of the creative team, utterly eclipsed by the highly publicized star and the director's more bewitching effect on critics.

To the public we were virtually nonexistent. Since we were generally hired week to week and frequently involved in "adaptations" of already existing literary material such as plays or novels, or occasionally maintained by the studio in contractual "stables," we were used as mechanics rather than artists. Many producers and directors regarded us as necessary evils, perfectly confident that they could easily write their own films—"if they could only spare the time." But their time was far more valuable than ours, and their rewards invariably far higher.

This was before the days when many writers became hyphenated into writer-directors or writer-producers. In the thirties, we were still craftsmen who had developed the exact technique of putting a moving picture on paper: every move, every word of dialogue, and in most cases every camera angle. We had to set down the precise blueprints from which a hundred or more studio technicians in various departments could know the exact requirements of the film; budgets, schedules, set construction, wardrobe, special effects, makeup, and a hundred other crafts would be involved. All this before the cast ever saw the script. This is still true today.

Stage plays required visual expansion and adaptation for the understanding of a much larger audience. Novels had to be distilled into visual drama; mood and the mental processes of the characters, dramatically interpreted for the camera to record and embellish. Occasionally a film script could, by clarity and believability of motivations, improve the fuzzy meanderings of a novel.

Producers frequently used writers in layers on the basis that there was safety in numbers. Some writers were considered specialists in construction, plotting; some in creating action, some in pure dialogue. In the case of a comedy, "gag-men" would be employed for the final polish, and often on a drama to add a touch of comedy relief. This is why film credits so often bear two or more names.

The harassed film hack increasingly found himself a victim of producers' abuses, and this led to the formation of the Screenwriters' Guild. To many, it seemed grotesque that writers should need any kind of labor union. Obviously, the important ones didn't, most of the time. But collective action gave us bargaining power to establish minimum wages and a fair break in advertising and publicity. The struggle still goes on. Perhaps the battle will never be entirely won, but it is important that there will always be an organization to help protect people who live by their typewriters.

Our infant guild faced all kinds of threats to its existence. But the most serious threat, almost from its inception, was a growing disease far more dangerous than producers' opposition. We faced an internal struggle, and in the friction of political differences almost succumbed to ideological self-destruction. A hard core of highly talented writers had become oriented toward communism. Others found a philosophy of strong individualism in the equally hardcore leanings of an ultra-right. Between the flashy oratory of the fringes sat the complacent middle moderates, concerned with survival in their craft, unpolitically oriented, internationally uninformed, and not in the least sure why the plight of the Russian invaders of Finland should be more important to us than improving our own working conditions and earning capacities. The moderates suffered from what was to many an uninspired conviction that a writers' guild should concern itself with the problems of writers. In this unenlightened multitude I found myself.

Many of the articulate left were certainly tools of professional organizers, trained rabble-rousers who inoculated the emotionally vulnerable with the virus of causes. How could you be a writer and not have an almost godlike concern with the fall of any sparrow of humanity in any corner of the earth? And so involvement for many came easily. We were all troubled by our own complaisance. Life in this Lotus Land seemed embarrassingly shameful when men and women out in the great world were finding things worth fighting and dying for.

Our sleep was becoming more and more troubled by distant thunder—Nazi drums at vast torchlighted gatherings geographically far away but brought closer by newsreel scenes; gentle, elderly Jews, who should have been presiding over prayers in the light of religious candlesticks, being made to polish the pavements under the delighted scrutiny of brown-shirted, jack-booted bully-boys. The horrors related by every arriving refugee were no longer bad dreams—or exaggerations.

Yet many outstanding Americans leaned toward what they considered the new sense of order. Order! Trains that ran on time. They dreamed of a disciplined press that would brook no disgusting carnivals, such as had been made of the Lindbergh baby's kidnapping case in the American tabloids. Charles Lindbergh himself, subjected to a vulgar circus of publicity and public curiosity, found in the Germany of the rising swastika what appeared to be dignity, discipline, and order. He accepted their Iron Cross and enjoyed hobnobbing with such dashing fellow flyers as Goering. He came home full of praise for the new order. The "lone eagle" was not alone. Men like Colonel McCormick, newspaper giant of Chicago, who had seen the ugly gangster violence and corruption of Prohibition days, could somehow equate Capone's mobs with the Red Menace. To many of these wealthy and well-established Americans, Hitler and Mussolini were considered the brave walls that would stem the flood of Marxism. As to the brewing war—why concern oneself with the fate of Frenchmen and Britons? Let them sleep in the beds their history had made them. Consider the health of America First! The policy became organized. Few listened to the warnings of President Franklin D. Roosevelt—that the frontier of our democracy was the Rhine.

But Hollywood's intellectual community listened, and felt deeply concerned. What useful part could one play in the cataclysmic events that lay ahead? How could we help those hunted creatures glimpsed in newsreels? And what about our own underprivileged? What about the sharecroppers? What about the Mexican "wetbacks" who fed the pools of cheap labor? What about the Negroes (who had not yet found pride in the word "black")? What about "lynch law" in the South? What about poverty? Illiteracy? Suddenly it seemed essential to be concerned with every facet of injustice at home and abroad. Such were the well-meant motivations that brought important actors, actresses, writers, directors, and even some producers to meetings at the luxurious swimming-pooled homes of the new socially-conscious.

Meetings which were occasionally addressed by men with a distinctly non-Hollywood appearance. They were professionals—and it didn't require a hard guess to conjecture professional "what." They would have looked far more at home organizing longshoremen strikes—or Molotov cocktail parties. They were there to give us "orientation courses" in "economics." At first these thick-shouldered, hard-eyed realists seemed a breath of fresh air among the parlor pinks and swimming-pool liberals, but gradually one began to feel queasy. Where was the invisible borderline over which one stepped into treason?

To this day I'm not quite sure how I avoided being signed into the Communist party. I was politically starry-eyed enough to have been swept along with the tide that carried so many good friends into the arms of the Party—*if* the Communists had tried a little harder. Perhaps my ideological lack of sophistication and my ties with the arch-Republican De Mille made me untrustworthy fodder from their standpoint. Perhaps I asked too many questions at preliminary gatherings, wanted to know too much about their cure-alls for injustice in our country, and the world. But probably it was my good luck not to join any parties—uninvited!

Moscow might be the Mecca toward which we were expected to bow, but when Stalin signed the Berlin-Moscow pact which freed Hitler to plan his war, when such opposite forces could join hands for political expediency, however brief, one either hung up one's ideals like an outgrown Boy Scout uniform or accepted some mystic Big Brotherism without qualm or question. The surprising thing is how many brilliant and respected creative people did just that.

The other aspect that troubled me deeply was how a well-organized minority was turning our young guild into a forum for propagandizing and soliciting contributions for every cause but our own. We seemed to exist for the sole purpose of collecting donations and signing petitions. Our grievances against dishonest producers who used every trick in the book to avoid paying writers seemed to have become trivial in the face of great crusades. Guild meetings were filled from dusk to dawn with the endless eloquence of lunatic fringes, and the left was always better organized, better trained. They sat in "diamond" formation. When one speaker would finish, another took over in a different section of the room. It made them sound as if they outnumbered every one else. They also timed their proposals for resolutions, holding "hot" items until the conservatives were exhausted and on their way home. Thus passage was assured of resolutions that had nothing whatever to do with the true purpose of our union. These lads had iron bottoms, it seemed, because they never went home! When anyone else would propose limitation on debate, or the hour in which new legislation and business could be introduced, we'd be hooted down and ridiculed by the brilliant polemics of the "bleeding hearts."

These were the conditions which led to the formation of a new nonpolitical group within our guild, a "moderate" party of middle-of-the-roaders who wanted to return the energy of the union to the problems of writers. In time, we would manage to get ourselves elected to office, and the left-wingers would be overrun by the McCarthy witch-hunt, that miserably misguided purge on the part of a politico sick with ambition.

Thirteen

ONE DAY IN 1938, the impossible happened. A Hollywood promise was kept! It was De Mille's promise to recruit me into his next writing team, the one which would reconstruct the Union Pacific Railroad. That historical saga of nation-girdling steel rails had always fascinated film makers—John Ford had produced *The Iron Horse* on this same theme, but that epic, De Mille assured me, good as it was, had barely scratched the surface.

Epic Americana had always been, would always be box-office gold. Well, almost always. Dad had hit pay dirt with *The Covered Wagon*, yet missed with *Old Ironsides* and *The Rough Riders*. De Mille had shrewdly lifted his own sights from bathtub to Yankee mythology with *The Plainsman* and *The Buccaneer*. He now felt audiences were ripe for sweeping vistas of continent-taming tribulations. The thirties had regained prosperity without grandeur, sanity without sense of destiny. We needed to draw spiritual nourishment for the present from the past. We needed to regain a sense of purpose in the long hangover from Prohibition and the materialistic disestablishment of the Depression. We had boozed away the American dream with Scott Fitzgerald and tasted the lusty cynicism of Hemingway and Dos Passos. Ripe time to produce chauvinistic fairy tales—thundering with rescuing cavalry, Old Glory cracking above the horse soldiers bugling into the wind, racing to save the settlers from the savages. *Union Pacific* would have such staples of the epic feast, and more—the symphony of thudding sledges driving home the spikes.

De Mille took one up from among the desk clutter that included Sitting Bull's peace pipe and Wild Bill Hickok's Philadelphia Derringer. "Know what this is, Jesse?"

"A railroad spike."

He looked displeased. However correct, I had certainly diminished the spade by so-calling it. I would have done better with something like "A pin to secure the future of a nation."

"A railroad spike," he mocked. "What would you call the quill that signed the Declaration of Independence? A feather?"

Jeanie MacPherson suppressed a titter of pleasure. She should have known that laughter at the cost of another's discomfort would soon cut both ways.

The plump, aging film authoress always wore only one color at a time, and today it was purple. Purple shoes, purple silk stockings, purple silk dress, purple straw hat transfixed with a purple-jeweled hatpin. She looked like a paragraph of purple prose. An ancient boa drooped a pair of molting vixens down her heavy purple bosom.

Her riveted gaze was on the boss, but De Mille peered past us, through us, imagining one of those camera shots that were always somehow nobler in his mind than anything that ever reached the screen.

"Wind-combed prairie—like a vast, almost uncrossable sea between east and west. A moat of separation bridged only sporadically by the occasional Pony Express rider—or the rocking Concord stages of the Wells Fargo—racing the arrows of death!" He was, as always, enjoying the taste of his own rhetoric.

"But, Mr. De Mille . . ." I was about to inject some dangerous quibble with the continuity of his history. Fortunately he ignored the attempted interruption, booming on, "Sweat, blood, and steel. That's what built the Union Pacific! Yes, and whisky and sin—in portable hells of corruption following the railroad builders, siphoning their wages away in the saloons, brothels, and gambling dens under the tents that followed the ever westward-pushing end of track!"

This subject, he assured us, striding his spacious office like some impatient Nelson pressing toward his Trafalgar, had everything, everything that a film maker could dream of! His eyes flicked to Jeanie for confirmation.

Ecstatic at this attention, the fading scribe of so many of his early films seemed to be verging on a kind of mental orgasm. "Oohh, yes, C. B. . . ." she moaned. Poor Jeanie, no longer toothsome, long since fallen from favor, haunted his corridors like a ghost of paradise lost, hoping for occasional invitations to be present at meetings like this one. One felt that she had forgotten more about the putting together of De Mille film scripts than any other person would ever learn, but her time had somehow passed. Now she was a pensioner, hovering at the feast, expecting only sporadic crumbs of attention.

The great man no longer saw her—or me. His mind's eye still searched for the impossible "shot"—a continent-wide vista of thousands of extras, laying track in front of the puffing engine with its great funnel stack and huge cow-catcher. Uncountable multitudes of builders crossing immeasurable spaces to bring inestimable wealth through the box office. But now and always, De Mille's verbal vistas, so glibly conjured, would be limited by the means of a mere film company to reproduce. The vast tribes of Sioux and Cheyenne he envisioned would become a mere few hundred extras. No doubt this diminution of grandeur would be truer to historic reality. Life was and would always be smaller than the concepts of Cecil B. De Mille.

"Once the range belonged to the red man and the buffalo he harvested with arrows. The shaggy herds fed him, clothed him, housed him." His finger stabbed at the purple priestess in his temple of relics. "Get that, Jeanie!"

"Oh yes, C. B.!" Her pencil trembled so violently it could hardly scribble. I wondered why on this occasion he had not had the usual speed stenographer present. Jeanie was having trouble. Pencils fell from her hands, notebook sprawled down in a splatter of pages. I knelt to help her.

"Goddamn it, Jeanie, if you can't hold a pencil in your hand, write with it in your teeth!" De Mille exploded.

The hurt in her face was awful to see. I knew of their long and stormy personal relationship. She had first gained favor by performing in that notorious brawl with Geraldine Farrar in De Mille's *Carmen,* back in 1915. He had simply told them to go to it, and the gals staged the wildest hair-pulling match in film history. Next year Jeanie gave up greasepaint for ink. Since then she had written his next ten films, and by now had twenty-eight De Mille screen credits. Then suddenly she had become obsolete. Other writers took her place, but he kept her on to haunt the perimeters of his script conferences. Gods didn't fire aging handmaidens.

A moment later his anger had left him. Cruelty was doused in remorse. He even sounded somehow apologetic. "I'm just trying to get you fellahs to *see* how it was. Get the dust of history out of your brains and start smelling drama! You don't just build a railroad—tap tap, and away we go. It's the biggest team action since the pyramids! The graders out in front. A shovel-brigade advance guard piling up the mounds of earth. Then come the ties. There wasn't a sliver of timber on those plains, every tie had to be freighted down from Minnesota and Michigan. It took forty freight cars of supplies to lay one mile of track! Stone from Wisconsin, steel rails from Pennsylvania . . . Where was I?" He knew, but he had to be sure we were listening.

"The graders, C. B.," Jeanie prompted primly, having collected her implements and herself, pencil now poised.

"We were laying the ties, goddamn it!" he snarled.

"Well, we had to grade first, and . . ."

"Don't tell me what I'm telling you!" he snapped, cutting her off.

She subsided. He, collecting himself, thrust his head forward from powerful shoulders, jangling the coins ominously in his pocket. "The ties are down—now for the rails! Three men to each, hefting 'em from the rail car. Down they clang on the ties, and the sledges beat their anvil chorus driving home the spikes!" His face looked pink enough to have been doing the job he described. "Now come the 'gandy dancers,' tamping down the earth between the ties, and you hear a thousand voices chanting the hymn of the railroad builders. 'Drill ye terriers, drill!' "

"That's the theme of your picture, C. B.!" Jeanie cried out.

"What?" He swiveled a gimlet eye at her. "Jesus God, will you not interrupt me!"

"But it is. I mean, Irish laborers fresh from the old sod and potato famines and things, landing on our shores, fighting the Civil War with clay pipes, I mean in their mouths, and the smell of peat . . ."

"Pete, who the hell's he?" He looked at me helplessly.

"Peat, C. B. What they burn!"

He spun back to her. "You mean they bring it with them?"

"No, I just mean—they smell of it. Well, if you've ever been in Ireland, Mr. De Mille . . ." Jeanie was always either offended, hurt, or sarcastic.

"I have been every place including the lost continent of Atlantis, and I would like to finish saying what I want to see in this picture!"

"I was just trying to help, C. B.!"

"Well try helping by shutting up, will you?" he commanded.

Her lips snapped tight, tears clouded her eyes. He went on.

"Get this—and get it into your guts and your souls! The theme of this picture. Lads from the Old World come to the New—to fight its war and bind its wounds—with bandages of steel! Steel track—red with the blood of the lads who lay it—forging a nation and a destiny

—lads who could scarcely pronounce its name. America!" It had come out like a nasal battle cry.

Jeanie's clasped hands burst into applause. An ecstatic yelp broke from her. "Oh, C. B., you used *my* idea!"

"I'm using history, goddamn it! If anyone can get it on paper, which of course they can't."

"I could," she offered, looking as though she might be making a mysterious proposal. He ignored it, turning to me.

"Do you begin to get what I see in this, Jesse?"

"I think so," I said.

"You don't." He sighed bitterly. "Nobody does. But by God I'll get it out of you! You and the other writers. I want history! Not dry old books about the past."

I did not quibble with the self-contradiction. He was surging on.

"I want train wrecks. I want to see the explosions of steam and bursting boilers! Iron guts! I want to boil on those prairies, and freeze in the Sierras. I want to smash through the barricades of mountain ranges of snow and ice. I want a love story that nobody has ever got on the screen, and I want human drama! Suspense. Not just 'Will they make it, or won't they make it?' which any damn fool can write. I want a snake under every bed!" (I had not yet learned the meaning of this last instruction, but I would.) His voice lowered to a rasping whisper. "I want to see Abe Lincoln's dream—come to life!"

"We might start with him. Lincoln in the White House, I mean," Jeanie piped suddenly.

"Good, Jeanie! Good! Get on to research and get me every word Lincoln ever said about the transcontinental railroad! Or anyone else. For or against. The congressmen. Senators. Good and bad. Even Democrats!"

"Yes, C. B.! And C. B. . . ."

He turned back to her. Somehow one sensed she was overplaying her ace.

"When you mentioned the love story . . . I thought, a southern belle. You know, impoverished from the war. Has gone west and . . . meets one of the very soldiers who had served with that General . . . Sherman? Yes, Sherman. When he burned down the flower of southern chivalry, I mean their houses and . . ."

"Shut up, Jeanie!" he roared. "If you have to think of the oldest plot in the world, do it on your own time!" He was suddenly livid with rage. "Now get out!"

She rose, trembling, things starting to fall from her hands again. I bent to retrieve glasses, pencils, eraser. Accustomed as she must have been to his outbursts, this wound of pride appeared mortal. She was puffed with pain and outraged injustice, yet she kept a superb dignity. A Boadicea could not have responded to a Roman insult with more majesty. She waved away the pencils I'd salvaged from the floor.

"I shan't need them, Jesse. He doesn't require my services any more. Good day, Mr. De Mille." Her exit was magnificent, only spoiled by an overtheatrical sob as she went through the door.

"Alas, poor Jeanie," he said. There was no doubt of how well he had known her, or that he was already regretting the outburst. "She'll get over it and come back for more. She always does."

Perhaps she would. But I conceived that I might not. That in the fullness of time no one would be spared the lash of his tantrums. I even considered leaving at that moment. But his words held me. The voice, now drained of anger, had lowered into the majestic cadences of the consummate actor.

"Four thousand years ago—the pyramids rose to feed the vanity of man. Later the Great Wall of China rose to calm the fears of man. The Union Pacific was built to supply the needs of man—by uniting a nation."

He waited as though for some applause. I had taken down the words with Jeanie's pencil. "Not a bad foreword for the picture, sir."

"It was on a bit of paper that Jeanie handed me this morning," he confessed. "She hasn't forgotten everything I taught her." He flipped down the key of his intercom. "Get Jeanie on the phone."

A moment later the box buzzed. She must have been recovering in the outer office among the sympathetic secretaries.

Her voice was a haughty hurt concession to long association. "Yes, Mr. De Mille?"

"I just read that thing about the pyramids to Jesse. He likes it and so do I."

By the silence, she could have fainted with joy. Then she choked out something like "Thank you."

"Come in if you like, fellah." Men, women, children, and dogs were all "fellah" to him.

"Just as soon as I've powdered my nose, C. B.!" Her voice returned to a cheerful chirp.

He hung up, eyes lifted to heaven at the miracle of his own compassion. "If that woman doesn't drive you screaming, raving insane—if you can keep from strangling her with your bare hands—she occasionally comes up with something usable." He shuddered at what he had to bear. "I will take care of my enemies if God will protect me from my friends." A line he always used as though he'd invented it.

Next day I met the rest of the Union Pacific writing team. They did not include Jeanie, for I heard that after she was restored to grace, the Boss had again lost patience and banished her from his presence for a month. On salary, however.

De Mille had assembled a strong battery of scribes. They included old Jack Cunningham, a wheezing, bone-dry veteran who was working on the "adaptation" of Ernest Haycox's book. Our screenplay would be based upon the book of the same name, although we might not use any part of it. On the advice of his attorneys, De Mille always bought some published work related to the subject matter. It was supposed to give him legal protection against possible claims of plagiarism. This probably made some sense, since any time he announced a subject for his next film, amateur scribes would drench him with a flood of submissions. Unsolicited scripts were almost always returned unopened and unread, but by their very submission of a story with a similar background the writer might claim that De Mille had used one of their incidents in his picture—and sue him for his shirt. This legal maneuver, incidentally, almost always eliminated his screenwriters from the "original screenplay category" in the annual Academy Awards.

Other writers assigned to Union Pacific included Walter De Leon, small, worried, seasoned, good at dialogue and ferreting out nuggets from mountains of research, and C. Gardner Sullivan, the methodical giant who composed sequences of short shots and elaborately prepared camera angles that were calculated to give De Mille pictures a tremendous sense of visual pace. These men were "pros" at the peak of their skills, and I wondered why De Mille had bothered to include me at all. I soon found out. He used writers like a general who counted no costs and spared no feelings. Casualties were generally high in wounds of the ego. Some writers were quite literally driven to drink, or into massive epic sulks or sudden resignations. He was always looking for (here comes that awful word again) "freshness."

"You're here to get some poetry into this film, Jesse!"

Poetry or not, I soon learned there was no safety in numbers. We would be assigned to create sections, then write in tandem—one polishing behind another. And somehow neither he nor we were ever satisfied. One might rewrite a scene thirty times and still not have arrived at the mysterious ingredient he was seeking. Perhaps it didn't exist, like the treasure in the fable of the father who kept his sons turning the earth of his orchards in search of it, only to find that the treasure was the orchard itself.

When we reached the "Final Revised Final," our script didn't seem much better than it had been in the beginning. The elephants' labor had produced only a rather stereotyped mouse. But from De Mille's standpoint the finished product was highly successful. And his standpoint was the audiences. We won't mention the critics. Eventually one learned his formula and could produce a script with that peculiar combination of glorious hokum, history, and suspense that he called "drama." No deep delver into psychological motivations of character or subtleties of shading, he aimed at audiences who loved a circus salted with history, in packages larger than life. Given his target and his times, he probably succeeded better than almost anyone. It is easy to snicker and toss off psychiatry-couched phrases about his movies being garish, over-simple, outrageously ornate, yet to date there has been no time when the old De Mille films have not been playing in one or more parts of the world. They succeeded in fulfilling the purpose of their elaborate preparation—they entertained. And that may not be a bad epitaph for dead movie makers.

Bill Pine, our associate producer, had a face like pummeled putty and the air of one who had seen it all. He liked to remind you that he'd been a marine, and a newspaperman of the old school. You could imagine him in the squashed hat, breathing whisky and cynicism in some Chicago bar with Ben Hecht or Papa Hemingway. You knew that for him life had revealed itself in the raw. His toughness was a kind of mystique, the invisible mask through which he smirked at a world that could neither hurt nor delude him. But he was a stout friend to writers, and his shoulder was a useful wailing wall. When he was not soothing our souls with the balm of bourbon, the old newshawk in Bill was constantly unearthing some strange fact of life or history to include in our already overcrowded script.

One day he told the boss that he had discovered the existence of an engine driver who actually might be the last survivor of the original Union Pacific Railroad. De Mille, Bill Pine, and I set off in one of the Paramount chauffeured limousines for Long Beach—an hour's drive from Hollywood. I had prepared a list of questions for the ninety-eight-year-old, for the opportunity to sit at the knee of history is given to few.

Our car drew up before a modest bungalow in the style of the twenties. Bleached bougainvillaea clung to a rotting lattice above the entrance. The smell of drying seaweed and of the nearby oil derricks hung in the scorched air.

We were admitted by a pudding-faced woman of fifty. Grandpa hadn't been at all well this week, she whined. It was this heat wave—and wasn't it simply terrible? It wore a body to death. Well, most everybody except Grandpa. The doctors had said he'd never get past eighty, and here he was, getting on to a hundred and still going. But the heat wouldn't lengthen his life none—and that was for sure!

Her own grandchildren lurked about the parlor, peering at us from behind early Grand Rapids furniture. Their faces bore traces of the dried residue of strawberry ice cream. Flies droned in concert. We were guided to a bedroom.

Here, in mercifully dim light, the old man creaked in a rocker, skeletonized, the skull stretching a mummified vellum of skin. He nodded acceptance of our presence as we were introduced with, "This here's that Ceesil Dee Milley, an' his moom pitcher folks, Grandaddy."

We took chairs as respectfully as if we had entered an undertaking establishment and were seating ourselves around a distinguished corpse. One lamp had a glass multicolored shade, above which was the framed advice: "To your own self be true." The cushion on the bed had a painted silk cover representing Niagara Falls. A yellowing photograph showed the old man's son as a sergeant in World War I.

"Hope you won't mind a few questions, sir," De Mille launched in politely.

"Oh, Grandaddy loves to talk, don't you, Grandaddy?" pudding face assured us. "Only with the heat and all, he's a little under the weather." Her pudgy hand plied a bamboo fan above his whispy white threads of hair.

"I'm alright, Minna," he wheezed quarrelsomely.

"Who wouldn't eat whose dinner?" she accused.

De Mille, growing impatient, cut in, "Perhaps you could tell us in your own words about your experiences during the building of the railroad?"

The old man drew thin lids over almost colorless eyes. "Which one? I seen more than a man can remember. Weren't just one, y'know."

"The Union Pacific," Bill Pine injected.

"That one." His face crinkled into what might have been a smile. The hands, which lay like withered claws across the blanket over his knees, stirred. You could imagine them reaching for the throttle of some funnel-stacked engine. "Yes . . ." he nodded. "That were one. I couldn't tell you what year it were. So many of 'em." The eyes opened—pale silver, like the belly of catfish. "It were thirsty work," he muttered.

"I'll get you a nice lemonade, Grandaddy," pudding face offered.

"Never seen a lemon—west of Saint Loo. Not any place," he insisted as though someone had argued. The silence stretched through dust and fly drone. From the parlor the children could be heard stamping heavily.

"Why don't you just tell these folks some of the stories, Grandaddy—like you used to tell the children?" pudding face wheedled.

"Stories? Weren't no stories."

A crash from the other room followed by bawling voices sent her racing out to restore order. We waited for him to continue.

"No stories," he grumbled. "It was there, and there weren't no stories to it. The damn fools made up the stories after. Damn fools who never was nowhere."

"What about the Indians?" prompted Bill, the interviewing reporter once again.

"Indians? What ones?"

"The Sioux and Cheyenne who attacked the trains."

A curious dry snuffling sound came from his lips, barely recognizable as laughter. "I heard tell some of 'em stretched a rope 'cross the track. Friend of mine drivin' old Seventy-Three—or was it Nineteen? Didn't see nothin' myself. How he told it, was these Indian fellers stretched a rope, thinkin' to stop the train, they bein' on their ponies. This rope, it were made o' buffalo hide or such. Thought they'd catch themselves a train," he chortled. "How he told it, they stretched it across the track, afore the old puffer he were drivin' come along. This engineer seen 'em, but he weren't a'stoppin', no siree! On he come, till the puffer hit smack dab into that rope an' four Indians flew off kickin'! He never stopped to say pleased to meetcha. Course the man were a born liar, so I couldn't swear to it bein' true," he hissed, vastly amused.

"Get that, Jesse?" De Mille sotto voce.

"But did they ever attack *you?*" Bill Pine persisted.

"The Rebs? Nope. War were over by then," he drifted vaguely.

His granddaughter returned about then with a pitcher of iceless lemonade. "Kids left the fridge open again," she complained, passing the tumblers around.

The old man came to life suddenly. "The attack I do recollect, were with General George McClellan. Lincoln wanted him to git a move on—an' jump them Rebs at Winchester. But Mac wouldn't move no place till he had railroads and bridges built behind him, 'case he'd have to hightail it real sudden. I were along there with one o' his engines. Can't recollect which year it were. But nobody done no attackin'. Not then. Mac he had what they called the 'go slows,' " he snorted in amused recollection. "Yes siree—that's how they called h'it. The 'go slows'! Sure way for a man to die in bed!" he chortled in pure delight.

"We were asking about the Indians during the building of the Union Pacific," Bill prompted. From the other room the children's voices suddenly entangled in an angry brawl of argument. The granddaughter left at a run, and a cannonade of slaps soon changed the angry cries to the howls of the punished.

"Injuns never bothered me none," the ancient observed. "Though I heard tell how they done one of our firemen. He were out o' his cab—alongside the track answerin' nature's call. Then right an' sudden he got it. Not even time to pull up his breeches."

"Did they scalp him?" Bill inquired hopefully.

"Nothin' to scalp. He were bald as a jaybird, weren't he?"

A flicked glance at De Mille revealed that his own polished pate had slightly reddened. But he was beaming benevolently over his beaker of warm lemonade.

We waited in this tawdry Mecca for the word of the Prophet, aware of the loudening tick of the clock. That mechanical heartbeat under the layers of heat that filled the room. The old man's lips moved again, tears spilled from undisciplined ducts. "Hell of a place for a man to die in, west of Omaha. That were where nowhere meets up with nothin', like the feller said. But we was too busy to think much on it." His head dropped forward.

We noted with horror that our oracle was sinking into sleep.

"Were you at Ogden, Utah, when they drove the golden spike, sir?" De Mille shouted respectfully.

The engine driver jerked awake. "Where?"

"Ogden! When the Union Pacific joined rails with the Central Pacific?"

"Never seen no gold spike," he muttered peevishly, a child who had been deprived of some special dessert.

De Mille produced one of his gold-plated spikes from a briefcase. "Here's one you can keep, sir."

The old man turned it over and over in his heavily knobbed hands. "Got the look o' gold—but if she were, you wouldn't be handin' it out, I reckon." He gripped the spike tightly. "Feller I knew were at Ogden. Said after they drove in that gold one joinin' the track east to west, they yanked it straight out again. Mebbe they figured the prairie dogs'd take off with it. Like pack rats. When I were a boy in Indiana, I seen their nests. Brass buttons, a copper penny, and a whistle."

We waited for an enlargement on this, but none came.

"What about the end of track?" Bill prompted.

"End of track. Weren't none. Soon as rails went down others kept comin'. No end to it. An' the heat. Not like this here. Never been no heat like that. Nor cold neither when y'got in the mountains . . ."

In the mountains! Yes, the mountains, he had said, always there for him, back behind this soggy afternoon stirred by the hand of a fattening grandchild with a Hawaiian bamboo fan. Him and the Irish and the Chinese. The boasters and the gamblers and liars. Crystal towers of the Sierras—were they always there beneath the bright-caged galaxies and the moaning wind off the long plains? There, like the joke about the timid general, and the wail of an engine's whistle, lonely as a cry in the nights, the nights that ended in sun-red banners over the sage. For them, the distance would only have been distance that could be captured, tamed, and crossed. Another day, another drink. The sun, only a coin to be spent across a bar for whisky. Not an arc light illuminating the long valleys of one's life, the wasteland of years, because one had not yet built a railroad or fought in a war.

This ancient's years had only the simplicity of doing, no fact beyond the crossing of one day into another—over the moat of night. For the ones who had done it, the doing was all! It needed no words, no orators burnishing meanings and images before which men might kneel to their own yesterdays. But had it been enough? Perhaps. They would be the last to know, or have need of knowing. Why all the freezing, sweltering, dying? To what end? Let meanings be woven later on the loom of words. For them, it had been enough to have a coin in the pocket, a cud in the cheek, a tune to pass the midnights, a job that needed doing. And now, an afternoon in a shabby bungalow, where the nearness of death was obscured by small memories of large events.

In days to come—would there be hands again to hold throttles across cold mountains and burning plains? How could we repay so great a debt to the architects of our country?

"Well, I'm not quite sure what we got out of that, Bill," De Mille said in the car that was driving us back to the studio.

"I tried to keep him on the subject, boss," Bill Pine apologized. "He seemed more interested in the Civil War than the Union Pacific."

"That picture's already been made," De Mille snapped.

We cruised back on the well-measured air in our white-walled tires through forests of oil derricks, toward the theatrical sunset above the upward sweep of distant hills that formed the backdrop of Hollywood.

"Did *you* get anything out of it, Jesse?" De Mille asked.

"Yes, I think I did, sir."

"What?" demanded De Mille.

"It's not easy to put into words."

"A feeling of how it was—to have been there?" Bill inquired.

"Not exactly that. Something else. How people who have done something special—or have been a part of it—like building a railroad or fighting a war—lived in a language of action, or they probably couldn't have done it. Not that this is anything you can put on the screen. Or maybe it will be there anyway. I'd just like to write and thank him, and I won't know how to say for what."

De Mille smiled across at me. This was something he could understand. "I think we haven't wasted an afternoon," he said.

Fourteen

THOU SHALT HAVE NO OTHER GODS BEFORE ME! The first of the Ten Commandments certainly applied to De Mille. Neither gods, nor wives, nor home lives, nor personal problems. Our time was his day or night, and we were expected to lunch at the De Mille table every day. This seven-foot unfestive board occupied a central position in the Paramount commissary. Our arrivals were processional. A silence would fall over the vast room of crowded tables as we filed in behind the boss, scripts under our arms, and took our prescribed places. It was never a simple matter of eating. Eating was generally next to impossible! It was like having lunch on stage, difficult to chew and argue at the same time, and we were always having to defend the morning's work. A great recipe for ulcers. De Mille kept a Bible beside his plate. ("The source of all drama—and the lexicon of human behavior, good and bad!")

I was never certain if he had memorized it completely or only selected obscure quotations, "which only the most anti-literate, feeble-minded Bolshevik could fail to know." On his left sat his current field secretary, who was expected to record our exchanges with the speed of light. My place was at his right. Occasionally Jeanie would be invited to join us, and always his associate producer, in those days Bill Pine (later, and to the very end, Henry Wilcoxon). All writers had to be there, often our unit casting director, and almost always our research expert. These last two were expected to read the boss's mind, answer questions before they were asked, and have instant information on almost everything from Babylonian sandal strings in the tenth century B.C. to the current political situation in Albania.

The most trying times for us were when De Mille invited some

VIP guest to join us. Everyone expected the court of De Mille to be turbulent. He did his utmost never to disappoint his audience. The visitor would be treated to a spectacle of slashing argument and bleeding self-respect. New York banker, Washington politico, railroad president, oil tycoon, listened fascinated to question games calculated to make us appear mentally-handicapped baboons clustered about the feet of Socrates. The Boss enjoyed himself vastly, and the guest would leave with something of the feeling of an ancient Roman who had attended blood sports at the Colosseum.

Nights brought their own torments. Customarily he would have current films projected every evening at nine o'clock in his private home theater on De Mille Drive. The walls in this combination office-library bristled with weapons. It had its own entrance and was connected to the main house at the end of a long corridor. We were nightly expected to drive up the winding road, high above old Hollywood, and await the Master in the projection room, which we entered by a rear "tradesman's entrance." Invitations to these evenings were graciously offered but might as well have been royal command performances. Every time I failed to attend, the boss was sure to bring up some pertinent detail at lunch the following day. Hadn't I thought that so-and-so had given an interesting performance? Shouldn't we consider him for the part of such-and-such in our own film? What had I thought of the dialogue? I'd be forced to answer that I'd missed the running.

A sigh that started from his toes. "How sad that Jesse despises the art of film making. He'll avoid showings at all costs to preserve himself from the possibility of increasing his usefulness to our project."

Nobody at the table dared risk more than a wan smile. His turn could be next! All in all, it was safer to abandon private life.

At day's end one would slip out of the studio as soon as the Boss was safely out the gate, race home for dinner, collect a wife, and speed back to the citadel by nine. A wife was always an asset on these occasions, since De Mille turned on instant charm at sight of any female and her presence could prevent a wearying late-night conference.

The problem was always to keep him out of the "kitchen" when you were preparing the first draft. You had to avoid him long enough to get something on paper good enough to survive the countless attacks and rewrites that lay ahead. De Mille was incapable of liking anything that he had not personally destroyed. Certainly he needed to feel a sense of paternalistic participation. When we had been sufficiently impregnated with the quality and spirit of his concepts we were allowed to get on with our job.

Involvement was so essential to him that he could scarcely bear the interruption of weekends taking his writers out of orbit. At least three out of four weekends a month, one was likely to end up in a cloistered corner of his Saturday world, in range of the booted stride and the deceptively friendly inquiry: "How's it going, fellah?"

He seldom spent weekends in the De Mille Drive house. He was either at the ranch or aboard his sailing yacht. This huge plaything was always ready to put out to sea with its superb crew that included the greatest French chef in the West.

But before being invited on a yachting weekend it was likely you'd be initiated to "The Ranch." A place of ritual dictated by personal eccentricity, its customs were as unvarying as a Bourbon Court. One would drive up a deviously winding road in The Little Tajunga—a brush-thick, rattlesnake-crawling area of hot hills. It was burnt dry. The surprise was to round a bend and see a considerable stretch of green lawn fronting a large Swiss chalet. Here he had dammed a small stream into a natural swimming pool. His lawn was cropped by wild deer, who no doubt felt, and were, far safer as guests of De Mille than ranging the mountain sides vulnerable to hunters' guns. Among the grazing deer, magnificent peacocks paraded like silent-film prima donnas, reincarnations of leading ladies strutting for his diversion as featherly gaudy as ever, and as bad-tempered, spoiled, and beautiful. These peacocks, I was told, were occasionally expected to make the supreme sacrifice—peacock tongues for breakfast!

So this was Paradise, as he had named it. Paradise certainly for De Mille, by whose decree no man was ever permitted to bring his wife! He himself never brought his own.

No wives, eh? On this first visit I arrived confident of an orgy in the old movie tradition. The hope was bolstered when I was conducted to one of the many guest rooms and found a purple silk Russian blouse laid out on the bed. The unsmiling manservant informed me that our host expected all his guests to wear such colorful attire to dinner, with evening trousers. Not a bad beginning! No doubt after sunset the place would swarm with girl extras, garlanded nudes like his debauched maidens of the golden-calf sequence in his silent version of *The Ten Commandments*. I envisioned De Mille presiding like a great satyr above a carpet writhing with bare bodies, spilling purple wine over us from his own hospitable hand, applauding our participation in some ornate orgy while the great organ in the living room sent bacchanalian chords throbbing up its pipes thick as elephant penises, and the smoke of incense, sandalwood, and myrrh fogged the beams.

The dream proved only a dream. The only ladies who appeared were our overworked studio secretaries, who had packed typewriters and shorthand books along with their evening gowns. We were here to work, work, and work only, under the surveillance of the Boss, who was never more than a few strides away. He occupied a private bungalow separated from the main house by a short path. It was fabled to be equipped with all the erotic paraphernalia known to man. A mirrored bedroom, cupboards full of women's boots, whips, and the like. I never saw the inside of his bungalow and always suspected these reports of elaborate erotica had been fabricated by wishful thinkers, based on no more substantial evidence than the fact that his films generally included scenes where someone got a fair crack of the whip. His fetishes, if any, were a passionate hatred of red nail polish on actresses and a penchant for small, well-shaped feet. All agents knew this and warned their actresses accordingly.

Still, I harbored expectations when we gathered for dinner attired in our variously-colored Russian blouses. Even in dinner gowns, our secretaries were regrettably businesslike and undebauchable. Someone touched the great organ and an imperious thunder shivered the beams. The door opened. De Mille, attended by one of his own secretaries, arrived in a coal-black silk Russian shirt, a .45 revolver slung from his waist.

"Rattlesnakes," he explained, removing a cape and donning a pair of specially made cocktail gloves. He turned his attention to shaking a cocktail, a feat accomplished to the rhythm of the musical bells on his gloves.

"How is the railroad going, gentlemen?"

"Fine, Mr. De Mille," I ventured.

"Tomorrow I want to go over every word of the new love scene, Jesse."

"I haven't finished, sir. Just started today. It won't be ready, I'm afraid."

The narrow glint of eye points widened to wonder. "Why not? Get up at six o'clock as I do. The mountain air is crystal wine in the morning. You'll write like an angel! I'll be up chopping wood at that hour. Then a swim in the ice-cold pool. By that time you'll have the scene ready. Good God, we've discussed it enough, haven't we?

You've got all the notes and a houseful of charming ladies to type copies for you."

I nodded, accepting the cocktail. It was very powerful. Five more, plus a few glasses of California wine—and he seemed transmuted into a mysterious superhost. My chair had suddenly developed the lurch and pitch of a running camel. I held on, hoping not to be sick.

"A little game for your diversion, gentlemen," he announced with mellow grandeur.

Ah, thought I, now for the naked girl out of the pie. Bobbing breasts, nipples dusted with gold.

He gestured to the butler. "Let us have a cordial for the eye, Albert!"

The words were promising. We waited. Moments later the butler returned bearing trays. They contained an array of dazzling, multicolored, flashing, unmounted jewels.

"From the De Mille collection," he announced. "Choose the most valuable stone on the trays. Come, gentlemen, we are all connoisseurs of beauty here. Which is it? Diamond, sapphire, emerald, ruby, pearl? Your choice! Now who would care to make the first guess?"

Through the thickness of inebriation I calculated that this game was childishly obvious. The large stones would be beautiful fakes, the small ones real. One would be expected to select the largest, flashiest. I took up an unimpressive green stone. No doubt a rare emerald. "This!"

"A peridot. Quite worthless," he laughed. "Keep it if you like, Jesse. But that large flashing ember beside it is one of the finest rubies ever mined in Ceylon. Worth the treasure chests of Croesus."

Everyone laughed. At me, at the idea of the priceless gems we fingered like marbles. I had the uncomfortable feeling that our laughter, this brief intimacy, the good fellowship of the night, might in the morning be remembered to our sorrow. But the feeling was fleeting. We were all a bit drugged with amplitude and gem-handling. Every wine he'd served had its special provenance. In this rarefied atmosphere, in our brilliant satin shirts, one began to feel larger than life and dangerously overconfident. Particularly after downing Napoleon Brandy from a bottle dated 1812.

"Y'know what's wrong with your pictures, Mr. De Mille?" I offered helpfully.

"Tell me, Jesse," he said, leaning back in his chair, a black prince among his knights.

"Too much muchness. Overcrowded. No straight lines."

He beamed tolerance, amusement.

Jack Cunningham pressed a gentle elbow into my orange-silk-shirted rib-cage. He had been to Paradise before, and knew the pitfalls. The well-laid traps. But I was in no condition for precaution.

"Simplicity!" I heard myself bray pompously. "It can be more effective—I mean affecting—than all the cluttered baroque architecture of overplotted relationships, and overcluttered clanvases . . . I mean screens."

"Go on . . ." The De Mille smile had become glacial.

"What Jesse means . . ." Someone had begun a life-saving operation which I quickly thwarted.

"I know what I mean—and I mean what I know." What verbal escrime! "And that is what I know I mean—that you can't see the forest for the trees!"

He weighed this on scales of respectful consideration. The smile glittered again. "Can't we, Jesse?"

"We can't. Indeed we can't! Simplishity!" I heard a fist hit the table, overemphasizing the point. Mine. It happily avoided breaking anything, but some of the gems leaped precariously above their red-velvet-lined trays. "Yes, the trees. Our script is getting to be like a jungle. There's so much happening—you can't find your way forward. Don't know where you are! What we should try for—to find a clean straight line—and follow it. Like the railmen followed . . ." I couldn't remember what they followed. "And the Magi. One star, sir. Not the whole damned Milky Way . . ."

Someone had arms around me. No nude extra girl. C. Gardner Sullivan was walking me under the sharp pinfire brightness of the California heavens. The lawn swayed gently underfoot. The air was wonderfully fresh! Fresh? Well, that was what always was wanted. Freshness. Ideas. Air! A symphony of crickets throbbed from the hills. I would have fallen if he hadn't held me.

"Where are we, Gardner?"

"Paradise."

"Christ."

"You won't have been the first," he comforted.

"Somebody should've put a foot in my mouth."

"You did," he chuckled.

"Will I be fired? I mean, for blasphemy or something?"

He considered it carefully, shook his head. "That would be too easy."

The dipper descended toward us in a roar of wind from the towers of the night. It would not have been surprising if it had bounced off my skull, but when you'd been drunk enough to tell God how to run His universe you didn't worry any more. It would have been useless in all events.

Next day I fought Chinese New Years in my head, hanging over the typewriter like the rail of a ship. The scene resisted every attempt to get itself written. In the end, I put some pieces together, worked out a few bridges of dialogue and hoped for the best, awaiting the footfalls that were not long in bringing De Mille to the door. He carried an axe over his shoulder, his face rosy, sweat-beaded. A lively, bustling woman in her forties trotted at his heels, notebook in hand. Gladys Rosson, his personal secretary, had been with him longest and followed his many business and financial interests outside of the film world.

They scrutinized me as I rose unsteadily from my typewriter.

"Ah, Jesse, finished with the scene? Worked all night, did you?"

"No sir. But I did get an early start. I've got a first draft." You were careful never to tell De Mille anything was finished. Not before he'd put his changes into it.

"May I?" he beamed benevolently, reaching a hand for the sheaf of papers.

I gave them to him. He set down the axe and seated himself to read. Habitually he read slowly. A heavy weight of morning heat filled the room. Insect noises crackled from the hills. One might even discern the hard metallic buzz, the sun-baked death warning of a rattlesnake somewhere in the distance. Neither Gladys nor I dared speak. De Mille finished and reread without a word. At length he sighed deeply, and put down the pages.

"I'm afraid, Jesse, you've lost the forest for the trees. Would 'cluttered' be the word? Overcrowded? No straight line of progression like the railroader?" His tone was unusually gentle, a silken whip. "I suggest you give it a bit more clear thought, meanwhile we'll let Gardner have a try, shall we? You'd better spend the day and evening reading some of Jeanie's old scripts. It might help you to a better grasp of how we write a De Mille screen drama." He inclined his head slightly, like an actor who had found a perfect curtain line, and made his exit, axe on shoulder, followed by the initiated Gladys Rosson, who knew a hack from a handsaw.

Fifteen

From the inception of my first De Mille assignment one aspect of the writing haunted my life: the invention of bits of "business" (sometimes referred to in contemporary showbizese as "schticks"). Business, the great director explained, was something for the actors to do with their hands while they spoke their lines. It could even replace lines, as it had in silent films. A character is involved in a dispute. Furiously he plunges his knife into a barrelhead instead of his enemy's barrel chest. He doesn't have to say, "I'm gonna get you, you son of a bitch"; the quivering knife has said it for him.

Several men are sitting on a porch in a western street when a stranger rides slowly past. One of the men spits contemptuously. An attitude revealed. Or suppose our spitter fashions a bit of twine into a hangman's noose and shows it to a henchman? His henchman mounts casually (in Westerns all moves are casual until they become sanguinary), sets out in the direction taken by the passing stranger. Business used to advance story.

Some business enhances character. Nervous habits or personal idiosyncrasies can tell much. A girl constantly smoothing her hair. A man always checking to see that his fly is buttoned before entering a room. Little clues to personality. Timelessly indulged, timelessly noted. Probably the earliest example of good business was Pontius Pilate's endless hand-washings after the trial of Christ, a habit also indulged in by Lady Macbeth. The classic film example is George Raft's repeated tossing of a coin throughout *Scarface*. He tossed it even during his dying fall. It indicated a cavalier noncaring attitude to life and, finally, death.

Good actors generally devise their own bits of business as they create their characters. Some directors invent it for them. But De Mille didn't let his writers off that easily. I was expected to think up and describe a unique and appropriate bit of business, a personal idiosyncrasy, for practically every character in the film.

Easy? Of course. One might think up a dozen small actions for actors in a few minutes, but to satisfy De Mille was something else. He simply wouldn't buy anything that he had ever seen used before. Since desperation is often the father of nonsense, his attitude gave birth to some pretty desperate suggestions.

The one character in *Union Pacific* that gave me the greatest difficulty was the gambler-heavy to be played by Brian Donlevy. With meticulous obsession De Mille would begin and end almost every script conference with the question, "Well, Jesse, what does Donlevy do with his hands?"

I don't know why this particular problem had become exclusively mine, but the other writers were more than pleased that it had. I tried everything from having him pick his teeth with his Bowie knife to bending gold coins between his powerful fingers. I tried having him build houses of cards which were always knocked down to punctuate some threat or other. The suggestions grew more puerile as panic increased. Everything I could think of, De Mille had either seen already or didn't want to see. No, I must find something "fresh"! But since, in his words, I hated films too much ever to see one, I couldn't be expected to get any ideas from them—old or new, could I?

The never-joyous lunch-table was becoming a perpetual bloodbath for me, to the vast exhilaration of my colleagues.

"Jesse refuses to tell me what Brian Donlevy does with his hands, gentlemen! Don't you find that rather selfish on his part?" (Polite reaction of suppressed mirth.) "And, as the starting date of the film approaches, I find myself increasingly curious. But I suppose you will say, 'Oh, let the director think up everything. Write a few "hellos" and "let's gos" in a scene, and let the old man find some way to keep the audience in their seats.' Well, damn it, I happen to believe that good screenwriting means finding ways to make an actor REAL on the screen! Not with a lot of talk—but with actions large and small—or I might as well hire a few clothing-store dummies and dub in the lines!"

And then, with total change of pace, he would switch from anger to pathos, his voice almost pleading. "Is it too much to ask that you find something, anything that I can photograph—for Donlevy to do with his hands?"

Rude possibilities suggested themselves. If De Mille asked me just once more, I might just for once tell him what Donlevy could do with his hands! Picture it on the big screen—Donlevy, the terror of the dance hall girls, the fastest grope in the West! That would keep a few fingers busy. Oh, the possibilities were infinite. What could a virile "heavy" do with his hands? A true-life incident came to mind. The famous actor Lee Tracy had once from his hotel window in Mexico City used his to open his fly and let fly on a pack of peons parading for Independence Day. But I was enjoying the refreshing experience of being on steady salary month after month. Self-preservation makes cowards of us all.

De Mille even took to phoning me at home in the small hours of the night. No hellos. No apologies for having awakened me. Only the cold nocturnal ear-stab of the ringing phone and the rasping voice, slightly nasal, insisting, demanding, "What does Donlevy do with his hands?" He scrawled notes to me on the subject, one decorated with a threatening skull and bones beneath which he wrote: "Business is what actors do that I can photograph! *Not* what they think or feel!"

One early morning the phone jangled me awake. The familiar voice. "Have you got it yet?"

"I may have, Mr. De Mille," I muttered dopily. "He smokes a cigar."

"What . . . ?" His voice clawed the night.

"He fondles a drink," I added.

"*What* . . . ?" he roared again through the receiver. "Every cheap heavy that ever walked on a screen always does one or the other!"

"My idea is that Donlevy does both."

"Both . . . ? Jesse, are you drunk or insane?" The absurdity of his persistence had driven me beyond caution. I was improvising and I no longer cared. "Both," I reiterated. "He takes a cigar from his pocket, dips the bitten-off end into a shot glass of whisky. Then . . . then he puts the whisky-soaked end in his mouth. And lights the tip!"

"Now why would he do that?" the Boss demanded.

"Well," I faltered weakly, "that way he can smoke and drink at the same time."

There was a pause like eternity.

"I've never seen anyone do that—on or off the screen," he said with cold finality.

"That would make it 'fresh' wouldn't it, sir?"

"Let's see . . ." You could almost hear him weighing it. "He takes out cigar. A beat. Speaks. Dips. Another pause. Cigar goes into mouth . . ." Then silence at the other end of the phone.

I plunged on, beginning to sense victory, "And once this habit's been established you can start on a close-up of the cigar dipping into the glass and you'll know who it is *before* you pull back and reveal him. Also . . ."

"Yes . . . ?" He waited.

"It's erotic."

"What?" A new interest infiltrated the tone.

"It has connotations. I mean, a faintly phallic suggestion the censors would be sure to miss. But it would be there for the smart members of the audience. You'd be suggesting the stallion in this guy, always looking for the chance to—to dip his cigar."

The chance to bamboozle a censor was always irresistible. "Good, Jesse! Put it in the script at once! We'll try it!" he hissed ecstatically.

Relief swept over me like a soothing balm. I could slide back into sleep, knowing there would be no more phone calls to dredge crazy notions from a tired mind.

"Great, Mr. De Mille," I mumbled. "See you tomorrow."

"Yes, Jesse, tomorrow and tomorrow. By the way, I want you to come up with a new kind of fight for Joel McCrea and the bruiser who leads the strikers. Something with some freshness to it, like that cigar dipping! Bring me an absolutely original fight by ten o'clock tomorrow morning. Good night!"

Good night? My bedside clock said almost two A.M. Good it wouldn't be.

Sixteen

Iron Eyes Cody, our Indian technical adviser, was getting busier every day. He was training Akim Tamiroff to use a bullwhip, Lynne Overman to throw a knife, Joel McCrea and Bob Preston to make fast draws without shooting off their toes, and Indian extras to use bows and arrows.

Filming had finally begun. Iron Eyes and I were prowling through the scene of the Indian attack, scheduled to be shot the following day. In accordance with our script, flat- and freight-cars had been carefully derailed. Tomorrow they would be consumed in smoke and flame and the attacking fury of real and bogus Sioux. Amid the carload of impedimenta that the railroad was supposed to be toting west, I spotted a ridiculous prop. A wooden cigar-store Indian! I'm not sure why so many of the nineteenth-century tobacconists sported carved Indians in front of their shops—perhaps it was a tribute to those neighborly redskins who introduced Sir Walter Raleigh to the pleasures of the weed—but the carved, life-sized effigy of a brave brandishing his tomahawk gave me an idea. When Iron Eyes led his ethnic allies in the looting of the boxcar, why not have him come face to face with this wooden Indian?

We tried it, and the confrontation was hilarious. Iron Eyes' look of bewilderment on meeting the wooden stare was one of the funniest reactions I've ever seen. We demonstrated for De Mille, and it put the Boss in a glorious humor all day. He bestowed upon us both his highest award: a mint commemorative silver fifty-cent piece of the Virginia Dare issue. It was said De Mille had bought up the entire issue so that the gift of these rare coins was somehow equivalent to being handed a gold bar. I received several during my years with De Mille. Then, years later in a lean period, I took them to a coin store.

Movie queen greets Swedish royalty, 1927-style. Pola Negri (second from right), on the set of *Hotel Imperial*, stands next to Crown Prince Gustav of Sweden. Crown Princess Louise is on the left beside her compatriot, the film's director, Mauritz Stiller. On the right is studio manager Milton Hoffman. *(Courtesy of Pola Negri)*

A slightly posed-looking on-set shot of studio bigwigs. The men are Jesse L. Lasky, Milton Hoffman again, Hector Turnbull (Lasky's brother-in-law and story editor) and Ben (B. P.) Schulberg, general manager of Famous Players-Lasky's West Coast studio. The young ladies in 1929's latest fashions are Lois Wilson and Betty Bronson. *(British Film Institute)*

Beaming with maternal pride, Jesse L. Lasky's mother at a premiere with her son and his friends Doug Fairbanks and Mary Pickford. *(Author's collection)*

One of those fabulous open-air parties at the Lasky beach house —the moon was only a tin one, but the stars were genuine enough. Possessors of outstanding eyesight might spot Philip Holmes, up-and-coming young actor, with Fay Wray of *King Kong* fame; screenwriter John Monk Saunders dancing with Bess Lasky; Jesse, Jr., dancing with starlet Doris Hill; on the far right, Doug Fairbanks, Sr., with Jesse Lasky, Sr.; and Gene Raymond, songstress Jeanette MacDonald, romantic lead Ricardo Cortez, director Frank Tuttle, etcetera, etcetera . . .

. . . and inside the beach house Bess Lasky collected house-guests and antique furniture. *(Author's collection)*

Stag corner (almost) at a Hollywood fiesta. Left to right: Maurice Chevalier, Leslie Howard, two unidentified gentlemen, studio manager Mike Levy, Elsa Maxwell (with mustache), comedienne Polly Moran, Jimmy Durante, Jesse L. Lasky, Fredric March, Frank Borzage and, amazingly mustacheless, Groucho Marx. *(Author's collection)*

Nice, 1928: The suave gentleman in the homburg is French film producer and studio owner Édouard Corniglion-Molinier, later air minister of France; on the other side of the Laskys, Rex Ingram, the great silent-film director. *(Author's collection)*

Another happily posed studio group; this time with Lasky are Spencer Tracy, Colleen Moore, and William Howard, respectively stars and director of the just-completed *The Power and the Glory* (1932). *(Courtesy of Colleen Moore)*

Foujita sketched Jesse, Jr., hatless–inexplicably, he saw him as a cowboy and added the hat afterward.

Adolph Zukor, the czar of Paramount, on a tour of the European exchanges with his first vice-president at this lunch given for the heads of the foreign offices. Jesse, Jr., is seated at far left; standing second from left is his father's secretary, Randy Rogers; Al Kaufman is seated at far right. *(Author's collection)*

Jean Harlow and Sid Grauman. No important star could afford not to have left a footprint in the cement outside Grauman's Chinese Theatre. . . .

. . . or indeed not to stay on the right side of Louella Parsons. *(British Film Institute)*

Director and stars of *Secret Agent*, for which writer Jesse Lasky, Jr., wrote the American dialogue during his brief prewar stay in Britain. Left to right, Madeleine Carroll, Peter Lorre, Alfred Hitchcock, Robert Young (1936). *(British Film Institute)*

Happy birthday, Jeanie MacPherson! The actress-turned-scribe with the Boss, a neophyte, and an arbitrarily selected number of candles. *(De Mille Foundation)*

The treasury must have held out on the Boss; the coins' value proved mainly sentimental.

Those two super comedians, Akim Tamiroff and Lynne Overman, were perfect foils for each other, as De Mille had discovered in *The Buccaneer:* Overman, a lean, parchment-dry, nasal-voiced Yankee, who delivered his lines with a rasping twang and sublime timing; and Tamiroff, the burly Russian, an exotic bear of a man with a basso-profundo growl like spring thunder. They could stretch a double-take like the last day of summer. But they were born competitors who naturally fought for every second of attention. So that's how we wrote them in the script—friendly rivals, each trying to get the last word, to milk the last laugh in every scene. We wrote Lynne Overman as the dirty, buckskinned Yankee scout, Tamiroff as a flamboyant Mexican. The rushes were hilarious. Then one day the beautiful friendship of the two artists almost came to an abrupt end.

The scene called for the pair to walk the length of a railroad car, each topping the other with bits of business as they went. All went sublimely until they reached the narrow door through which they must exit into the next car. Through numerous rehearsals each of them tried desperately to be last through that door, to steal the scene with a final roll of the eyes or gesture of the hand. For such masters of mime it required hardly more than a twitch or a shrug to wipe out the man who had exited first.

Of course this jockeying at the door threw the scene into chaos. Funny as it was, it spoiled the pace of the sequence. Yet neither man was prepared to lose that final exit.

Usually, with important performers De Mille avoided direct criticism. He was always more occupied with inanimate details: props, positioning of extras, etc. "I'm too old to teach actors how to act," he would say, when some flaw in a reading was pointed out to him. But this time he was growing understandably irritated with his pair of comics, and by the sixth rehearsal it was ceasing to be funny.

"Akim!" he called angrily, "I want you to exit first! You got that? Let Lynne follow you!"

"But Mr. De Mille, it will give me a weakness of character!" the raucous Russian complained.

De Mille became icily firm. "I'm not wasting any more time on that damned exit. You'll do it my way! And no more rehearsals. Now let's line up and shoot the scene before I start shooting my actors!"

Akim convulsed as though a knife had been buried in his heart. Lynne Overman's pursed lips suddenly seemed to have swallowed a canary. With the mere hoist of an eyebrow he could now demolish his helpless rival.

While the stand-ins took over and the shot was lined up, the two men made final repairs to makeup and costume. By now they were no longer speaking to each other. At last they took their places.

"All right, gentlemen. I want to get this in ONE take! And no three-ring circus at the exit, please. Akim, off first. Then you get right out after him, Lynne. Got it?"

They had. The ritual of starting the cameras.

"Lights."

"We're rolling."

"Scene numbers." Clapperboard man in.

"*Union Pacific*—scene 96—take one . . ."

"Action."

With a sense of impending trouble, we all crowded as near as we could behind the camera line—waiting.

It started perfectly. The pair sauntered down the car, making the most of every moment, obedient to the actions laid out in the script—and reached the narrow Pullman car door. We held our breaths. But Akim knew when an order had to be obeyed. He stepped around Lynne Overman, ready to go off first. Then in the final instant an incredible thing happened. As he looked back at Lynne (and over his shoulders at the camera) Akim's huge ears suddenly waggled like a pair of wings. Then, completely deadpan, he obediently made the required exit. The effect was sidesplitting. Overman was dead as a herring. The whole company howled, choked, wept with laughter. Even De Mille could not suppress a chuckle.

The ingenious Tamiroff had simply rigged threads to a pair of false ears; the scissors of our film editor, Anne Bauchens, removed the moment—to save saga from becoming slapstick.

Since it was my first De Mille picture I had not realized that harrowing happenings were indigenous to his filmings. About halfway through, in the most difficult part of the action sequences, the Boss was suddenly afflicted with prostate trouble, and had to undergo what was in those days a very serious operation. It looked as though the film would be stopped, canceled, or indefinitely postponed. Aside from second-unit action long shots being filmed in Utah by Arthur Rossen, De Mille would not consider allowing any man to take over for him. Not while he still held the breath of life!

Production was shut down while all waited uncertainly for hospital bulletins. They weren't too encouraging. It was said that the boss languished in terrible pain and was allowed to see no one but his wife, Constance, that gracious and gentle lady generally far separated from his working life.

Then one morning an ambulance nosed through Paramount Studio's De Mille Gate and word spread around the lot: The Boss had returned. We hastened to the set to witness a display of sheer guts and stamina. His face a gaunt mask, De Mille, still aboard his litter, was strapped to the platform on the great camera boom. Packed in ice, the invalid could be raised on this contraption, lowered, or whisked to any part of the set in seconds! A self-propelled Nemesis awesomely swooping about. Now there was no escape from his watchful eye, no safe hiding place! I might be chatting with some pretty actress behind a wind machine when suddenly the angry invalid would be whipped through the air, descending in his ice-packed cradle to hiss in my ear, "Why are you wasting my time, Jesse? Get those crowd lines ready, for heaven's sake! You're supposed to be a writer. There are laws in this state against taking money under false pretences!"

Many times on later films it seemed to me that De Mille's rages must be pure self-indulgence, even calculated cruelty; on this occasion I and everyone else forgave him his irascibility. If ever a man deserved a medal for courage it was De Mille as he directed from his mobile bed of pain.

For me it was only the beginning of a relationship, strange, productive, remunerative, sometimes inspiring, other times soul-destroying and mind-boggling. Yet while he lived I would seldom manage to escape what he liked to refer to as "the bondage of great deeds." A kind of bondage, perhaps, but no great deeds that come to mind—at least from me!

One evening toward the end of the thirties, Katherine De Mille, who had once shared the educational glories of the Hollywood School for Girls with me, phoned to say she wanted to bring someone over to meet me. Actually, I'd met him before in brief encounters on the sets of *Union Pacific*. But any encounter, however brief, with Anthony Quinn—playing any part, however small—would have revealed that he had a formidable future. The young Tony was a walking eruption of talent with cougar grace and features like carvings on an Aztec pyramid, all blended with Irish charm and the magnetism of the born actor.

For Tony acting was more than a career drive; it was part of his insatiable appetite for living. Nobody ever seemed more ready and equipped to devour, swallow, and digest life and art. There appeared to be nothing that didn't interest him, nothing he could not absorb to the enrichment of that sponge of a mind, widening, deepening that exuberant personality, increasing his range as an actor and his fascination as a man. It also made him vulnerable to a plunge into one failure that I shared with him—but we'll come to that later.

Tony could read six books of verse in a night and memorize much of the content. As a performer he could scarcely make a wrong move, but as a prospective husband for De Mille's beloved adopted daughter, it seemed unlikely that any move could be right. Like most mighty, self-made men De Mille would wish to conjoin his children to powerful dynasties. John De Mille, also an adopted child, was at that time married to a member of the Giannini banking family. De Mille had helped the Bank of America keep on its financial feet during the slippery Depression days. Now, had he needed it, he could have raised a few million dollars by a telephone call. His own daughter, the attractive Cecilia, horsewoman and leader of local society, was then married to a son of the president of the Union Pacific Railroad. By Hollywood standards the De Milles were a royal family, even admissible to such theatrically unpolluted precincts as the Los Angeles Country Club, where the chosen were never the "Chosen People" and film folk were strictly verboten! The De Milles and the Harold Lloyds were among the few who had bridged the social gulf between old Los Angeles and Hollywood. Quite fitting, since one of his ancestors had spanned the English Channel with William the Conqueror.

As a prospective son-in-law Tony Quinn had two strikes against him. Not only was he an actor (a suspect breed in the De Mille private world); far worse, he was a Democrat. But the director general found in Katherine a will as stubborn as his own, or perhaps he shared the general concept that few Hollywood marriages, his own excepted, were fashioned to endure a lifetime anyway. At any rate, he finally agreed to Katherine's marriage.

When told that the newlyweds had accepted the gift of a splendid home on De Mille Drive, situated on a slightly lower level than De Mille's own rambling palazzo, John Barrymore sonorously declaimed: "And every night, Tony, your father-in-law will step out on his balcony, and urinate upon you—a golden stream in the moonlight!"

But as his incomparable son-in-law surged onward and upward in his art, De Mille's respect rose with him.

Tony's background and memories of the Depression could hardly have left him without a core of social consciousness, intensified during his years of work with the Actor's Lab, where he studied and eventually taught.

It is curious to consider that Roosevelt's Works Progress Administration created jobs in the Depression years not only for blue-collar workers but for artists, giving them a security unknown since Renaissance Italy. In New York the theater had a rebirth of vitality, and in this atmosphere of Art for Art's Sake—and getting paid for it—the Actors' Studio grew and flourished. A new generation of players was inoculated by Lee Strasberg with "Method" acting. "The Method," as is well known, imposes a profound self-analysis upon the actor in which he digs deeply into himself and the character he portrays, seeking innermost motivations beyond superficial aspects.

Everyone was on a "dig"—the actors into themselves, the writers into the hard realities of working-class drama in the footsteps of the newly risen prophet Clifford Odets. The theater of entertainment was becoming the theater of significance; the cradle for the antihero was beginning to rock. Even in folly-famed Hollywood, film folk would find things to be very serious about, and no one could be more intensely serious about something serious than my friend Tony Quinn. He told me this story himself:

Raoul Walsh was directing the picture. This rugged veteran, who had once been an assistant to D. W. Griffith, packed his films with action and broad comedy. He didn't want to know about such subtleties as psychological nuances and profound probings into character. His target was the solar plexus rather than the cerebellum, and his films never missed the mark. *What Price Glory?*, *High Sierra*, *They Drive by Night*, *They Died with Their Boots On* were typical of his hard-hitting style.

Walsh enjoyed the useful distinction of looking as tough as he was. His craggy face was enhanced by a black eyepatch which he had acquired on a drive to a desert location from a jackrabbit who had leaped through Walsh's windshield. It gave him an image somewhere between Long John Silver and Moshe Dayan. Walsh shuffled about his sets like a boxer looking for a chance to deliver a Sunday punch, his one good eye missing no possibility that could embellish the action of his movie.

Tony, as I recall, was playing an Italian—a stock hood, a small part, requiring little more than opening a door and entering a room. Walsh was looking through the viewfinder, his eye trained on the star, when Tony approached him. Tony—at the "Who am I?" stage of his Strasbergian self-analysis, started bombarding Walsh with questions. How did he relate to these people in the room? What was the background of his character? Where had he lived as a small child? Who were his parents? Were they happily married—or married at all? What were his drives, motivations, obsessions, fears?

Raoul listened patiently, blinked, lit a cigarette. Then the gravel baritone grunted, "I tell you what you do, Tony. You just open that door, walk in that room, and give 'em the garlic—right in the puss!"

This, Tony assured me, gave him exactly what he needed to know. No complications. All basic. Visual. Direct. Tony followed the suggestion, and some of these doors he subsequently opened led to Academy Awards.

De Mille used to love to quote somebody (perhaps Shaw?) with the line "An actress is something more than a woman, but an actor is something less than a man." He believed it no more deeply than his other verbal extravagances, useful only for the demolition of egos. In Tony's case he came to consider the actor an extension of the man. To writers he was generally less generous. I once heard him observe, "Authors, authors, everywhere—and not a scribe to think!"

Seventeen

ONE DAY IN 1939, I was called into the Boss's office to find him studying the Gettysburg Address. It was not impossible that he was going to ask me to rewrite it. We had just finished *Union Pacific* and he was looking for a new subject. "Sit down, Jesse," he snapped, absorbing the Great Emancipator's words through an enormous magnifying glass. "What do you know of American history?"

"Well, sir, it just happens that I–"

"I'm running a film at the house tonight. *Ruggles of Red Gap.* I suggest you attend."

I couldn't quite see the tie-up. "I've seen it, Mr. De Mille."

"How many times?" he demanded.

"Once," I admitted, all chance of escape destroyed.

"And what would you say was the most memorable moment in the picture?" He set down the Gettysburg document on the cluttered desk.

"Charles Laughton speaking the Gettysburg Address?" I offered smugly.

He grunted, almost displeased that I had managed the right guess.

"May I ask the connection, sir?"

He leaned back in his chair. "I have agreed to prepare a documentary for the New York World's Fair. It's to be the official exhibition of the Motion Picture Industry. I'm calling it *Land of Liberty*."

"World's Fair . . . That doesn't give us much time. When do you start filming?"

"I don't. We'll use stock film from every picture dealing with American history ever produced anywhere by anyone on earth! Jeanie will select footage and write a narration."

"Sounds like a sizable assignment."

He nodded. "Jeanie's asked for you to work with her. I agreed."

Nobody had felt it necessary to ask me.

"Anne Bauchens has already started a rough assembly of film clips. We've got everything but time. I want the history of the United States, stressing the theme of liberty, on my desk by five o'clock today."

"The whole history?" I was properly staggered.

"Jeanie's got all the books you'll need. Get at it. Dr. Shotwell, our technical adviser, arrives on Monday. Chair of History at Columbia University, and author of *The History of History*. That means he knows nothing about drama—so don't let him influence you!"

In the end Laughton's rendering of the Gettysburg Address became the high point of the film; De Mille used the soundtrack from *Ruggles of Red Gap* over shots of the Gettysburg cemetery.

Laughton had always been a favorite of De Mille's, ever since my father first signed him from the London stage, overriding objections that he was not the leading-man type.

In 1932 De Mille had cast him as Nero in *The Sign of the Cross.* When the director arrived on his lavish set of Ancient Rome on the eve of its burning, he found Laughton in toga and laurel wreath spouting Latin verse to the twanging of a prop lyre. Worried that the sardonic Briton was not taking a De Millian moment seriously enough, the Boss delivered one of his spontaneous discourses on the impermanence of man's mightiest works when pitted against divine power, as demonstrated throughout the debacles of history. Gray was wrong, he suggested. The paths of glory led not to the grave, but through the grave to eternity! He terminated with this inspiring conclusion: "When I stand among the ruins of Ancient Rome—so perishable—I cannot help but feel how much we need our faith. Faith is man's only strength. With it I feel that God is in me, and I am in God!"

Laughton weighed this with deceptive gravity. Then the lips pursed out of their famed pout to observe, "Really? How cozy!" De Mille admired him ever since—but never used him again.

Jeanie and I were busy assembling film with the help of Anne Bauchens. The veteran lady film editor was not happy, but she clearly felt it was not her place to voice criticisms. Would that she had, instead of remaining silent as we beavered away, selecting footage to illustrate our narration. In fact Jeanie and I, the perfectly matched combination of crusty age and youthful overconfidence, were committing the most basic of errors. We had written our narration in its entirety before seeing a foot of film, and, worse still, instead of letting the words support the pictures we were forcing the pictures to duplicate the words.

We screened battle scenes until our eyes were ready to fall out, and gorged ourselves on cliché vignettes of immigrants hoisting their eyes to the Statue of Liberty as they sailed into New York harbor, escaping from the oppressions and pogroms of the Old World.

We drooled over film scenes of succulent, spit-turned wild turkeys, supplied to pilgrims by obliging redskins who would eventually be rewarded by decimation. We wrote poems over shots of roaring crucibles of molten steel that would swell the bellies of American industry, and sang ourselves silly over seawide stretches of wind-caressed wheat. We hosannaed the deeds and inventions of American science, the masterworks and the miracles, always harking back to the sagacious founding fathers in their wigs and knee breeches, spelling out man's inalienable rights. After an inevitable pause at Niagara Falls, we plunged westward to wallow in the scenic celebrity of the Grand Canyon, then southeast to the Lincoln and Jefferson memorials, always chewing the cud of liberty among the sacred cows in the pastures of patriotism. Dr. Shotwell, meanwhile, combed our turgid pasages for factual inaccuracies. We thought we were building a monument to history. We were fat for the kill.

De Mille arrived at the projection room to view the rough assembly of film, beaming with benevolence. Our confidence soared. Jeanie started reading the narration. But she had scarcely got through three speeches when he suddenly rose from his seat and began to stride up and down the aisle. At first I thought he was in some kind of pain, for his face writhed in pure torment. But the show must go on, and we continued to read our ringing speeches against the heroic tableaux on the screen.

Finally he slumped into a seat, snarling an order at the projectionist which brought the film to a flickering halt. Lights came on. We sat in silence.

"*You* may call this *Land of Liberty*. I call it the most rank exhibition of amateurishness and monumental stupidity I have yet seen on this earth!"

I enviously watched the blissfully unconcerned acrobatics of a large fly.

"You fellahs have reduced the story of America to a lunatic's valentine accompanied by greeting-card drivel. You are either totally insane, or dedicated to the destruction of my reputation as a film maker. I should like an explanation!"

Jeanie, attired in red, white, and blue for the occasion, lifted her voice from a sniffle to a wail. "You have my resignation, Mr. De Mille!" She rose like an offended flag and flounced off toward the door. In a voice like thunder, De Mille ordered her to sit down. She complied meekly.

I was, meanwhile, suffering from the sudden realization that I couldn't truly disagree with him. Sometimes it happens that something which one has labored too hard to create needs the perspective of a second pair of eyes to make one see it in its true light. Too often the creator falls in love with the sound of his own voice, the form of his own work, the choice of his own words. But his passion can be cooled in an instant when the veil is lifted by a judicious critic.

Dr. Shotwell was exhibiting a superb detachment. After all, his responsibility was only for accuracy of content. But De Mille was playing no favorites. His barrage caught the innocent bystander.

"At least from you, Doctor, I expected some vestige of reality!"

The iron-gray academic descended from his cloud. "I can assure you, Mr. De Mille, that the material covered in the narration is quite authentic. I believe, within its limitations, it offers valid and acceptable historical concepts."

"And I assure you, sir, and I think most audiences will share my view," said De Mille, "that I would prefer to be wrong and dramatic to right and dull!"

Dr. Shotwell snapped shut his briefcase. "Then, Mr. De Mille, I can't be of further use here. My responsibility is to be right—*if* dull."

De Mille smiled for the first time. "I'd say, from reading your works, that history was never dull. However, you didn't have the help of this lady and gentleman. Now, I suggest we strip ourselves of prides and preconceptions and get on with the job. We've all insulted each other, which isn't a bad start for a good working relationship. I want to make a documentary that will excite and thrill, not just the people who love history, but the people who hate it! I don't want to violate truth, but I don't want to employ it to put audiences to sleep. So if *you'll* keep us accurate, Dr. Shotwell, *I'll* try to restrain our writers from gilding every lily."

He extended a hand to the historian, who accepted it. Jeanie huffed and puffed, but she was too old a pro to blow the house down. And

De Mille, always at his best when loyalty was the issue, did not change writers in midstream. He started Jeanie and me back at the beginning, and this time kept a strong supervisory hand on the reins. Whatever else audiences came away feeling about *Land of Liberty*, I don't think they found it dull.

Eighteen

IF YOU HAPPEN not to be Canadian you could live out your life without ever having heard of Riel and his Rebellion of 1885, but if you were a screenwriter in that torrid Hollywood summertime of 1939, hammering your head in search of a suitably De Millian epic about the Northwest Mounted Police, a stumble upon the Riel Rebellion would have been on a par with Columbus' first sight of America.

The problem with the subject of *Northwest Mounted Police* had been to find something more spectacular than the usual long, quiet, dogged, lonely manhunts for which the Mounties were justifiably famed—"getting your man" by tireless pursuit across tundra and forest was just not big enough for one of the Boss's spectaculars. Now we had the missing link—rebellion! This minor event could be blown up, dramatically speaking, until it threatened to engulf all Canada with blood and flame.

We distilled our epic into a nutshell sentence for the Maestro. "A young nation, threatened by the flames of rebellion, deposits its destiny into the protection of a handful of men in scarlet tunics—The Northwest Mounted Police!"

"You've just lost me the entire American market," the Boss grumbled. "If you ever want anyone in town to pay fifty cents to see this picture, you'll have to put in an American character.

"Not just an American star playing a Canadian, and not just an American 'heavy.' He must be a hero important enough to be played by a major star."

We tried out and discarded a number of possible and impossible solutions, and finally came up with—a Texas Ranger, the perfect southwestern equivalent of a Mountie, pursuing his man across the border into Canada. And since the pursued heavy is up to a spot of gunrunning to Riel's rebels, everything ties together. Mountie and Ranger after the same man—and the same girl, of course. Add to the stew good and bad Indians, half-breeds, and one of the best props ever, a Gatling gun (to quote our script, "She squirt lead like hurricane"). Add to these infallibles a waterfall or two, a canoe chase, a pretty English nurse in scarlet-lined cape (Madeleine Carroll), a lithe half-breed girl (Paulette Goddard), the comical Lynne Overman, this time a skittish Scottish trader, versus Akim Tamiroff as a fractious French Canadian trapper. Add male stars, Gary Cooper, Preston Foster, and, for the girl's handsome brother with a weakness for squaw meat, young Robert Preston. Stir slowly and serve in Technicolor.

Where now are those old, bold formulas, which stirred the hearts of less sophisticated audiences and lined the pockets of fortunate stockholders? When you see these old movies (perhaps badly chopped down to fit some television slot, or rerun in a back-wash theater destined for conversion into a bingo palazzo), you may wonder if the creators of these fairy tales of virtue-versus-evil were as naive as their works? Hardly. We were giving the customers what they wanted, and the proof of our puddings was that people were crowding the movie houses to, as it were, eat them. Today's escapists can find no priest's hole deep enough to hide from the century—and so reach for their cosmos in sex and drug dreams, replacing the lamb with the goat.

De Mille, seeking a more primal tint of virility on his palette, had decided on a new combination of writers. Alan LeMay was lured from short-story writing for *Collier's* and the *Saturday Evening Post*. Lacking any screenwriting experience, he was assigned to collaborate with me. Having survived two De Mille pictures I was now considered almost seasoned. This meant, among other things, an acquired ability to roll with the insults. And, as the Boss put it, I was supposed to keep Alan from "going too far wrong." Tried-and-true script carpenter C. Gardner Sullivan was assigned to clean up the mistakes behind us.

I am frequently asked how two people can actually write together. Obviously methods of collaboration differ with the personal preferences of the collaborators. Sometimes one talks and the other types. Sometimes they type in separate rooms, then exchange drafts for polishing. The perfect collaboration, like a perfect marriage, requires diplomatic genius and extrasensory perception. The combined writers are supposed to augment and stretch each other's abilities without inhibiting creativity or ever offending each other. Since producers were frequently the common enemies, strong alliances were pretty essential to artistic survival.

Though not quite Damon and Pythias, Alan and I got on well. We learned to cover for each other when one or the other suffered a hangover, making him unfit for De Mille consumption, and kept the script moving forward, avoiding undercutting each other during conferences, without, however, falling into the hypocrisy of agreeing on every word. Alan had only one serious problem—the magazine writer's inability to "talk a scene." When story discussions became unavoidable, as they so often did at the De Mille lunch table, I would do most of the verbal dramatizing, while Alan confined himself to moving his thick hands in gestures of drawing on some invisible canvas. Alan's inarticulation troubled De Mille, but generally when we got the scenes on paper, the Boss was well enough pleased.

One day we brought him a scene, one of those jaw-to-jaw showdowns between heavy and hero.

As Bill Pine later explained it, some oil well had failed to gush on schedule—one was always at the mercy of outside influences—but we weren't to know that.

"I've never heard such sissy dialogue outside of a young lady's tatting squabble!" shouted De Mille.

"Then, C. B., you won't have to hear any more from me," blazed Alan, rising to leave.

"Don't you dare get mad at me!" rasped the Boss, "*I'm* the only one who gets mad on a De Mille picture."

Some of the Boss's tantrums and games had more damaging results. Generally he was extremely expert in gauging the boiling points of his stars, but a month before we were supposed to start filming, he overplayed his hand with the two key members of the cast, Gary Cooper and Preston Foster.

De Mille had never quite made up his mind which man he wanted in which part—the Texas Ranger and the Mountie. In the end he called the two actors into his office together. Surveying this splendid pair, each six foot plus, each extremely popular at the box office, he was carried away by a sudden mischievous whim.

"All right, gentlemen. You've both read the script. The two parts are just about equal. The Mountie gets the girl. The Ranger gets his man. You fellows fight it out between you who plays which."

There was deathly silence, as the two actors took in the fact that

De Mille admired them equally, and neither one had the special admiration which he inwardly needed. Without a word they both walked out of the office and off the picture.

Pine, the associate producer, eventually persuaded them to return, but not until De Mille had repaired the damage by sending each a confidential message that he wanted him to take what De Mille had personally decided would be the *stronger* of the two parts. Prides were soothed. Gary accepted the Texan, and Preston Foster the sergeant of Mounties.

De Mille was now almost ready to start shooting, but we had still not solved a major script problem. The situation: Madeleine Carroll and Gary Cooper were in a canoe paddling downriver. A few strokes behind was a virtual armada of canoes bristling with scalp-hungry redskins. Ahead of them was a waterfall equal to Niagara. The luckless pair had a choice—capture by the Indians, or a plunge over the falls, without benefit of barrel. De Mille wanted us to find a truly spectacular escape. Something never before seen in a film. A nagging problem for the writers!

We suggested upsetting the canoe, the two swimming to the bank, hiding under the reeds. They could even breathe through the long, hollow reeds while hiding under water. De Mille would have none of it. He wanted, he warned, "the scene to grab me by the hair of my head (difficult to imagine) and yank me out of my seat!"

We sat in his office, swathed in glum dejection. Short of parachutes, which probably hadn't been invented at the period of our story, our stars were literally for the hatchet or the high dive. And so would be the writers if we didn't come up with an idea soon.

The buzzer snarled on the Boss's desk. Wilfred Buckland, now retired and in his mid-eighties, had stopped by to see him. Alan and I rose, seizing the chance to escape, but De Mille gestured us back to our seats, then growled through the intercom to send Buckland in.

The old gentleman made a shuffling appearance, blinking at the models of sets and the sketches which he might himself have prepared, long ago when he had been the first art director in Hollywood. He was a bulky man, with a fine crest of silver-white hair and lively blue eyes behind pince-nez that gave him the look of a somewhat ancient Theodore Roosevelt. In other lands he would have been weighted down with honors for his contribution to film art and industry. He was in fact neglected, jobless, left virtually penniless by the Depression. His son Bill had fared even worse. He'd attended

Exeter Academy and Princeton, and been the toast of the deb parties, but the high life had vanished with the family fortunes and he had returned to California in time to see his mother, the stunning actress Vida Buckland, die of cancer. He had cultivated only two talents, social charm and tennis. From the latter he tried to earn a living teaching on public courts. When this failed he began to accept the bottled consolation offered by old friends. Then one day, while job-hunting on Hollywood Boulevard, his mind fragmented. He was collected sobbing on the pavement and confined to a public sanitarium, where he was given shock treatment.

None of this could have been guessed from Wilfred's jaunty appearance in worn corduroy jacket, exchanging jokes about old times with De Mille. But eventually the Boss took the opportunity to tell him our problem. The leonine head nodded, the lips crinkled with some personal inner gust of dry whimsical humor. One could never be sure when the old man was being serious.

"And so, Wilfred," De Mille concluded, "as usual my writers have failed to find me anything—anything at all—that will enable Madeleine Carroll and Gary Cooper to survive the redskins, and ME to survive an audience's boredom. Perhaps you could give them some ideas?"

The sparkle in the old man's eyes was definitely amusement. "Send 'em over the waterfall, C. B.!" Buckland suggested.

"Who, my writers? Damn good idea!"

"No, your actors," Buckland replied. Was he making a joke? His pencil was out and he was sketching the scene, making it graphic as he talked. "The canoe goes over. Like this." Quick sketch of precipice. "Then, just as it plunges down, Cooper grabs a tree limb which happens to be stretched across the falls—here. With one hand he seizes it—and with the other arm he holds the girl. Their weight makes the limb swing—right through the downpour of water—and . . ." He thought a moment. "And whips them safely into a . . ." He paused again, searching, and found, ". . . a cavern! Here, behind the falls."

We stared at each other. De Mille was taking it seriously!

"Right through the cascading water, Wilfred?"

"Why not, C. B.? They'll be a little damp, of course." That smile again. It had to be a leg-pull.

The Boss growled around to us, "What do you gentlemen think of it?"

"Could an audience believe it?" I snorted.

De Mille mused, "An audience will believe what it sees." He was now totally absorbed in the challenge of creating such an incredible visual effect. "The Indians would see the canoe disappear. They'd paddle to shore—run to the edge of the falls and look over in time to see"—his mind was already photographing the event—"the wreckage of the smashed canoe, dancing in the rapids below like confetti in a wind tunnel."

Alan had turned black, a pigmental metamorphosis indicative of deep internal consternation. I looked at Wilfred. De Mille turned to us. "Well, gentlemen, has anyone any better ideas?"

Alan, never much of a rhetorician and now ready to explode, gesticulated in a kind of angry sign language that suggested it would be a better idea if we all cut our own throats. I fumbled a few wild suggestions. Ignoring us, De Mille turned his attention back to Wilfred.

"Now let's take it step by step. Intercut a long shot of doubles in the canoe. Process shot—stars against spray. Now back to long-shot, with appropriate intercuts of pursuing Indians. Then close on actors again. Then a special effect, possibly of a miniature of two dolls swinging through mist and spray. Then a shot of cavern, as the actors swing in on the branch and drop, soaked but safe . . ."

De Mille had made his decision. Ours not to reason why. The mechanics of the stunt were too fascinating to him. Plausibility no longer entered the question.

About the time the picture went into production Wilfred's son Bill was released from Camarillo, the state institute for the mentally ill. He appeared to be cured. The doctors urged that he should find some not too exacting employment as the best possible means of reorientation into the workaday world. I asked De Mille if he couldn't be used as one of the assistants to an assistant on our picture.

The Boss's eyes narrowed to knife-thin slits. I think he saw himself as a chief of staff on the eve of launching a war, which was not, after all, too far fetched a comparison to starting a film.

"Would you trust him to deliver a message to Garcia?" he demanded melodramatically.

"I think so," I said, after weighing the possibility.

"Don't think. Know!" he challenged.

This was of course pure pyrotechnics, for De Mille would have been the last man on earth to deny Bill an opportunity to find himself again. I also knew he had sent old Wilfred a check in gratitude for the "great canoe escape," as we had come to call it.

Production moved well, and the work seemed the exact tonic that Bill needed. I thought he was getting better every day. We saw each other frequently on the set, when I was called over to do rewrites.

Gary Cooper was always intensely alert for the false ring of a single word. De Mille had me devote a lot of time to Gary's questions —which generally paid off. You had to hit the exact style of his delivery. He was best at delivering a kind of folksy humor: "I wouldn't jump to conclusions. Liable to be a feller's last jump!" was a line of mine that he liked to repeat far better than I did.

But there were other speeches in which he did not feel so comfortable. Words had to fit him like his own clothes. One scene had to be rewritten over and over again, and when I finally thought I'd found a simple version that totally suited him, he drew a line through two of my best speeches. Opposite one he scrawled the single word "Yup." By the other dialogue he'd scrawled "Nope." I thought at first that these were meant as his comment on my lines, but not so. They were Gary's own rewrite. He'd reduced his entire dialogue in the scene to those two terse words.

In high good humor, Gary invited me to the coke machine to celebrate. Never given to flamboyant extravagance, he deposited his two nickels, passed me one of the cokes, and said, "Yours is five cents, Jess."

He died a wealthy man. Also a beloved one.

The filming of *Northwest Mounted Police* had reached its end. Bill Buckland rejoined the unemployed, and the bottle. I could feel him drifting into a private world more kindly than ours. But it is in the nature of things to close one's eyes to danger signs, and I hoped the end would be happy like the beginning, when we'd shared the best of growing up in Hollywood, empty film sets like oversized playgrounds of a Disneyland long before Disney landed in L.A., complete with canvas castles and whole villages built in one-dimensional false facades.

We had always been laden with overactive imaginations, and now we laughed, recalling the skeletal scarecrow we'd put together in the cellar of our La Brea House. We'd constructed it of an old cow skull, its bleached bones, and a sheet amply smeared with red paint. Unbelievably, the homemade horror had so terrified its creators that nobody could persuade us to enter the cellar for a week! We laughed over the Halloween party when Bill's father had greeted us with a white cotton glove packed with ice, muttering through his skull mask, "Shake hands with the corpse, boys!"

Old Wilfred had been a great pistol marksman, with a shooting range in his cellar where he'd taught us to squeeze pistol triggers with such precision that we could shoot the head off a rattlesnake (a by no means useless accomplishment, since the wild hills stopped just behind our garden walls and serpents, coyotes, and skunks used to wander in regularly to see how the other half lived).

Halloweens and birthdays, Bill and I had never been apart. Our parties were shared by the De Mille girls, Doug Fairbanks, Jr., Phillips Holmes, my cousin Ruth, and Evelyn Flebbe (now Scott). Sons and daughters of the pioneers scattered in '39. Expanding Hollywood had raised walls between old playmates. Memories were the ghosts of happier days in a smaller world.

Old Wilfred invited me over for a spaghetti dinner in their debt-laden house. Bill was extremely quiet, but Wilfred was full of inquiries as to how the waterfall escape had actually worked.

"Mr. De Mille considers it the best spectacle sequence since the closing of the Red Sea in *The Ten Commandments*." I was referring to the silent film version.

"But you don't, I see!" The old man was still enjoying what must have been his monstrous spoof on the current industry that hardly remembered him.

"I'm only one of the writers." I thought Bill's eyes were focused on something at the top of the stairs. Something that only he saw. And indeed neither his father nor I could get his attention all the rest of the evening. I finally wished them good night and left, full of the firm resolution to spend more time with my old pal. But the pressure of preparing endless crowd lines for dubbing sessions was keeping me too heavily hung up at the studio.

One afternoon, while we were lunching at the De Mille table, Florence Cole, the Boss's secretary, came over from the office and whispered something into his ear. His face went pale, for a few moments empty of all expression. Then he recovered himself, nodded her away, and turned to me.

"Jesse . . . Bill Buckland was shot dead early this morning. By his father. Then Wilfred killed himself."

Not the kind of ending our Hollywood would devise or sanction —madness and poverty were still far from film fashions in the forties.

De Mille's hand on my shoulder brought back the reality of the crowded commissary, where Roman senators bumped knees with chorus girls and agents table-hopped from star to star. He was speaking in the kindliest tone I'd ever heard him use.

"Wilfred was getting old. I guess he was worried that Bill was breaking down again. That he'd die leaving his son to face a lifetime in and out of state institutions. So he put a bullet through Bill's head while he slept—and a second through his own."

Another face came into mind: Vida Buckland, Bill's lovely actress mother, rolling bandages beside Bess in their Red Cross uniforms during World War I. The Bucklands had been one of filmland's first families and who now would ever know or care? I'm not even sure whether Hollywood's first art director had his name on one of those brass stars on Hollywood Boulevard.

The movie theater where *Northwest Mounted Police* was to have its first preview was at Westwood Village. It turned out to be a little too close to home. In fact there shouldn't have been any preview! Not that night. Not after what was reported to have taken place the evening before at Ciro's on Sunset Strip. Practically everyone in Hollywood knew, or said they knew, what happened at that nightclub. Everyone except the De Mille unit, who were too busy making the preview arrangements to collect the daily gossip.

It was scurrilously alleged that Paulette Goddard had participated in a unrehearsed love scene with a famous director at Ciro's. Waiters and guests were said to have formed a circle of delighted voyeurs around this spontaneous floorshow. Hardly believable to anyone who knew Paulette, who, aside from being a lady of taste, would under no circumstances have fed her reputation to the Hollywood locusts. I exhume this piece of gossip, not for its entertainment value, but to explain the curious events that took place at our preview.

The trouble began when our film reached the torrid seduction scene between Paulette, as the half-breed, and Robert Preston, as the young Mountie. Even in terms of those more florid times it must be admitted that it contained some of the most overripe dialogue in the picture, and it cannot be considered altogether surprising that when Paulette dragged Preston into her arms with the threat "I think I eat your heart maybe!" a roar of salacious mirth rocked the house. The situation was not improved by the loud voice of one of those murderous jesters who cannot resist such opportunities.

"Didn't you get enough last night?" he shouted.

The audience shrieked in ribald appreciation. There was worse to come.

"Ronnie," Paulette whispered, "a terrible bad thing happen for us."

This brought another explosion of mirth, scarcely helped by Preston's answer, "It seems pretty nice to me."

We held our breaths for the next line, as Preston drew her tight into an embrace and whispered, "I'd come to you if you were on the other side of the moon."

Chirped the anonymous quipster unhesitatingly, "Try Ciro's, it's nearer!"

The audience rolled in the aisles, and we held our breaths as the disheveled Mountie delivered himself of this horror: "Listen, you little wildcat. You're the only real thing that ever happened to me. And nobody—nothing—could ever make me let you go!"

"Not even the head waiter!" shouted the clown in the balcony.

It was the *coup de grâce*. The preview viewers never recovered. And in such a mood, they came to the preposterous escape sequence —over the waterfall! They guffawed until they wept. Our virile drama had become the greatest unintentional comedy since East Lynne. They were still laughing when the film faded out, and we faded out into the night, determined never to show our faces in the Hollywood film world again, but to crawl into the dead navel of some defunct volcano, and there hibernate until another ice age should have expunged from the earth the memory of our shame.

De Mille, however, confronted this defeat with cool practical analysis. A lost battle need not be a lost war. Gossip unsubstantiated would soon enough be forgotten. He readjusted the order of a few shots, made a few judicious trims, and took his film to another preview in Santa Barbara, a citadel of well-furbished respectability which would never have heard the slander. This time the preview was an unqualified success. And so was *Northwest Mounted Police* when it went into roadshow release. Paulette was hired by De Mille for his next film.

Nineteen

CALIFORNIA HAD ALWAYS BEEN a kind of game reserve for madmen. The lunatic fringe found their perfect habitat on the fringe of the Pacific. But sometimes they were not easily kept at bay. A mysterious crank "writer" who believed De Mille had once stolen his story material and used it in *The King of Kings* had the habit of making sporadic appearances to threaten the Boss with vengeance. On occasion this literary avenger—call him "Worfell"—would be found lurking in the shrubbery near De Mille's house. Sometimes he would slip into the studio hidden in the back of a truck, or turn up in a crowd of extras, to cast dangerous glances at De Mille. But unless he cast something more substantial than a glance, the police said, they were powerless to arrest him.

Worfell had once even found employment as a waiter on an ocean liner on which De Mille was traveling to Egypt.

"I am Worfell . . . !" he had hissed at the director general over the *saumon fumé*—no doubt expecting that this revelation would panic De Mille. He had not counted on the Boss's poor memory for names and faces. De Mille extended a hand politely, assuming this seagoing waiter to be some former employee or other. The would-be terrorist must have felt terribly let down. When Worfell slunk away, Gladys Rosson identified the stranger. It didn't improve De Mille's appetite for the rest of the voyage.

Not only madmen but con-men flourished in the perpetual sunshine, and no one could be more vulnerable at times to a blast of bunkum than the great dream merchants. In the days when my father was still vice president of Paramount, he and De Mille together got involved with another mysterious character.

Like candy manufacturers developing a sweet tooth, like a politico believing his own speech, those showmen, whose careers were made by conning audiences and each other, all too easily became ripe victims for any spiv adventurer who could cog the dice, mark the cards, or sell a bathtub to a whale. These mighty monsters of hype were susceptible suckers for any Jack-be-nimble with a flair for melodrama and the gift of the gab. Perhaps one breathed in the virus with the balmy air of Southern California, where oranges grew larger than life, where cults and kooks flourished secure in the illusion that nobody dies in the sun.

Our very architecture was the stuff of dreams. Ancient Egypt bumped temples with Spanish Colonial. Norman buttresses sprouted from palm groves. Tudor cottages squatted amid bamboo. It was a climate for Magi and miracles.

My father could have used a miracle in that summer of the early thirties. His fortune had gone down with the stock market and he was losing his grip on the tiller of Paramount production. This may help explain how and why he became involved in the "Willows" affair.

The true names of some participants have been changed in this account to protect the guilty. When I later asked De Mille about meeting Willows, he didn't deny it. Nor, on the other hand, was he in the least willing to enlarge on the episode. I promised him and my father not to reveal the story during their lifetimes.

One morning, as he sat at his desk at the studio, my father received a phone call from a highly respectable Los Angeles businessman. Los Angeles, mark you, not Hollywood. Mr. Vanderman, as we shall call him, was no flamboyant juggler of film funds, but a conservative financier. He was phoning with an important request—Mr. Lasky should make time that afternoon to listen to certain proposals from a Mr. Willows. Vanderman emphasized that, however unorthodox they might sound, they deserved serious consideration. Vanderman had already arranged a meeting between Willows and De Mille. Although the formerly close companions were not at this time on the best of terms, Lasky always had a justifiable respect for De Mille's business acumen in any venture, in or out of the film world, and an introduction from Vanderman was equivalent to a tip on the stock market. My father was a gambler at heart, anyway. Whoever this Willows was, he could not have arrived under more favorable auguries.

Promptly at three o'clock, Willows entered the office. He requested at once that for the next forty-five minutes Mr. Lasky allow no phone calls or interruptions. Furthermore the office curtains must be drawn to prevent eavesdropping. Mr. Lasky considered this a bit unnecessary. The executive building was backed by a high wall, and unless the eavesdropper arrived on stilts it would be impossible to . . .

Willows indicated an upper window of an apartment house across the street.

"With fieldglasses they could even read our lips," he said laconically. The instructions were passed to the secretary, Randy Rogers. My father indicated his visitor to a chair.

Willows was small and compressed-looking with a string-taut frame, face gaunt above padded shoulders, and cropped gray wiry hair. He bore himself with archaic formality, and his English was overprecise, like a cultured European trying to pass an oral examination. His eyes were opaque. He fixed a long cigarette delicately between thumb and first finger.

"With your permission?"

The producer waved his own cigar in a gesture to go ahead. Willows lit up without smiling. It seemed possible he never smiled. A long moment ticked away as they regarded each other through the blue tobacco fog. Then he spoke with quiet directness. He was taking Mr. Lasky into his confidence, he explained, only upon the recommendation of certain persons.

"Mr. Vanderman?" my father inquired, enjoying the aroma of adventure.

"And others. Persons connected with your Department of State. But let me introduce myself. The name Willows is used only as a convenience."

One may imagine that at this point my father reached to a superb onyx ash tray, the gift of some grateful opportunist, and tapped the fine ash off his Corona Corona Super Perfecto. The star of his blue sapphire, which exactly matched his eyes, exuded a comforting sparkle. "Who are you, then?"

Willows glanced about as though ensuring that there was no ear in the wall, then lowered his voice. "I am one of the few surviving blood relations of His Imperial Highness, the Czar of Russia."

As my father later told it, he was not sure whether at this disclosure he was expected to fall to his knees. He could almost imagine a flourish of invisible trumpets followed by the majestic cadences of the Russian Imperial Anthem.

"No doubt you will question the truth of what I am going to tell you." The hands lifted in a palms-out gesture of concession. "This is understandable."

A meeting worthy of the opening of a Victorian detective film. Something with Clive Brook or Basil Rathbone in the leading role.

"Go ahead," the producer urged, totally intrigued.

"I ask only one favor. If when you have heard what I tell, you wish not to believe—you will say nothing ever to anyone. I must have on this your promise!" The tone had become almost commanding.

"Go on," Lasky nodded, curiosity at war with suspicion.

"I take you back in history to Russia of the revolution. When Dornilov was killed in action and Alexeyev died, the resistance in south Russia was headed by General Denikin. At this time I had the honor to serve with his army. But when in November 1920, the Bolshevik force crossed the Strait of Perekop, we lost the power to defend the Crimea. We knew we must escape, yes? Already the Czechs had brought to Siberia the gold reserves they captured at Kazan. Our country was in ruins. The White Army was finished."

It needed only the film maker's imagination to see a military cap, decorated with the double-headed eagle, above the deep-set eyes. Mist. Black-green fir trees against snow. The bedraggled remnant of a broken army. Gentlemen officers hounded out of their country by the hordes they had so recently led, and misled. And in the dark forests, trampled paths blotched with blood, sprouting the fingers of corpses like tubers signaling the end of a season of civilization.

All this could be conjured into the mind's eye in a second by a man who had produced Emil Jannings' great film *The Last Command*, directed by Josef von Sternberg. You could believe in almost anything if you had guided the making of a film about it. Showmanship.

My father tuned back in on the continuing revelation.

"But all of the treasure of the nobility had not been captured by the Reds. There was much more that could be taken safely out of the country. Yes, we had a few handfuls of jewels, gold coins. But the rest—the great paintings, candlesticks of pure gold, Sèvres table services, jeweled crosses from our private chapels and icons. All the great pieces that we had been able to move must now be hidden. Yes! Like pirates, no? And there, where we hid it, it remains—to this day. Waiting."

My father's skepticism must surely have shown through the expensive cigar smoke. "Why do you come to me?"

"Why?"

"Yes, why? Your story is hardly original enough to make a film. Besides, we already own *From Double Eagle to Red Flag.*

"I come for two reasons, Mr. Lasky. The first is because you are strong. The second because you are weak."

My father rose with an air of finality. Even a tottering tycoon was not to be glibly analyzed by this preposterous stranger with his wild talk. But Willows ignored the gesture of dismissal.

"Permit me to explain. You are strong because you still have a position of power in your company. You are weak because you know you could soon lose it. And you have lost all your money also in the collapse of the stock market. You see, I have investigated before trusting."

"You're very well informed," my father admitted.

Willows nodded. "Otherwise I would not be here. But I need your help. A favor still in your power to give. And you need what I can give. The promise of financial security."

"The favor, Mr. Willows."

Willows looked grimly pleased, but still unsmiling. "You will make the arrangement that a writer is hired by your company—to prepare the scenario for a film. He is to be put under contract for six months, a year—at a nominal fee . . ."

"How nominal?" my father asked guardedly.

"Three hundred dollars a week." The shrug left open the possibility of negotiation up or down.

"And who is the writer?"

"Myself. This scenario—it is for a film to be made on location. In the Crimea, on the Black Sea. You begin to understand . . ."

"How is De Mille involved?"

"He has a very large yacht, and a reputation that would not be questioned. He might even be persuaded to go on the location journey himself—as 'director.' The crew will be selected by myself. Old associates, sprinkled with a few real film people to avoid suspicion. This is the essential. And one night, in darkness—I know the Crimea like the palm of my hand because there we had once a summerhouse —the yacht sends a boat into shore. My friends who are still on the inside will be ready. They will have the shipment prepared for us to remove."

"Suppose the Reds catch on and remove your friends first?"

Willows came near to the edge of a smile, indicated only by a slight enlivening spark at the back of his deep-set eyes.

"A risk we all take. But you and Mr. De Mille and Mr. Vanderman risk only money."

My father weighed the words, but the old devil enthusiasm was beginning to chase reason away. A showman does not analyze like a lab technician, testing every atom under the microscope of common sense.

"And how long would this 'scenario' take you to prepare?" He was trying to keep the growing excitement from showing in his voice.

"Impossible to say, Mr. Lasky. But I have the intention to take care of you." He suddenly thrust a hand into his inside pocket as though toward a shoulder holster. Could this be a total madman? Eyes locked, as the hand remained hidden. Then slowly Willows drew out an envelope. "This will symbolize financial security for yourself and your family in the future—should we fail. I do not wish you to have worries about money. So we call this—like a token of payment. Yes?"

So saying, he opened the envelope and gently poured a glittering stream of gems on the gray desk blotter. My father stared at them, noting perhaps that they quite outshone the hazy star sapphire on his own finger. He lifted one or two to the light. They were impressively luminescent.

"I don't know anything about gems," he admitted.

"It is in any case unnecessary." Willows scooped them back into the envelope. "You must not, I repeat, under any circumstances allow anyone to see these, or know they are in your possession. Only if I fail to return from the location journey are you to open this envelope. Meanwhile, in your presence, I shall seal it."

He proceeded to do so, using his own sealing wax and a heavy gold ring. There flicked into my father's mind a performance by a long-ago friend and employer, the magician Herman the Great. Words drifting back through the veil of years—"and now we shall seal and lock the casket in your presence. If any gentleman from the audience would care to test the . . ." A forty-week season's tour with sister Blanche and Mother Sarah, watching the dapper Frenchman baffle audiences with sleight-of-hand and grand illusions. The comparison was not reassuring.

"Did you give Mr. Vanderman and Mr. De Mille similar envelopes?"

"Their financial insecurity is not, one may say, in the same situation, Mr. Lasky. What I give you is not their concern. No?"

"And what you give them is not mine?"

The too-thin shoulders moved slightly. "As I have said, Mr. De Mille supplies the yacht and plan of production. Mr. Vanderman will arrange any extra finance that may become necessary, and you will make the contract for the scenario. We will permit the Red spies to believe we go to the Black Sea to make this picture."

How easy the man was making it sound. As though my father could just press a button and switch on a contract. Not in these times, when his every move was under another kind of scrutiny—that of spies from the New York office. He had been warned by his few friends there that one wrong move could upset the apple cart. How would he like to stand before a blue-jowled rank of board members and explain hiring Willows?

"I have stockholders to answer to, Mr. Willows. We don't just hand out six-month contracts for mythical films. I mean, scenarios that can't be used."

"How many scenarios have you had to put on the shelf? That you have paid for over many weeks?"

"I'll have to give this a bit of thought."

"You must. But not too long. There are three other heads of studios that have been suggested to me—if you decide against it. Which, I hope for your sake, you will not. Meanwhile, not a word, please, about the envelope I leave with you. It is, after all, no more than a small pledge—which I shall redeem later with something more negotiable."

My father stared at the envelope. The wax puffed out around the image where Willows had put the pressure of his double-eagle seal.

"Like what?"

"A small painting—a seventeenth-century portrait by Rembrandt. Or perhaps bonds of your government—paid up. But I think Mrs. Lasky would more appreciate—say—an Old Master, being herself a painter of importance."

"You know quite a lot about the Laskys."

"It was necessary," he nodded, almost apologetically, then suddenly bowed and walked out.

It has ever been man's nature that the intensity of his needs is in inverse proportion to the sobriety of his judgment. With a safe bank account and firm hold on his executive desk, my father might have laughed Willows out of California. But he was in no laughing mood. Willows looked like the golden straw that had to be grasped. You didn't build a worldwide film empire out of a barn in an orange grove without believing in the star of destiny that gamblers call luck. A week or two later, Willows had his contract.

Each day he could be seen arriving at the studio, driven in an old Mercedes Benz by a bulky foreign-looking chauffeur. Formerly a

Cossack batman, no doubt. He kept punctilious hours, supplied his own secretary, a nondescript-looking woman. He never lunched in the commissary or fraternized with the other writers, who were naturally curious about him. And he eventually produced a bulky, amateurish treatment that had for its setting . . . a yacht in the Black Sea.

One night my father even brought him home to dinner. We were fascinated, Bess and I, for he kept a secret about as well as a child would, and had revealed all on the first night after his meeting.

When I entered the room, Willows looked me up and down like an inspecting officer. "You wish to be a writer? Then you must experience the world. One day when my business with your father is finished, you will go with me to Tibet. There you will learn the inner secret that will give you power over your own thoughts. To a writer most useful. No?"

I nodded politely. Hearing him discussing paintings with my mother, it was plain he could be all things to all people. As I listened to the stiffly accented English over the carefully poised coffee cup, I wondered which of his masks was the real one.

"Masterpiece," he was declaring, "is not too much to say." His left hand traced the outline of the vase in one of mother's still lifes. "White bowls have been painted before. But in this porcelain, you capture the soul, yes, the essence, no? Of a dynasty. It is a gift the artist's hand brings to us from God!" Bess had been the most skeptical of us all, but not any longer.

This state of suspended expectation might have continued indefinitely, with Mr. Willows on salary, eternally developing his "scenario." But the steady worsening of my father's position in the company brought a sudden decision. Increasing insecurity moved him to inquire as to the true value of the jewels. He had convinced himself that De Mille and Vanderman had received similar envelopes, whether or not they'd ever admit it. And if they had, it was unthinkable to suppose that such astute businessmen would not have had their assets appraised.

So the moment came when Randy and I were given the priceless envelope to show a jeweler friend. He poured out the stones onto black velvet and nodded enigmatically. Glass screwed in eye, he took a closer look. Nodded again.

"Well?" we prompted.

"Well," he shrugged. "Zircons."

"What . . . ?"

"Semiprecious. Worth a couple of hundred dollars at most."

"Are you sure?"

"Sure I'm sure. What are they, props for a movie?"

We brought the envelope back home. My father's face went white. He'd just lost his paddle in the middle of a rapids, his Santa Claus had suddenly been debearded, and the fairies at the bottom of his garden had been fireflies all the time. Hurt gave way to rage. "I want Willows at my house tonight! Nine o'clock. And tell him he'd better not be late!"

Randy went off to make the phone call. "Suppose he gets violent?" I asked. "You gave him a promise not to show them to anyone, remember?"

"Which, thank goodness, I broke! We'll rig a hidden intercom, and leave the key open so you two can listen. Randy had better take down every word." The drama of it was already lifting his spirit. "I want a transcript that can be signed under oath. In case I have to take him to court for fraud or grand larceny."

That evening, in the best tradition of spy movies, Randy and I crouched by a newly installed intercom in the bathroom adjoining the library. I had suggested the precaution of a loaded pistol, but the Lasky sense of drama could not quite be stretched that far. Seated on the toilet lid, Randy followed every word, straining to hear as the voices rose and fell. I squatted on the edge of the tub, our ancient shower baptizing me gently as I fed him sharpened pencils.

My father broached the discovery with magnificent coolness. When he reached the point of what the jeweler had said, his words were served on the rocks.

We waited tensely through the pause that followed. Randy's pencil hovered, ready to pounce on the pad. I could imagine Willows casually lighting one of those long cigarettes. When he spoke his voice filtered in to us, totally devoid of emotion.

"But of course the gems are worthless, Mr. Lasky. Would I take the risk of endangering you and your family by planting jewels of high value in your possession? You may underrate the efficiency of the Communist agents, but I cannot afford to. What did I say to you when I gave them to you? Try to remember, please."

"You said they were a pledge. Security for the future for my family, Willows."

"Your memory is correct, sir. A pledge for items of true value. To be redeemed. Honored—when it is safe and practical. Do you think we are not under observation? Every hour? Perhaps even at this moment? Do you think our every word could not be overheard?"

I exchanged a grimace with Randy. The voice swept smoothly on—a teacher being patient with a child.

"No, my dear sir. With great care and also expense we prepared this plan. It is essential that the Red agents should know what we are doing, up to the last moment before the motor boat carries me into the shore. We expect to be under observation. But if they found out I had in my possession *real* jewels—they would guess in one second from where they came. And they would know the true purpose of the location trip." He paused. You could hear the breathing. Then the words sounded again. "The stones that I gave to you were like the display in a window. To suggest what is inside. Now, I suppose you have told your discovery to our associates, Vanderman and De Mille?"

"No, Willows. I thought I'd give you an opportunity of making your explanation first."

"You must tell them! They could explain that these are merely copies of the real stones. That is why I did not want you to show the envelope to anybody. Also, it was important to know if *you* could be trusted."

"I, trusted?" My father's voice exploded. "You're the one who put the fakes in my pocket, Willows!"

"Mrs. Lasky wears a *copy* of her large emerald, no? The real one, she keeps in her safe."

"By jove, you're too well informed, Willows!" my father exclaimed.

"It is necessary, or I would not pry into your private family affairs, only for your own safety. Remember, the stakes are high. Many lives have already been lost. Now I ask myself—if you have lost faith in me, and the plan—should you be permitted to continue?"

"My company has paid you a substantial salary for quite a few months, Willows. You can hardly call that a lack of faith." Dad's voice seemed somehow inoculated with new confidence.

"The money is not important," Willows dismissed. "It is trust. Suppose this jeweler should talk? Or your son? Or your secretary? You put trust in everyone but me. For this reason I must consider, Would it not be better if you were to withdraw, and I to find somebody else? It would mean a postponement, of course. But when one has waited so long . . ." The thought trailed away, leaving the question that Willows was asking himself hanging between Randy and me in the bathroom.

"I had to know the answers." My father sounded almost apologetic. "You've explained yourself. Now I'm satisfied. I am prepared to go on."

There was a long silent moment of indecision. Finally Willows spoke.

"Then we will say no more about it, Mr. Lasky."

My father didn't, except to re-swear Randy and me to silence, and no mention of the false jewels was made to Vanderman or De Mille. If you were going to believe any part of it, you had to believe it all.

As time dragged on, Willows, when asked, would say only that his scenario was still being polished. From which his sponsor assumed that arrangements were not yet finalized.

Then one morning Vanderman phoned. I'm sorry I couldn't have recorded the conversation. My father was still at breakfast. His kidneys and scrambled eggs went unfinished. Vanderman asked if he had seen the morning papers. An item about a man having been arrested in Santa Barbara on a charge of fraud. The man, representing himself as a Hollywood film writer, had recently married a wealthy widow some years older than himself. He had secured from her a huge donation to start the first Mohammedan mosque in Santa Barbara. He had also invested her money in a platinum mine in Alaska. Vanderman's voice faltered at the next bit. Among his several aliases the man was known as Willows. He had served prison terms for similar offenses in various parts of the United States.

Vanderman was deeply embarrassed, but, said he, the sources who recommended Willows had been impeccable. In all events, it was hastily agreed to lock the skeleton into a cupboard of silence.

Several weeks later we were lunching at Lucy's on Melrose Avenue. My father was leaving for New York that night to attend a board of directors meeting. He was going over some last-minute arrangements with Randy. A troubled look invaded his eyes.

"There's one question I hope won't arise at the board meeting."

Randy gave a sharpening twirl to one of the points of his mustache. "Pertaining to the employment of a certain writer, Mr. Lasky?"

"Did you ever read the script?" I asked.

"Of course. And you know what, Jesse? It wasn't all that bad. A good basis for a moving picture. I even thought of a title. *The Magnificent Fraud.*" He grinned across at me, then added, "Lincoln was surely right. You *can* fool some of the people some of the time."

Twenty

THE GRACEFUL SCHOONER-RIGGED YACHT rose and fell on the blue belly of the Pacific. Riding at anchor in the lee of Santa Catalina Island, it found some protection from tormenting winds that provided occasional invisible tightropes for sea gulls. Also, nausea for seagoing screenwriters. Our portable typewriters wallowed and waltzed under our hands, and our pencils spilled, rolling into the scuppers. All of this De Mille, the sublime sailor, loftily ignored. He might, one suspected, have felt even happier breasting the teeth of a gale that would have driven lesser mortals cringing to shelter. But in the absence of gales we had him to drive us, in this case to speedier output of script pages for *Reap the Wild Wind.*

The nautical atmosphere was supposed to give us the final boost of inspiration to finish the script with flying jibs. What it gave us was the confines of a sixty-foot yacht in which there was no safe hiding place from his swaggering surveillance. The mere sound of a pecking typewriter was enough to bring our skipper-cum-boss looming over one's shoulder, eyes devouring the tentative beginnings of a scene, with the cheery demand, "Ready for me, fellah?"

He knew we knew he knew exactly how unready we generally were. *Reap the Wild Wind* had been a problem project from its inception. The probable reason was that the story we were adapting seemed to have everything! Action, love, suspense, adventure, history. And what do you add to the story that has everything? Normally, a tightening of episodes, a sharpening of dialogue and character would have been sufficient to ready this saga for the screen. But De Mille wanted a complete rewrite. Referring to Thelma Strable, the authoress of the original, he had warned, "Listen like the Sphinx. Then forget every word she says! No 'slick fiction' writer ever heard of 'drama.' They don't know the meaning of the word! She's given us pretty pictures of sails and seas and sunsets shining through a lady's auburn hair. What I want in this subject are storms and sinkings and salvage. I want to smell the brine and hear the creak of rigging. I want to feel the bite of hurricanes. I want the birth of America's lifeline on the seas—and to see it threatened by the toughest tribe of murdering pirate-wreckers that ever gutted a ship to steal a cargo!"

His eyes narrowed toward the horizon of waters, his hands rested upon the spokes of the wheel.

"I want to see the teeth of a reef bite through a ship's bottom—photographed from under water!"

"But, sir . . ." I started to broach a worried protest at the technical difficulties.

"We'll do it with miniatures in the Paramount tank if we have to!" Today he had no time for trivia. He was busy molding mood. "I want broken skulls and skulduggery! I want it to contrast with the tinkle of teacups in Charlestown drawing-rooms. And I want two love stories. The first—ending in death and drowning. The second—a man and a woman finding and losing, and finding each other again. Through hell to heaven! Did you get any of that?" He swiveled a snarl at Bernice, the efficient field secretary, who had not missed a turgid word, as he well knew.

These notes she would later comb through for substance, and circulate the proceeds among the writers, research staff, and all other departments concerned. For instance, the art director would be alerted to the suggested underwater scene, so he would not be found unprepared when sketches were demanded for camera setups.

None of this concerned Miss Strable, whose *Saturday Evening Post* serial Paramount had purchased for De Mille. Adaptations are always tricky affairs. Translating the original material into the language of visual action, giving it fresh air and movement, variety of locale. Theater audiences will sit through long dialogue scenes. Cinema audiences won't—or shouldn't have to!

If Sherlock Holmes on the stage exhibits a fingerprint, he must talk about it. On the screen, one close-up is worth a thousand whorls. Some books offer only the basis for a film, not a blueprint. Long descriptions of a character's thoughts must be translated into dialogue or action, leaving messages to be delivered by telegram and analyses on the couch.

Charles Bennett, former actor-playwright, joined us on the scripting of *Reap*. British, flamboyantly theatrical, he fascinated De Mille with his verbal description of contemplated scenes.

I'd first met Charles Bennett in the so-called "Balkan Corridor" of the old Shepherd's Bush Gaumont British Studio in London when I was working for Hitchcock. Like so many others, success had brought him our way. Hollywood was like a colonial outpost anyway. You almost never met anyone who was born there. A dinner party might include a Polish actress, a Russian composer, a Hungarian playwright, and an English author. It was said that you needed a German passport to get into Universal when its founder, old "Papa" Carl Laemmle, was in charge. Hollywood was the goal of every international beauty, and it picked the brains of the world, who enjoyed the climate, if not the intellectual atmosphere, at a time when much of Europe was shrinking into political coffins.

But the jauntiest émigrés were the Brits, who grew more British in the California sun. Their cricket, tea, and talent contributed much to making Hollywood's product internationally successful.

The newly arrived Charles Bennett would appear wreathed in scarves, draped in a dashing blazer, or dustily booted, fresh from a polo match. He flew planes, rode like a Cossack, and could on occasion come dangerously near stealing scenes from the Boss, who had always been second to none in "office performances."

Charles would swagger and glower in an impersonation of the heavy to be played by Raymond Massey. Then Charles would mince out a delicious imitation of Paulette Goddard's Florida belle. He'd ape Ray Milland's effete aristocrat, or the heavy-shouldered, jaw-jutting challenge of John Wayne's First Mate. But too often his office performances were better than the scenes themselves. The written word missed the swaggerings, struttings, eye rollings of our spellbinding Charles. De Mille would complain that we hadn't got it on paper, quite ignoring the fact that this would have been next to impossible.

The nautical nature of our subject was compounding the headaches. With his hobby of sailing, De Mille saw himself as a combination of Magellan and Sir Thomas Lipton. He became obsessed with the technicalities of seamanship, and the rest of us did our best to get into the spirit of things by salting conversation with helms, halyards, mizzen masts, and marlin spikes. We lurched about the studio corridors like tars, three sheets to the wind, and Bernice Mosk took to preparing lists of words and phrases which would be understandable mainly to sea gulls.

Our "blue water" jargon was greatly supplemented by the arrival of Captain Fred Ellis, the technical adviser. We nearly lost him prematurely, however, when he only narrowly survived the shock of discovering that the script called for the peak and throat halyards to be tied close together on the starboard side fife rail! (Paulette, in a fit of pique, was to part both lines with a single blow of an axe.)

Not wishing again to be caught in the old *Union Pacific* problem, I devised a bit of business for the heavy that only an actor as good as Raymond Massey could cope with. I gave him a shark's tooth on a hawser-thick watch chain, and he would emphasize his threats and decisions by stabbing it into some keg top or table—and finalize his warnings by yanking it out of the wood. This operation required about the same effort as removing a harpoon from a killer whale, the while he was to utter such salty delights as: "Listen, you dried-up old crawfish—you and The Lamb find out where Tolliver casts anchor. Take three or four horn-fisted galley growlers and port his helm!" (Tug out shark's tooth and glower hard.)

Leading ladies in De Mille films were always subjected to punishment that would delight the marquis de Sade, but the doses we devised for them in *Reap* might have alerted any perceptive psychoanalyst to someone's need of vengeance against wife and mother. When not being buffeted by typhoons and tempests, Paulette was publicly spanked by Milland, who later threw her overboard into the harbor for good measure.

Susan Hayward, in her first important part, played a character who would be called upon to stow away in a sea-chest on a ship that would be sunk. It furnished one of the most macabre shots of the day: her long red hair streaming out into the helmeted gaze of the divers exploring the submerged wreck.

De Mille, as always, had supervised the progress of our screenplay with growing dissatisfaction. He was increasingly certain that we lacked what he considered a truly grand climax. Tossing miserably in our narrow bunks in his yacht, *The Seaward*, we racked our imaginations for a suitably spectacular episode that would top the already action-crowded procession of scenes. His feeling was that audiences are likely to be eye- and bottom-weary by the end of a multi-reel epic, so one last effect, one final spectacle was needed to ensure that they would be left with spines tingling, and the need to tell all their friends to *run,* not walk, to the nearest neighborhood box office to see his exciting movie. This "word-of-mouth" advertising was considered essential to the financial success of a film. Adjective-drenched ads, even favorable reviews, could only be expected to reach a small portion of the potential viewers, many of whom couldn't read anyway.

De Mille sipped an ice tea on the never-still deck and leaned back in his director's chair, surveying the Catalina Island shoreline as we sat about doodling on pads and listening.

"I couldn't sleep last night," he intoned sadly. Assuming that the cause of his insomnia was not the tossing of *The Seaward*, which would customarily have soothed his restless spirit like a cradle of the deep, we waited.

"I kept asking myself the question. What, in *Reap the Wild Wind*, would galvanize headhunters in an Amazon River jungle?" (The phrase was not totally incomprehensible. De Mille films were so widely popular that it was said they were carried by dugout canoe and projected on 16-mm. screens in the furthest corners of the earth.)

"What," he continued, "would fascinate Eskimos in their igloos, harness harassed housewives, rivet restless children? What can we offer to match"—shudders of horror—"our great waterfall escape in *Northwest Mounted*, or our train wreck in *Union Pacific?* The opening of the Red Sea in my silent picture, *The Ten Commandments?* Because until we've got that, gentlemen, we just haven't got a moving picture."

He paused quite enjoying the mind-screws he had applied. He and we knew that the script was already action-packed to the bursting point. Storms. Shipwrecks. Sinkings. Drownings. Races to salvage cargoes from wrecks. Fisticuffs. Spankings. And plenty of juicy love scenes. What more could he ask? And what more could we dream up, now that he had asked?

"I refer to the situation at the end of your script," he said ominously. "When the court trial adjourns to the wreck, and your two leading men dive to search for the evidence—of murder! They screw on their helmets, plunge overside, go down, find the evidence—a girl's body—and what happens next? That was the question that kept me awake, gentlemen, and I am curious as to whether any of you can provide an answer. Because if you can't, we have a five-million-dollar moving picture without an end!"

We had indeed been grappling with the question and found a solution of sorts. We had devised an undersea struggle between the two helmeted stars, whacking at each other's life lines with hatchets, while the wreck kept slipping off the undersea rocks where it was precariously balanced, like a melting ice cube falling to the bottom of a glass.

"I'm waiting for your answer, gentlemen," De Mille prompted. "That is, *if* you have one?"

I glanced at the other writers. They seemed disinclined to commit themselves. Our plan of the underwater combat, however spectacular, could hardly be considered original. Still, someone had to tell it.

"We do have an answer, sir," I said.

"Ah . . . ?" He beamed. "Then perhaps you will share it with me."

Neither Alan LeMay nor Charles made a move to aid or abet me. I plunged on.

"The two divers have gone down into the sunken ship, looking for evidence," I began, then stopped.

"I know the story," he inserted impatiently. "Get to the point, Jesse. What do they do?"

Alan's eyes were closed. Charles Bennett was sprawling out of his chair, scarf tucked Britishly into his blazer, face benign.

"The discovery of the body—explodes them into violent action, sir. One seizes an axe . . . The other a knife . . ."

"And they go into a life-or-death struggle. That is your great plan, is it? To end this picture, or me? Because it's exactly what everyone expects, and it's as old as Noah's ark! So if you can't do better than that, I'd say we haven't got a moving picture."

I saw myself out of a job for Christmas. And I'd just bought a new house whose long-term payments depended on steady employment.

Then Charles Bennett came to the rescue.

"But you haven't heard the end of our plan, C. B."

I shifted my glance down from the swaying top of the masthead. De Mille regarded Charles with amused expectation.

"Haven't I?"

"No. The underwater fight between the two divers is what you'd expect to happen. Indeed, it is what *starts* to happen. But in the moment, the first instant that the divers start to hack at each other, suddenly you see behind them—rising out of the belly of the dead ship, one great long red tentacle—and then another." Charles had come to his feet now, his hand snaking through the air to illustrate his words.

"Then, faster than a striking cobra, it sweeps around the body of one of the men. It heaves him up, light as a doll in the fist of a giant—for giant it is—a giant squid! The largest monster of the deep. Great eyes like illuminated green balloons, full of malevolent intelligence.

Massive, slack, big as a circus tent, but with tentacles strong enough to squeeze an elephant to pulp! And now Steve and Jack are fighting for their own lives, against the most terrible creature nature has ever produced. The enemies have become allies against the common danger . . . this ink-throwing behemoth, this leviathan! The sea bottom has become an arena where man is pitted against nature. Nature, with yellow glazed eyes, and probing tentacles thick as pine trees!"

De Mille looked ecstatic. "And in Technicolor," he breathed. We sat in stunned silence, as well we might, for Charles had not even mentioned his great idea to us. Hardly surprising, since he had not, until that moment, thought of it.

A month later we were again being unhappily rocked on De Mille's cradle of the deep. The weather was worse, *The Seaward* no more seaworthy, and script problems as prickly as ever.

The Paramount prop department was straining all resources to produce the giant squid. It was to have controllable rubber tentacles fourteen feet long, operated hydraulically so that it could obey the orders of the director. The underwater scenes were to be photographed through the glass wall of the studio tank. Real fish were being screen-tested. Most were enthusiastic performers, although some persisted in violating the first rule of acting, by swimming directly toward the camera and peering into the lens.

All these exotic preparations had little effect upon the writers. De Mille was not yet happy with our script, perhaps he never would be. Specifically, he was displeased with the love scenes. And for this, blame was heavily leveled on me. The Boss had decided, not unjustly, that I had "lost my poetry." As always, he was looking for that elusive "fresh" quality—some new imagery and color of language that he could not define. An unearthly beauty that would yet sound natural from the lips of "real people."

And what was real to him, would be to his audiences, he believed.

These sessions at sea were supposed to inspire us. Nightly, smoky suns plunged into long vistas of lavender ocean. Santa Catalina viewed from our rocking decks became a fantasy isle of fairy lights and romantic contours. The pavilion where weekending stenographers eluded or sought the groping attentions of beefy bosses became at this distance a silhouetted dome worthy of Istanbul. Distance definitely lent enchantment to that teeming trippers' isle. But enchantment seemed to have eluded our script. We had been too obsessed with creating suspense and action. We had been overdrenched in research. We wrote with one eye on the interminable lists of nautical gadgets and phrases. And De Mille, inevitably, was the first to realize that good was not yet good enough!

One evening he brought out a bottle. Of rum. It looked like the same that had on a previous occasion been my undoing at the De Mille ranch.

"From the keg broached by Morgan after the rape of Panama," he growled, understandably troubled at trickling out such liquid pearls for literate swine.

I accepted a tot from the master's hand. It had a strange taste of dusty molasses.

"Y'know how many bottles exist in the world, Jesse?"

"One, sir?" I tried hopefully.

"None. After this is gone."

Maybe he refilled it, I speculated.

I accepted four tots in the rocking cabin, while he recited a favorite poem. It was called "Evolution," and I've never heard it since, nor discovered who wrote it, but it was full of splendid images of a love affair that spanned eternity—from the caves of Neolithic man to Del Monico's in 1890s New York. Hearing him recite it through the haze of Morgan's lubricant had the proper effect. I began to roll off a few turgid lines of my own.

He looked pleased.

"Now, Jesse—write me some love scenes!"

With a formal bow, he bore the elixir of the great corsair out of the cabin. I was alone, swayed increasingly by the swell that undulated around the rim of the island. A rag of music floated over the water from the dance band playing in the Casino. "I found my love in Avalon—Upon the shore . . ."

A lot of guys must be finding love in Avalon tonight. Its beaches, powdered with lights behind imported palm trees, accommodated more amorous turbulence than a hundred great Beds of Ware.

And wouldn't I rather be there than here? Here, with a snootful of rum and a command to produce some verbal pitter-patter for our stars. I took up my leaky pen.

Next morning De Mille was up and pounding at my cabin door before my eyes were open. They hadn't been closed for long. I must have been writing most of the night.

He read through the sprawl of pages and looked pleased.

"Now," he said gently, "you've got something. Too much, of course. Too fancy. For real people. But with scissors and a paste pot we can make some of this work."

With coffee and toast soaking up the aftertaste of old molasses, we moved up to the deck to edit, polish, cut, and paste. Everyone went to work on dialogue bridges—transition bits—and in a couple of hours the scenes were done.

Contentedly De Mille shuffled the script into a pile and beamed around at one and all: Alan, Charles, the research people, and the secretaries.

"Fellahs, I think we can go home," he said.

He gave the appropriate orders to the crew and sent word to the galley that we'd have lunch, then sail on the wind for San Pedro. I think if we'd known how we might all have gone into a hornpipe of pure joy on that teak deck.

Then, as simply as taking candy from a baby, that malevolent Channel wind suddenly freshened and whisked away the one and only copy of our glued-together scenes. Over the taff rail and into the Pacific.

We stood paralyzed. The only copy! The final result of weeks, months of writing—welded together into an accepted final draft, and . . .

"Every man overboard!"

The command had come from De Mille—and every man jack of us obeyed. Dressed as we were, we jumped or dived into the Pacific to flounder about in the swell, seizing soggy pages before they sank. A small boat came creaking down the davits, and as we salvaged our script sheets, like priceless scrolls from Dead Sea caves, they were passed on up the side of *The Seaward* to De Mille. He gave them a stern glance, then passed them to the two secretaries, who were armed with towels, blotters, and sponges.

Soon most of the pages hung fluttering gently from clothespins on a line, though some were lost. Of course, I'd like to think that accounted for a certain lack of memorable magic in the scenes that finally appeared on film.

And if certain surviving lines, like "When you entered the room—it was like all the winds of the Caribbean, and I was shipwrecked at once," sound a bit soggy, think of where they'd been!

Today you wouldn't need dialogue. You could accomplish the same result with a simple direction to the actors: *Their eyes meet across the rims of their empty glasses. He nods toward the bedroom. She shrugs, follows him in. To bed.*

Hey ho.

Twenty-One

AS LIGHTLY AS A WALT DISNEY Fox creeping up on its unwary prey, the winter of '41 descended upon Hollywood. Our town was an imperfect isolation ward that year. Distant sounds were beginning to reach it. Ghostly drum-taps from faraway battlefields. But we were always expert at closing our eyes and ears to realities, near or far.

My father was trying desperately to find some film company who would back a moving picture of the life of Sergeant Alvin York, the World War I hero. Better than most, Dad sensed the stillness before the gathering storm. Hollywoodites were like sleepers, unaware that the forces of their awakening were already in motion. Nobody, the Moguls insisted, wanted war films. Patriotism hung like a dusty long rifle above the hearth. Nobody wanted old-fashioned, jingoistic nationalism! In vain Dad argued with the powers that were. The life of Sergeant York wasn't just a story of a war hero, it held the seed of self-questioning that many people would face if war should come again. York had been a pacifist, a religious conscientious objector. But in lone meditation on a Tennessee mountaintop, he had sought and found his own answer—in his Bible.

The executives only wagged their cigars. War pictures were out of date. Everything worth saying had been said. In *The Big Parade, What Price Glory?, All Quiet on the Western Front.* All had sung the familiar theme voiced by General Sherman. "War is hell." "Nobody wins but the worms." People wanted to forget their troubles—drown 'em in pure entertainment. So Dad had continued peddling the project that nobody wanted—until he told the story to Harry Warner, who phoned his brother, Jack.

Sergeant York would be the most successful film my father ever made, yet ironically in the end bring him his greatest personal disaster. Every step of setting it up was paved with problems. Sergeant

York held the altruistic belief that his life story—as had his life—belonged to his country. A mountain man, of deep faith in God, he put no trust in Hollywood, which as everyone knew was populated by rogues and sinners. Only after my father had visited him in the mountains of Tennessee and proved his mettle in a turkey-shoot, did the sergeant consent to consider.

There was one actor whom he would accept to portray his life, Gary Cooper. The problem was, Gary wasn't available or deeply interested. Dad finally resorted to desperate subterfuge. He used York's name on a spurious telegram to Gary saying he was the man—then signed Gary's name to a telegram to York. The exchange of admiration brought agreements, with one further wrinkle. Gary, albeit willing, was still not available. Warner Brothers stepped in to break through that barrier.

Sam Goldwyn, who owned Gary Cooper's contract, agreed to loan his star to Warner's for *Sergeant York*, if Warner's would loan Bette Davis to Sam for *The Little Foxes*. The exchange proved fair enough. (Even then, the blending of elements by which an independent producer got his film into production required a seasoning of showmanship, chicanery, gusto, and pure luck.)

It was a strange time, that winter of '41. The terrors of Hitler loose in the world, and we in Hollywood only half aware. Mostly, indeed, citizens of Pompeii on the Pacific, we chose to ignore the rising rumbles of the volcano. Never had Hollywood parties been more lavish. Never were salaries more soaring. Never had production been so heavy. Even writers were in great demand. You could get a job by answering the telephone. A friend of mine composed an idea in his shower, dictated two pages and had it sold by evening—for fifty thousand dollars. That was exceptional, but the deal I made with an original I had knocked out during a weekend—a Western about the bull-freighters, called *Ox Train*—brought in twenty-five thousand. Dore Schary, brilliant writer and rising young producer at Metro, purchased it the following morning.

But I had to ask for a collaborator on the script, because that autumn I'd begun to lead a double life. After a day of scriptwriting at MGM studio in Culver City I would drive out the studio gate, the studio gate policeman would salute me respectfully, and an hour later I would drive into the Los Angeles Armory, change into the suntans of a buck private in the 2nd Regiment California State Infantry, and salute the same studio gate guard, who had meanwhile changed into the uniform of a lieutenant!

Our State Guard, a militia regiment, was like a French foreign legion. California was swarming with émigrés that year. Refugees from every country in Europe, who had seen Nazism and fascism in action. Some had already fought it. They knew, far better than we did, that this war would never be contained in continental boundaries. They wanted to prepare to serve their new country when the time came. But many were too old or physically unfit or politically unacceptable to find a place in the regular army in peacetime. We had not yet come to the day when "if he can walk he can pull a trigger." The California State Militia offered a service—of sorts. You bought your own uniform and you provided your own transportation. You were given a modicum of training and issued a rifle, a bayonet, and obsolete web belts and canteens.

Seldom had a more motley crew been assembled in the name of home defense. Our part-time volunteer warriors' occupations were as varied as their origins. Filmland was strongly represented. Writers, actors, directors, cameramen, and even grips, electricians, and carpenters. Some of our most professional-looking officers were extras or bit players who, having been frequently cast as officers, had acquired—if nothing else—a military bearing. Everyone could salute but few had ever fired a weapon, and those few, mainly in World War I—and not a few of *those* had served the kaiser!

Aside from the film folk there were a couple of Mexican prizefighters, three truck drivers, a member of the sheriff's office, a post office official, a floor-walker from Bullocks Wilshire, and a mysterious renegade ex-mercenary who had, he assured us, once served in China—in the Horse Marines. My own ephemeral claim to military fame stemmed from a brief attendance at Page Military Academy and a short man's enthusiasm for Napoleon. I had also acquired a reserve commission as second lieutenant in the U.S. Army Signal Corps years earlier. I had applied to be activated and been turned down as too old, too inexperienced, and too physically unfit. So I offered myself as a private to the 2nd California Infantry. I never heard of *them* ever turning anyone down.

I soon recruited one of my best friends, a good-looking young insurance salesman whose sister was a quite famous film star, Elissa Landi. Toni had been born an Italian count, which title he had abandoned when he migrated to California. Toni's mother was a daughter of Emperor Franz Josef of Austria. The Hapsburg family resemblance was evident in both Toni and Elissa.

He had attended public school and university in England, and there acquired a British accent. He had seen brief service in the

Royal Navy in World War I. He had rowed and boxed at Cambridge, played polo against Will Rogers, and sold insurance to the reigning monarchs of Hollywood. He carried an air of mysterious adventure that would have done credit to a secret agent, and he definitely added tone to our foreign legion.

From the beginning, Toni and I enjoyed spectacular promotions. We became platoon sergeants before we had fired a rifle. He was considered a great "catch" for our team—since Victor McLaglen, the screen tough guy, was forming a Black Horse Troop of cavalry, and would have traded three actors to get Toni!

Evenings we paraded about the environs of the armory, practicing close-order drill, riot drill, and guard duty, in preparation for the unlikely event that we might one day be called upon to defend Southern California. Our liberal friends regarded us as virtual stormtroopers and almost everyone else considered us total idiots.

But letters from London told of English friends being killed on the beaches of Belgium and Greece, or shot down over the Channel. Country after country was falling to the Nazis—while we marched around our armory.

Or drank ourselves silly at the moonlit poolside parties of Bel Air and fabricated our escapist films. It was surreal—a burlesque. Earning a four-figure salary for writing:

"*Fade in: Western desert.*
Three riders approaching."

And rushing off to present arms to our ancient colonel, Rupert Hughes, otherwise a renowned novelist. And knowing there was not one single cartridge in the whole regiment!

You wondered about it, threading into the crowded MGM commissary in that vintage year. There was Mickey Rooney lunching with Judy Garland. Cute-as-hell kids. Clark Gable waving you over to ask if you wanted to slip out and shoot skeet for an hour after lunch, which of course you did—he was easily the best shot in Culver City. Louis B. Mayer, Emperor of MGM, had built up the greatest stable of stars to be found anywhere. Walking through that commissary in 'forty-one, you could have seen picking at their salads Jimmy Stewart, Hedy Lamarr (in a sarong for *White Cargo*), Greer Garson, Lionel Barrymore, Katharine Hepburn, Irene Dunne, Red Skelton, William Powell, Wallace Beery, Spencer Tracy, Walter Pidgeon,

Robert Taylor, Lewis Stone, Gene Kelly, George Murphy, Van Johnson, Marsha Hunt, Robert Benchley, Dame May Whitty, Esther Williams—a terrycloth robe covering her sleek bathing suit; Mary Astor (whose name my father had invented); June Allyson, the eternal girl next door; Spring Byington, Gladys Cooper, Barry Nelson, Desi Arnaz, and so many others. Including Louis B. himself, not everyone's cup of tea—sentimentally patriotic, with a face like an overconfident owl—who was still keeping a firm hand on the helm of his company, and studying the rhumba to keep up with beautiful Lorena Danker, who was to become the next Mrs. Mayer.

Toughness and sentimentality, cheek by jowl. Mayer's appetite for Americanism, for his brand of the tattered dream, was insatiable. The great critic Bosley Crowther had called him "violent, stubborn, arrogant, unmercifully rude, ruthless, tyrannical, hardheaded, and a stayr at sex." The judgment seems superficial.

This giant who had come out of a Russian ghetto was a far more complex manifestation of the results of humble origin, wretched discrimination, and self-grown determination. He was quick to weep, tough to beat, and capable of being a formidable father-image to the vast family of stars and workers who sustained his greatness in the film world. He was physically formidable, an amateur boxer ever ready to take a swing at anyone who might at the instant seem to deserve it. He was also extremely generous on occasions and fanatically loyal. A promise once made was likely to be kept. In the pattern of other greats, like Jack Warner, Harry Cohn, Darryl Zanuck, he was a showman who felt his great debt to the American society in which he had been permitted to grow so powerful.

A vintage year for MGM. The heaviest concentration of talent in Hollywood—the studio seemed incapable of turning out anything that wasn't a hit. Its greatest creative genius, Irving Thalberg, had died five years earlier, at thirty-seven, but his spirit still dominated the studio that his great productions had brought to number-one success. To Louis B., Thalberg had been like a son, fragile, brilliant, considered one of the few authentic geniuses in our town.

Mayer had acquired a film giant for a son-in-law, David Selznick, my father's one-time assistant. While he was still at Paramount, David married Irene Mayer, the MGM boss's daughter. Later, when he set up to produce independently, Mayer made it a condition of loaning him Clark Gable for *Gone with the Wind* that the film would be released through MGM. So in 1939 MGM had got itself the biggest money-maker in Hollywood history without having had to invest a penny of its own money. No wonder it was at the top of the heap that winter of '41!

One of the joys of working at MGM then was lunching at the Writers' Table. You might find yourself sitting between the ebullient Bill Saroyan and Bill Faulkner. Saroyan had put up a basketball cage on the wall of his office so he could practice shooting baskets while relaxing from scripting *The Human Comedy* from his own book.

William Faulkner had rather embarrassed the studio by having a clause inserted into his contract that he should be permitted to write at home. In those days writers were expected to occupy the sumptuous offices provided for them, but in the case of such an eminent American novelist, an exception was made. However, home for Faulkner turned out to be, not a suite in the Beverly Wilshire or a rented palace on Beverly Drive, but, literally, his home, deep in the Deep South. When he was asked to step over to Louis B.'s office, the step could take a month.

Our crypts of creativity were guarded by efficient and often beautiful secretaries. Even that wasn't enough for one prominent writing team. They hired a brace of gorgeous extras to sit in evening dress in their outer office. This ensured uninterrupted writing, since nobody who came to see the writers ever bothered to get further than the girls.

If I had to select Hollywood's greatest period I suppose that this would have been it. Every studio grinding out hits, like *Mrs. Miniver*, *Good-bye, Mr. Chips*, *A Woman's Face*, *Waterloo Bridge*, *Dr. Jekyll and Mr. Hyde*, *The Grapes of Wrath*. Stars were earning their top salaries, pampered, protected, and groomed by the executives, who regarded them as priceless commodities, and the most famous writers in the world had been lured west by the irresistible salaries. Many, indeed, found in Hollywood a kind of negative inspiration for their bitterest, if not their best books, like Liam O'Flaherty's *Hollywood Cemetery*. The sumptuousness of it all gave creative people a sense of plush isolation.

This opulence sharply contrasted with the military asceticism of evenings at the old armory, but the fun of amateur soldiering was beginning to wear thin. One evening some local Clausewitz reached the sensible conclusion that even part-time soldiers should not remain perpetually innocent of the facts of war. There were some of the regiment who had never once fired a shot. Certainly none had yet fired the rather archaic Enfield rifles we had been issued. We knew the nomenclature, and had reached the advanced stage at which we could even respond to the command "Fix bayonets!" without castrating ourselves or beheading the man in the rank behind us. Nonetheless we were still unfit to protect the corner drugstore from a determined assault by a company of Campfire Girls.

So Rupert Hughes, colonel commanding the regiment, somehow contrived to get a few rounds of live ammunition, which I suppose he paid for himself, and complex logistics were worked out to portage a few hundred of us into the Mojave Desert for a weekend of bivouacking and maneuvers. We would play hide-and-seek amid the sage-clad Mojave hills, trying to avoid capture and cactus quills in our behinds, and there we would be indoctrinated into the mysteries of firing at targets. Not live ones, of course.

So, thanks to the trucks privately owned by some privates, we found a patch of reasonably open desert in a bowl of hills to bivouac on Saturday night. The stars blazed above, and the campfires below. Toni Landi and I had found an old iron bedframe rusting away, and we set it up in the open for our company commander, an act of unabashed ingratiation. This tactical triumph was interrupted by a minor riot which developed over a major poker game. One of our Mexican boxers, no doubt wishing to preserve his fists from damage in such an unprofessional foray, drew a switchblade on his brother-in-law. Sides were taken and the cream of the regiment was very nearly curdled, until somebody produced and uncorked a gallon of down-to-earth vino.

Tempers subsided. Toni, as first sergeant, confined the two miscreants to "quarters." Quarters? We had placed our bedrolls on the sandy crust of the desert floor, where we might become live bait for enterprising rattlesnakes and scorpions.

Still, I've always enjoyed rolling up in a "tarp" where everything distant becomes near and important in the listening to silence. Silence above sputtering embers—and the rising music of coyotes—suddenly mingling with reveille.

Soon enough the cooks got bacon frying, and as sunrise flowered above the lavender-tinted sage, our CO was roused from his iron bedstead and hoisted himself into the burnished morning.

Sunday morning. The crystal air began to heat in long translucent rays. A December scorcher! My platoon set off to attack a rival detachment, commanded by a German chef who normally compounded pastries at the Ambassador Hotel. We won by default, for as we moved to outflank each other in the best Napoleonic tradition, the chef suffered a mild case of heat prostration.

I considered dispatching a runner to Toni Landi at regimental HQ for litter-bearers, but decided against it. Toni would surely exaggerate it into a major medical crisis, for he was justifiably notorious for his tall stories. In fact he could make a cut finger sound like the assassination of Archduke Francis Ferdinand at Sarajevo. But you could never be sure if, when you least expected it, he might just be telling the truth! We'd all watched him do the curious stamp, stamp, stamp, about-face of the British army, and heard that he had performed similarly mounting guard at Buckingham Palace under the eye of King George! Knowing, however, that his military service had been in the Royal Navy, it seemed safer to reserve judgment.

In a regiment that had so little, we had something that other militia bodies, who had everything, had not. We had in Landi the greatest tall-tale teller since Baron von Munchausen.

While we were deciding what to do about the collapsed pastry cook, a runner came trotting across the sand, gasping that Sergeant Landi wanted all units to report to HQ at once, on the double!

All units? The designation in itself was a typical Landi-ism, since the whole heat-prostrating maneuver had scarcely engaged one battalion.

We struggled in. Toni was waiting, regarding us severely as we literally fell into formation. I announced all present or accounted for. If this was going to be the long-heralded target practice, our battalion was in the soup. Too many men had wasted their ammunition on jackrabbits, who had suffered no ill effects. We waited a brief eternity until Toni spoke.

"Men," he said theatrically, "the Imperial Japanese Air Force has just sunk the American fleet at Pearl Harbor."

Such an announcement from anyone else would have merely passed as a tasteless joke. From Toni it came as the master's supreme work of fabrication, and we began to laugh uncontrollably. "This time he's gone too far," my corporal choked.

But surely even Toni was overplaying the joke as he continued, stony-faced. "The 2nd Regiment has been ordered to return to Los Angeles at once. In the absence of regular army units, the fate of Southern California may rest in our hands."

We shrieked. His famous sister Elissa could not have matched this performance. We were enjoying ourselves so much, in fact, that we did not immediately hear the sound of sirens.

"Must be coming to lock up Toni!" someone guffawed.

"Shut up and listen to the radio!" somebody else shouted.

We broke ranks, crowding around the crackling radio in the one and only regimental jeep. It was a rebroadcast of the first news bulletin, and from it we knew that for once, just once, the truth was wilder than any yarn Toni could have conceived, that Sunday morning of December 7, 1941.

I think our first reaction was sheer exhilaration. Perhaps man's first love has always been war, until he gets a taste of it. Our amateur army siren-screaming through the small towns, empty Enfields slung on our shoulders, suddenly shared stature with the taxi-cab troops who'd halted the German drive on Paris. We were the minutemen responding to Paul Revere. We were Lincoln's blue-bellies, rushing to the salvation of Washington; Wellington's infantry, pouring out to Waterloo.

And in the little outlying towns, as our convoy bumped through, we heard the sound of cheering for the saviors of California. Quite a change from the laughter generally brought on by state guardsmen. We felt intoxicated with importance, drunk on glory.

The return to the armory was sobering. We lacked everything. Men were getting hungry. "When the hell do we eat?"

A diet of valor was hardly sufficient. With no facilities to feed our legions, Toni and I deployed to the nearest drive-in and purchased hamburgers for all. The regiment had not even been provided with funds to keep the armory's night-watchmen in coffee.

This war was getting expensive.

Then I saw the enemy, a wave of them, pouring into our building. Khaki-clad Japanese shouting and gesticulating! The advance guard of the Imperial Japanese Army? We stood paralyzed, armed only with hamburgers. Had an enemy landing been effected at San Diego?

Not quite. They were the Japanese gardeners of Beverly Hills and West Los Angeles, that some overpatriotic citizens had rounded up and delivered to us—for safekeeping.

Safekeeping! Where? How? Nobody knew the answer to that. Orders were shouted and countermanded. Confusion not only rained, it poured. The Japanese were bowing and hissing their innocence. Our officers would have gladly locked them up, but short of hiring hotel rooms, there was no place to put them. Somebody offered the embarrassing suggestion that we call the police. Somebody else said, "Whoever heard of an army calling the police?" Somebody else suddenly realized that Los Angeles was supposed to be in a blackout. Every light in the armory went out.

This was war. "Fix bayonets!" screamed some madman. A fat Japanese seized me about the waist, howling. I thought I was being attacked, but somebody had nicked him, trying to fix a bayonet in the dark. The first casualty on American soil—happily only a scratch. Nobody could find a light switch. At last some genius remembered the jeep parked in the armory and turned on its lights. An elderly Japanese humbly suggested that we confine them to their homes. This seemed a most practical idea, so we did.

Most California Japanese were loyal citizens, as it turned out. Nobody poisoned the water supply, blew up bridges, or set fire to oil wells. But the Japanese Imperial Forces had certainly fumbled their great opportunity by failing to invade Los Angeles that first night, for within the next few hours our own regular army troops poured into California, cigar-shaped barrage balloons blossomed in the cloudless skies, and the guardsmen were sent home.

I went back to MGM to complete the final script of *Omaha Trail*, rather an anticlimax after saving California from the gardeners. But my civilian days were numbered. A war department telegram activated me as a second lieutenant in the U.S. Army Signal Corps.

And so with cameras grinding, Hollywood plunged into war. For most it was not at first a very far plunge. The cinema battlefronts were Army Photographic Centers in Hollywood and New York. Many film folk merely exchanged their sports jackets for uniforms, their substantial salaries for army pay, and went right on doing the same jobs as always. Film editors edited, cameramen photographed, directors directed, actors acted, producers produced, and writers wrote. Only the product had changed, from entertainment films to training films. Directors who had once pampered pompous prima donnas might now be called upon to guide an instructional epic on the challenging problem of *Disposal of Human Waste*. You might find them positioning prop turds as carefully as they had once adjusted the shawl of some seductress.

"I'm doing the same thing as always," George Cukor confessed—"except instead of Joan Crawford in *A Woman's Face*, my star is a gas mask."

An army had to be trained rapidly and film was considered the natural short-cut. Every branch of the service was demanding training series dealing with its own particular techniques. West Pointers assigned as technical advisers began to sound like movie tycoons as they chatted glibly about "inserts" and "close-ups" and "dubbing" and "dissolves." There were moments when it seemed so many troops were involved in filming that there were scarcely any available to send over to the fighting.

Writers who had commanded four-figure salaries were creating minor masterpieces on such subjects as *The Loading of Box Cars.* Every subject was covered, from military police to military courtesy, from the dangers of syphilis to infantry-toughening series like *Kill or Be Killed!* With the army, navy, and marines making movies, you couldn't, it seemed, load a gun, cook a meal, repair a clutch, or sew on a button unless you had gone through a film course on the subject. One GI was so overindoctrinated after the film course on bayonet fighting that when he finally got into combat he chased enemies for miles trying to stick them, completely forgetting that his rifle was full of cartridges.

My first assignment was to script films on the mysteries of rigging and maintaining barrage balloons. It took me to Coast Artillery Camp Tyson, Tennessee, where I promptly lost a month's pay playing poker. On return to our Signal Corps Center, I was assigned to set up courses to train writers to write training films. It seemed a pretty dreary way to spend a war.

Particularly when you heard about Hollywoodians who'd gone overseas. Men like Lew Ayres, who even as a conscientious objector was risking his life stretcher-bearing wounded marines in the Central Pacific; Doug Fairbanks, Jr., serving with Mountbattten in Burma; Clark Gable and Jimmy Stewart, flying missions over Europe; Si Bartlett, on the staff of General LeMay. Almost everyone seemed to be going somewhere, while my typewriter commandos churned out dreary scripts, and endured the bickering of the various army branches, each of them trying to produce bigger and better training films than the other.

Even Dad seemed disappointed that my military career was to be spent in the studio he had built at Astoria, while I was "billeted" at a New York hotel. With my roommate, Jerry Hopper, who had been head of film editing at Paramount, I'd take the subway to war each morning. It was frustrating, and terribly embarrassing. Each evening we'd drown our shame in drink, until it seemed we should earn wound stripes for hangovers.

We began to pull strings to get ourselves sent overseas. I could see myself forging a great career in Europe via a smattering of languages. I savored a vision of being holed up in the cellars of a wrecked chateau while shells exploded above, wine-tasting for some division commander.

"A young Beaujolais, sir. You'll find it quite drinkable, I believe."

"Hmm, yes. Excellent, Lieutenant. See what you think of that cognac before we counterattack."

Then one day opportunity finally knocked. A new friend I'd met through scriptwriting for the infantry, Major General "Buck" Lanham, was alerted to a command in Patton's First Army, and he put in for me to go as his combat photo officer.

I waited, but the usual snafu developed. My overseas orders arrived all right, but somebody must have reshuffled the deck. I was to entrain to San Francisco and ship out as a replacement to a Signal Corps battalion in MacArthur's army in the Southwest Pacific. There'd be no wine cellars in the New Guinea jungles.

But at least this meant going somewhere: a troop train across the continent, then farewell to my father on the set at Warner's, where he was starting to produce *Rhapsody in Blue*, a filmed biography of George Gershwin. Gershwin had been a constant visitor at our New York apartment in the late twenties and Bess had given him painting lessons. I sat around in uniform, glumly listening to my father swap yarns with Irving Rapper, the director, and Oscar Levant, who was playing himself in the film. Already I felt displaced. I didn't belong here any more. Or at home, either.

A few days later, our troop transport nosed through the Golden Gate. Dad had sailed from here once, with the first hundred men to head for the gold rush at Nome, Alaska.

In my pocket was a letter from Franklin D. Roosevelt. It was a printed form letter, and a similar well-wish had been handed to every man as he came abroad. It went with us like a touchstone, and since the troop-jammed ship had no escort or self-protection against subs, no comfort of convoy, the letter was the only talisman we had. The only protection.

A time for old-fashioned sentiments.

Some three weeks later, we marched down the gangplank at Brisbane. A Digger shook us by the hand, a savagely lean-cheeked ghost of Tobruk. Everyone gave him a coin to drink our health (at his suggestion). We'd need health. And a hope that we might again see those fantastically attractive Aussie girls, who were known to be Yank-crazy. But after one night's tenting on the dog track outside the city, I was in a flying boxcar (C-47) pushing over Townsville and the liquid rainbow Coral Sea.

As we clambered out on the busy airstrip (still subjected to occasional raids by the Zeros) a powerful man hefting a valpack, an air force brigadier general, turned just in front of me. Suddenly he smiled with recognition—it was Merian C. Cooper. With Ernest

Schoedsack he had produced several films for my father's company, among the most important documentaries ever made.

"Small world, Jess."

"You making a documentary here, Coop? Sorry—I mean, General."

"You writing a script, Jess? Sorry, I mean Lieutenant."

We had scarcely more than a moment. His plane was leaving. You couldn't quite get away from Hollywood, even in New Guinea.

The next old friend I met was another Cooper. Gary. He was passing through with a USO show.

"Dammed back kept me out of your army"—he smiled his thin smile. His old back ailment had been so painful at times that the great man of action had had to be helped out of his chair. He'd just finished one war at Warner Brothers, as Sergeant York, and was on his way back to start another at Paramount for De Mille, *The Story of Doctor Wassell.* I wouldn't be available to write "Yup" and "Nope" for him in that one.

A few days later Captain Jack Hively and I with a combat photo detachment were edging around the tail of New Guinea in a landing craft to Milne Bay, recently taken from the Japanese. From there we sailed to join the Confederates—the 112th Texas Cavalry, staging on Goodenough Island for the invasion of New Britain, at Arawe Bay.

Our arrival in this particular theater of operations had inauspicious beginnings. Stepping into the tent assigned to us, we discovered a huge boa constrictor curled around the center pole.

We'd already set down our carbines and pistols at the entrance, a *faux pas* in any man's army. Any move to retrieve them might rouse the malevolent reptile. Jack had been a film director in civilian life and a university football player, and was now my superior officer. I knew he would have the answer. He did.

"Call for help," he advised. "And don't make a goddamn move till it gets here."

We started judicious shouting for the guard, while the boa constrictor watched us with a beady eye. After an eternity a bone-lean, six-foot Texan slouched in laconically. With trembling finger I indicated the creature braided around the pole.

"Oh that there's Joe," he drawled. "Regimental mascot. Right useful, too. Keeps the rats away. Figure we ought to take him along where we're goin'. Might scare off some of the Nips."

He administered a friendly scratch to the metallic nose, and the monster almost purred.

Happily, the Texans were generous souls and overlooked our cowardly Yankee origins to the point of making us Honorary Confederates. We would invade New Britain under the Lone Star flag of Texas, against which, one presumed, nobody would dare fire a shot.

General MacArthur did not share this confidence. He had employed a brilliant phrase to describe this operation: "a reconnaissance in force." To the unmilitary reader I dare interpret this as the greatest hedging of a bet ever attempted. Our regimental combat team would land with some "spare parts" and "reconnoiter" an enemy-held island. If we should be destroyed or pushed out, the "reconnaissance" could not be listed as a defeat, since we would have gained the priceless information that the Japanese were present in force. But if we succeeded in holding on, the reconnaissance could be exploited into an invasion. And while the Japanese were busy trying to push us off, a second landing would take place higher up at Cape Gloucester. It should have been called "Operation Guinea Pig."

The first time I saw MacArthur he was squinting benevolently at us as we embarked, and smoking a curious corncob pipe. He looked detached, aloof, Olympian. I had rather expected that on launching us on such a precarious adventure, he could at least have made some sort of farewell speech, something extemporaneous, like "You who are about to die—salute me!"

He spoke not a word.

What this war needed was a good scriptwriter, I decided.

Two days later the good scriptwriter was trying his best to become even a bad soldier. We made quite a heavy investment in that useless bit of coral beach, but as Brigadier General Cunningham pointed out, we couldn't go back anyway. The sea was behind us, and there was no place to go back to.

Dug in on that fringe of jungle with our backs to the beaches, the 112th Cavalry seemed likely to follow in the footsteps of the defenders of the Alamo. Reinforcement was difficult to ferry over because the Japanese Imperial Air Force controlled the sky with swarms of Zeros. But rescue was on the way. A detachment of highly trained jungle fighters was filtered across from Finschhafen under cover of darkness.

They landed behind us, passed through our lines, and slipped into the jungle. They worked around behind the Japanese positions and infiltrated them, which took the pressure off us and made life a lot easier for us all.

How many times had I and other film people perpetuated the fable of embattled settlers rescued from red Indians by the U.S. Cavalry? That night our cliché came home to roost, for when the dawn rose over Arawe we saw that our rescuers were in fact a detachment of American Indians, come to get the 112th Cavalry out of trouble. United by the common cause, they had come from a score of different tribes, many of whom were traditional enemies who did not even have a common tongue.

I resolved that if I got out of New Britain I would never again write a scene in which the army arrived in the nick of time to save the settlers from the redskins. But the promise was broken on my first film after the war—*Unconquered.* It proves, I suppose, that nobody can trust a Hollywood promise.

At least one Hollywood-made illusion survived wartime for at least one member of a wartime audience. A couple of years and several campaigns later, the MacArthur island-hopping technique had us poised for a thrust at the Philippines. We had joined the convoy off Manus in the Admiralties, staging for the invasion of Leyte Gulf. Combat cameramen had been brought from all over the Pacific and some from the Central Pacific with the XXIV Corps to record the keeping of the MacArthurian promise: "I shall return."

I was attached to the 96th Infantry, and embarrassingly in command of the combat photographic mission—embarrassingly, because my officers included ranks up to lieutenant colonel. I had to salute almost everyone before giving them orders.

We were watching an old movie on shipboard: *Northwest Mounted Police.* The captive audience (for there was no escape except into the steaming hold) bore up rather better than I would have expected. Our old film seemed unbearably heroic. As the hot breath of jungle night steamed across dark waters, once again I faced that awful waterfall escape! But the troop audience watched spellbound, applauded lustily at the end. As we moved below decks, the ham in me could not resist a moment of revelation. Suddenly it seemed important to tell someone that I'd been involved in writing that movie.

Briefly, in the press of men going below, a soldier was delayed beside me. His neck was turkey red under his steel helmet, and wrinkled enough to hold a three-day rain. He looked the kind of man you'd be glad to be near in an invasion.

Cecil B. De Mille directing *Union Pacific* (1938) from a stretcher. Here, in mellow mood, he displays one of the gold-plated railroad spikes, with which he rewarded admirers and VIPs, to Bill Pine, associate producer, and a set visitor. *(De Mille Foundation)*

Paulette Goddard and Robert Preston have a torrid moment in *Northwest Mounted Police* (1939). *(De Mille Foundation)*

Top: Nobody enjoyed the Paramount commissary lunches at the De Mille table except De Mille. To Jesse, Jr.'s right, Donald Hayne, speechwriter and official De Mille biographer; Jesse's co-scriptwriter Fred Frank; and research supervisor Henry Noerdlinger. *(De Mille Foundation)*

Middle: On the set of *Unconquered*. De Mille examines production sketches, surrounded by nervous staff. *(De Mille Foundation)*

Bottom: The end product. Paulette Goddard and Gary Cooper in *Unconquered*. *(De Mille Foundation)*

The rubber squid neatly upstaging Ray Milland and John Wayne in *Reap the Wild Wind* (1941). *(De Mille Foundation)*

Two mementos of Jesse Lasky, Jr.'s 1950 Roman interlude: TOP LEFT: Fashionably deglamorized Italian actresses, led by Valentina Cortese, in *Women Without Names* . . .

. . . and, BOTTOM LEFT, less artistic but more glamorous, Maria Montez as she appeared, for the last time, in *City of Violence*. *(British Film Institute)*

RIGHT: De Mille's own peacocks supplied the feathers for the gown Hedy Lamarr wore in *Samson and Delilah* (1948). *(De Mille Foundation)*

Samson (Victor Mature) does a little sparring with old Jackie.
(De Mille Foundation)

Hedy Lamarr, George Sanders, and producer-actor Henry Wilcoxon consider an appeal from Olive Deering on behalf of Samson. (*De Mille Foundation*)

An orgy interrupted—*The Ten Commandments*, 1956 (in the center, Edward G. Robinson). *(De Mille Foundation)*

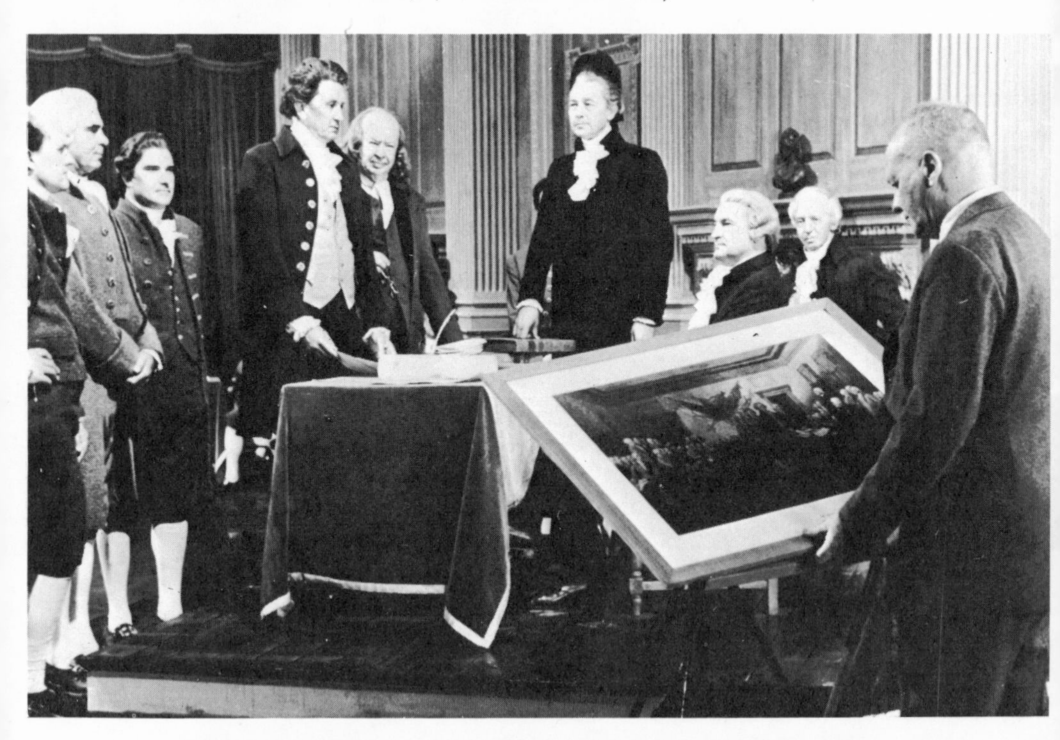

Director John Farrow recomposing the Declaration of Independence for the movie *John Paul Jones* (with Charles Coburn as Benjamin Franklin) from a famous painting of the incident. *(British Film Institute)*

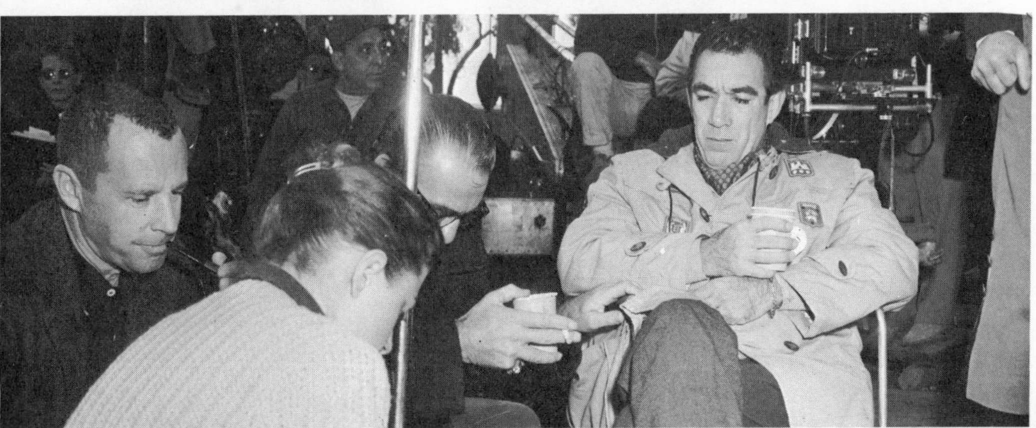

TOP: That floating hell for screenwriters, De Mille's yacht, *The Seaward*, *(British Film Institute)*

MIDDLE: An understandably unhappy-looking Anthony Quinn, supervising on-set rewrites for *The Buccaneer*. (*De Mille Foundation*)

BOTTOM LEFT: Jesse and Barbara (Pat) Lasky, husband-and-wife writing team at Twentieth Century-Fox, circa 1960. *(Author's collection)*

BOTTOM RIGHT: Jesse, Barbara, and earliest childhood pal, Douglas Fairbanks, Jr., circa 1975. *(Author's collection)*

Probably the last existing photograph of the three original partners in The Jesse Lasky Feature Players who in 1913 produced the first feature film made in Hollywood. From left, Jesse L. Lasky, Sr., Samuel Goldwyn, Cecil B. De Mille. *(Author's collection)*

"Did you like that movie, soldier?" I asked.

He swiveled eyes around and down like a periscope. "Yup."

That "yup" could not have been more laconically emitted by Gary himself. The beat went on interminably, then he added suddenly, "Why?"

"I wrote it," I said, somewhat too majestically.

He survived the disclosure, but stared down just a shade more curiously. "How's that, Captain?"

"The words."

"You sayin' you wrote down them words they talked up there on the screen?"

"Yes, and the movements, the action, the story."

This brought an immense grin. Infinite disbelief curved his lips. "You tryin' to tell me *you* wrote down what Gary Cupper said?"

I let a nonchalant glance slide across the rail to the dark profile of jungle shoreline. "Much of it. Often I'd even be called onto the set to give Gary new words to say."

The long face wagged positive negation. "Ain't no man tells Cupper what to say."

Hollywood had done its job, fabricating heroic concepts, making life appear braver than it was, strong men stronger, honor brighter, truth truer. Hollywood's real power was that audiences could believe it and its supermen, the Errol Flynns, the John Waynes, the Gary Coopers. Today, we are more concerned with man's true weakness of nature. The scope of cinema has extended inward, replacing illusion with a greater honesty.

And through this exploration of the human psyche, man as he is rather than as he might wish to imagine himself, Hollywood took the road to maturity. There were still beautiful toys in the attic, to be shared with the public. Change would come gradually over some fifteen lush years that lay ahead. But change there would be—for many of us an extension of the experiences we had known in a more real world. Most who had come back from war were, for better or worse, different than they had been. In this difference was the seed of ways of thinking and believing that would outgrow the old Hollywood. In time.

Twenty-Two

SHERMAN'S CONCLUSION that "war is hell" could have read "war is hell on marriage." My own broke up soon after I returned home from overseas in '45.

Home was no longer where the heart was, anyway. That revelation would be paid for, for years to come. Yet alimony, however crippling it would become in the years ahead, was not the only damage. From a career-expectation standpoint there was no reason to doubt that the big earning days in my mid-thirties were not only beginning, but would, like the prosperous dream capital itself, go on forever. That was why I chose not to contest the burden of alimony imposed on me. The money trees of Hollywood were heavy with fruit and always would be, so why worry about the future? One was home and alive and would, as before the war, be in demand to go on writing movies. One thought then!

The town wasn't physically much changed—only more crowded—but the enthusiasm of old friends seldom survived the first welcome-home toasts. Everyone wanted to forget the war, yet some couldn't. We hung on in bars, exchanging muted exaggerations with strangers. There was a feeling of basic dislocation—of being broken off from old roots. We felt unable to pick up the pieces of our old life, unready to plant seeds for the new. We were emotional tumbleweed.

Some younger GIs who had been wild and free and loose before the war rushed back to seize the stability of children, marriage, mortgages to be paid off, the GI education bill. Solid life patterns, and a vote for Daddy-loves-you Eisenhower.

But if the war had interrupted wild-oat sowing for the young, it had offered older men an often secretly welcomed dislocation: escape from comfortable monotonies—jobs, wives, obligations. The return to civilian life could be a letdown. Foundations in Hollywood had always been flimsy. You went up too briefly, down too quickly, always accustoming yourself to the peaks of income, then—bingo! one bad part, bad script, bad break, and you couldn't walk up to your best friend without his thinking it might be a touch. That was the chronic Hollywood disease, and the war years hadn't changed it. The sense of disorientation clung long after the uniform had been confined to mothballs.

These were the feelings I was trying to sort out in a novel called *Spindrift*—the spray after the storm, blown to nowhere on the whim of the wind. A blend of confession and apology. Meantime all my efforts failed to land a job as a screenwriter, brought me back to a beginning. I found myself sitting in De Mille's office again. Had it been four years? He, at least, seemed hardly changed.

"You don't have to tell me what they talked about in the foxholes, Jesse. I know. They talked about my fight for liberty—right here in Hollywood. My struggle to preserve 'the right to work'!"

He was referring to his famous battle with the American Federation of Radio Artists, who had voted to assess each member one dollar, to be used to oppose a proposition on the California ballot to abolish the "closed shop." De Mille's refusal to pay the buck had led to his being banned from the air. The loss of his Lux Radio Theatre amounted to some hundred thousand dollars per year. A fair price to pay for any principle.

I did not, however, correct him on the point of what "they had talked about in the foxholes." We sat a long moment, letting time flow between us. All the questions that couldn't be asked. One, of course, would be about my coming divorce, of which he would disapprove. Another matter of principle.

"How was the war, Jesse?" he tried finally.

"The Japanese weren't as terrifying as working for you used to be, sir."

I had my job back. He had already signed Charles Bennett and Fredric M. Frank to work on the script of *Unconquered*. On a film of such scope there would always be room for one more.

He took from his pocket a small, carefully folded morsel of paper and passed it over to me. I read aloud: "Where Liberty dwells, there is my country."

He nodded, then challenged suddenly. "Who said that, Jesse?"

"You, sir?"

"Ben Franklin!" But my error had not displeased him.

He pressed a button on his intercom. "Get me Henry Noerdlinger!"

Florence Cole's voice responded crisply, "Yes, sir."

"Henry's our new research man. He's not afraid to say, 'No, Mr. De Mille.' " De Mille beamed.

In a moment a giant Swiss with the frame of a fullback entered the office. He had an expression of poised granite.

De Mille showed him the scrap of paper.

"When did Ben Franklin say that about liberty? Do you know?"

Henry faced him squarely, unblinking. "No, Mr. De Mille. But I'll find out."

De Mille favored me with a what-did-I-tell-youish grimace. The giant receded quietly.

"He speaks half the languages in the world—and what he doesn't know he knows where to find someone who does."

With Henry aboard, our research tentacles could stretch around the world. He would issue regular bulletins of his findings on all pertinent subjects. He maintained a full liaison with the large department of research that serviced all units in the studio. He was our bulwark and our shield. De Mille expected his writers to assimilate the most detailed information on everything related to our subject. It is curious that with all this preparation our moving pictures somehow never came out looking as authoritative as they occasionally were. The special De Mille brand of theatricality ultimately submerged all but the pageantry. But the efforts we made through Henry and his sources to master minutiae were exhaustive and exhausting. It hardly mattered in the end. The critic always concluded—De Mille had done it again!

But to the boss, *Unconquered* had become more than a film. It was a cause embracing his struggle with AFRA, which had assumed the dimensions of a battle for free men's survival in a world threatened by Red submersion. With associates like Donald Hayne, his biographer and speechwriter, he formed the De Mille Foundation for Political Freedom, dedicated to promoting and protecting the "right to work." He wanted this union-curbing policy to be incorporated in the legislation of every state's constitution. In many states he succeeded. But while he was fighting his battle for the right to work, others were losing the battle for the right to exist, as Senator McCarthy began setting up his guillotines. His basket would soon be full of reputations.

In the newest addition to his stable of writers De Mille found a strong ally. Fred Frank was a devout Republican, a compact logician, a mule-stubborn scriptwriter as hardheaded as the boss. His conservatism was deep-rooted and practical.

We churned out a massive (190-page) screenplay under the master's eye. The film opened with dear old C. Aubrey Smith, that paragon of British virtues, as a judge at the Old Bailey (recreated on stage nine) offering murderess Paulette Goddard the choice between the gallows and indentured servitude in America. Her decision was not exactly surprising.

Unconquered packed a mighty cast. Gary Cooper, more or less playing himself in three-cornered hat and seasoned buckskins, Howard da Silva as a vicious heavy, Ward Bond as an honest blacksmith, Boris Karloff in a bit of offbeat casting as chief of the Seneca Tribe. Rugged Henry Wilcoxon doubled as De Mille's associate producer while playing a scarlet-clad British officer. Like all De Mille films, it would be loved by audiences, hated by critics, and rewarding to Paramount stockholders.

The filming produced a notable incident. On the Fort Pitt set. De Mille had positioned an energetic drummer boy high up on the stockade. The lad was beating the alarm—something of an overstatement, since the fort had been under attack for a considerable time and every man, woman, and child was busy repelling the assault.

It had been a difficult enough scene to get on film anyway. Battles generally are. There's always too wide a margin for error. A hammy death-fall by some extra, an accident to one of the stunt men, a wrist watch revealed beneath an eighteenth-century sleeve—all these can ruin an expensive take, and cause the scene to be reshot a dozen times. Only that morning a gallant charge by naked braves had turned into a burlesque when one of the noble savages accidentally slipped into a pratfall. Battle scenes are a director's nightmare, the chance of error being increased by the ratio of people involved. De Mille, ever obsessed with his passion for detail, had been forced to shout "Cut!" over and over again. Tempers were growing frayed as costs mounted. If we didn't get the "master shot" soon, we'd be into overtime, which could cost thousands of dollars.

Cameras rolled on the twenty-first take. Everyone held his breath, crossed his fingers. Again, the weary Indians rushed the stockade. Using their canoes as ladders, they swarmed up the walls and grappled with the defenders. Stunt men did spectacular drops from the top, supposedly hit by bullets or tomahawks. It was going magnificently. The defenders were heaving water along the bucket line to dowse flames—but nobody dowsed the flame on the arrow that arched straight down into the drumhead under the lad's thundering sticks!

De Mille closed his eyes, lifting clenched fists to a heaven that could be so careless as to ruin his best take. He was about to yell "Cut!" when he caught his breath. The drummer boy had *not* stopped beating! The camera did not miss the small white gloved hands rattling on, even as the flames rose from the drumhead igniting the very sticks themselves! The fury of the attacking redskins broke like a wave out of the inferno. It was superb. At last the Boss yelled "Cut!"

The lad plunged his charred gloved fists into a pail of water. Everyone rushed to him. Especially dour Roy Burns, the unit manager—who calculated that some fifty thousand dollars had just been saved by getting that shot.

A doctor examined the boy's burns, happily not serious. De Mille came over to the unruffled lad and bestowed one of his famous mint fifty-cent pieces as if it were a Congressional Medal of Honor.

"For courage far above and beyond the call of duty!" he said. The boy grinned.

"Aw, them gloves were kinda thick anyhow. Didn't hurt much."

Still photographers recorded the incident for publicity.

"I guess America won't have to worry as long as there are boys like you growing up," the Boss said, and everyone applauded.

Henry Wilcoxon and I watched the award almost with envy. That lad could grow up and tell his grandchildren he had once beaten a fiery drum for C. B. De Mille in the autumn of Hollywood's grandeur. And of course he would be called to work in every De Mille picture to come. And it was easy to believe that there would always be another. The old man was indestructible, as everyone must know—even God.

As production wore on, nerves generally grew increasingly frayed and the wrath of our god began to fall increasingly upon the shortcomings of the scriptwriters. I was not married at the time and was dating a vivacious young starlet, Marie Johnson, a protégée of Howard Hughes at RKO. One night she gave me a gift, a rather ostentatious gold cigarette holder. Next day at the De Mille table, instead of pulling out one of my customary grimy pipes, I smoked with it. There were snickers and smirks which I rose above. The following day after lunch all the staff—writers, research people, field secretaries, and the like—suddenly produced similar long holders. Everyone had a good laugh at my expense, including De Mille. Enough to disinfect me against any further illusions of romantic grandeur.

Once bitten, I should have been twice shy of attempting any flamboyance within range of the Boss's unpredictable responses. This time my indiscretion was self-indulgence in that "lowest form of humor." No worse choice of time or place could have been imagined.

We had been on the set of *Unconquered* doing some further script repairs and were watching a take that had gone wrong for the nineteenth time. Paulette Goddard had run the usual gauntlet of maladventures to which De Mille heroines were traditionally subjected. She had been sentenced by C. Aubrey Smith, bullwhipped by Howard da Silva, mauled by soldiers, manhandled by redskins, and finally, as their captive, tied to a stake. There, the lady would surely have been for burning if Gary Cooper had not materialized from a puff of powder smoke!

At this point in the action, dicing with words for her life, he demands of Boris Karloff (playing Guyasuta, the Seneca chief) that the white woman should be set free. Expectedly, Guyasuta refuses, opposing the threat of white man's magic with the power of his great medicine man, Sioto (played by Mark Lawrence). In a contest of magic—red man's against white man's—a showdown is reached. Gary wagers, on the life of the girl and his own, that his talisman will prove his occult superiority.

His prop is a simple pocket compass. Standing before Guyasuta, who is wearing more steel weapons than a porcupine has quills, Gary challenges the medicine man to change his needle's direction away from Guyasuta. As everyone (but Guyasuta and his medicine man) knows, a compass needle oriented to the pull of steel cannot be swerved. In frustrated fury, Guyasuta urged on his medicine man with increasing vehemence.

"Make needle point! Make needle point!"

I couldn't resist a whisper to Fred Frank, "How can he? The poor bastard can't even sew!"

The tense weariness of the moment made the remark seem irresistibly funny, and the two of us collapsed with unjustified mirth.

De Mille, who had been intently following the rehearsal, now rasped furiously, "What do you find so funny, Jesse?"

"It's nothing, sir."

"Nothing. You're easily entertained, I'd say." His voice had lifted to include almost everyone on the set in his auto-da-fé. "Our writers have something more entertaining than the scene they've prepared for my direction! I think it unfair that the pleasure should not be shared with the rest of us. So, Jesse, tell us all what you find so amusing."

One recalled the story of the whispering extra girls on one of his films who had responded to a similar demand with the admission that they had been speculating as to when "the bald old bastard" would let them break for lunch! It seemed unlikely he would be similarly amused this time. He wasn't.

"Then perhaps *I* should make needle point, too!" he purred. "To the gate by which you leave this studio."

But before the threat was put into effect I was exonerated by the reasonable suggestion that I devote my flashes of humor to the screenplay—which could only result in its improvement.

Conclusion: De Mille of de Gods grinds slowly! I refrained from sharing that one with him.

For a time production continued smoothly enough. The writers were released from front-line duty on the set to the welcome rear-echelon function of trying to create a story line for the next film script, back in our offices.

Then one hot summer afternoon, a secretary interrupted us with the troubling word that the Boss required us on the set again. At once! We gathered up scripts, pencils, and pads, and raced off to the dread arena.

We knew at once that the crisis was major. Filming had come to a dead halt. Paulette, in bright green ball gown, had been rehearsing an exit that didn't work. It didn't work because the line we had written her (which had seemed bright enough in cold print) came off flat and soggy when actually spoken. A new speech was required, and from the frenzied scribbling of various people trying to lend a word, it was apparent that the Boss had worked himself into a mood wherein the Bard himself could not have delivered satisfaction.

"I know it's too much to expect from writers—to supply usable words for actors and actresses to speak," he began. "Originality, like hope, is abandoned by all authors who enter my employ!" Unrestrained mirth from everyone in earshot. "Well, gentlemen, if you want me to finish this picture, I suggest you, or somebody, find me a line to cover Paulette's exit!"

We went to work, madly scribbling suggestions, our creativity hardly assisted by his stalking up and down behind us. And the whole crew waiting. Each offering was rejected as quickly as it was submitted.

"I am not asking for the soliloquy of Hamlet or the Song of Solomon! Just something short and fresh that a 'real person' might say! But I suppose it's hopeless. Let us then hope that the color of the gown will brighten her exit."

Paulette came to our rescue. "Green is such a cool color," she suggested.

"Perfect!" He beamed. "Exactly what I've been looking for! Which, of course, my overpaid men of letters couldn't be expected to think of. Writers must never be asked to write!"

Paulette beamed gently up at the great man. "Oh, but they did write it, C. B. They just whispered the line to me. We're all glad you like it."

Yes, indeed. An actress *could* be something more than a woman.

This story has nothing to do with *Unconquered*, but I had to put it in somewhere.

Henry Hathaway, as tough-minded a director as any of that vanishing breed who filled the screen with crashing horsemen and powder smoke, told me of his first brush with the master of invective. Henry was serving De Mille as a young third assistant director. It was his first film job with the Boss and he wanted to be on his toes, jump to the command, make a great impression. His chance came when De Mille suddenly spotted him and called, "You!"

Henry leaped to the old man's side, "Sir!"

"Go over to the main office and . . ."

Before the sentence was finished Henry was off like a shot. De Mille's voice whip-cracked him to a stop three steps from the sound-stage door.

"Wait! Just what do you think you're going to do when you get there?"

"Well, I . . ." Henry stammered. "You said to go and so I got going . . ."

"Good," De Mille snapped. "Just keep going, fellah. Right through the gate, and don't bother to come back!"

Years later, when Henry reminded De Mille of the story, the Boss was truly surprised. "Would I have done a thing like that?" he appealed to the assembly of those who knew him.

"Yes, Mr. De Mille," we chorused in unison.

"I guess I would," he sighed.

Actually, on that occasion Henry Hathaway had kept going, and got halfway around the world, pausing only when he reached India, by which time he had run out of funds—and in fact cabled me for a loan (which he repaid!). He stayed in India long enough to pick up a smattering of knowledge that later suited him for one of Paramount's most desired directorial assignments, *The Lives of a Bengal Lancer*. He was the only man I ever knew who thanked the Boss for firing him.

Twenty-Three

"What would you say is the greatest love story ever told?"

I could not think of an immediate answer. After a moment De Mille repeated the question, this time less benevolently. That afternoon in the summer of '48, his inner office, a deathly still cell of interrogation, was the only quiet place in the De Mille building, for all round this throne room the hive of office suites, breached by a long corridor, perpetually droned with the throb of commerce and creation—a symphony of typewriters, phrases of dictation, and ringing phones poured out of any door that might be opened.

"I'm waiting," he reminded me.

"Romeo and Juliet?" I tried.

He looked ready to hit me. "Thalberg made that years ago!"

You never could be sure how many guesses you got in these games. I searched for a visible clue, and settled on the huge Bible on his desk. Of course. The Book of Esther. He had always been fascinated by its filmic possibilities, and no one could say it wasn't a formidable love story. My suggestion was sheathed in reasonable confidence.

"I ought to brain you!" he exploded, reaching for a curious weapon, apparently the jawbone from the skull of some animal. Of course! The jawbone of an ass . . .

"Samson and Delilah," I ventured.

He lowered the osseous weapon. "In my school days any five-year-old could have given the answer in two seconds. But I suppose today nobody studies anything but the works of Lenin and Marx."

Suddenly abandoning sarcasm and posturing, he told me the familiar story of the strong man as it appears in the Book of Judges—simply, divested of lily-gilding dramatics, in terms that made it as current as the morning news. I knew he had found his next epic, a parable of strength and weakness, foolishness and faith.

But there was one major structural fault:

The Bible story, starting from Judges 14, refers to three women in Samson's life. The first is the daughter of the Philistines, "who pleased him well"—so well that he goes down to Timnath (pausing en route to kill a young lion) and takes her as his wife. At the wedding feast he proposes a riddle, wagering thirty suits of new clothing with the thirty Philistine wedding guests. But the Philistines are not about to lose a bet to any mere Hebrew. They wouldn't even want him in their country club, let alone married to one of their sisters. So they persuade Samson's wife to entice the answer from her husband.

She does, and they win the wager. Samson guesses where their information came from and cries havoc. To pacify him, his bride's father pleads that he "take her younger sister instead," pointing out that she is fairer anyway. But Samson rejects this young charmer, and then, in a frenzy of frustration he unleashes a holocaust, destroying houses, hosts, fields, and guests.

The Bible does not mention whether or not the younger sister died in the conflagration; but one may presume that if she survived the carnage, it would not have been unlikely that she vowed vengeance against the man who not only destroyed her family, but, far worse, scorned the offer of her hand in marriage.

Thereafter Samson becomes an outlaw, harrying his enemies with a variety of weaponry, ranging from foxes with their tails set on fire to the familiar jawbone of an ass, and once even carrying off the gates of Gaza. But for all his strength he still has a weakness. The Bible tells us that "he loved a woman in the valley of Sorek, whose name was Delilah." The story of how she tempted his secret from him, made him vulnerable to capture and blinding, and how finally, when his hair grew long again, he pulled down the temple to die with his enemies is known to every child.

But from a film dramatist's point of view, there is one great hole in the story: the gap in his love life. After his marital breakup, seemingly years later, he becomes involved in another affair, with that woman in the valley of Sorek. The opening has no connection with the end. Episodic, and hell to cast, since no major female star would want to appear only in the last half of the film.

But—take dramatic license, give that spurned little sister a name, and the whole story falls together into a perfect structure. Call her Delilah.

Now she has an understandable motive—vengeance! The woman

scorned becomes the instrument of high tragedy. We understand why Delilah seduces the secret from Samson. We have the magic formula—love becomes hate becomes love! We can now prepare the treatment and screenplay for an ideal De Mille film.

During the writing, the Boss again underwent hospitalization, but the script moved swiftly to conclusion, and he gave it his blessing from his sick bed. Never had a De Mille script been readied so quickly, or so painlessly for its authors.

Then the Boss recovered his normally robust health and with it his prickly disposition, and went back to his desk to tackle the problems of casting.

In those days our unit casting director was Joe Egli, a mild giant, subject to epileptic fits. When overcome by a seizure, Joe would clutch the nearest bystander in a stranglehold. Occasionally it happened to be De Mille! A lesser mortal might certainly have protected himself from these sudden, bone-crushing embraces by getting rid of Joe. But De Mille stoically endured those terrible moments when the stricken giant fell foaming at the mouth, while we tried to manipulate handkerchiefs between his teeth to prevent his biting his tongue.

Despite this tragic illness, Joe was one of the best casting directors in Hollywood; yet all his efforts and those of the agents who hovered about the unit had not yet put together a complete cast that De Mille would approve.

We had made a good start with Hedy Lamarr. Considered to be the most beautiful woman in Hollywood or anywhere else, Hedy had partially achieved her reputation with that famous nude swimming sequence. Everyone had wanted to know the identity of the beautiful nymph streaking into the limpid lake. The answers were seasoned with mystery. "Hedwig Kiesler" was said to have been the mistress of the richest arms merchant in Europe. In the ten years since her first American film, *Algiers* (1938), Hedy Lamarr had starred in some twenty successful movies.

De Mille was not sure how good an actress she was, but that was never his first consideration. She filled the eye of the beholder with such breathless beauty that her acting hardly mattered.

The spectacular face and figure were enhanced by a miraculous grace. She could fall into a pose as naturally and easily as though she had been rehearsing it for weeks. She seldom needed correction. De Mille said she was like a gazelle—incapable of a clumsy or wrong move. But as was the case for many screen beauties, the lovely surface hid troubled depths.

That year of *Samson and Delilah*, however, found Hedy as nearly fulfilled as she would ever be. Admired, adored, worshipped by all of us who worked with her.

De Mille personally selected peacock plumes, feather by feather, from his own stately birds of Paradise to adorn her. The result was the most glamorous gown Hollywood had ever seen.

After reading the script, Hedy scrawled on the title page of my work copy, "Jesse, I hope I do justice to your Delilah—Good luck to both of us!" Having Hedy in that part was everybody's good luck.

De Mille's choice for Samson was less exuberantly received. Victor Mature had never been taken very seriously as an actor by anyone—probably not even himself. Perhaps he had been a victim of his own publicity. When some press hawk tagged him "the beautiful hunk of flesh," any serious consideration of his thespian talent was forever submerged. But he had the physique to match De Mille's concept of Samson—or at least De Mille's concept of what the public's concept ought to be. And when the Boss decided what the public wanted, there could be no argument.

The selection of Angela Lansbury to play the older sister was perfect. Also George Sanders, as the Seran of Gaza, boss of the Philistines; he had just the right touch of nonchalance to lift a cup in toast to Delilah—while Samson pulled the temple down on his head.

The one part that hadn't been and apparently couldn't be cast was the hometown-girl-next-door, the honest Hebrew maiden that Samson should have married. She had to look like what any Jewish mother would choose for her son, practical, religious, unglamorous, and marvelous about the house. Miriam, the good girl, marriage with whom would have deprived the Bible of its most spectacular love story.

You might think such a part would hardly require casting genius! The trouble was that all the young contract actresses whom the studio wanted used were pure Irish-American! Or so De Mille insisted. It was enough to bring on one of Joe Egli's fits. And it did.

Henry Wilcoxon, serving De Mille as associate producer as well as playing Ahtur, Samson's Philistine rival in the film, was hard-pressed. Harry was almost always hard-pressed. Beneath a visage that would have perfectly graced Mount Rushmore, the granite eagle was sweating blood. If someone didn't find the right girl soon the film might have to be postponed—which could mean just about doubling the three-million-dollar costs already envisaged. But Harry was a born trouble-shooter. He thrived on crises, appearing to keep his head when all about him were losing theirs and blaming it on him—quite the best quality for an associate producer.

"Biff" Wilcoxon had originally been imported from England to play Richard the Lion-Hearted in De Mille's *The Crusades.* It was a crusade from which he never returned. But surely his amaranthine true-life role of right hand to the Boss required the most courage of all. It was just lucky for all that he had it.

Candidate after candidate for the important part of Miriam was introduced and rejected. Desperation increased. Then, happily, I had an idea.

Betty, my New Yorker second wife, and I had received an unexpected phone call from an old friend, Olive Deering. A superb actress trained in the Jewish theater, she and her husband, New York actor Leo Penn, had just arrived in California and badly needed work.

I broached Olive's name to De Mille with the assurance that she was definitely "Old Testament." A veritable Ruth, an Esther, a Rachel—so why not a Miriam?

"I want a Jewess!" he grumbled petulantly, "A Jewish Jewess! If there is such a thing."

"She's a walking synagogue," I assured him. "Rebecca at the well! If you'll only just see her, sir."

He didn't look too happy. My reputation as a judge of casting had never been particularly high in De Mille circles.

"All right, get her over here," he growled.

I hardly needed Harry's warning that De Mille would have my scalp if Olive turned out to be insufficiently Semitic.

She arrived with Leo, and after due briefing and plenty of warnings of what not to do or say, we were summoned into the throne room.

I had cautioned against the hated red nail polish, too much lipstick, or too high heels. Her hair fell biblically about her shoulders.

My final whispered precaution was, "Remember, you're supposed to look Jewish!"

"That's a relief," she laughed. "For most parts they say I look too Jewish!"

Florence buzzed. The voice growled through the intercom. We were gestured to enter.

I introduced Olive informally, as De Mille rose with deceptive politeness—deceptive because an instant later he had reseated himself in his traditionally squeaky swivel chair, kicked on a spotlight to blaze into her face.

But Olive bore up wonderfully against this Gestapo-ish gesture, which had floored so many young actresses. She returned his penetrating glance with placid poise. At last he kicked off the terrible spotlight, and again became a hospitable host, showing her Dan Grosbeck's wonderful visuals of the characters. The boss demonstrated biblical props. He swirled a diaphanous scarf through the air.

"Gauze," he announced. "Gets its name from Gaza."

She appeared properly fascinated. I could tell we had got off on the right foot, when he pantomimed Miriam's entrance into the film, with an imaginary waterjug on his shoulder and a smile of infinite sweetness. He saw her out at last, with the grace of a papal legate, but nodded at me to remain. He returned to his desk, and I awaited the word.

"Well," he said finally. "You say she can act. I suppose that's possible." Earth-shattering praise, from him.

"She was one of the stars of the Jewish Theatre. Practically a Sarah Bernhardt!"

"She'd have to be. Because no camera on God's earth could photograph that face."

But–she's–she's so Old Testament, sir . . ."

"Jesse, you have brought me the one actress in the world who cannot, I repeat *cannot*, be photographed from *any* angle!"

Behind the performance I could tell that he was completely sold on Olive, and in a perverse way it infuriated him. He kept probing for some fault or failing.

"What about politics? Where does she stand? In the Kremlin?"

"Her dedication is to the theater, sir. And her husband has every medal in the book. He led the bombers over Germany. Wounded. Shot down. Back in the air as soon as he could get out of hospital. He's–all American!"

De Mille buzzed Florence. "Get Henry Wilcoxon in here!"

Henry marched in, a curious inverted chamber pot on his head.

"I was trying out the new design for the Philistine helmets," he explained. "They still haven't got it quite right."

De Mille nodded, his smile mysterious. "I think we've found our Miriam, Henry."

And so we had. Olive could hardly have been better. A thorough professional, imbued with her role, she moved through the Hollywood sets like a daughter of Dan, the perfect foil for Hedy's dashing Delilah.

Then came a terrible day. A mysterious phone call from Washington. One of those invisible zombies who destroyed reputations in the darkness of anonymity had launched a suspicion, and poisoned it with a rumor. Olive's name had appeared on "one of the lists"!

Those fatal, ephemeral lists. There were so many at the time that it would have been virtually impossible for anyone's name not to have made one of them. Yet, admittedly—the mere fact of inclusion could be serious enough in those days.

Some members of the staff had turned visibly paler under their suntans at the possibility that we were harboring a traitor. If Olive seemed an unlikely candidate to overthrow the U.S. government by force, it had to be remembered that Senator McCarthy and Martin Dies had revealed that even priests, generals, and scrub-ladies were not immune to subversion. Traitors lurked under every bed, and many in them!

Expectedly, De Mille concentrated the first interrogation (it took place in the commissary) on the source of Olive's introduction into the unit . . . me. "Jesse, I have one question—and I want it answered with a simple yes or no. Is she clean?" The contemporary use of the phrase was political.

I crossed over to the table where Olive was lunching alone. "Something's come up," I began. "A political question."

She nodded, knowing exactly what I was about to say.

"It's De Mille who wants to know."

"Tell him not to worry." Her smile was beautiful.

With vast relief I crossed back to the De Mille table. "All clear, sir."

He beamed around the table. "Get Washington. Tell them—if she's a De Mille actress, she's clean."

The Boss regarded it as a matter of noblesse oblige to protect his own people from everyone. Except from himself!

Henry Wilcoxon could bear witness to that.

We were rehearsing a scene in which Samson was called upon to attack an entire company of Philistines single-handed.

Somehow the scene didn't quite produce enough realistic violence to satisfy the Boss. After watching the flabby flailing of the stunt man doubling for Vic Mature, armed with a rubber "jawbone of an ass," De Mille grabbed up one of the actual bone props and attacked Henry Wilcoxon, armed only with javelin and shield. "Defend yourself, Harry!" he shouted.

His loyal associate underwent a terrible bashing, but the stunt men and extras got the idea. On the next "take" they fought like furies. For that scene the blood was not all provided by the makeup department.

A few days later, trouble again developed. Victor Mature, normally a docile actor, unexpectedly refused to go before the camera. The Bible and our script both called for Samson to kill a young lion in single combat.

Obviously the sequence would be shot partly with doubles. There would be a rolling grapple with a man in a lion's suit. There would be the use of a disembodied claw that could rake Vic's face in close-up. But to make the struggle appear real, it would be absolutely necessary to get a few scenes of Mature fighting a real lion, in person, and unfortunately Mature didn't share the lion's enthusiasm for the tussle.

De Mille flicked a glance around the set, looking for a candidate to set an example. There stood Henry, who would have wrestled a battalion of lions at a nod from De Mille, but he would not do. The director's eyes cast about for somebody smaller, the smallest available victim, to make his point to the star. His eyes settled on me.

"Jesse, wrestle that lion!"

I looked toward old Jackie. A reputedly harmless toothless film veteran himself. Absolutely safe, as everybody knew. But did Jackie know? I appreciated Vic's reluctance. But an order from De Mille was never preceded by "Will you?" Mine not to reason why! I turned uncertainly toward the amiable-looking King of Beasts.

The trainer whispered a word in Jackie's ear. The tawny creature arose, freed from his leash. I inched to meet him. Yellow eyes glazed in unfriendliness. Was the beast acting? The trainer's hand reached to a chair, just in case.

"Now you'll see how dangerous old Jackie is, Vic," De Mille smiled.

As I took a halting step nearer, powerful jaws widened, yellowing teeth bared. I hoped that De Mille would not expect me to place my head between those jaws. Happily it was not necessary to come to grips with the situation, for old Jackie was only yawning, and anyway the gesture had sufficed. Vic threw off his robe, flexing his famous muscles, and stepped ahead of me toward Jackie and the cameras. What actor could let a writer steal the scene?

As the filming drew toward its end, we terminated the writing chores by preparing long lists of crowd lines. Too much shouting by extras during actual photography could spoil the balance of sound, drown out important speeches. Also, there was the constant danger, when extras ad-libbed, that somebody might shout something silly or obscene. So on all De Mille films the shouts and yells were prepared on paper, to be dubbed in later by actors. Like Olympic weightlifters reduced to the ignominy of carrying luggage, we toiled over fifty ways to say, "Go on, Samson, fight that lion! He can't lay a claw on you!"

And then, quite suddenly, it was over. De Mille glanced through the last of these boring lists, nodded, beamed around the lunch table. "Well, that's it, fellahs. Good job. You're finished. Collect your final check and go home after lunch."

We stared at him. We were fired? Terminated? Sacked? It was unprecedented. We were accustomed to completing one assignment and being instantly started on another.

"You mean we'll be—off salary?"

He nodded blandly. "Nothing more to do on this one. And I haven't decided on the next. So, I'll see you next year, perhaps. When we're ready to start another script."

Just like that. After years of diligence and opulence. Working till nine or later most nights. Saturdays on the ranch. Or the yacht. Nightly projections at his house. All ended—to be cast adrift on the seas of unemployment as casually as a dismissal of strangers. It was too much.

It was also illegal. Our Writers' Guild required that if we had been employed over a prescribed length of time we must receive two weeks' severance pay. It was our right and our due. After lunch we contacted Roy Burns, the unit business manager on the production, into whose lap fell union problems. Roy's head began wagging even before the ultimatum had tumbled from our lips. We certainly would not, could not, impose technicalities of our "pinko" guild on the "old man" who loved us like children! Blood had to be thicker than ink! He conveyed the image of a gallant mellow, aging champion of humanity, being beaten down by storms of impersonal pecunious legislation. We held our ground. So did he.

"For *two lousy weeks*' pay you'd stick a knife into *him!* A man whose sole consideration is sacrifice and loyalty to his fellow workers —no mention the cost?" (Everyone around De Mille eventually started talking that way.)

We informed Roy that we were no longer fellow workers in any case, since we had just been kicked out into the cold.

"My God," wailed Roy. "After all he's done for you—you bring up money! I never heard of such a thing!"

"You heard of it when you read the basic agreement with our Guild. Two weeks' notice, or two weeks' salary."

His face became ashen. He looked sick with disgust. "I wash my hands of this!" he declared, and left, his whole soul repelled by our crass commercialism.

Moments later the famous booted stride thundered toward us down the hall. De Mille knocked and entered without waiting for invitation.

"Gentlemen," he murmured, surveying us with infinite sadness. "Do I correctly understand that some trivial technicality has been allowed to threaten a great working relationship?"

Fred Frank and I explained quietly, even regretfully, that the initiative was not ours—but a basic working agreement between our guild and the studio. We had no option in the matter.

He closed his eyes a moment, wounded to the core.

"Caesar had his Brutus—" he said. "I have you."

There didn't seem to be any suitable answer to that, so we waited silently.

His hand moved slowly toward his pocket.

"There was a quite different speech I had planned for our farewell. I was going to have spoken about the deep values shared in a creative relationship. The brotherhood of effort that doesn't watch clocks or count pennies, but gives all to the endeavor. All the perspiration and inspiration that builds the great result! I was going to say thank you for giving me your devotion, and a script to be proud of—a film that will outlive us, and inspire perhaps some few in the vast faceless masses of humanity who await it. I was going to say, 'Thank you for giving me *Samson and Delilah*—and I hope you will accept—for your devotion and effort—above and beyond the call of mere duty—these tokens of my appreciation and esteem!' "

So saying, Cecil B. De Mille, whose mere word had caused golden bathtubs to be filled with asses' milk, or castles to rise from orange groves, bestowed on each of us, one of his mint fifty-cent pieces—in lieu of two weeks' salary.

Twenty-Four

THE "OLD GLORY"-CLAD huntsmen were riding high. They thundered through turgid meadows of publicity after the red foxes threatening the chickens in every pot, the two cars in every garage, the futures of the freckle-faced Little Leaguers and their dads who had so recently saved the very fat and fabric and substance of the land from little yellow men and brown- and black-shirted high steppers in jack-boots. Now, it seemed, our security was vulnerable to pen pricks and typewriter taps of eggheads, scribes, and thespians from the socially too conscious fringes of Manhattan-spawned theater groups and our local swimming-pool pinks. We were, we were assured, in danger more dire than in those cataclysmic days of war and death, for now the foe wore no uniforms nor subscribed to Geneva conventions. So the self-appointed guardians of our survival must hound and break up the predators, snout and tooth. The name of the game was "Un-Americanism" and the referee was blowing the whistle on everyone. The players didn't wear numbers or uniforms, and the losers could be anybody that somebody just happened not to like.

With a prevalence of witches, the only problem was, Which witch to hunt? That too-bright young producer who had risen too quickly, that story editor who hired only guess-what-kind-of-writers (which perfectly explained why she hadn't hired you). The actor who got the part you were up for; even the director who banged the red-headed starlet who let him. It was the essence of McCarthyism to accept the postulation of a vast conspiracy against which the loyal could be protected only by the weapon of vigilant investigation. Innocents were swept to the burnings along with anyone allegedly dedicated to overthrowing the government. It was enough to have attended a meeting of the Hollywood Anti-Nazi League, or to have contributed to a Fund for Chinese Orphans, or to have signed a petition against child-beating prepared by the Hollywood League for Democratic Action. It was almost enough to have worked in films. The Sermon on the Mount would have been suspect.

The mainstream of McCarthyism reached a degree of senseless savagery that made Cotton Mather's Salem trials look like amateur theatricals. For some there would be imprisonment; for others, exile. Small fish though we must have been from the standpoint of a serious Communist threat, the persecution of Hollywood celebrities, large and small, had become irresistible fodder for ambitious politicos. Even Helen Douglas, wife of actor Melvyn Douglas and a Democratic congresswoman from California, was a target for a rising young Republican lawyer, Richard Nixon.

I, too, faced a congressional committee, and was cleared only when I proved that at the time I was cited as having attended a Communist Front meeting in Los Angeles, I was actually taking part in the invasion of the Philippines under General MacArthur.

Perhaps the most ludicrous aspect was the investigation into the Red Menace supposedly infiltrating our Hollywood product. Propaganda? It was hard enough to inject any food for serious thought into movies in those days, let alone a corruptive shove into the arms of Marxism.

However, these tragic years gave birth to at least one perfect comedy, in 1956.

Our "middle-of-the-roaders" in the Writers' Guild of America, West, had been voted into power. Men like Charles Brackett, Irving Stone, James M. Cain, Philip Dunne, and many others had plotted a victory for moderation. I had become vice president of the Screen Branch.

Our most inflated occasion was, and still is, the festival of the Academy Awards, which made us into a kind of Pamplona for the running of human bulls, headed for professional death or triumph.

On this particular "night of nights" in 1956, the usual black-tie event at Grauman's Chinese Theatre, the president of the Screen Branch, Ed North, had been unavoidably called out of town. I was drafted as his stand-in, and one of my duties was to accept the Oscar in place of any writer who happened not to be present to receive a prize, and to pronounce a few well-chosen banalities.

Reluctantly I set forth in my old sports car, my speech memorized, to represent the Guild. The president had already given me an advance hint that a writer called Robert Rich was expected to be a winner. The name sounded familiar, but I couldn't quite place him; but in a guild of almost two thousand, one couldn't expect to know everybody. Word had reached the Guild that Robert Rich would not be present, since his wife was having a baby and he had to be at the hospital.

The evening went its usual way. Starlets falling out of their dresses, losers hiding their sulks, winners struggling to appear modest.

Lovely Deborah Kerr, perhaps because she was married to a very fine screenwriter herself (Peter Viertel), was presenting the Oscar for writing. I waited while the man from Price Waterhouse went through the traditional opening of the sealed envelope.

"And the winner—for the Best Motion Picture Story is"—suspense overstretched like a tired rubber band—"Robert Rich!"

Down the aisle I hurried, amid polite applause, and up to the stage, while Deborah Kerr announced to the audience and, via TV, the world that in the unavoidable absence of Mr. Rich, Jesse Lasky, Jr., vice president of the etc., etc., would accept the award. More polite applause. Well, everyone has a *few* friends in Hollywood. I reached the enormous stage, to be bussed on the cheek by Miss Kerr, which ought to be worth an evening's trouble in anybody's book, and accepted the glittering Oscar.

I made some speech to the effect that "my good friend," that wonderfully creative writer Bob Rich, had been called to the hospital to attend the result of another important creative effort—his newborn son or daughter. The award given for the Best Motion Picture Story, *The Brave One*, produced by the King Brothers for RKO, was well earned. Set in Mexico, the film had been directed by Irving Rapper and featured Michael Ray, Firmin Rivera, and Joi Lansing. Everyone applauded, and the Oscar and I left. I locked the precious statuette in the trunk of my car until I could deliver it to the Guild the following day for Rich to collect.

Next morning I was awakened by a phone call from the Guild office. They had checked for Robert Rich's address—and found, to their consternation, that his name didn't appear in any of our membership lists!

Then who had phoned the Guild as Robert Rich and regretted that he would not be able to be present should he win the award? And who had the King Brothers hired to write the excellent movie? Robert Rich had to be *some*body! The nationwide press would be trumpeting his name this morning. How would we feel when we were forced to inform the Academy that nobody in our guild had the foggiest idea who or where this Rich was? Someone tried the King Brothers, but they could not be contacted. Next, the Academy was checked. No, all it knew was that its writer-membership had voted for him. Which put the phantom squarely back in our laps. We checked the hospitals, but none had any record of a Mrs. Robert Rich.

Then the worst happened. *Life*, *Time*, and *Newsweek* got hold of the story that I had collected an Oscar for a non-existent screenwriter. My telephone began to hum. The national press must have been pretty short of news that week, since the incident was inflated from a curious mystery into a national enigma. Who was Robert Rich? They ran photos of me clutching the award in his name, and quoted the speech which suggested that I knew him like a brother.

Now, every community has its fringe of lunacy—that surrealist wilderness where fantasies haunt lonely minds, provoked by images of celebrity. With poisoned pens and faceless voices on the telephone, they hurl obscenities, or pant anonymously, deriving thrills from threats. In Hollywood they flourished like the green bay tree!

Enter the cranks.

Weird phone calls whispered breathily that they knew Robert Rich, were calling for him in fact, demanding the Oscar. (I had returned it to the Academy to be locked in its safe.) The phone calls grew worse: They became obscene, then threatening.

"Jesse Lasky—this is Robert Rich. I want my award. Meet me at the north corner of Pershing Square at midnight tonight, or I'll get you. I swear you'll never see the light of tomorrow, Jesse boy, if you hold out on me . . ."

One weird whisper promised to "fuck your corpse!" Another mailed me a shoe box in which was a miniature scaffold and hangman's rope, perfectly noosed. It bore the cut-out letters: "To Jesse Lasky, Jr., from Robert Rich. Use it on yerself, shithead. You got that Oscar buried in yer garden. I'm gonna put you there beside where it be." The only certainty was that *this* Robert Rich had not been given the Oscar for grammar!

Located by now, the King Brothers protested their own ignorance. It seemed incredible, yet they insisted they had not actually met Robert Rich either. He had submitted through an accredited agent. The agent himself wasn't sure if Robert Rich was a pen-name. He had sent the check to a bank. He saw no reason why he should give any further information about his unknown client. The affair languished, and finally blew over.

Rich was one of the writers who had been driven into exile in Mexico during the McCarthy days. Several of them had continued writing, and they sold their words under *noms de plume*. Since most of them were top writers, they had no difficulty finding agents to peddle their wares. It was whispered about that Robert Rich was one of the best of these banished scribes, the author of that superb book *Johnny Got His Gun*, but the official writing credit has to this day not been established.

Dear Dalton Trumbo: If you should ever read these lines, you may know how much trouble you caused me (if indeed it was you) back in those torrid days. But if you weren't Robert Rich, I'd like to know who was. Occasionally when the telephone peals in the dead of night I think of those terrible, gasping words: "This is Rob Rich, Jesse boy —I'm gonna get you for stealin' my Oscar!"

Twenty-Five

AROUND ABOUT 1949, Hollywood discovered Italy. Tyrone Power, one of the most attractive stars of all time, had swashed his buckles in the Tiber, making *Prince of Foxes*. It was said that enterprising *paesani* had foxily sold the Fox company soda-water—for a princely sum—to water their horses. Doubtless the Italians made the most of such an opportunity to milk those early runaway productions which sought greener fields in Rome than were offered by home sweet home.

There were a multitude of reasons for that cinematic immigration. American stars had discovered personal tax benefits in working and living abroad. The Hollywood unions had begun to price themselves out of popularity with budget makers. Labor costs were cheaper in Europe. Cheaper? Extras could be harvested by the gross—whole villages of them, while at home a pretty tomato still cost twenty-five dollars a day. More than this, there was a certain artistic aroma about shooting in Rome, Paris, London, or Madrid. The vultures of culture began crying for films in settings where they were set. Gone were the days when a tycoon could mumble, "Brazil? Nuts. A rock is a rock, a tree is a tree. Shoot it in Griffin Park."

Visconti and De Sica had upset tradition with films like *Shoeshine* and *The Bicycle Thief*, put together for peanuts, and now actually making money in American art houses. World-wide production at cut-rate costs was on the way in, and foreign governments were shrewdly offering tempting inducements to Hollywood's peripatetic producers. Government support was nothing new to Europe, where, because markets were smaller, various forms of subsidy had generally stimulated anemic production. England had inaugurated the Eady Plan, by which a percentage of box-office takings was passed back to the producer. Such conditions were balm to Hollywood fugitives from the injustice of mounting costs. Oil had always been pampered as a vital industry, with favorable tax benefits, yet films, which did so much to sustain and promote the American image abroad, were the constant victims of unsympathetic tax legislation. So when the once-mighty moguls began boarding jets, blinking through giant dark glasses at the brightness of foreign skies, the Hollywood horn of plenty began to bleat in a ghost town, and the men who had made up the world's most highly trained film crews joined the unemployed.

We who had grown up out of a few miles of dusty citrus orchards looked as though we might soon be living on orange juice. Of course there was still film production in Hollywood—and television production to take up some of the slack—but things would never again be the same.

The exodus brought a new language, unfamiliar terminology. You began to hear about "coproduction deals," and phrases like "below the line," referring to those costs that didn't include stars' salaries, scriptwriting, casts, and director's fees. Below the line, a concept unknown to the old-time major studios, meant expenses of travel, housing (in hotels), feeding, costuming, extras, food, sets, and locations. And foreign crews. So, if an American producer could provide script, principal actors, and director, the bulk of his production cost could be provided by the Europeans.

The distributors, whose task had always been to sell the product, were hurting anyway. Television was seriously cutting into film box-office receipts. The great companies had compounded their own self-destruction by selling their backlogs of old films to the television networks. This short-term sagacity helped to show profits without involving the risk and expense of making new films. Probably never in the history of industry has any group committed such efficient suicide. The Christians, feeding their own children to the lions, thus gave the lions greater strength to devour them all the more! People began to stay home to watch old movies on television instead of paying to see new ones in the theaters. The writing was on the walls of the great sound stages. One might go and live—or stay and die.

And for every one of the legitimate movie makers who packed their briefcases, practitioners of a new art began to appear. The title of "producer" had once only been won through years of experience and showmanship, plus a flair for business. Producers had been professionals, expected to know their job even to editing and scoring the final product.

All such qualifications were now obsolete. Production dealing and wheeling in Europe opened the doors to self-styled producers of a very different ilk. Promoters. Adventurers. Carpetbaggers. Men whose sole qualification for film making was a nose for somebody else's money. High-grade thieves and con-men who could talk up enough front money to set a deal with a writer. Then, scenario in hand (if not yet paid for), this promoter would try to set up a "package." In other words, lure in a star, or stars, and director. If he succeeded, he might then talk himself into distribution guarantees which would help him complete his financing. Some even got pictures made and released; but many left investors and writers high and dry, and took off with lined pockets for another capital, to play the shell game again. These pirates increased the risk of investing capital, and the reluctance of investors to pitch their pence to honest independents. This destroyed much of the stability that the film world had left, turned a craft into a jungle. How many bamboozled investors moan in this wilderness, and how many writers remain unpaid for their work? The Writers' Guild's "unfair list" of substandard movie men, rigidly restricted to Guild members, reads like a *Who's Who* of the industry. Their victims dream of those final payments never met, those promised percentages never seen. We victims are thicker than ghosts on old battlefields.

But if Hollywood was showing signs of serious illness, it could not yet be said to be dying. The time would come when "Western" towns would be built in Yugoslavia, Italy, and Spain, to accommodate the runaways, when one quite legitimate producer I knew would say, "The script calls for a setting in Arizona. But who can afford to make a picture about Arizona in Arizona? If I can get a deal in Rome we can make it!" But as yet the spaghetti Westerns had not yet been invented, so the invitation to go abroad and prepare a script for a film about Venice, in Venice, sounded pretty adventurous to me.

My producer was an independent named Nat Wachsberger, a Belgian, who had lured John Brahm, a German, to direct. Our stars were to be the popular Maria Montez, born in the West Indies, and Paul Christian, a Swiss. We even had an outstanding Italian actor to play the heavy. A truly international production.

The story left everything to be desired. *Robin Hood* in a gondola! The canals made things a bit more original. The real star was Venice itself, a city imperceptibly changed since the sixteenth century, in which period our adventure story was to be set. In the hands of John Brahm *The Thief of Venice* should at least have been a visual masterpiece.

What we didn't have was enough money. Ever.

In the beginning Nat had found a private backer who was expected to put up unlimited funds.

Soon after arriving in Italy, I was introduced to this "angel," at Montecatini. Anyone who survived this watering place must have had bowels of steel, for the systematic regime of taking the waters had similar effects to a diet of castor oil. Nevertheless the aging clientele appeared to hop about with the sprightliness of mountain goats, and developed the speed of Olympic sprinters to answer the demands imposed on them by the stringent regime.

We stood in the palatial lobby of a *fin-de-siècle* hotel intermittently rocked by the thunderous functioning of mighty plumbing in action. Our great investor appeared old and bulky, and was reported to be an important ex-Fascist who had nimbly survived the fall of Il Duce with fortunes intact. He explained through my multilingual producer that his main concern with the screenplay to be written was that it should provide a sufficient number of parts for young women. Apparently he maintained a harem of mistresses who had all been promised key roles in the film he was backing, and, he stressed, these parts must be equal in importance!

I next met him in Rome, this time splendidly ensconced in the bosom of a very considerable family. He sat in a halo of grandchildren, perspiring under damp jet-dyed hair, while we demolished a ten-course meal that lasted most of the day. Nat was understandably concerned that the promised financial injection had not yet found its way into the company account. He might well have been!

A fortnight later, while typing in my hotel room on the Lido, we received news of an inconsiderate act on the part of our backer. There would be no further need to pad the script out with female parts now. Our patron had dropped dead. I always wondered whether it was the overexcreting in Montecatini, the overeating in Rome, or the overcopulating incognito that finally did him in. In any event, from that day forward the film never recovered its financial equilibrium.

After the affluence of a great Hollywood corporation like Paramount, the unstable state of an independent European production was shattering. While I labored to produce a screenplay and John Brahm hunted locations, Nat was darting about Europe in quest of alms. Even when we knew his foragings were successful, his payments to us would be several weeks overdue, making it necessary for us to be slow-pay with the hotel bill. One weekend I found myself a veritable hostage in another *fin-de-siècle* room on the Lido. Nat had vanished before breakfast, leaving me and his luggage as collateral. I was beginning to feel like death in Venice when the clerk, who resembled Al Capone, informed me smoothly that unless I was prepared to take care of certain bills currently outstanding, including Nat's, he would prefer that I should also transfer my own luggage to the safekeeping of the concierge. John and I soon became aware of a certain vigilance that would doubtless have erupted into firm action had any of our expeditions to the city taken the direction of the railroad station or airport!

Happily Nat returned with the bacon, and promptly paid everyone—up to about two weeks' short of currently due amounts. Since this appeared to be a kind of custom of his, one day during a gondola journey down the Grand Canal, I turned to him and asked, "Nat, you always do pay eventually, and I'm sure you always intend to, but why always keep me two weeks behind?"

A wistful look dwelt briefly on his plump face. Eloquent shoulders lifted in a gesture to emphasize the destructibility of man against the will of universal destiny.

"Suppose, darling—God forbid—during the two weeks, you should die?"

I saw his point.

On another occasion he returned from a successful foray after funds and took us to lunch at the best restaurant in Venice.

Considering the possibility that payment of the lunch bill might leave him less opulent, I dared remind him that my salary was now about five weeks in arrears. He considered this, nodded, and mysteriously invited me to extend my palm toward him under the table. Mystified, I obeyed. An icy kiss of coinage chilled my hand. I drew it back into view stacked with gold louis. Payments in such gold coinage, should one have been caught, could be worth a jail sentence in almost any language—to an American citizen it could mean rack and ruin.

I pressed the dangerous coins back into Nat's hand. "Christ, do you want to get me imprisoned for ten years?"

He beamed enigmatically. "Some great works have been written in prison cells, darling. Look as Oscar Wilde!"

At last the first draft was completed, and Nat treated us all to a few days in Monte Carlo. We were to be his guests at the great Gala. It seemed he wanted to exhibit us to some potential backers. Living proof of a live project. He told us to meet him at the bar at seven o'clock for a briefing—black tie, of course. When I informed him I hadn't brought one with me, he ordered me to find a dinner jacket or not show up.

If you've ever tried renting a dinner jacket in Monte Carlo on the afternoon before a Gala, and you happen to be a size thirty-seven short, you can appreciate my surge of hope when I spotted one of the hotel waiters just a little under my size. Francs and cloth changed hands, and I got me to the bar on time. Nat raised his eyebrow slightly at the fit of my jacket—they weren't wearing nipped-in waists that season—but I assured him I would manage beautifully as long as I didn't have to signal for a taxi, and that I was safe until midnight, when the waiter I'd borrowed it from went back on duty.

"Waiter?" Nat choked. He was definitely not amused. I was exiled to a side table and snubbed for the rest of the evening.

That is, until the great Darryl Zanuck spotted me and surged over for an enthusiastic greeting. If he noticed my suit, he apparently didn't subscribe to the doctrine that clothes make the man. I was promoted back to Nat's table of backers. As I shook hands with the first, my sleeve ripped at the shoulder. The finances for *The Thief of Venice* remained unstable.

We returned to Venice to complete the final draft and to meet Maria Montez, who was arriving from Hollywood. Maria Montez had figured in many Hollywood "tits and sand" epics of the forties, and she bore herself appropriately. Many top performers appear as glamorless creatures off-screen, reserving their flashy appeal for the camera. Some even make a fetish of anonymity, striving to go unrecognized, and if recognized, to be considered "real folksy," an apple-pie-baking, sugar-borrowing next-door neighbor "just like everyone else."

Not so Montez. She oozed patent, blatant allure. She was a panther of pleasure, more suggestive than the brand names of perfumes. She was a schoolboy's wet dream, a traveling salesman's fantasy. She glided into a room, hips undulating, eyes like dark cauldrons in which the virtue of a saint could be dissolved. The titles of her films said it all: *South of Tahiti*, *Arabian Nights*, *White Savage*, *Cobra Woman*, *Gypsy Wildcat*, *Sudan*, *Tangier*, *Siren of Atlantis*. Actually, she was a shrewd, hardheaded businesswoman, marketing a highly salable commodity: herself.

The very first night of her arrival caused a near riot. Nat had taken us all to dinner, and it was one of those Venetian evenings that have since time immemorial gilded the minds of poets and painters. The sun had taken a last fiery dive into the lagoon and the sky was smoky with the afterglow. At the water-steps of San Marco, boarding the privately rented motorboat that would speed us back to the Lido, Maria stood poised against an infinity of golden light. Lifting her skirt just a shade higher than the maneuver of stepping across to the tossing craft might require, she raised one lovely bare arm in farewell salutation to Venice in general and to a cloud of young men in particular.

A typical pack of young Italians, who, three years after the war, were growing up with almost no expectation of employment, or the means to court any marriageable young woman. Impoverished, without hope, disgruntled, their sole means of existence to prey upon the seasonal invasions of tourists from whom they had acquired the usual concept of Yankee affluence. Understandably they equated this with the single American industry that had established itself in practically every corner of economically recovering Italy, the cause "for the pause that refreshes." Their haunted, beautiful faces turned to the spectacle of the Hollywood Goddess whose generosity was according them a wonderful display of silken thigh. And quite suddenly she became the embodiment of all their frustration. A terrible cry broke from them, yelped and howled into the descending darkness . . .

"Coca Cola! Coca Cola! Coca Cola!" The cry held all their longing for that fabled way of life, embodied in two glorious American products—a drink and a movie queen.

Maria was of course delighted. Higher the skirt, more undulation of the magnificent hips. And then the joyous cry lowered to a kind of carnal growl, no longer gay but ugly, even threatening. And not a *carabiniere* in sight.

In another minute they might have rushed her and ripped the flimsy clothes from the provocative body. Our alert producer dragged Maria into the boat and signaled the boatman to cast off. Not a moment too soon. The dark profile of the ageless city diminished, domes and towers highlighted by the rising moon. At last the barking howls of the wolf pack blended into the reassuring churn of the motor launch bearing us across the widening lagoon. I recalled how Jean Harlow had similarly overstimulated another mob in Venice, California, long ago. The world kept changing, yet some patterns remained the same.

Maria was looking back toward the city, pleased by the sensation she had caused on her first evening. Watching her, I never dreamed that this was to be her last major film. Within months she would be discovered dead in an over-hot bathtub, and there would be rumors that she had taken her own life. Having known Maria, I think that unlikely, however; I'm sure she enjoyed life far too much to part with it intentionally. A more likely explanation is that she suffered from a heart condition. Beauty can be a flame that consumes itself. To anyone who knew them, it would be hard to imagine the Jean Harlows and Maria Montezes as aging ladies.

When the script was finished, Betty and I headed for Rome. There at the hotel a cable was waiting. It read: COME HOME STOP ALL IS FORGIVEN, and it was signed DE MILLE.

I didn't. And missed the opportunity to work on the only one of his screenplays that won its writers an Academy Award—*The Greatest Show on Earth.*

At that moment in time Roman life was at its most sparkling, and we had decided to stay on for a while and sample the *dolce vita.* It contrasted irresistibly with the bondage of De Mille's great deeds. In film-mad Rome no Hollywood screenwriter with good credits would have found any difficulty picking up assignments. You had only to seat yourself on the Via Veneto, in the vicinity of the Hotel Excelsior, contemplate the navel of some passing sex kitten, appear faintly uninterested in the prospect of employment, puff a cloud of expensive pipe-smoke, and you could take your choice of the offers. All kinds! At every table around you some film was being promoted. Projects being launched. Productions put together. Practically everyone but the waiters had a script that needed a rewrite, a rewrite that needed a polish, or a treatment that needed a screenplay. Even film money was, for once, apparently plentiful.

Without leaving his seat at the table or putting down his Negroni, an enterprising producer could firm a deal with a writer at the next table, a passing director on the pavement, and finally a star descending from her sports car. It was like a marketplace, with every commodity of film making within the distance of a glance. Before I was fully aware of it I had committed myself to write two scripts. The first, *City of Violence,* was for a Hungarian producer. It was to be set in Naples and star Maria Montez. The second was for a Romanian producer who had contracted the services of an outstanding Hungarian director, Géza Radvanyi, and was to be called *Women Without Names.* It would deal with displaced persons, and have an international cast of excellent names, headed by Simone Simon, Françoise Rosay, and Valentina Cortese.

To my embarrassment I was even paid in cash! The wads of Italian banknotes could scarcely be stuffed into a briefcase—they soared into the millions, though the rate of exchange in American dollars was a bit less impressive.

We summered in Rome, suffering a heatwave that stopped the fountains and kept me popping in and out of a cold bath, with my typewriter set up next to the tub. And the money that had come so easily, easily went.

But this carnival of European production was not all as hilarious as it looked. On the ground floor of our hotel near the Piazza del Popolo lived an American bit-player. In Hollywood he had always been a solid family man, but unluckily he had come over without his wife, and plunged rather too deep into the action. He had drunk himself off two films and was in financial trouble. We used to meet in the little hotel bar, and he would hit me for small loans. Then, one terrible day, walking past his ground floor window, I noticed that in spite of the sweltering heat his window was tight closed. Then I saw why. Thrust through a jagged hole in the glass was a blood-soaked hand. In a fit of alcoholic despondency my friend had cut his wrists, then, changing his mind, broken the window to attract attention.

The hotel called an ambulance, and he was rushed to the hospital. He recovered, and the American Embassy sent for his wife to come over and bring him home to Hollywood. He wasn't the only person to suffer from transplanting.

Meanwhile my film scripts went into production. I watched Géza Radvanyi filming *Women Without Names*. He was a highly talented director, but extremely sensitive about the fact that my script included full and carefully prescribed camera angles, and he refused to have it circulated on the set. My secretary was instructed to prepare a second script that left out all camera angles. Thus he could compose them himself on the spot, which certainly was impressive. I was glad to see, however, that he kept one copy of my script *with* the camera angles in his dressing room for secret reference before his "creative decisions." The De Mille training in preparing all aspects of filming on paper would soon be outmoded. Most contemporary directors would be outraged if a writer brought them a script that indicated camera angles, business, or detailed action.

European film finance was a law unto itself. *City of Violence* I wrote as a coproduction of German, Italian, and American companies. The German company, Comedia, was represented and financed by Henry Lester, a Berlin-born, half Italian charmer, who held an American passport as a result of having served in the American army. The American coproducer was the Belgian-born Nat Wachsberger. The filming in Germany and Italy was a Tower of Babel, since each company represented had its own production manager, none of whom spoke a common language. The only one who could make himself understood in all three—with a Hungarian accent—was William Szekely, overall producer-director.

To complete the Italian financing, Henry Lester had to provide $200,000 in a hurry, or Wachsberger threatened to walk out with his American stars, Alan Curtis and Maria Montez. At that time stringent currency regulations plagued all countries. Lester was faced with converting German marks to dollars in the Munich black market. Happily, he had an impressive secretary, one Baron Wolf Dieter von Oppen, who knew his way around the black forest of money changing.

On the night that Henry was to take the train to Rome, traveling with a beautiful German actress an unlocked compartment away, the baron was to deliver the cash to the station. But the train pulled out of Munich, and no baron! As it slipped into a smaller station on the outskirts, it paused again. An anxious Henry peered out the window to see his noble secretary running hell-for-leather, waving a fat attaché case. The train started to pull out. The baron attempted to pass the case through the window. It burst open, scattering $200,000 in illegal currency over the outskirts of Munich. Incredibly, the baron managed to scoop up most of it, jam it back into the case, and shove it through the window of the moving train, as he hot-footed along beside it.

Henry collapsed on the seat, clutching the illegal film financing.

"How do you expect to get that out of the country?" the beautiful actress inquired.

"I'll think of something," replied Henry, thinking of nothing.

"Not with me, you won't!" she affirmed, retreating to her own compartment and locking the door with a resounding click. "I have promised to follow you to Italy, not to prison!" she called through the door.

Henry placed the attaché case on the seat beside him. When the currency-control officer entered at the border his question was brief. "Are you carrying any currency, *ja*, or *nein?*"

"No," Henry replied in his best American accent.

With the money available, the film progressed in Italy. But Lester and Wachsberger remained mutually cautious of each other. They had opposite suites at the Hotel Excelsior and lived in a perpetual state of suspicion. When it came to Henry's ears that Wachsberger had allegedly ransacked his room hoping to find some evidence of treachery, Henry returned the compliment with a key bribed from the same hotel maid, no doubt. But all he found was Maria Montez's contract. It was enough. She had been paid only half the amount that Henry had been given to understand from the budget.

When the picture was finally completed, Wachsberger was required to put up the tail-end money, some 10 million lire. Since Henry claimed to have financed most of the production, the money was due him to pay off outstanding lab charges, etc. Nat showed reluctance to pay, but as a mutual precaution in an uneasy partnership it had been previously agreed to process the German negative in Italy under Nat's supervision—and the English one in Germany under Henry's supervision. These were to be exchanged—after the discharge of mutual financial obligations.

Since Nat refused to pay, Henry refused to hand over his negative. Nat refused to hand over his. This put Henry in a pickle, since he had firm playing dates set in Germany, as Nat well knew. Henry was forced to give in. At a formal meeting in Rome, the negatives were finally exchanged.

Wachsberger's exuberance was short-lived. Henry advised him to examine each reel of his negative carefully. To Nat's dismay he discovered that Henry had removed one important scene from each reel! Nat paid over the 10 million lire.

To this day Wachsberger and Lester renew their friendship at every Cannes Film Festival. Both men subscribe to the industry tradition: Never have an enemy for longer than two years; you may need him for a friend!

That hot Italian summer's work left me feeling drained and homesick. I was debating whether to do another script in Europe when another cable arrived from De Mille. This one was much longer than the first had been. It told me that he had decided to tackle a new version of *The Ten Commandments* as his next film after *The Greatest Show on Earth*. It concluded with the wonderful words: "COME WADE WITH ME IN THE RED SEA."

I cabled back instant acceptance. I could hardly wait to get back. I had suddenly realized how much I missed Hollywood. At least the home-grown flamboyance had come to seem more genuine than the table-top machinations of the Via Veneto. And strangely, I found I missed the Boss, the sense of importance that he gave to every undertaking, the hard critical guidance, even when it resulted in something less than what the critics would call art. The total dedication to the job of making what was always, for him, not just a film to show a profit, but by his own lights, in his own way of thinking—a greatest show on earth. Show! Not just another movie.

And so, with a big De Mille assignment awaiting me, I stood in the office of Air France in Paris. I was trying to VIP myself and Betty into reservations on the first plane heading for home, but all flights were heavily booked. No matter. I flung weight. I dropped names. I bullied. I threatened. I won. We were given the last two places aboard a flight leaving the next day to fly to New York via the Canaries, and thence to Los Angeles.

We celebrated by accepting an invitation from a swashbuckling ex-gunrunner, ex-people runner, who had smuggled human contraband through the British blockade of Palestine and was pouring his precariously gotten gains into the fleshpots of Montmartre. We joined him for a noisy night on the town.

I emerged from a sleep of oblivion, with aching head and depleted pocket, to the insistent ringing of the telephone. I answered it, and the fog cleared with a flash of lightning news. We had, regretfully, been removed from our flight departing today. No, they could do nothing, monsieur.

These, then, were the wages of sin! But I was not to be so easily put off. I told Betty to pack everything and give up the room. As planned, I would go down to Air France and give them the word. De Mille is waiting! That would stop any nonsense. They'd put the pilots off before I'd let them remove us!

Defeat ignominious. All my puff and pompous insistence was getting nowhere. My *dernier mot* merely elicited a helpless shrug.

In vain I insisted that what M'sieur De Mille wants M'sieur De Mille gets, whether it's a writer for one of his films or a president of the U.S. Didn't they know that Eisenhower was his personal selection? If they gave me any further trouble I would see that the whole affair went higher—much higher!

The harassed office staff conferred for the last time, and stood polite but firm. Weather conditions required carrying extra fuel. The last two reservations had therefore to be removed, and these, regrettably, were us.

Deflated, I returned to the hotel, and persuaded the clerk to let the valises be carried back to the room we had overconfidently vacated.

That night we went out to dinner with an old friend, Henry

Hathaway, who was also returning to Hollywood the following day, and suggested that we book on his plane and all fly back together.

As we left the restaurant, somewhat mollified by the best Parisian food and wine, I noticed a headline in the evening paper. An Air France plane had crashed in the Canaries that afternoon, killing a famous French boxer and a violinist, along with everyone else aboard. I checked the flight. It was the one we had been booked on and removed from, and which I had so desperately tried to talk our way back aboard.

Twenty-Six

Back in Hollywood again I was stunned to discover that De Mille wasn't actually ready to start any writers on *The Ten Commandments*. He would contact me when he was, but meanwhile I was, as the saying went, "between pictures."

Like some dowager hag with cracked, caked makeup over a leathery suntan, Hollywood had begun to age ungracefully. It looked smaller after the months abroad. Peeling stucco walls and faded tiles. Smaller, busier, and far less ready to welcome its returning native. Perhaps I was feeling a little scared of the place. Being scared had always come easy in my hometown. The fear that old friends might—should one need them—not be friends any more. When the fat salaries you had earned had been nibbled to death by alimony. When you had bought things you couldn't afford so that everyone could see how successful you were. And then, suddenly, no job, when your last several credits hadn't been all that stupendous. Bank loans were never easily forthcoming for writers, unless they were so rich they didn't need them. No, you couldn't borrow on a story idea, or even an original, completed film script. Your work was worthless until somebody wanted to buy it.

You consoled yourself a shade desperately with the knowledge that Hollywood was still Movie Capital of the World, grinding out the world's most expensive entertainment. Television was still a parvenu, stunted by minuscule budgets. Still, I was scared. We were suddenly very broke, having counted on coming home to instant employment. And in Hollywood you had to *look* successful, sound successful, even smell successful, or you were dead. A producer, a prospective employer could smell unemployment as a wild animal smells fear. One whiff and down went your salary. He'd "buy you for peanuts."

I began to make too many nervous phone calls to my agent.

But fortunately the shadows were worse than the substance. The first offer came from Hunt Stromberg at Columbia Studio, over on Gower Street. A name to conjure with. Hunt had been one of the giants at Metro. His credits read like the Blue Book of fine films. But for some unknown reason he was beginning to slip. Columbia Studio was his banana peel, his Last Chance Saloon. I found him a gentle, thoughtful, kindly gentleman, much like Dad, who was also again having his troubles. Perhaps the downgrade mellowed the Moguls.

The assignment was a flashy piece of mythical-kingdom baloney, directed by Phil Karlson and with Tony Quinn playing the heavy. They made the film come out better than it deserved, but *Mask of the Avenger* certainly did nothing for my own career. Still, it was a step toward that ever-illusive mirage, security, for the praises heaped on it as a "workmanlike" job got me two more assignments on equally unrewarding projects, this time for Eddie Small. "Little" Eddie Small had an independent production deal ,with Columbia distributing and footing most of the costs. Eddie was reputed to be fantastically rich, and to possess a sure touch for commercial film making. An enigmatic, sparsely verbal, dwarf-high presence, he invariably wore a hat tilted to his eyebrows. He spoke in a kind of shorthand, an oral code that omitted all but the barest clues to what he was trying to communicate. After reading over a section of script, he'd mutter something to the effect of, "Important. Important. Where the guy does that—change it." You might never find out what guy, or what it was he'd done that had to be changed.

I worked at his Palm Springs home, a small palace in the blazing desert. Betty swam round and round the kidney-shaped pool while I pounded out something called *The Brigand,* and something else called *Lorna Doone.* Phil Karlson's direction again lifted these two from being mere escapist hash, and in *The Brigand* Tony Quinn gave another of his superb performances, a whale of an artist swimming in a goldfish bowl. Since both films produced comfortable profits, Columbia Pictures offered me a long-term writing contract. Security with a capital "S" was in my clutches at last.

A contract meant you couldn't even be fired, except once a year when the option came up and the salary raise came due. It meant you'd never have to worry in betweentimes about a steady flow of income to stoke the furnaces of extravagance. Why, on a long-term contract you could even save up for that "rainy day." Not that you would, but you could con yourself into believing you would.

The Columbia offer, which included regular semiannual raises, was flattering, since that company had by then reduced its stable of term-contracted scribes to one: the highly versatile James Poe. Besides, Betty and I had fallen in love with a house in the fashionable Up-lifter's Estate in Pacific Palisades, which we couldn't afford. The house had everything but a swimming pool, which could be added later. It was in the heart of the party-hopping belt, and around the corner from an excellent tennis club. Pacific Palisades was a fair stretch from the Hollywood studios, so naturally we'd need two cars. But with a seven-year contract, even banks would loan you money.

"Grab it, sweetheart," my agent advised—the contract, not the house.

I grabbed them both and plunged into a sewer of hack writing as trouble-shooter on every piece of rubbish that needed a polish, a brush-up, a once-over, a rewrite, a sharpening; an addition of gags, of action, of schmaltz, of sex; or a trim for budget reasons. My contract automatically denied me any choice as to what I could refuse or accept. I soon ran up a string of inglorious credits: *Mission over Korea, The Iron Glove, Never Trust A Gambler*. There were others, heaven knows how many; on some I managed to avoid taking credit.

My work was going from bad to positively mediocre. But alimony to my first wife (which had started at a mere 40 percent of my gross earnings—before taxes, agent's fees, Guild dues, motion picture charity contributions) was being paid on the dot. This virtually insured eventual bankruptcy, but I was still young enough and the Hollywood industry was still profitable enough to blind me to the inevitable disaster.

I was getting out of debt—except for long-term payments on the house, the car, the furniture, etc. I acquired a business manager, a tax accountant, a pedigreed boxer (dog) with a penchant for biting other people's tires, two country-club memberships, and a regular Sunday tennis game at Paul Henried's with Charles Schneer, the Columbia producer, and Frank Rosenberg, a Warner Brothers producer, Emmet Lavery, the writer, and Ed Hinton. A good-looking character actor, Ed was extremely popular with the "racket barons of Brentwood" until he committed the sin of not showing up for Sunday tennis. He'd been filming on location on Catalina Island, and, worried about being late, had begged a ride in a friend's private aircraft. It crashed into the sea on takeoff. As a naval officer, Ed had survived a direct hit that sunk his ship at Pearl Harbor.

Most of tennis-playing Hollywood attended the funeral. "Not like big Ed to ruin our Sunday game," somebody said.

Along with my contract I had acquired tired eyesight, a heart murmur, bad digestion, and soulless self-discipline at the typewriter. Somehow my hangovers from Hollywood parties made my daily diet of film tripe more endurable. And hangovers were easy to come by in those days. Everyone was giving parties. We attended swimming parties, beach parties, tennis parties, country-club parties, buffet parties, cocktail parties, masquerade parties, game parties, lawn parties, come-as-you-are, come-as-you-aren't! We attended parties given by an eccentric millionaire, Hal Hayes, who had built his own bomb shelter in the side of a mountain, stocked, it was said, with champagne, ladies' lingerie, and Russian dictionaries in case he should ever have to face the unwelcome invaders after being the sole Californian to survive the fallout. Armageddon with a harem. He also affected an indoor waterfall and a guest list of everyone and anyone who was pretty enough to be somebody. At one of his parties I heard a lady columnist scream amid a tight-packed multitude of fashionable bodies, "But *nobody's* here, dahling!"

That meant nobody had yet started a fight, danced in the nude, or tried to drown himself in somebody's indoor swimming pool. But the term "Hollywood party" was often a gross inaccuracy. So-called "events" were frequently hosted by rich dilettantes trying to become star-crossed Elsa Maxwells, but the guest lists often consisted less of authentic film folk than of hangers-on, pretenders, and has-beens. Working Hollywoodites had to go to bed early—and often alone—when they were on a picture. Actresses had to make a photogenic appearance at the studio by six A.M. (four-thirty or five A.M. if they were going on an all-day location) for makeup, wardrobe, hairdressing—and be ready, with part memorized, on the set by eight A.M. They weren't about to conduct themselves like debauchees in a Scott Fitzgerald novel, not if they hoped to stay in demand. The wildest parties generally turned out to be "Hollywood" mainly in respect to geography. Oil, real estate, cafe society, call girls, fortune hunters, and fringe filmites, peppered with a few weak-minded characters like me. There were few we missed and few we shouldn't have.

A jaded, corrosive time. A sense of rot. Of hopelessness. A tired writer delivering junk for very hard cash. Until one day the boss of Columbia summoned me to his office.

Harry Cohn, as absolute a monarch as Hollywood ever knew, ran

Columbia like a private police state. He was tough, feared, ruthless and courageous, unbearably crude, profane, quirky, a hammer-headed power-machine who held total financial and physical control over his self-made empire. He chewed cigars and relatives. It was said that he would fire and blacklist a man for mentioning *verboten* subjects like death or disease in his private studio dining-room, where a coterie of privileged henchmen vied for his favors. It was said he had listening devices on all sound stages and could tune in any conversation on the set, then boom in over a loudspeaker if he heard anything that displeased him. It was said that every evening he personally toured his big studio, trying to catch anyone who might have left on a light (in the Wurtzel tradition). It was said that some of his best movies were made and previewed in spite of his disapprovals. This I would doubt. Harry Cohn was far too autocratic to allow anything to happen at Columbia that he had not personally sanctioned. Sam Briskin, the producer, called him "the last of the pirates." Yet others insisted that a nod or handshake from him was worth more than a contract.

Certainly, Cohn's vision was sound. His taste was somehow universal. His success was enormous.

His discoveries included Rita Hayworth and Kim Novak. And whatever else could be said against him, nobody would have accused him of being less than a monolith of sheer guts. It took guts to undertake films like *From Here to Eternity*, with singer Frank Sinatra playing a straight acting role, or signing up young Stanley Kramer for a twenty-five-million-dollar deal to produce pictures of a quality hardly ever equaled.

He was lying on a massage table being pounded by a masseur when I entered the private suite of offices in the Gower Street studio. I had worked in his film factory for over a year, and never yet exchanged a word with the mighty man.

"You used to write some big pictures for De Mille," he said, without looking at me. The powerful hands of the masseur pummeled thick shoulders.

"Yes, sir."

The look that swiveled around was distinctly unpleasant. I had heard he hated politeness. Considered it phoney. But I reminded myself of the highly creative men, writers like Sidney Buchman, directors like Frank Capra, who flourished under the "wild bull" of Gower Street. There had to be some sensitivity under that skin.

"I need a story for Rita. I've got a commitment to start her in a picture and the script is a piece of shit."

I assumed this might be another of those miserable salvage jobs that had become my customary Columbia fare. "Is it something you want rewritten, sir?"

"Nobody could rewrite it. Anyway, Rita hates it. And she's right. I want you to come up with a fresh subject. Something that has balls and is big. You get the idea?"

"A famous character, perhaps?"

"You got something in mind?"

"Salomé."

"Who the fuck is that?"

I changed my pronunciation. "Sa-*lo*-me?"

He grunted. "How fast can I get a story—I mean the whole goddamn picture in treatment?"

"Well . . . how much time have I got?"

"Till Monday. And don't screw around with any story editor. Bring it to me."

"Monday? But I'd have to research it, and . . ."

"You giving me a Rita Hayworth story on Monday or not?"

"I'll do my best."

"Well, don't stand here talking. Get started. Oh, yes. I talked to your producer. I've pulled you off that crap you were assigned to."

At least this ill wind had blown me one bit of good. That weekend I left the telephone off the hook. Adaptations of the famous biblical story were numerous; many great writers—Flaubert, Sudermann, Wilde—provided clues to character from which plots and conflicts could be developed. By Monday I handed in my screen story to Harry Cohn. He read it while I waited in his outer office. Then I was admitted.

The eyes were dark and penetrating, the shoulders in the gray suit enormous, the smile was foreboding, ready to deliver an accolade or a crushing ultimatum. Nobody could fail to be unnerved by such a concentration of personal power. The cigar protruded from behind the colored pocket handkerchief like a deadly weapon. If he reaches for it—duck! I thought. I did not notice that there was another person in the office, a small man with his hat on, slouched in a chair. Not at first. I was too absorbed in the compliments. Yes, compliments.

"I like your story. Rita will too. I sent her a copy."

"And you really like it. Sir—?"

"Yeah. We'll use it. It's good."

He liked it! A credit on a Rita Hayworth picture would be like moving out of the slums of Columbia into a room at the top.

"Then you'll want me to start on the screenplay. How long will I have? I mean how much time, sir?"

"No time. The screenplay's already assigned. To Harry Kleiner. I got a commitment with him, too." He nodded to the little man in the chair. I couldn't believe it. The disappointment certainly showed in my face, because suddenly granite-Cohn softened. The smile was total charm.

"I tell you what you do, Jesse. You take two weeks' holiday and charge it to Columbia Pictures." I heard myself thanking him profusely. A shade too profusely, because, my agent later pointed out, that the studio owed me the two weeks' holiday anyway—under the terms of my contract.

That disappointment was somewhat leavened a year or so later when *Salome* received its big press preview, right on Hollywood Boulevard. It was packed. The word had been allowed to seep out that a new Rita Hayworth film was being "sneaked." Everyone who should have, had crowded in—and so had at least one person who shouldn't have.

The film started well. It was not one of William Dieterle's best pictures, but it was opulent enough, and the cast included Charles Laughton playing Herod. I suppose Laughton, like Brando or Orson Welles, could never make a really wrong move in front of a camera. I was retasting the disappointment of only having received a "Screen Story" credit when suddenly it happened. The film had reached the moment when John the Baptist's head was carried into the throne room on a platter.

Then, from high in the balcony, a clear voice piped, "Dig that crazy dessert!"

The audience roared, and they never stopped until the lights went on. The preview was a shambles, which certainly didn't help the critical reaction in the press. It was a good screenplay, too. What they hadn't screened were the clowns in the balcony. There's one in every crowd.

The bullet-headed, tight-knit young writer from the next office joined me for coffee brewed by a sexy secretary whose legs beat her typing. He was never very busy in the afternoons, having done most of his work between midnight and seven A.M. He only came to the studio to leave pages for Harry Cohn. While I contemplated my own empty page in the typewriter, he scrawled in the book he had written: "To Jesse Lasky (no Jr.), who could have written a far better book than this if he only thought he could." The book was *From Here to Eternity*, which the studio was preparing to film, and nobody could have written a better one. James Jones lived in a caravan trailer with a retired lady English teacher who had kept him virtually incarcerated to get that book out of him.

"Why the hell don't you get out of this trap and start writing?" he challenged me over the coffee.

"Lack of character. Anyway, nobody ever gets out. We talk about it. About how we're going to escape to Majorca or Connecticut. It's only talk. We're in too deep. Besides, I've got a Columbia contract. There's no way out of that."

Jim pointed out the window. A removal van was taking home the personal effects of one of Harry Cohn's top executives. The movingmen's arms were loaded to their chins with boxes of long, unsmoked cigars. One of the Briskins had died a few days before. "That's one way out," he said. But in a studio contract job you mostly felt too young to die and too old to run. The kill you were weekly fattened for was a slow kind, progressing from numbed senses to a lowering of the moral pulse and finally plain inertia. It was called "doing a job" —but the difference in Hollywood was that you were overpaid for it. You had fallen into a gold-plated rut. I'd even given up expecting that De Mille would ever get around to calling me for *The Ten Commandments.*

But the surest truth of show business is that you never know what is going to happen next, and the good things you expect generally don't until you've given up hope anything ever will. My salvation was a sudden loan-out to Twentieth Century-Fox. Since I was a Columbia contract writer, Fox paid my studio a considerable amount over my regular salary to borrow me. It had all been arranged by my agent.

"I saw you were getting stale, sweetheart. So I had a word with this Fox producer who was looking for someone who could do a quality Western, quick and cheap. He read some of your old scripts —and you're in. Now thank all the nice people at Columbia for being so nice about loaning their best . . ." He broke off.

"Hack," I suggested.

"You said it, baby, not me."

Still, the assignment was a breath of fresh air. This Western was to be based on an excellent magazine story, and to star Robert Wagner, Dale Robertson, and Rory Calhoun. Great actors and great guys. *The Silver Whip* was a lot better than anything I'd had my name on recently.

The Twentieth Century-Fox studio had grown into the Versailles of filmdom. It sprawled over a vast expanse of hills. Driving through it was a world tour. You passed Egyptian monuments, French villages, English villages, New York streets, Shanghai docks, ships, Chinese junks floating in tanks—the aftermath of uncountable epics. Even a real southern mansion in a garden setting, where Shirley Temple and Bill Robinson had tapped their way through *The Little Colonel*. What the Twentieth Century-Fox studio had was space. To get to the commissary or a producer's office you walked through gardens or down rows of bungalows. It was a city in itself, set on the edge of plush Beverly Hills. Like a symbol of its own opulence, an oil rig in the exact center of the studio pumped day and night, presumably dredging up subterranean fortunes to match the plush product of the great company. I was housed in an office grander than my home, a private bungalow shared with a secretary. If Columbia had seemed like a compact absolute monarchy, Twentieth was a kind of empire. Its czar was equally powerful—yet, one felt, not as totally, personally involved on every level as Harry Cohn.

Darryl Zanuck was quite another cut of man. He had been a highly successful screenwriter himself. A dynamic bantam out of Wahoo, Indiana, Zanuck had risen from scripting for the dog star Rin Tin Tin at Warner's to the production throne of Twentieth, which he founded in 1933. Zanuck had the vision; Joseph Schenck had the money. Zanuck was also a sportsman, a big-game hunter, a two-goal polo player, a connoisseur of French wines, women, and the gastronomic arts as practiced on the French Riviera. He customarily sported polo-neck sweaters and polo boots, and carried a kind of headless polo stick, with which the horseless headsman could practice shots while nervously pacing through story conferences in an office scarcely smaller than a polo field. Except for the oversized cigar, he looked like an Ernest Hemingway description of a combat colonel in mufti. Wiry, nervous, and capable of sudden verbal bombardments, though without De Mille's sarcasm, he personally produced some of the best films ever made in Hollywood. He was a movie-makers' movie-maker, always ready to gamble on a hunch, and the hunches almost always paid off. He must have liked my screenplay *The Silver Whip*, because he called me into his enormous office one morning and assigned me to one of his favorite projects.

The picture was an action melodrama called *Hell and High Water*—all about a privately owned anti-Communist submarine that sets out on a private war against the Reds. The second film to be made in cinemascope, it would have everything, including Richard Widmark, but it would need a hard-hitting, tough-talking script. It needed bite, sparse verbiage, and closely packed action. Samuel Fuller had directed two minor classics, *Fixed Bayonets* and *The Steel Helmet*. He'd been a combat infantryman and his films reflected the war he knew. He was highly creative and inventive, with a flair for tough realism in the best tradition of such two-fisted directors as John Ford and Henry Hathaway.

Zanuck warned me that before committing himself, Sammy would have to like my script, at least well enough to rewrite it.

For me, the two big problems of the script were two of its main characters: the English atomic scientist and his daughter. It was bad enough to justify the presence of a woman aboard with this submarine load of sweaty characters—you had to believe in her and her scientist father. And secondly, they had to sound authentically British. I worked the speeches over and over, then finally checked out the dialogue with English writer and actor friends. I thought I was finished.

Until Zanuck sent for me. He prowled about the huge office, whacking everything but me with that damned polo practicing stick. Then to my surprise he announced that he liked the script. So did Sammy. So did everyone. Only one small problem. He had discovered a new star, Bella Darvi, who happened to be French, and he had decided to cast her in the part written for the English girl.

Now how fast could I change the leading lady from British to French?

"What about her father? The British scientist?"

"He's a French scientist now. Put a *Légion d'honneur* in his buttonhole. I'll send Bella to go over her own words with you. I want her to be comfortable with every line, so keep changing them until she is." He gave the pigskins a tremendous clout with his polo stick. The victory shot at the Uplifter's Club next Sunday, no doubt.

"What other films has she done, sir? So I could get an idea of how she works."

"No others. Never acted in her life. I just discovered her. In France. I just gave her a name. Dar from Darryl—Vi from Virginia, my wife."

I refrained from murmuring, "And Bella from Lugosi?"

He read my mind. "The Bella's her own. Bella Wegier, Polish model. But for Christ's sake don't change the script all around. Just her nationality. Sammy will make any changes he wants himself."

For once on an assignment everything was coming up roses. A top-notch director, a super cast—and a French discovery, the current favorite of the sultan of Fox.

My secretary brewed endless pots of continental coffee, and chilled the golden wines of the Guasti region of California, while I translated English dialogue into my broken French; then Bella would polish the French, and I would translate it into broken English until the words seemed to fit her like Parisian gloves. I was beginning to love Hollywood again.

Meanwhile, back at the ranch—the De Mille ranch—one could imagine a distant rumble like summer thunder, as the word drifted down from his mountain. The Boss was ready to start writers on *The Ten Commandments*. The halcyon days of scripting for Zanuck, like all good things, were coming to an end.

Twenty-Seven

NINETEEN FIFTY-FOUR. WE WERE MOBILIZING at Paramount Studios, like an army staging for invasion. All the complex human pre-production components—the writers, research people, sketch artists, designers, art directors, technicians—were being assembled, selected, assigned their special tasks. The word had spread throughout the industry. De Mille was starting another big one, perhaps the biggest of all.

The mounting of an epic film production is a cumbersome affair. Not that many "blockbusters" are mounted these days, certainly not the old extravagant studio kind. Today's film makers cut themselves adrift from sound stages and studio costs. They go on location, improvise, take advantage of natural conditions wherever they happen to choose to shoot. But De Mille scripts had to be total blueprints for epics, which would crown not only the Paramount sound stages, but also, via second-unit filming, deserts in California and Egypt and the rocky heights of Sinai.

The manual for all these far-flung operations would be our screenplay, three hundred and eight pages in final draft, fully annotated for source references, and detailing many props, costume notes, and every camera setup that might be required. De Mille might vary these later, but they had to be there on paper so that every member of the company would know what was expected of him.

The selection of source material imposed the weight of popular belief, tenets, dogmas, doctrinal opinion, and general gospel truth upon us. You didn't mess about with the recorded word of God, and this script would include dialogues between God and Moses as revealed in the books of the Old Testament, referred to in the New Testament, and recorded in the Koran. We were, De Mille affrmed, not merely writing for film audiences this time, but for the ages! Our every word must be weighed against his concept of "the eternal truths," especially in the early stages when research outweighed drama. We felt so inoculated with significance that we hardly dared write at all, certainly not with such profane tools as pencils and typewriters. Besides, one was always safe until words were put on paper.

The silent version of *The Ten Commandments* had used the biblical story only as a prologue. It was a modern (1923) morality play, demonstrating that whoever broke the commandments would by them be broken.

In the prologue, old Theodore Roberts had played Moses as a staff-brandishing prophet, straight out of William Blake. Granite-limbed Charles De Roche made a magnificent pharaoh with well-oiled biceps. Some reviewers called it the greatest film ever made.

For sheer spectacle, it certainly outdid anything of its day. The art directors had reared Egyptian temples on the sand dunes of Santa Cruz, California. From the gates of this bogus city the greatest swarm of chariots ever assembled, possibly even larger than Rameses had originally used, was flung in pursuit of the marching Hebrew tribes.

The Red Sea opening had been ingeniously accomplished in the studio tank by sheets of gelatine which restrained two walls of water. When the gelatine dissolved, the walls collapsed and the waters rushed inward to close the gap in the sea. Opening the Red Sea was dead easy. Just run the film backward. A spectacular effect. The people flowed down the path through the sea by a "process shot"—superimposing one negative upon another.

California extras were cheap enough to be hired—and drowned—by the thousands. The chariot army that pursued the Hebrews, however, was provided by a regiment of U.S. field artillery, and when De Mille revealed to their colonel that his men would have to race chariots down an almost vertical cliff of sand, he was understandably unenthusiastic. Danger might be a soldier's daily bread, but to risk life and limb to create a sequence for a Hollywood movie was something else!

De Mille showed proper amazement. What risk? Why, a ten-year-old child could ride a horse down a cliff like that! To demonstrate, De Mille summoned one—his little daughter, Cecilia.

"Cessie, I want you to ride a horse down that sand cliff," he suggested, almost casually.

The child bobbed her pretty head. "Yes, father."

The colonel held his breath as the little girl clambered onto a giant steed and set it into a canter directly toward the almost sheer drop—and over the edge! Down she zigzagged, slipping, skidding, slithering, but reaching the bottom quite unscathed.

The colonel had seen enough. With crisp military decision he ordered the three hundred chariot drivers to follow in the hoofprints of the child's horse, and De Mille's cameras captured one of the most spectacular scenes ever filmed. Chariot after chariot rolled, bounded, capsized, tangling in wild sprawls of horses and men. Some even made it down without upsetting. It is not recorded how many artillerymen were sent to the hospital.

What the colonel didn't know was that little Cecilia De Mille was, even then, one of the greatest horsewomen in the United States, with ribbons and prizes for just about everything that could be done in a saddle.

Two new faces had been added to our writing team. Aside from Fred Frank, the Boss had hired Aeneas MacKenzie, a peppery Scotsman who had drifted to Hollywood after World War I, attached himself to the young film industry, and never gone home again. Aeneas was a fine film dramatist and a walking encyclopedia of obscure information. Ask him to recite the third word on a Tibetan prayer-wheel. Ask him how often Bonnie Prince Charlie changed his kilt. Ask him to quote in nonstop Latin the heraldic emblems of every Royal Family in 1900. The composition of the eye of a fly. The precise measurement of powder to load a Snaphance. Ask him anything, and he would rattle off an answer which you would have a hell of a time disproving. When he joined us he was aging and nearly blind, but he had never forgotten anything he had ever seen, heard, or read—not a bad trait for a screenwriter. The fourth team member, Jack Gariss, had recently emerged from William de Mille's film department at the University of Southern California. He was huge and bearded, and both looked and was a tower of erudition, exuding infinite tranquillity and mysticism. I had more De Mille writing experience than just about any living writer. All in all, no previous De Mille writing team had ever been better equipped to survey the forest of research for *The Ten Commandments*.

Our chief research coordinator, Henry Noerdlinger, was well prepared to brief us. His documentation for the film script was so rich and extensive that it was later published by the University of Southern California Press. He had assembled over nine hundred and fifty volumes of information that had to be distilled into pertinent notes for us and all departments concerned. We were drenched in history, legend and archeological conclusions. We immersed ourselves in the works of Flavius Josephus, Philo Judaeus, and Eusebius of Caesarea. The Bible, the Koran, the Midrash, and the Talmud were our bedside reading. Our conversations became peppered with such esoteric verbosity as the Logos Doctrine, Memphite theology, and the concept of *ma'at* (an expression of ideas, which, although inexpressible, were morally good, and with which God-kings were endowed).

Our thoroughness was dictated by a proper caution. Moses himself is revered by followers of three great religions: Judaism, Christianity, and Islam. The author of the Fourth Gospel quotes Jesus as saying: "Had ye believed Moses, ye would have believed me: for he wrote of me. But if ye believed not his words, how shall ye believe my words?" (John 5:46)—only one of numerous references to Moses and The Ten Commandments in the New Testament.

We approached the subject with the reverence of travelers entering a holy place, and at first it cramped our literary style.

The problem for the filmwriter confronting history is to stretch threads without rupturing credibility, to invent without distorting accepted facts. Yet facts themselves are suspect. What was the truth of any historical event? Accounts of great happenings were influenced by many considerations. Political, religious, or the local tyrant's whim. The survival of scribes and recorders depended upon adherence to currently accepted doctrine. One age would have burned you for revelations and conclusions essential to the common sense of another. Faced by a sea of often contradictory historical conclusions, the screenwriter can only hold his aching head and, in the end, having absorbed some few grains of information, seize the freedom he needs and try to tell a whacking good story.

In the end. But not the beginning. First the subject must be explored from many points of view. Such surprisingly diverse authorities as Martin Buber, Sigmund Freud, Henry George, and Winston Churchill have recorded interesting conclusions on the personality of Moses and the significance of the heritage of the Laws. But the great clue from which we could erect our dramatic hypothesis was supplied by the archeologist James Breasted. He deduced from altered reliefs on a temple wall at Karnak that the pharaoh Sethi I, the father of Rameses II, had another, older son, the heir to the throne. But Rameses eliminated his big brother through intrigue, and the name of this unknown prince of Egypt was forever expunged from walls and monuments. Since the Bible, the Koran, Philo, Josephus, the Midrash Rabbah, and Eusebius supported the probability that Moses was reared as a prince of Egypt, we gratefully invoked dramatic license to extend and develop his relationships with members of the Egyptian court. The film story of *The Ten Commandments* was born.

You may ask how four men write one movie. I suppose you could ask how more than one artist managed to paint some of those oversized Italian paintings of the sixteenth century. Each man works on a different area. Then when the sequences are finished the survivor goes over his collaborators' sections to ensure some ultimate consistency of style. I don't recommend this as the best way to produce a deeply subjective masterpiece.

My area of the screenplay was based upon a rather bogus assumption. The Boss decided, a shade arbitrarily, that for his own purposes I was the company Hebrew. The fact that I'd never been bar mitzvah, or even inside a synagogue, and had in boarding-school days been a leader of the Christian Endeavor Society, was completely ignored. He needed a Jew, so Jesse was elected. At least the name was biblically authentic enough. In vain my warnings: Although I might conceivably "pass" in our Gentile unit, to a Jew would I be considered a Jew? He overrode such technical quibbles.

My own feelings, when it has been necessary to have them, have always been somewhat ambivalent. The Laskys were Jews by heritage rather than practice. Neither Bess nor Dad were religious in the church-going sense, perhaps because Dad's pioneer forebears had found no synagogues when their covered wagon reached California in 1848. Bess's father had fled Russia because of religious persecution, then sent his daughters to be educated at the Sacred Heart Convent in Boston. My mother did not actually convert, yet she always felt deeply and mystically inclined to Catholicism. Her father may have been Orthodox, but it was in the nature of Bess, the artist, to search toward sources of inspiration beyond the borders of physical reality, in those metaphysical gardens of beauty reflected in her later "cosmic" paintings and poetry.

With increasing age and decreasing fortunes, Dad found his dedication to worldly pursuits slackening, too. He, too, began to search through religious studies for some meaning, some path toward the faith he needed to bear the kind of blows which had driven other defeated giants to suicide. He explored various "thought" religions that evolved out of Christian Science for meanings to replace the old buoyant optimism which was becoming harder to justify. His faith in God was personal and strong, sustaining him when his faith in his brother man was proved unjustified, which was constantly. Dad loved and trusted practically everyone, and was always surprised when they failed him. He trusted the tax lawyers whose negligence brought him financial ruin. He even trusted the Internal Revenue Department to favor him through his honest declaration of assets and failure to hide anything (cheating tax-men he considered un-American). But nothing would shake his beautiful Christian faith that bread cast upon the waters would be returned.

Once it was established in De Mille's mind that I was the unit Jew, however, he would brook no protests. If there was an essentially Jewish script problem, Jesse was the fixer. His puttees flashing as he paced the office jingling a pocket full of gold coins, he would say, "Jesse, I want you to write me the first feast of the Passover. Write it from the heart of a Hebrew."

"I'm trying to study about the Jewish religion, but I still don't know much about it, sir."

"You know what you feel," he snapped.

"I'm not even sure of that."

"Better get sure, fellah. You can't just work from books and research. You've got to—dig. Into yourself. Your ancestors. Just as I go back to that baron at Hastings, fighting beside William the Conqueror, when I need courage."

I returned to my office, picked up my writing board, and stared at the empty page. I groped hard for some atavistic root into my Hebraic ancestry. The first Passover feast would of course be different from any that came after. A reference in the Mishnah says that it differed from that celebrated later, which acquired the quality of a memorial, a Thanksgiving for deliverance from bondage.

Obviously, it must have concentrated on an invocation of protection from the avenging Lord who smote the first-born of Egypt. It could hardly have been a festive occasion. Rather an hour of awe, weighted by the terrors of the night, and the first groping sense of termination of four hundred years of bondage in the land of the Nile.

No screenwriter could have approached it without a deep sense of reverence and emotion. Here was the human drama, the birth of a tradition that would endure through the anguish of pogrom and persecution. The strength to endure dispersion and ghetto. In this spirit you took up your pen and tried to create a scene that would come as much from the heart as from cerebral research. Impossible, perhaps, to do full justice to such a moment, but certainly the scene I brought De Mille was not without emotional involvement, or even, one dared hope, a spark of merit.

I sat in the cluttered office, watching his face for some clue of reaction. The ever-disconcerting squeak of his swivel chair did not contribute to my confidence. He read with painful slowness, as though deliberately stretching me on the rack of suspense. Then suddenly he was seized by one of those senseless rages that seemed to sweep away reason, turn a self-contained gentleman into an incoherent fury, hissing accusations. I had failed in every respect! Such incompetence could only be deliberate treason! Where was the drama? The importance? The significance? I had reduced a great moment in the saga of mankind to Hollywood theatrics! He could scarcely speak. Then, with spluttering finality, De Mille spat on my scene!

I walked out. I returned to my own office and began to pack the books that had come from my personal library. He had not only insulted my work, he had sunk to the level of an incoherent, angry child. I felt debased, offended to the core. It was the last of enough last straws to weave a basket.

There was a quiet knock on the door. Harry Wilcoxon or Roy Burns, no doubt. They would by now have heard of the whole episode and be coming to calm the troubled waters with a few well-chosen drops of verbal oil. Only this time it wouldn't work.

I opened the door. And faced De Mille. He smiled rather wanly, no trace of tantrum now. All was suddenly mellow, bathed in the chrome-yellow light of eternal beneficence, suggesting a well-kept pact between God and all his humbler creatures.

"May I come in, Jesse?"

Hardly necessary to ask. The office was his, in his building, in his town. He wouldn't get any answer from me either. Stab back with the ice pick of silence!

He stepped in, glancing about.

"Packing, Jesse?"

I nodded, maintaining my vow. I was a Trappist of hurt pride.

"These books. All yours, I presume? Not removing any De Mille property?"

If this was a joke . . . !

"All mine." I grunted.

"And the Bible?"

"It happens to be inscribed, 'To dear Jesse. From Mother. September 1924.' "

You could almost hear the turning wheels of his mind. Of course he was sorry for what had happened. But it wouldn't have been his style to simply say so. Anyway it didn't matter. I was resigned to resign. He looked at the briefcases I had been packing.

"You're—walking out on me—just because of . . . a petty difference of opinion on a scene? I can't believe it."

"Try." I was as rude as I'd ever dared be.

"Haven't we worked together long enough? I mean, not to have to waste time being diplomatic to each other? Long enough not to have to worry about hurt feelings? Good God, Jesse, you're not Jeanie MacPherson. You're a young pro! Tough and realistic. How many years has it been?"

"That's not important. What happened—happened."

He nodded, conceding, I thought, the point, if there was any point. Then a curious smile came over his face, and he said, " 'And the Lord God took dust and mixed it with spittle—and from this he made a *man*.' You will find something like that in the Bible your mother gave you, Jesse. A man. Not a spoiled child, but an adult, who can stand up against criticism, resist petty feelings of offense, shrug off the flea-bites of injustice. You came to me as a young poet. I don't think a poet ever stops being a poet. Nor should he. But over the layer of sensitivity is built an armor of use. This is man's equipment—and it is not a bad shield to carry when you gallop on Pegasus, Jesse. So grant me the privilege of mixing spittle and dust—at times."

It was flattering to be the target of what must have been one of his greatest performances. It was effective, too, because in spite of his weaknesses, it seemed to show that at his best, there could be a princely capacity of acknowledging error without the embarrassment of a clumsy apology.

"Where in the Bible did you find that quotation, Mr. De Mille?"

"You'll have to look for yourself, Jesse—and keep looking." Then he rested a hand on my shoulder, smiled mysteriously, and walked out. I unpacked and stayed to finish the scene. And the picture. But the strangest thing is, I never have discovered that particular quotation in my Bible.

The cast for *The Ten Commandments* was his largest, costliest, and in most respects carefully selected. Charlton Heston had won De Mille's boundless admiration for his performance in *The Greatest*

Show on Earth. The Boss liked his looks, his acting ability, and his reputation as a highly respectable husband and father.

De Mille regarded a stable home life as a particularly American decorum. He harbored the Victorian distaste for divorce. Although he himself might form attachments, some of which graduated into the respectability of lifelong associations, he never conceived of breaking up his marriage. The devoted attention he paid to wanton debauchery in his movies was always counterbalanced by the final triumph of virtue. He sold the same message as the great illustrator Norman Rockwell, but using Babylon instead of the small-town drugstore. He wanted his pillars of virtue to be rugged in appearance. Heston had the cragged face that could "age" believably from prince to prophet—via a series of false beards—and he had a voice that could outrumble the thunder.

For Nefertiti, the Egyptian princess, Anne Baxter was less physically ideal, but could be counted upon to deliver a flawless performance.

The casting of Rameses, the pharaoh, was sheer genius. De Mille had wanted to find a physically powerful specimen with a voice that could seem to emerge from the depths of a Gustave Doré chasm. When he saw Yul Brynner in *The King and I*, it was love at first sight. The shaven head, the air of inscrutable mystery—it was perfection. Yul's origin was shrouded in rumor. Was he a Russian? A Tartar prince? A gypsy? A Manchurian acrobat? These and other exotic possibilities were carefully nurtured by efficient publicity men. As I recall, Yul never committed himself either to admission or to denial.

We acquired Yvonne De Carlo to play Sephora, the daughter of Jethro, who became Moses' wife. Edward G. Robinson, an old friend of mine, was playing Dathan, the dissembler, which saddled him with the most difficult moment in the script.

Consider that moment: The Children of Israel have, by the will of God and the intercession of Moses, escaped from bondage. They have seen the sea opened for them and had a miraculous pillar of fire protect them as a rear guard. They have seen the great chariot army of their enemy drowned beneath collapsing cliffs of water. And they have been promised by their unfailing leader that he will descend from Mount Sinai to bring them God's Law. Yet, after all that has happened, in a mere thirty days of awaiting Moses at the foot of the mountain, they lose their faith so completely as to become vulnerable to the quisling Dathan's slanderous lies and propaganda. He sells them the preposterous idea that the return to slavery in Egypt as worshippers of a golden calf is their only salvation. Could anyone have been so gullible? Well, the Bible says so.

At the end of a long film, to sway this multitude by one speech, to turn them, from an inspired host marching to freedom with God and Prophet into carousing, faithless sinners, required a magic performance.

Such chronicles are all very well when bound in a holy book, but the screen is something else: a magnifying glass for skepticism. Eddie accomplished the impossible with the reading of that speech.

At the time of my second divorce Eddie Robinson was one of the friends who did not drop me like a hot potato, or whatever it is that domestic casualties are dropped like. When later on, I thanked him for this, he just said, "You gave me the greatest exit a 'heavy' ever had. No actor would break friendship with a writer who created a tempest, then an earthquake, then opened a fissure and had me fall through into hell. Even in *Little Caesar* I never had an exit as good as that!" True, cousin Mervyn LeRoy had only provided a gutter for the great gangster's demise.

The cast of *The Ten Commandments* was full of old friends. Sir Cedric Hardwicke was hired to play the pharaoh, Sethi. Then there was Olive Deering, playing another Miriam, the sister of Moses. And Nina Foch to play the Egyptian mother who would draw the baby Moses from the bulrushes in our studio Nile. Chuck Heston's own baby son was cast to play the infant. There was Vincent Price to perform Baka, the unfortunate master-builder who is slain by Moses. Henry Wilcoxon, our associate producer, would also be in grease-paint again, to double as Captain of Chariots. And even my brother, Bill, was summoned by De Mille. Bill had a reputation for training wild falcons, and it was his job to control the birds that would ride the wrists of our pharaohs. He had always been a great bird handler, except for the night a falcon escaped from his own wrist at one of my parties and dive-bombed the hors d'oeuvres.

One morning I was studying the daily installment of our conference notes. They stretched for about six pages, and, as usual, the numerous passages of profanity had been replaced with strings of miscellaneous symbols by Bernice Mosk, De Mille's ever-vigilant and bowdlerizing field secretary. They read something like this:

"JESSE: Don't you think, sir, we're too long about the orgy? I think we should go right from everybody rolling around to . . ."
"DE MILLE: I think you're!*©/(?)"%=%=&%©!"

"You don't look too happy, Jesse." Bernice had silently drifted in, a sphinxlike presence behind my shoulder.

"He never lets me finish," I grumbled.

"Should he?"

Mystery was Bernice's stock-in-trade. My principal source of information on the set, she always knew more about what was happening in the unit than the Boss himself, and she knew when to declassify a secret.

"Guess who's going where," she began.

"The Boss?"

"And Harry and Chuck and Yul and me, and maybe even you."

"With cameras?" I probed.

She nodded. "You guessed it. The Land of the Nile."

"How do I find out if I'm going?"

"Why not ask Mr. De Mille?"

"Well, how will he know where I found out from? I mean, if I mention that I know—about Egypt?"

"It will probably be declassified by the time you see him."

It was. He wandered about among the props and bric-a-brac in one of his most benevolent moods. He even confided to me that the expedition might be politically sensitive, since President Naguib had originally granted permission for *The Ten Commandments* to be filmed on location in Egypt, on the reasonable grounds that whole villages of Egyptians would find employment impersonating the mixed multitudes of the Exodus. But Colonel Nasser had seized power since, and there were reports that Naguib might now be under detention or arrest. Fortunately the new Egyptian leader seemed disposed to honor the agreement of his predecessor. It had even been confirmed that units of the Egyptian army would drive the chariots, as the U.S. Field Artillery had done for the silent version.

"Then when will we be leaving, sir?" I inquired confidently.

"We? Oh, you thought you'd be going, too?"

"You once invited me to come wade with you in the Red Sea," I reminded him.

He looked troubled. "I'll need you to stay here and polish the script. So it will be ready when I get back."

He could hardly have missed seeing my disappointment. I had already daydreamed the climb up Mount Sinai. Surely a place for mystical revelation, though the only voice I would hear would be De Mille's.

He shook his head. I wondered if there might not be something he was hiding.

"What would you like me to bring you from the Land of the Nile, fellah?" he asked suddenly.

I weighed numerous possibilities, and foolishly decided to let modesty outweigh greed.

"A stone."

"What, the Rosetta Stone? That's in the British Museum."

"A pebble—from the top of Mount Sinai, where Moses might have set his foot."

It was during that famous second-unit trip to Egypt that there occurred the incident which is so well known that I am almost embarrassed to repeat it here. In brief, it concerned a moment when the Exodus crowds were pouring out of Egypt. The principal camera, because of a technical fault, failed to get the shot. When De Mille sent for Henry Wilcoxon, who was in charge of the second camera unit on the hill, and asked, "Did you get that, Harry?" there was breathless suspense, then the legendary reply: "Ready when you are, Mr. De Mille." Apocryphal, no doubt. Wilcoxon was far too efficient a right hand to have failed in a crisis, but it made a good story.

I didn't expect De Mille to remember my pebble. But on his return from Egypt he gave me a bit of granite set in a silver mounting on a black wooden stand. "From the top of the mountain—where Moses might have set foot," he said with a smile.

I looked at it. No inscription? No well-chosen words on a small silver plaque?

"You make up the words, Jesse. You're the writer."

I still have it. Without any inscription.

My old boss had suffered a heart attack in Egypt, but true to his custom had not changed his life-style of overwork and overindulged rages. He was driving the company as furiously as ever. This, however, did not deter every extra in town from trying to get on the picture. It was common knowledge that a job on a De Mille production ensured the longest possible stretch of employment. Long, but not always pleasant.

The golden-calf sequence, for example, was no ordinary film orgy. It was more like a marathon misery contest. Not only was it planned to involve hundreds of extras and run for some fifteen minutes of screen time, but De Mille shrewdly recognized it as the opportunity to capitalize upon the most impeccable of sources to produce the most unrestrained scenes of debauchery the censor would allow. His passion for perfection turned three days of shooting, already generous for a single scene, into three weeks of purgatory.

The set had begun more to resemble a battlefield than a pasture of pleasure. With hair matted with muck and bodies drenched with fake wine, the unhappy extra girls rolled and writhed with sweaty muscle-men in what was supposed to be the bacchanal to end all bacchanalia. After weeks of rape and ravishment the girls were becoming understandably weary. Their mud-caked biblical rags were shredded to ribbons, their body makeup would scarcely wash off any more, and they were black and blue from the gropes, pinches, and clutches of overenthusiastic partners. Worst of all, they could not protest, for as I heard one lecherous Adonis chortle, they were "Only doing our best to give the old man one hell of a peep show!"

Never satisfied, De Mille thundered and railed, demanded more and more abandon. After an eternity of such goings-on, one lovely but exhausted girl was overheard moaning to her friend, "Who do you have to know to get *off* this damned movie?"

Twenty-Eight

YOU MAY IMAGINE the old movie moguls as floating in their gold-plated swimming pools, imbibing magnums of champagne as they contemplate their next casting-couch conquest, but the picture disintegrates beneath the lens of reality. On the way up they are clawing to get there; at the top they are clawing to stay there; on the way down they are struggling to arrest the skid into an oblivion deeper than the pit.

Even my father's huge success *The Great Caruso,* produced at MGM in 1951, failed to resuscitate either his finances or his prestige. When he had first decided to undertake that project, he borrowed money on his life insurance to option the screen rights to Dorothy Caruso's biography of her famous husband. The price, paid in installments, came to $100,000. My father believed the rags-to-riches rise of the exuberant tenor couldn't miss, but Hollywood powers had not seen eye to eye with him. One by one the big companies turned down the project.

Faced with having to make another hefty payment or lose the book rights, he went to see his old friend Louis B. Mayer. L. B.'s own position had become shaky and he could not persuade the studio to commit themselves to the film—movies about opera singers had always been considered risky—but Mayer did get the studio to take over my father's payments on the Caruso book. This gave them an option on the book and my father's services without any obligation to make the film.

A few days later, Howard Hughes, who then owned RKO Studio, made my father a fantastic offer. Hughes had just contracted a great young operatic tenor and needed a vehicle for him. When he heard that my father had the rights to the Caruso book he offered him a three-picture deal that would run into the millions, if he would produce *The Great Caruso* for RKO with Hughes's new tenor.

My father was jubilant! An offer like this would whisk him off the Hollywood scrapheap, back into affluent security that would last the rest of his life. Head in the clouds, he stamped about the house on North Saltair, imitating a cornet blowing out a Sousa march. The Laskys were riding high again! My cautious sister, Betty, failed to be swept away by his exuberance—her feet had always been more firmly anchored to terra firma than brother Bill's or mine.

Totally confident, Dad rushed over to Culver City to see Louis B. In his pocket was an RKO check for $30,000 with which to buy back the option on the Caruso book.

The mighty Mayer, still sporting a brave white carnation in his buttonhole, was on the brink of a power eclipse. Mayer's battles with Nick Schenck, president of MGM, had resulted in Dore Schary, the brilliant young writer-producer, being eased onto Louis's production throne. Mayer was on his way out and he knew it. His favor to Dad had been one of his last acts of power.

Confronting the mogul of Metro in his tennis-court-sized office, Dad explained the Hughes offer. How the book nobody wanted would now bring him millions. Louis B. was full of congratulations. He confirmed that Dore considered the Caruso project old-fashioned, creaky, sentimental rubbish and had no interest in making it. Dad laid the RKO check on Mayer's desk and Mayer picked up the hotline to Dore Schary.

"Have to get approval from him to go to the toilet," he grumbled. He explained to Dore the situation and that Dad had brought a check to recover the option. Then he listened, attentively, his lips pursing, his sagging double chin pressing back against the edge of his collar. His cigar went cold on his lip. He peered across the desk at Dad, the hint of a tear in the corner of his eye. He was always very sentimental. Then he hung up soberly. "No deal, Jesse."

"What?" my father asked incredulously. "But you just said Dore always despised the idea of an opera picture. When you took over my option, it was more like a loan. Just helping me out until I could buy it back!"

"Now he wants to make it," Mayer said flatly.

"What do you mean, he wants to make it?" Dad demanded.

"He changed his mind."

"But why, Louis . . . ?"

Louis leaned forward, with solicitous frankness. "Why? I shouldn't tell you but I will. It's your funeral, Jesse, you got the right to know what you died from. MGM has signed that truck driver with a voice you heard and liked at the Hollywood Bowl concert. You yourself said he might be a good Caruso. He made one picture for us nobody went to see. He eats like a horse and nobody can handle him. He's meshuganah! But Dore is stuck with the commitment, so suddenly he gets the idea—since we got to make something with this bum, and we got the option on your Caruso, it's cheaper to make the picture than pay off Lanza's contract. He's assigning Joe Pasternak to produce."

Gone, the dream of the great three-picture deal with Howard Hughes! Dad would have been entirely out in the cold if Mayer hadn't persuaded Dore to let him produce "in association with Pasternak." His salary: $500 a week—no percentage of the profits.

The Great Caruso turned out to be one of the biggest hits Metro ever had. It virtually saved the company from going under in the increasingly lean years that followed the fall of Louis B. Mayer. Dad, who had found it, fought for it, and produced it, never again got another job in the film industry. Though he was honored and beloved, everyone figured he was old, broke, past it. For six more years he struggled on, trying in vain to put another deal together.

One day he phoned me with the suggestion that we go away together for the weekend. I was delighted. I had wanted to get away anyway after finishing work on *The Ten Commandments;* the only question had been—where? North, to the civilized bistros of San Francisco? South, to the fleshpots of Ensenada, for lobster and tequila? To Palm Springs, for sun-drenched tennis at the Racquet Club and turquoise crystal swimming pools? Dad settled the dilemma. Las Vegas—for fun, food, and a go at the gaming tables, his favorite vice.

My father may also have had in mind that, having recently completed the big De Mille film, my financial condition must be comparatively fat. But I was far leaner in the pocket than he could imagine, what with alimony, business managers, agents, taxes, and the cost of high living. No matter, we always had fun together, and I badly needed a change. We'd be like two bachelor pals, gunning my sports car out down the broad desert highway to Nevada's capital of chance. With each mile of distance between him and the film city, he began to feel more affluent, more successful, less old. He habitually drove like a lunatic, the heritage of early racing-car days. By the time we drew into the over-illuminated oasis of vice, he declared himself ready to lick the world.

The only thing we conquered were a few Bourbon old-fashioneds. The tables were instantly and consistently unfriendly. We soon had dropped all the money we had brought, and all the money he could persuade me to cash. Happily, we'd paid for our rooms in advance, because after several hours of heavy losing our credit was undergoing extremely close scrutiny by some heavy-shouldered types.

"What are you worried about, Jesse? Don't you know our luck's going to change at midnight? I'll bet you anything you like, right now. I'll show you five thousand dollars' winnings in chips right there on that table at the stroke of twelve!"

He didn't, but we still managed to drop a few hundred more between dice, blackjack, and roulette. We squandered another twenty-five bucks "on the greatest meal in Las Vegas"—nothing to my father was ever less than the greatest—and then we were back at the tables for more. Gluttons for punishment. We ended the first night in the hole. By the second we had doubled our losings. Even Dad's normally ebullient spirits were damp. It was not a loss that could easily be reported to Bess, who could never fathom anyone preferring chips to Chippendale.

We swam in the pool, inspected some rather nonstop female showgirl torsos, and considered the course for the last hours of our little holiday.

"How much have you got left in the bank?" he demanded.

I made a rapid calculation and told him the worst.

"Good. Then you could cash a check for another five hundred and I'll show you how to make a thousand dollars by sunset!"

I did and he didn't. My hard-earned De Mille money melted away under the bright chandeliers. Poor Dad. He could never believe in bad luck. It had been the same on the golf course. I had seen him drop $500 a hole to Al Jolson, and on another occasion he lost a thousand to W. C. Fields. The tough young actor Bruce Cabot almost managed a permanent income from playing golf with Dad, who was flattered by the attention of such a notable brawler and cocksman. Dad had a weakness for association with the sporting gentry, and tough guys and flashy girls were an environment that made him forget his age.

"Well, Jesse, shall we give it a last try? I mean, it can only get better. It has to!"

"Sorry, Dad," I said, no doubt sounding unbearably priggish.

"What d'you mean, sorry?"

His eyes had that same glassy look of rare anger that I had seen long ago when once I tried to stop him running some impossible rapids alone in a canoe on the River Balsas. He had hit me with a paddle, cursed me for a coward, and shoved off. And capsized in a whirlpool, to be dragged out half-drowned. I resolved that he would not drown our last waning resources tonight in Las Vegas.

"We're going home."

"Why, for goodness' sake?" Profanity was unknown to him.

"Because we've both lost far too much. I for one cannot and will not lose another penny. We're going home while we still have enough in our pockets to pay for gas or a car repair if we need it."

And suddenly there was the rapid change. The blue steel glint softened, becoming watery. He seemed to age.

"All right, Jess." And then a pathetic plea from the man who might so few years before have bought this desert hotel just to entertain a few friends. "Couldn't we have dinner first? I mean, before we drive home?"

Home to the town in which we both would be job-hunting on Monday. I weighed it. "How much money have you got left?"

He put his hand in his pocket, looking sheepish. "Two silver dollars. You?"

I had been cautious and could muster almost five. It would be enough for a modest dinner. We selected a small Italian restaurant away from the plush hotels. It was a gloomy dive, virtually deserted. The menu offered the usual array of steak and starch. We ordered a cheap California Chianti and pasta.

I hoped he would not notice in the gloom that against one wall was a pair of one-armed bandits and a single blackjack table. The croupier was a young woman wearing too much makeup and too little evening dress. She had a carrot-tint rinse, and restless eyes. Yet she was brassily pretty, and my father had not missed her—or the table.

"We could play a few hands and still have enough left to pay for the dinner," he suggested.

"If one of us eats."

"What do you mean? I'll show you how to win fifty dollars right now!" At least the sum of his insane optimism had been somewhat reduced.

"Dad, nobody's going to show anyone anything. We're going to finish dinner, pay for it, then—if there's anything left, I mean over a couple of bucks for emergency, *I'll* play it. Not you."

He looked ready to explode. But subsided. "All right. The cowardice comes from your mother's side."

"The caution."

"It's the same thing!" We finished dinner rather glumly. But by the time we had enjoyed the earthy wine our blood had warmed. We had two dollars left for a last play. I made it a condition that he wouldn't even come near me. He would remain at our table and have his coffee, while I quietly lost our last stake. He must have been feeling tired, because he agreed.

Feeling smug and prim from my last ultimatum to Dad I set down one silver dollar and awaited the deal. The girl dealer noticed the extra dollar I was saving for a second play.

"Bet them both, Captain," she said.

"What?"

"Bet the two bucks."

I did what I was told. It could hardly matter anyway. The blackjack hand was dealt. I had fourteen. About the worst hand you could have. I asked for another card.

"Stand, Captain," she said. What the hell was this Captain business, anyway?

"On fourteen? You'll slaughter me!"

"Stand, Captain," the husky voice repeated.

I glanced across at her for the first time. Her eye makeup was smeared. Anyone else would have said, "Look, give me that card!" but after three nights of being beaten by the tables another two dollars hardly mattered. I left it.

She reached over, and drew to her own hand. Twenty three—and broke. I scooped up my winnings.

"Leave it, Captain."

"What—the four dollars?"

She nodded. I did. She dealt. Blackjack! Twenty-one! She put down a stack of silver dollars. And again I was instructed to leave it. Seeing the piles of dollars mounting, my father was going wild with excitement, but sensibly he stayed away from me, realizing that, whatever my mysterious change of fortunes, Lady Luck might not wish to be interrupted. My winnings had now reached nearly seven hundred dollars.

"Take it, Captain," she said quietly.

"Hey, wait a minute, I'm ahead! I can afford to play all night. I'm not just pocketing winnings and walking." I was sounding like my father.

"Do it, Captain. Go home."

I looked from the gleaming stacks of silver dollars to the tired girl in the sleazy evening gown. "What kind of a deal is this?" I demanded.

The false eyelashes lifted. I looked into sad, violet eyes. Somewhat familiar, a phantom trying to surface in my recollection.

"Why?" I demanded.

"Why what?"

"Everything. The winnings, that Captain stuff! I've never won at cards in my life! You could have washed me out in one hand. So what's the game?"

"It's called memory. My memory against yours . . . which is pretty lousy, Captain."

"Something to do with the war? New Guinea? There weren't any women . . . except . . ."

"Nurses?" She smiled. "You're warm. Try naval nurse. A hospital ship taking wounded out of the Leyte Gulf campaign. You sailed with us, back to Dutch New Guinea. Hollandia. You wanted to date me—if we ever met in Sydney or San Francisco. But you probably forgot after you got home to your wife." She took a long drag from the cigarette. "I got married myself, right after VJ day. To a kid marine who thought he could beat Las Vegas. He lost. So did I. He died here. Some of his creditors offered me a job. I've learned to be a pretty good dealer, wouldn't you say?"

I wanted to cry. Just sit down and bawl. I ordered a drink and bought her one, and Dad one. We told her, if she ever came to Hollywood, all we would like to do for her. She just smiled, and touched my glass with her glass. "Good night, Captain," she said.

"Good night, Lady Luck. If I ever need you I hope you'll be somewhere around."

"Who knows?" She turned away, perhaps to fleece the next lamb who stepped up for slaughter. Dad and I drove back to Hollywood, not quite so poor.

The lucky streak didn't wear off. I got an immediate assignment. An agent friend, Harry Tattleman, was going to coproduce a film with Jane Russell at RKO. So I moved my writing board to RKO to script *Hot Blood*, a saga of authentic contemporary gypsy life.

To direct our film, Jane had picked Nicholas Ray, who had recently completed *Rebel Without A Cause*. Nick was among the first "new wave" American directors, tremendously creative, difficult to pin to a decision, but able to convey a mystical sense of omnipotence to his cast.

Gone now were the hard-boiled, tough-talking technicians who booted their casts around and fought to come in under budget. The new image was becoming half guru, half father confessor, and all amateur analyst. It was Nick Ray who had gotten such a great performance out of the insecure genius James Dean. My first meeting with him was certainly promising. Jane Russell sent me up to his Hollywood apartment. Experimental jazz thundered from a hi-fi in a room lit by red lanterns. Nick was sparring with a young prize fighter. They ignored me. Then suddenly we were discussing the film. He wanted a slice of life! He wanted to live with the gypsies and he wanted to infiltrate their caravans. The last thing he wanted was a "Hollywood" movie.

By way of research, I was to interview the king of the Los Angeles gypsies. The audience was arranged through the Los Angeles police department. They warned me that if the king picked my pockets I was not to complain to them. They had tipped him off that I worked for a newspaper, which would make me less pluckable than a plush Hollywood scribe.

I entered his caravan, which was unexpectedly sumptuous. The monarch, a stocky man in a panama hat, then proceeded to remove the two brass door knobs. I was glad I'd left my gold watch at home.

"I don't never trust no Gajos," said His Majesty. "You Gajos steal too much. A little bit—all right, maybe. But Gajos, steal even the nails from the Cross! Without the handle on the door you walk when I tell you, but not before!"

I could wish I'd had his royal foresight on occasions when my story ideas had been stolen! But then perhaps it was my luck to walk out of that caravan with the idea for a good film story that became *Hot Blood.*

Twenty-Nine

IN THAT SAME YEAR I accepted an assignment from Sam Bronston, an independent producer. *John Paul Jones* was an exciting subject, and besides I had added an expensive new sports car to our garage, a Ford Thunderbird—white with red leather upholstery, only the second of the model to be sold in California. Though I couldn't afford to pay for it, it was such a good deal that I couldn't afford to turn it down.

But the new film assignment would pay for it, and much more, including my eternal alimony.

Bronston had great ideas, but, at that moment, extremely limited finances. He was likable, experienced, a man of tremendous ups and downs. But his approach to *John Paul Jones*, the story of the Scottish fugitive who fathered the American navy, was inspired.

We flew to Washington to chat with the admiral who then headed the Joint Chiefs of Staff, and who we hoped would provide the essential naval cooperation. We visited the U.S. Naval Academy, where Jones's bones lie in state. He had been less honored in his lifetime—after the failure of Congress to pay him for his war services he had been forced to accept a commission from Empress Catherine of Russia.

His wartime deeds for the United States included a raid on the coast of Scotland, where, in the best piratical tradition, he ran off with the Selkirk silver. I think he was the first enemy to invade England since the Vikings—unless you care to count his countryman Bonnie Prince Charlie.

There was another purpose for our visit to Washington. Sam needed financing for his film, and he had set up a sound possibility of acquiring it. A potential backer was to meet us at our hotel suite that evening.

"Now," warned Sam, "I want you to put your best foot forward, Jesse—your historical foot. I've been warned that this possible investor happens to be an amateur American historian. He'll want the correct answers from you on every detail of our story."

"I hope I'll have them, Sam."

"Keep reading!" he urged, indicating the huge stack of history books I was carrying. "This man is a fiend on history. A serious university scholar. And a great American."

"And a financier," I added, opening a book.

"Naturally a financier! But that may depend on how we impress him with our knowledge of every detail of the period."

"We?" questioned I.

"You," he conceded. "My first concern is to get the picture made, yours is to write it. Accurately. Correctly. Historically . . ."

"Don't worry, Sam. I had my training from De Mille."

"That's just what I'm worried about!" he admitted.

I was still cramming for the great exam as our millionaire historian headed up to our suite.

"Be sure you put the books where he'll see them. You know, casually, not too obvious," Sam said nervously, straightening his somber tie, brushing a speck of invisible dust from his banker's blue suit. "Only we've got to be sure he sees how serious you are, Jesse. Maybe it wouldn't hurt to drop something about your academic background? Degrees from universities?"

"You start dropping that, and you'll never see his checkbook," I warned, as the door of our suite was buzzed.

A serious-looking, impressive young man was admitted. We exchanged a few polite pleasantries.

"Jesse can't be got out of his history books for five seconds. He's like a dope fiend about history! Practically lives in the archives. . . . Now, sir," Sam concluded, "what would you like for dinner tonight?"

Our distinguished guest suddenly changed. His face became furtive with a very different brand of dedication.

"Women!"

Sam, as proper a married man as I'd ever met in Hollywood, looked as though he'd been hit in the face.

"Women . . . ?" he said weakly.

"It isn't every night I get a weekend away from my wife!" our potential backer beamed.

Sam unhappily went to the telephone to contact some of the Film

Exchange men in Washington who might know the ropes, and I offered our prospect a stiff whisky—and had one myself.

In the end Sam's casting in that department must have fallen short of his film-casting, because I don't believe he ever extracted any gold from that angel.

But the ghost of John Paul Jones must have been looking after us better than the commodore ever looked after himself. Recently retired Admiral of the Fleet Chester W. Nimitz became our special Naval Technical Adviser on the screenplay, and the association of such a name helped open financial doors for Sam.

Our first meeting with the great man was to be at his home in Berkeley, an hour's flight from Hollywood. Our anticipatory nerves weren't helped by the fact that my new high-powered car had a vapor-lock and was stalling, and that we succeeded in being stopped by every traffic light between Beverly Hills and the airport. By the time we arrived the plane was ready to take off, but Sam, ever the devoted family man, insisted on taking time to fill our flight insurance forms. As we scurried to catch the plane, we thrust our airline tickets into the mailbox, and handed our insurance policies to the gate steward.

Consternation! Officials went racing about the L.A. air terminal, trying to find someone with the keys to the mailbox. At the last moment, success, and we were shoved aboard the plane with our insurance forms still in our pockets. Happily we reached Berkeley without incident. Sam bribed a taxi driver to race up to the admiral's home at top speed. On the way he warned me, "whatever you do, don't mention General MacArthur. They were enemies in the war."

When we arrived, the admiral was having his afternoon rest, and could not be disturbed, but Mrs. Nimitz, a gracious person, greeted us and offered us coffee.

Eventually he appeared, and, anxious to air my credentials, Sam proudly informed him, "Jesse saw service in the Pacific, Admiral!"

The white tufted eyebrows lifted politely. "Did you? Under whose command, Mr. Lasky?"

Sam closed his eyes and clutched my arm.

"Why, I . . . ah, oh. General . . . Aiken, sir." I had chosen the coward's way out. Sam's glare melted into relief.

"Ahh," beamed the admiral, "General MacArthur's army. Great man, MacArthur. I'll give you a photograph of us together. Signing some papers."

"Papers, sir?" I asked.

"Yes, the Japanese surrender."

When the first draft of the screenplay was ready, the producer faced two major problems. To lure the next injection of capital, he needed a top star. But to lure a star he might need a director. And before he could sign a director he would need money in the bank. It was a tossup which to try for first.

Sam decided to go for the star. Many great names were considered and rejected for one reason or another. Unavailability. Price. Unsuitability for the part. At last it was decided to try to get Glenn Ford. He was at that moment important enough to bring the package together and (horrible phrase) a name you could take to the bank. But Glenn Ford was also in great demand, and, said his agent, would probably not even read any screenplay we submitted, unless it happened to be by a writer whose work he tremendously respected. Unfortunately, as a Columbia star, Glenn Ford could not have been unaware of my numerous hack credits at that studio. The agent even went so far as to say that an acceptable name would be that of the great Ben Hecht. It seemed that Glenn Ford had met Hecht at a party and become deeply enamored of his work, as who wasn't? Now if Sam could get Ben Hecht to do even a rewrite—a polish—on my script, and put his name on it, Glenn Ford would read the screenplay, and surely accept the part!

A great chance for Sam, but a bit hard on me. He was full of apologies. He liked my script, everybody did. But he had to hook Ford; he hoped I wouldn't mind about Ben Hecht.

"He probably won't accept the job anyway," I said.

"He already has."

"Ben Hecht agreed to do a quick polish on somebody else's script?"

"Well—yes and no. Ben's a pretty important writer."

I didn't need Sam to tell me that.

"And he's actually too busy to write everything he writes himself. Not that he doesn't get the same amount. Fifty thousand dollars."

"More than twice what I got to do the whole story and screenplay, Sam!" I gasped, chilled to the heart.

"You think I'm happy?" the producer sighed. "You think *I* think the script needs a rewrite? But I told you, without Ben's name on it Glenn Ford won't even read it. And without Ford, what have I got? I'm trapped. The worst of it is, even if I have Ben Hecht, I may not get a Ben Hecht script, if you see what I mean."

"Go on, Sam," I said, forcing him to say it aloud.

"Ben has a kind of stable. Young writers. They work for peanuts. So when he hasn't time to do all the work himself, he supervises them. And when they've blocked it out he gives it the final once-over himself. I hope."

"All for fifty thousand."

"Don't make me feel worse than I do!"

"And suppose his bright young men make a botch of it?"

"If that happens, Ben made me a promise. He'll hire a room in a downtown Los Angeles hotel, where nobody can interrupt. He'll lay in a case of whisky and he'll personally write a brand-new script. In one weekend."

"I thought you only wanted a polish that he could put his name on." I was trying not to sound bitter.

"Did I say we have to keep what he writes? If we don't like it you can rewrite the rewrite. But by then we'll have the commitment from Ford."

So this was our Brave New World of independent production. At least Sam was being honest about it. God help the writer when the fly-by-night promoters took over.

One evening I unexpectedly ran into Ben Hecht at a party. "I liked your *John Paul Jones*," he said.

That was flattering. "But you're rewriting it, Ben."

"A few small changes. It won't kill you."

I waited until the host had stoked our drinks, then asked the big question. "You doing those changes yourself, Ben?"

He looked at the drink, then growled, "Don't worry so much. You'll live longer, kid."

In the end Sam didn't get Glenn Ford anyway. When the script with Ben's name on it was ready, the star had already accepted another assignment and left the country!

Worse was to follow. Nobody was happy with the new script, even Ben Hecht. So Sam and I put back most of the original, keeping the few good bits Ben had added himself. Sam now decided to go after "a great director" first.

I was a little astounded by Sam's choice. William Dieterle, the distinguished German-American director, hardly seemed ideal for so American an epic. Sam assured me that I was wrong. Hadn't Dieterle made *The Story of Louis Pasteur* without being a doctor? *Juarez* without being Mexican? *The Life of Émile Zola* without being French? *Midsummer Night's Dream* without being English? All outstanding films. I was grateful that Sam didn't include *Salome*.

Certainly Dieterle was a fascinating director. He was reported, too, to have some interesting quirks. He was totally guided by astrological predictions. He wouldn't even walk on a set if the heavens happened to have produced unfavorable signs that day. He directed in black gloves and, with his high domed head, his ivory complexion, and matted, jet-black hair presented a singularly Transylvanian appearance. Certainly he was hardly noted for humor and lightness, in or out of his films.

He had read the screenplay and was favorably disposed. Of course he wanted to meet and chat with me first. This meeting would be extremely important. I was asked to go to Dieterle's house in the San Fernando Valley, where he wanted to show me one of his films in his private projection room. Sam warned me that Dieterle had been assured that I was a deeply serious, scholarly writer. With this image in mind I put on a dark suit and the necktie of the Company of Military Historians, and set out to Dieterle's home. The sun was casting its last bloodred rays over San Fernando as I turned my car up the road that wound round and round Dieterle's private hill, higher and higher to an almost gothic chalet.

William Dieterle greeted me at the door, leading me into a high-ceilinged room that would have been more suitable to some Black Forest castle: dark wood, antlers on the walls, heavy Biedermeier furniture, bookshelves groaning under the weight of Germanic, leather-bound tomes, a sense of oppressive gloom. And, in the middle of a California summer, a roaring log fire in an open fireplace large enough to roast an ox. I restrained myself from taking off my jacket, hoping he would notice the significance of my tie.

"You will take something to drink, *ja?*"

One, I supposed, would not too greatly diminish my image as a serious American historical writer. Dieterle snapped his fingers. A small woman, barely larger than a dwarf, came bobbing in, bearing what appeared to be a huge wooden surfboard. It carried a single tall heavy goblet of cranberry-colored glass.

"It iss martini," another gnomish woman assured me, popping out of a doorway like a cuckoo from a clock. More fraus and frauleins kept materializing from dusty shadows. All eyes were upon me as I sipped what must have been the strongest martini ever made. Pure gin with some sweet vermouth, and not a hint of ice. An alcoholic soup. I lifted the glass to my host and drank, quicker, perhaps, than I had intended. As though by magic the surfboard reappeared with a second great glass beaker, more of the same. Nobody seemed to be drinking but me.

"Drink!" Dieterle commanded. His enormous face loomed high in the room, a Bavarian steeple of a man. You could imagine chimes would throb from him, and a procession of allegorical medieval figures, bearing hourglasses, swords, scythes, would march out of his mouth and reenter by one of his ears. The family faces bobbed out of the darkening shadow, like petit-point eyes peering from a tapestry forest. Nobody spoke. Again, as though by silent command, the enormous wooden trencher bore me another huge, hot martini.

Sometime later I found myself at a long oak dining table. Battalions of Rhenish wines surrounded me. I was eating something that may have been venison.

The director was speaking. "Years ago in Germany I haf made a film about a German classical composer. It iss using the music—not for entertainment—but to create the sense of the past. The ages. It iss four hours long in the uncut version, which tonight we shall project. Nein?"

I nodded, my forehead touching the plate. A dwarf leered around my chin, refilling my wine glass. Later I had a brief memory of a darkening projection room. I don't know how I reached it. I do remember that the chair was carved wood, very tall, lined with oxblood velvet cushions.

"Now we start!" said the sepulchral voice of the director.

There was a deep throb of organ chords from the sound track and I fell into a bottomless crevice of oblivion.

I awakened with a war hammer beating inside my skull and the hot dawn of the Valley blazing into an airless guest room. The house stirred gently alive with snores. I tiptoed out, crawled into my car, and drove home.

The phone was ringing as I arrived. It was Sam. He was very upset. "How in God's name could you have done it, Jesse? Got so drunk you fell unconscious out of your chair—at the opening of his great film he arranged especially for you to see! How could you?"

"It was easy, Sam," I groaned.

"What! Don't joke about this. It's damned serious. I think we may have lost Dieterle, thanks to your insulting behavior! I've arranged to go up and see him tonight myself. To apologize. And I hope to God I can talk him back into doing *John Paul Jones*." His voice rose. . . . "A serious professional like you. It is incredible!"

"Sam, look out for those martinis. He uses pure wormwood."

"I don't drink. Certainly not when there's a moving picture at stake," he said righteously.

The report I got was that Sam had been taken directly from Dieterle's to the hospital.

It wasn't true, of course, but when I next saw him, several days later, his first words were, "I'm afraid we've lost Dieterle. And Jesse, you couldn't guess what happened!"

But of course I could.

Some months later Sam phoned to tell me that Johnny Farrow was going to direct *John Paul Jones*. Farrow had specialized in naval pictures, and had even served in the navy. He wanted me to go back on the film and make script changes necessitated by the Spanish location where the film would be made. I was dying to go, but it was too late. I had started on another writing job, this time for my friend Yul Brynner.

It had come about when Yul invited me to lunch at Lucey's. I considered his offer over a grilled swordfish steak. He was going to prepare, direct, and star in a film for De Mille. I knew the Boss was much taken with Yul, but this was beyond any expectations. De Mille would supervise, Henry Wilcoxon produce, and—they would like me to write.

"Write what?"

"*The Buccaneer*," he rumbled.

"De Mille already made it. With Fredric March—in 1938. Tony Quinn played one of the pirates. I even wrote a few lines for it."

"This won't be anything like that," Yul assured me. "It will be a musical—or rather a film with music. Songs that come in naturally. I have a lot of ideas to make this original. Do things that have never been done before. De Mille will give us a free hand."

"I wasn't planning on doing any more scripts for the Boss. Not for a while."

The great shoulders hunched the shaven head nearer.

"It won't be for him, Jesse. For me. And Harry."

Perhaps I'd had too long a training in saying "yes."

For the first three months, there were no regrets. De Mille stayed away from us. Occasionally he would bestow on us an almost coy grin when we met in the commissary. "You fellahs got anything you'd like to show me?"

Of course I knew he would at some point want to be included. I had from the first an uneasy feeling in my bones that, when finally invited, he would make his presence felt. He wanted us to call for help, to ask his advice, to consult, to make him feel a part of the act of conception, but Yul wanted to present him with a *fait accompli*, and, against Henry Wilcoxon's better judgment, Yul and I continued to avoid him like the plague. I couldn't help worrying, though, that there was bound to be a day of reckoning, when we had our first meeting with De Mille.

Yul brushed aside such trivial concerns. "Don't worry, Jesse. I will tell him the story. The Old Man will listen to me. I'm like—his son."

"Ask his son how well the old man listens," I suggested.

"I told you—don't worry!"

As it turned out, I hadn't worried enough.

The meeting opened with deceptive calm. De Mille arrived, slightly stooped, hair whiter since his heart attack in Egypt, too benevolent, too pleasant for words. Bernice Mosk walked at his elbow like his gunbearer, her notebooks ready to record his reactions to the story we had prepared. Harry sensed the storm signals, but we counted on Yul's performance to pull us through.

At first it looked as though he might. His storytelling was superb. It would have thrilled any audience.

Except one. You could see De Mille's growing anger. It burned slow at first. The gentle sabotage of polite interruptions, delicately seasoned with sarcasm, at crucial points in the story.

"I'm curious as to when we will hear of the presence of a woman. I take it, you do have—a love story? Somewhere in your"—too long a pause—"drama?"

We all chimed in that we did—and if he would only be a bit patient, we were approaching the introduction of that element. But patient he wasn't, and we never did get to our love story. De Mille's interruptions became quicker, sharper, more insulting. And suddenly he was citing every weakness of the story we had scarcely begun to tell. No, he wouldn't wait, because neither would an audience, he said. I saw the cold rage mounting in Yul. More than a story had fallen to bits. A relationship had crumbled.

And suddenly Yul was resigning as director, and De Mille was saying that if we weren't prepared to write a screen story that people would sit through, he would find writers who could!

It was our own fault for hoping that this time things could be different.

Our failure seemed at first to call for nothing less than some form of hari-kari, but we accepted the inevitable, went back to the beginning, and refashioned our story with De Mille's approval at every step.

"If you go too far wrong, even I won't be able to get you back on the track," he had warned. So we wrote it the way he wanted, which was less fun, less creatively free, and less original. In fact it wasn't original at all. It was a musicless, slightly updated copy of his old film, and it would no doubt have been a fantastic financial success.

Yul had moved out of the unit, but not off the picture. Contractually bound to perform the role of Lafitte, he was a good enough trouper to make the best of a bad situation. But on this, as on many other occasions, the Boss was not prepared to forgive and forget. We had all offended him, and he contrived to punish us in a manner worthy of Machiavelli.

We were all lunching with the Boss in the commissary, Yul at table with us. De Mille repeated his frequently asked question. Who would be our choice to direct *The Buccaneer* now that Yul had bowed out? All insisted, as always, that only De Mille himself could do justice to this epic fragment of Americana.

But, like Caesar thrice refusing the crown, he always declined. And on this particular day his eyes rose from the cold lobster to settle on his son-in-law, Anthony Quinn, who was at that instant striding across the lunchroom.

"Tony!" he called. "How'd y'like to direct *The Buccaneer*?"

I glanced over at Yul. His face was impassive.

It took Tony all of two minutes to accept, although he had never directed a film in his life. Brilliant actor that he was, to take over a project that had been hand-tailored to De Mille specifications, an old fashioned spectacle-epic, was extremely risky, but Tony was not a man to be intimidated by such considerations.

Why had the Boss asked him? To punish Yul for walking out as director? To put him in the position of being guided by another actor who had never directed a film before? And for Tony, too, it might be a kind of punishment, since nothing could be more difficult to handle than this cumbersome juggernaut of sea battles and land battles, of buccaneers and New Orleans balls, of British red-coated armies and historical clichés.

But Tony no doubt conceived that the sow's ear could be turned into a silk purse—that a thirties melodrama would be converted into a modern psychodrama.

So we started to rewrite. But the basic structure just wouldn't wear contemporary clothes. The more we rewrote, the less we seemed to have. As an actor of the new school, Tony wanted to create something modern and spontaneous. In spite of Yul's failure with the Boss, Tony figured he had the power to get away with it. He even tried to improvise the battle of New Orelans. We had reached a state of artistic anarchy.

In his enthusiasm and creative fervor, Tony kept searching for new and more original solutions. Nightly we would throw away the scripted scenes we'd agreed upon in the morning. And rewrite. There were so many versions of every scene that only Bernice Mosk could put them in some form of order so that filming could continue.

Claire Bloom heroically performed a part that would have defied any actress on earth, that of the female pirate in love with Lafitte. Written and rewritten to death, this buccaneer's moll became a kind of combination of Carmen and Miss Julie, yet Claire made her believable. Yul tried hard, and occasionally breathed life into our Freudian Lafitte. Wise old hands like Chuck Heston and Charles Boyer secretly hid the original dialogue scenes in their boots, so that they had something prepared when attempted improvisations ended in chaos. Inger Stevens, a lovely Swedish-American actress more in love with Tony Quinn than with the vapid character we had built for her, played a southern belle with a cracked chime and some morsels of dialogue that would have destroyed Ethel Barrymore.

> ANNETTE: Jean, my father was sent down here by the President to bring some unity to this country—and here I am in love with a man who is helping to destroy everything he is trying to build up.

To which Lafitte was made to reply, "Who, me?"

Well, we kept throwing away the script, but the great spontaneous lines that were supposed to replace it were somehow never born. (Well, hardly ever: *The Buccaneer* had moments of surprising poignancy.) It was as though a mortally wounded composer was struggling to play the note that had never been sounded on the instrument that had never been built.

The Buccaneer was to some extent redeemed by its technical achievements. Harry's well-supervised special-effects men had created wonderful "Congreve rockets" on trolleys. Stunt men were blown off horses. American Legion "Highlanders" marched behind their pipes into the hottest musketry in the history of cinema battlefields, and died to the last man.

Throughout this film I was in a bad emotional state, compounded of a number of elements, one of which was sheer exhaustion. I think we'd rewritten and discarded about fifty scripts—I lost count. The strain of having to work on the set, changing words as the filming progressed all around, was enormous. So was the heartbreak of seeing the rushes. De Mille on one occasion murmured, after viewing some turgid moment of ad-libbed verbal violence, "The only one in this film who should have been hung was the writer." I couldn't honestly disagree with him. If Claire Bloom hadn't provided me with occasional contributions of whisky and sympathy, I wouldn't have got through it.

I had become extremely worried about my father. His lawyers had advised him to take a capital gain on the profits of *Sergeant York*. He lost his case by a decision of the state supreme court. Those high-powered lawyers neglected to file an appeal within the allotted period of time! It left my father the clear option of suing his legal tax team for the carelessness that had caused his ruin, but such vindictive action was not in his nature. The film pioneer whose company had virtually created Hollywood was a rather more complex personality than superficial observation might suggest. The adventurer, the gambler, the showman, the sportsman, were all facades real enough in themselves, yet hiding still another personality.

Now, at seventy-seven, he had signed everything over to the tax collectors to pay for the success of *Sergeant York*. The layers of his material life had been stripped from him skin by skin. Gone, the memberships in his beloved clubs: The Santa Monica Beach Club, the valuable Hillcrest Country Club where oil had been struck under the fairway, The Riviera Golf Club. Signed over with his own power-of-attorney were the stock portfolios which could have insured his retirement, and every penny of his life insurance. The zealous tax collectors, with whom he had somehow equated a kind of benevolent and loving Uncle Sam, had even cut off his income from his own autobiography in its first printing! *I Blow My Own Horn* was the government's horn now.

As on that grim Depression day in Santa Monica years before, Bess confided her concern to me. Self-concern would have been the last thing Dad would ever have shown.

"When he stays home on Saturday nights you have to worry," she said with an effort at humor she didn't really feel. "The trouble is, he's acting his age," she added sadly. She was standing in the L-shaped living room of the last house they had built together. Around her were the few bits of old English furniture that had survived the auction rooms of the Depression. Her own landscapes and still-life paintings caught reflected sunshine through the wide glass windows, beyond which Dad sunbathed in the garden.

Bess, too, was trying to hide the mainstream of worry. "And he won't even tell me how much has been lost. He keeps saying, 'One more picture, *The Big Brass Band*, and we'll make it all back again.' "

"And you know it isn't true?" I asked. Realism had not always been Bess's strength.

"He isn't well and he won't tell us how sick he really is. He keeps saying he's fooled the doctors before. Every day, driving his old car from studio to studio, briefcase full of scripts and photographs—so heavy you can hardly get them off the floor. If it weren't for his religious reading, I know what he'd do! Go out and talk to him, Jesse. Maybe he'll tell you the truth."

He was lying on a slant board on the warm grass practicing deep breathing. Beside him, books dealing with Science of Mind, Religious Science, Unity, Christian Science.

"How are you, Dad?"

"I'm inspiring myself, Jess. You should try it sometime. I'll give you some books to read. You'll find what you need. And you're slumping! When will you learn to walk with a straight posture? Head up, shoulders back! And take deep breaths." He demonstrated, inflating his still-powerful chest. From all reports, the heart within it was tired.

"Things are going badly, aren't they?" I began.

"Who says so?"

"Everyone knows, Dad."

"I don't know! Let me tell you something: You're a fair-weather sailor, Jess. You think you carry your whole life in your pocket or your bank account! How small do you think God made this world —the size of a wallet?"

"Dad, let's be honest with each other . . ."

"It's all in your mind, Jess. The power to accept and build—or lay down and die. Cecil understands that, too. How's *The Buccaneer* going?"

"Not good. I don't know what's wrong. I can't seem to write anymore, not what they want. Or what I want either."

"You're only licked if you admit it."

The sun dappled the grass. Birds chattered in the avocado tree. The lead cherub balancing a sun dial on his head pouted a smile out of eighteenth-century England at Dad's beloved California. I could not find any faith or word of encouragement. Time was no healer.

"Remember when you swam out that day in Santa Monica, Jess, to try and save me?"

I nodded. "And you told me you were planning a picture called *Zoo in Budapest*."

"Well I made it, didn't I?"

"Yes, Dad."

"And everybody said it wouldn't be done. They said I was finished. What does that tell you?"

"*The Big Brass Band* will be made, too."

"You don't believe it, do you? Suppose I said one year from today you and I will be attending the Academy Awards together?"

"Dad . . ."

"If you could only learn to believe in yourself, it's all inside you. The talent, the courage, even the will. Everything. Do unto others, Jess, and take deep breaths!" He closed his eyes. His cataracts were troubling him, yet he insisted on staring at the sun. "Remember me to Cecil."

I did not then know the unhappy scene that had taken place with his one-time partner, De Mille. Young Barney Slater, one of my brightest young writer pals, had done a treatment for my father on *The Big Brass Band*. Desperate for investment, my father had gone to De Mille as a last resort, to solicit his old friend's support and possibly his participation.

There must have been times when he could have had it without asking. But now was different. De Mille had become moody, resenting the creeping limitation of his years. He was, except for rare flashes, a rather bitter old man. And yet he had everything—wealth, success, influence—everything but the old vitality.

My father and Barney Slater tried to read and tell him the story of *The Big Brass Band*. De Mille was being a very bad listener. He walked about. He showed his boredom. He asked questions, and at last he became insulting. He suggested to my father that, for a man who had had the best story sense in the business, he had forgotten his ABC's. To do this in the presence of a young writer was humiliating in the extreme. When Dad fought back, De Mille interrupted sarcastically, "I've made a few successful pictures myself, you know."

My father turned white and walked out of the office. Barney, who lingered behind to collect the sheafs of script that had been brushed to the floor, heard De Mille call after him, "Jesse, come back . . . we haven't finished talking . . ."

He never did go back, and De Mille never made the apology he might have wanted to make. He probably did not realize how desperately my father needed help, and it would have been unlike my father to admit it. In any event Barney Slater told me that he had closed himself up alone after that experience.

Meanwhile I was trapped in that nightmare production from which De Mille, although still executive producer, had cut all connections. His attitude was "You fellahs got yourselves into this, get yourselves out."

Yul was upset with his predicament. Harry was upset with everyone. Tony couldn't fathom how the more we tried to avoid an old-fashioned cliché movie, the more we became bogged down.

Then one day, as Bernice Mosk and I were struggling to write modern lines for one of the comic-opera moments in our pirate story, word came that De Mille wanted to see me in his office at once. Fired at last, hopefully, I thought. The end of the agony. All I wanted now was to escape. Some woman had phoned me on the set the day before, inviting me to make a return appearance at her literary lunch in Beverly Hills to autograph copies of my recent novel. I had declined, but phoned my father, asking him if he would like to accept the engagement with his autobiography. He always enjoyed speaking to groups, and the chance to autograph copies would give him back the sense of celebrity that he badly needed at the time. He gladly agreed to take my place.

All this was in my mind as I headed for the De Mille Building, threading between a straggle of Highlanders with bayonet-tipped muskets intermingled with Tennessee riflemen and pirates. Ours was Paramount's largest production at this time—largest, costliest, and most unpredictable! If De Mille fires me, I thought, I'll thank him. Then I'll phone Dad and suggest a holiday together. Las Vegas again, or perhaps this time Arizona. We both needed to get away from the taste of Hollywood disappointments. It was January. Ideal weather in northern Mexico. Some dove-shooting, then drop down to Gueymas for fishing in the gulf of Baja California. Feast on lobster and tamales, and talk.

Then back to Hollywood, where he'd feel refreshed for another try with Barney Slater's script for *The Big Brass Band*.

When I walked into De Mille's office he was pale and silent. He just looked at me.

"Jesse is dead, Jesse."

There wasn't any breath I could catch. He went on.

"He'd finished his lecture at the Beverly Hilton. The cheers, applause were ringing in his ears. He must have felt on top of the world. He autographed books. They followed him through the lobby. Applauding. He summoned his car. As he started to get in—a heart attack. He died in the ambulance on the way to the hospital. Think of it as the best way a man like him could ever have gone. An exit for a showman."

The news was on the radio as I drove home. I talked on the phone to Bess, and to my sister Betty. They were strong. Much stronger than I.

The show doesn't have to go on. Other things do. Bess, Betty, Bill, and I selected the coffin. The funeral was arranged and paid for by the Screen Producers Guild. Adolph Zukor, who would live well past a hundred, was there. So was De Mille, and the officers of the Guild.

The same people who had attended Dad's Testimonial Dinner on September 12th, 1951, when the Screen Producers Guild presented him with their first Milestone Award, inscribed, "To Jesse L. Lasky for his historic contribution to the American Motion Picture."

That glittering night in the Coconut Grove, old friends and ex-partners like Mary Pickford (with whom he had formed Pickford-Lasky), Goldwyn, and De Mille (with whom he had formed the first company to produce a film in Hollywood), stars he had discovered, unknowns he had raised to fame—all were there. That night "they said nice things about me," as he wrote in *I Blow My Own Horn*. And blow his own horn was exactly what he did. Rising to respond to the speeches of praise, Dad suddenly borrowed a cornet from the orchestra, and played a Sousa march, followed by his home state's unofficial anthem, "California Here I Come!"

The cheering admirers marveled at his ability to play the cornet so brilliantly after not touching it for half a century. Not one guessed that the shrewd showman had hidden one of the best trumpeters in California behind the curtain at his back.

Thirty

IT WAS TOLD LATER how one man had remained behind at the crypt. Long after everyone else had left, and the early darkness of the January evening had drawn across Hollywood like a last curtain, Cecil de Mille remained with his old partner.

My sister Betty, my brother Bill, my wife, and Bess and I drove home in the undertaker's hired cars. I did not see De Mille keeping his lonely vigil, but I believe he did. The strange texture of his association with my father had known many variations—since those days in 1913 when they had come west to produce Hollywood's first feature film—born in a barn. The State of California would preserve it as a historical landmark. And Beverly Hills would preserve my father's name on Lasky Drive—but the founding fathers of our town were making their final fade-outs.

In February 1958, *The Buccaneer* finished shooting, and I chose the Arizona desert to collapse in. A pastel setting where great hotels sprawled around turquoise swimming pools, where cavalcades of dudes strung over the dunes, trotted in to dunk their saddle sores. The still air shimmered with heat sparks. Sunsets blazed until at last the night's stars were veiled by the smoke from a thousand barbecues.

No wilderness, this, for truth-seeking prophets, no sanctuary for ascetics—but ideal for a Hollywood scriptwriter to dissolve into the landscape.

I cantered up a sandhill, dismounted to contemplate a horned toad, a miniature dinosaur basking untroubled in the stillness—until the stillness became troubled, fragmented by the nagging shriek of a siren, loudening as it approached from the direction of the Arizona Biltmore and screamed up the road through a cactus forest. It came from a pearl-gray ambulance, an oversized, glass-walled coffin on wheels. Within it, Harry Cohn, the king of Columbia Pictures, was dying.

So many of the great founders seemed to be dying now. Only the year before, Louis B. Mayer, still raging for his lost power. Then my father. It had never been easy to think of them as destructible.

There was still De Mille, however; he contacted me soon after my return to Hollywood. I drove up to the aging mansion on De Mille Drive, and the Boss received me in his library projection-room. He had not been well after returning from the New Orleans premiere of *The Buccaneer*, and his face was gray. I was grateful that he didn't comment on the things that had gone wrong in *The Buccaneer*. He had never been one to dwell on sins of the past. He walked slowly around a desk weighted by innumerable books.

"I want to talk about our next film, Jess."

At least he was not holding that debacle against me. He reached for a favorite pipe, one that I had brought him from London years before, but put it back without lighting it, as though reminding himself of doctor's orders to cut down on smoking.

"It's a subject I've thought of doing for years. Even talked to your father about it once. He could see what I saw in it. There was a man who had a story mind." He stood the pipe back into the enormous rack of gold-banded briars. "Henry Wilcoxon has dug up some wonderful material to produce a moving picture about the beginnings of the Boy Scouts. We'll call it *On My Honor*. Do I correctly remember you were once a Boy Scout, Jesse?"

The question was asked in precisely the same tone as when he had once asked, "Do you believe in God?" or "Are you a Hebrew?"

"Never a very distinguished one, sir. Tenderfoot in the Wolf Patrol."

He hadn't even bothered to listen to my answer. In his mind I had assumed the stature of an Eagle Scout.

"Lady Frances Baden-Powell will be coming to Hollywood as my guest. It will be important for you to have talks with her. What are you doing now? Any plans?"

"I've had an offer from Columbia Screen Gems. Bert Leonard wants me to join him as an assistant producer and head writer on one or two series. But I haven't accepted yet," I added hopefully.

"Go ahead," he nodded. "We won't be ready to start *On My Honor* for a while. Harry may send you over some reading on the subject."

"The Boy Scouts."

"Yes, you might begin by reading the Scout Oath. It starts: 'On My Honor . . .' "

"Yes, sir, I remember."

"Good! Most people have forgotten honor these days. Did you know the idea of the Boy Scouts was born to Baden-Powell during the Siege of Mafeking in 1900? He formed a corps of messenger boys with bicycles . . . You could say the message they carried at Mafeking went around the world . . ." He broke off, looking somehow exhausted.

"I hope you'll direct this one yourself, Mr. De Mille."

"I? Oh, no. I'll just try to help you fellahs see what I see. The Scout movement is a lot more than tying knots and making fires without matches. It's a hope—if there is any—for this old world. Did you ever see a film of mine called *The Godless Girl*?"

"A long time ago, sir."

"I was making films about young rebels before half these new directors were born! They forget that. Nineteen twenty-nine." His eyes were smiling slightly as though with some secret joke that couldn't be shared.

A few days later Florence Cole phoned me to say Mr. De Mille had died peacefully in the night.

Henry Wilcoxon, with the support of Cecilia, followed the Boss's wishes. Eventually I left Screen Gems to work on the screenplay. Bernice Mosk was assisting on research. We three were all that was left of the great De Mille unit at Paramount. I smoked the pipes he had left to me and we prepared an enormous script.

But when it was ready nobody wanted to know. The studios, short of production capital, were not interested in a De Mille epic without De Mille.

I met a young actress-writer during my frantic labors in the television tabernacle of Screen Gems. Barbara Hayden had written, directed, produced, and performed in the first live TV dramatic series made in Hollywood. *Mable's Fables* brought her an Emmy Award nomination, and no more security than any other creative talent in that hectic field. She came to one of our series as an actress in a piece of mine called *The Explosive Heart*.

It was a time of desperate problems with New York networks, and sponsors who were capable of phoning at the last minute and demanding total script changes. In a "joke" that describes the situation in those dreadful days, a secretary answers a long-distance phone call and soothes the terror-stricken producer with the words: "Good news. It wasn't New York, just a call from San Francisco to say your mother's dying."

There is, indeed, something peculiarly destructive to the mind and soul about the pressures of getting out one half-hour segment of a series every week—on a minuscule budget of money and time. Barbara turned out to be an indefatigable writer. We wrote scripts together for that series. Then we began to write together most of the time. Eventually, we became a husband-and-wife writing team. These shows called for virile violence, and police and fire departments involved would have found a woman's name on scripts quite inappropriate in those pre–Women's Lib times, so Barbara took the writing name of Pat Silver.

The golden age of the Hollywood writer was heading into its winter.

But Twentieth Century-Fox still had the appearance of a major film studio when Barbara and I were assigned to write a comedy film for Dick Shawn. We shared a studio suite larger than our Hollywood apartment. The other writers under assignment were few but impressive. Clifford Odets, the once-revolutionary New York playwright, and Carl Sandburg, the aging Chicago poet, were just down the corridor. It was easy to close one's eyes to the realities of the day in such a company. Like the Romanoffs shutting out the rumbles of revolution, we imagined ourselves still safe in our palace suite. Each evening after the day's writing, we would drive out in a speedy sports car down the Pacific Coast Highway, past Malibu and into the Malibu mountains, to be met by a withered, near-mummified ex-rodeo rider who boarded our pair of aging mounts, purchased from a "used horse lot." In the tack room we'd change into cowboy boots, corner our phlegmatic horses, throw on the saddles, and canter off into the sunset in imitation of some of our old scripts. We did not know how final was this sunset.

Ronald Reagan, now doing TV commercials for General Electric, invited us to ride on his enormous ranch. Other ex-stars, less fortunate, could be seen dismounting from their expensive limousines to join the unemployed lines at the "52-20 Club"—as the dole office was fondly known.

Like George Murphy, Reagan was politically oriented. I used to lunch with Ron, who as president of the Screen Actors Guild, served with Lou Greenspan and Jerry Wald of the Producers Guild in a dedicated group called the Motion Picture Industry Council. Historically unique, the MPIC represented one of the rare attempts of Hollywood to defend itself against the bad publicity attacks in the wake of the witch hunts. The valiant effort of the MPIC was never sufficiently supported by filmdom.

Reagan himself had built up a strong following over the years at Warner Brothers, playing mainly the companions of the leading stars, or loyal confidants of the rich and powerful. He hardly ever "got the girl."

So when Jack Warner heard that Reagan was running for governor of California, he shook his head dubiously. "Governor, no. Bad casting. The *friend* of the governor."

Through 1960 into '62 we were finding life in movieland increasingly less hopeful. There were fewer jobs, and the budgets of those few films that were scheduled were beginning to look like back to *The Squaw Man*! American production effort and money seemed to be mainly going abroad.

Barbara and I continued at Fox for another three assignments. Our films, which had been optimistically written as big-screen entertainment, were so cheaply produced that the last one, *Seven Women from Hell*, almost underwent a title change to *Six Women* to save on costs. Our story, set in the jungles of New Guinea, was filmed in a park in Hawaii, and the director ensured himself further employment by shooting the entire film in three weeks, and making ten Japanese actors suggest the presence of the entire imperial army.

The studios, like impoverished gentry, had begun to sell their real estate almost to the doors of their administration buildings.

The storm flags were up. Like top-heavy ships heading into the teeth of a gale, the studios were lightening ballast—heaving everything and everyone overboard—even their own captains. Almost the only projects to reach production were the movies made with cheap labor in far corners of the world.

Then, like the tent-folding Arabs, Barbara and I packed our pencils and dictionaries, and quietly stole away. We had written our last Hollywood film script.

Still there were other forms of writing. There was my novel *Naked in a Cactus Garden*. There was a verse-play production of *Ghost Town*, a long folk poem of mine that Barbara had dramatized. It wasn't too difficult to get a cast of film actors like Wright King, Susan Oliver, and Marvin Miller for a local theater production. And there was still television. Even some really good-quality television being produced by Quinn Martin. But after writing seven one-hour shows for Quinn, the pickings began to get leaner. The waits by the telephone for our agent's calls began to get longer. Then the phone would ring and we'd fall over the furniture to answer it.

"Look, kids. It's getting tighter all around town. The people you've worked with haven't got anything going at the moment—but Cheap and Nasty Productions out in the Valley are inviting writers to submit for a new series. Kind of a cowboy-detective-situation-comedy. You be out there at three o'clock tomorrow and they'll show you a pilot in the projection room. Then if you've got any ideas for it, submit a page or two! No, who said a full story line? We all know the Guild frowns on spec. writing. Just an idea. Four or five pages, maybe. If they don't like it, it's your property, sweetie."

The trouble was that they didn't have to like it. These flimsy ideas could be stolen as readily as fake jewelry from a dime-store counter, and some of those producers seemed to be afflicted with chronic kleptomania.

We were driving through the once-great capital of Twentieth Century-Fox. Not a single film was in production, but there was activity and plenty of it. Great machines were gouging out the earth, devouring, maiming, burying canvas cities in dusty heaps of scaffolding and plaster-of-paris bricks. A French World War I village being pulverized by a charge of bulldozers. A gracious section of Berkeley Square where Leslie Howard's coach once rattled him through time in my father's old film. An Egyptian temple falling under hammer-blows where *The Robe* had once exploded onto the first cinerama screen. Down crashed the Spanish village where Tyrone Power searched for truth in *The Razor's Edge*. The truth was a vast, ripping, grinding demolition on which would rise the profitable subdivisions of Century City.

We drove on to keep our appointment with an independent film producer who had contacted and contracted us by long-distance telephone from London. London, he had said, would be his base; and there he would want us to develop one or more film properties that could be produced in India, Yugoslavia, France, Spain, Rome, or Twickenham. Practically anywhere except in Hollywood. It was a strange offer of employment, and it had come from a stranger, who now commanded our presence to tell the story of his projected first film to potential backers and, it seemed, to watch him promote money.

In the setting up of a film, the writer serves as a kind of leper's bell, the first tinkle of an intent; someone's optimistic plan to prepare and produce a movie. He is therefore the person most vulnerable to rogues and incompetents, since at the writing stage financial backing is frequently more shadow than substance. He is too often hired by some shoestring adventurer who dreams that the script will produce enough front financing to launch a production and, incidentally, pay the writer. Sometimes it doesn't happen.

The "producer" who had just hired us hadn't stinted on that trip to Chicago he arranged so we could meet him—from the first-class air tickets to the chauffeur-driven limousine which whisked us from the airport to the hotel where he had arranged a corner suite. He had permanently reserved the best table in the room, where only the most important VIPs were to be found. Not unreasonable, we concluded, in view of the many scheduled interviews and meetings laid on for us.

Only once did a slip of the facade reveal an uncomfortable glimpse of the inner man. We had descended half an hour before one of our press interviews, badly in need of a quiet drink at the bar. We had just lifted our glasses to toast the fantastic turn in our fortunes when our dark angel appeared. "What are you doing there?" he hissed. "Important writers do not sit at bars!"

"What about Hemingway?" I stammered. "Dos Passos, Fitzgerald, Jack London? You've got to admit bars occupy an important place in the great American literary tradition."

"Not very funny," he decreed. "You are my writers, not Hemingway and Fitzgerald. You are not to be seen anywhere but at my table. Unnerstand?"

We surrendered to his whim in the spirit of *richesse oblige*. Besides, this ship of fortune was not a boat to be casually rocked. For the remainder of the Chicago visit we received the press in "first table" glory and played our required roles.

Now, with Richard, my eleven-year-old stepson, Barbara and I would fly to London—and hopefully be paid for the long weeks and months of work which lay ahead. (Naturally, we weren't. Not completely. About two-thirds of the way through the second-draft screenplay, our promoting producer failed to produce the cash to pay off his preproduction staff. He ran out of financing and made a rather sudden exit from London. There was nothing sure any more in the film world, where yesterday's promoters could become tomorrow's producers, or fugitives from the law, depending on which way the money was blowing.)

The plane lifted us above the veil of smog worn by the once-beautiful City of Angels, those angels who washed their feet in the Pacific and rested their eucalyptus wings on the foothills of the San Fernando.

How could one say good-bye to a state of mind?

To most of a lifetime?

But that, too, was the kind of business it had become, I thought, and would one ever stop asking or being asked, in the suburbs of Athens, or sea caves of Portugal, in Morocco or on the Mountains of the Moon . . . Whatever did happen to Hollywood?

FADE-OUT THE END

Index